# CONTEMPORARY CHICANO FICTION

## A CRITICAL SURVEY

# *Bilingual Press/Editorial Bilingüe*

Studies in the Language and Literature
of United States Hispanos

**General Editor**
Gary D. Keller

**Managing Editor**
Karen S. Van Hooft

**Senior Editor**
Mary M. Keller

**Editorial Board**
Ernestina N. Eger
Joshua A. Fishman
Francisco Jiménez
William Milan
Amado M. Padilla
Raymond V. Padilla
Eduardo Rivera
Richard V. Teschner
Guadalupe Valdés
Juan Clemente Zamora

**Address**
Bilingual Press
Box M, Campus Post Office
SUNY-Binghamton
Binghamton, New York 13901
(607) 724-9495

# CONTEMPORARY CHICANO FICTION

## A CRITICAL SURVEY

Edited by Vernon E. Lattin

*Bilingual Press/Editorial Bilingüe*
BINGHAMTON, NEW YORK

© 1986 by Bilingual Press/Editorial Bilingüe

All rights reserved. No part of this publication may be reproduced in any manner without permission in writing, except in the case of brief quotations embodied in critical articles and reviews.

ISBN: 0-916950-56-5
Printed simultaneously in a softcover edition. ISBN: 0-916950-57-3

Library of Congress Catalog Card Number: 85-71528

PRINTED IN THE UNITED STATES OF AMERICA

*Cover design by Christopher J. Bidlack*

**Acknowledgments**

*The editor wishes to thank the following persons and publications for permission to reprint material appearing in this volume:*

Society for the Study of the Multi-Ethnic Literature of the United States, for Ramón Saldívar, "A Dialectic of Difference: Toward a Theory of the Chicano Novel," *MELUS*, 6, 3 (Fall 1979), 73-92.

*De Colores*, José Armas, ed., for José Armas, "Chicano Writing: The New Mexico Narrative," 5, 1-2 (1980), 69-81; Juan D. Bruce-Novoa, "Miguel Méndez: Voices of Silence," 3, 4 (1977), 63-69; Justo S. Alarcón, "Las metamorfosis del diablo en *El diablo en Texas* de Aristeo Brito," 5, 1-2 (1980), 30-44; and Vernon E. Lattin, "Time and History in Candelaria's *Memories of the Alhambra*," 5, 1-2 (1980), 102-10.

*Minority Voices*, for Luther S. Luedtke, "*Pocho* and the American Dream," 1, 2 (Fall 1977), 1-16.

*Latin American Literary Review*, Yvette E. Miller, ed., for Norman D. Smith, "Buffalos and Cockroaches: Acosta's Siege at Aztlán," 5, 10 (Spring-Summer 1977), 85-97; Jane Rogers, "The Function of the La Llorona Motif in Anaya's *Bless Me, Ultima*," 5, 10 (Spring-Summer 1977), 64-69; Eliud Martínez, "Ron Arias' *The Road to Tamazunchale*: A Chicano Novel of the New Reality," 5, 10 (Spring-Summer 1977), 51-63; Erlinda Gonzales-Berry, "*Caras viejas y vino nuevo*: Journey Through a Disintegrating Barrio," 7, 14 (Spring-Summer 1979), 62-72; and Nasario García, "The Concept of Time in *Nambé—Year One*," 7, 13 (Fall-Winter 1978), 20-28.

*(Acknowledgments continue on next page.)*

**Acknowledgments** (continued)

*Critique*, for Vernon E. Lattin, "Paradise and Plums: Appearance and Reality in Barrio's *The Plum Plum Pickers*," 19, 1 (1977), 49-57.

Ralph F. Grajeda, for his "Tomás Rivera's Appropriation of the Chicano Past," *Modern Chicano Writers*, ed. Joseph Sommers and Tomás Ybarra-Frausto (Englewood Cliffs, NJ: Prentice-Hall, 1979), 74-85.

*Revista Chicano-Riqueña*, Nicolás Kanellos, ed., and Juan Rodríguez, for the latter's "The Problematic in Tomás Rivera's '... and the earth did not part,' " 6, 3 (verano 1978), 42-50.

*La Palabra*, Justo S. Alarcón, ed., for Francisca Rascón, "La caracterización de los personajes femeninos en '... y no se lo tragó la tierra,' " 1, 2 (otoño 1979), 43-50; and Yolanda Guerrero, "Literatura y sociedad: Análisis de *Generaciones y semblanzas*," 1, 2 (otoño 1979), 21-30.

*The Bilingual Review/La Revista Bilingüe*, Gary D. Keller, ed., for Erlinda Gonzales-Berry, "*Estampas del Valle:* From *Costumbrismo* to Self-Reflecting Literature," 7, 1 (Jan.-April 1980), 29-38.

*Cuadernos Americanos*, for Miriam Bornstein, "*Peregrinos de Aztlán:* Dialéctica estructural e ideológica," 39, 4 (julio-ago. 1980), 23-33; and Oscar U. Somoza, "Choque e interacción en *Caras viejas y vino nuevo* y *La verdad sin voz* de Alejandro Morales," 39, 4 (julio-ago. 1980), 34-40.

*Frontiers: A Journal of Women Studies*, Kathi George, ed., for Tomás Vallejos, "Estela Portillo Trambley's Fictive Search for Paradise," 5, 2 (Summer 1980), 54-58. (Special issue on "Chicanas in the National Landscape.")

# Table of Contents

| | |
|---|---|
| INTRODUCTION, *Vernon E. Lattin* | 9 |

### 1. Critical Overviews

| | |
|---|---|
| RAMON SALDIVAR, A Dialectic of Difference: Toward a Theory of the Chicano Novel | 13 |
| JOSE ARMAS, Chicano Writing: The New Mexico Narrative | 32 |
| MARVIN A. LEWIS, The Urban Experience in Selected Chicano Fiction | 46 |

### 2. The Early Writers in English: Villarreal, Acosta, Barrio

| | |
|---|---|
| LUTHER S. LUEDTKE, *Pocho* and the American Dream | 62 |
| NORMAN D. SMITH, Buffalos and Cockroaches: Acosta's Siege at Aztlán | 82 |
| ALURISTA, Acosta's *The Revolt of the Cockroach People:* The Case, the Novel, and History | 94 |
| VERNON E. LATTIN, Paradise and Plums: Appearance and Reality in Barrio's *The Plum Plum Pickers* | 105 |

### 3. Tomás Rivera and the Spanish Language Novel

| | |
|---|---|
| RALPH F. GRAJEDA, Tomás Rivera's Appropriation of the Chicano Past | 113 |
| ALFONSO RODRIGUEZ, Time As a Structural Device in Tomás Rivera's "... *y no se lo tragó la tierra*" | 126 |
| JUAN RODRIGUEZ, The Problematic in Tomás Rivera's "... *and the earth did not part*" | 131 |
| FRANCISCA RASCON, La caracterización de los personajes femeninos en "... *y no se lo tragó la tierra*" | 141 |

### 4. The Accomplished Voices

#### A. Rolando Hinojosa

| | |
|---|---|
| ERLINDA GONZALES-BERRY, *Estampas del Valle:* From *Costumbrismo* to Self-Reflecting Literature | 149 |
| YOLANDA GUERRERO, Literatura y sociedad: Análisis de *Generaciones y semblanzas* | 162 |

B. *Rudolfo Anaya*
    JOSE MONLEON, Ilusión y realidad en la obra de Rudolfo Anaya    171

    JANE ROGERS, The Function of the La Llorona Motif in Anaya's *Bless Me, Ultima*    200

C. *Miguel Méndez*
    JUAN D. BRUCE-NOVOA, Miguel Méndez: Voices of Silence    206

    MIRIAM BORNSTEIN, *Peregrinos de Aztlán:* Dialéctica estructural e ideológica    215

D. *Ron Arias*
    ELIUD MARTINEZ, Ron Arias' *The Road to Tamazunchale:* A Chicano Novel of the New Reality    226

    EVA MARGARITA NIETO, The Dialectics of Textual Interpolation in Ron Arias' *The Road to Tamazunchale*    239

E. *Aristeo Brito*
    MARVIN A. LEWIS, *El diablo en Texas:* Structure and Meaning    247

    JUSTO S. ALARCON, Las metamorfosis del diablo en *El diablo en Texas* de Aristeo Brito    253

F. *Estela Portillo Trambley*
    TOMAS VALLEJOS, Estela Portillo Trambley's Fictive Search for Paradise    269

G. *Nash Candelaria*
    VERNON E. LATTIN, Time and History in Candelaria's *Memories of the Alhambra*    278

H. *Alejandro Morales*
    ERLINDA GONZALES-BERRY, *Caras viejas y vino nuevo:* Journey Through a Disintegrating Barrio    289

    OSCAR U. SOMOZA, Choque e interacción en *La verdad sin voz* de Alejandro Morales    299

I. *Orlando Romero*
    NASARIO GARCIA, The Concept of Time in *Nambé—Year One*    306

**Bibliography**
    ERNESTINA N. EGER, A Selected Bibliography of Criticism of the Chicano Novel    316

# Introduction

The growth in both the quantity and quality of the Chicano novel since the publication of *Pocho* in 1959 has been phenomenal. This growth has been matched by a growing critical awareness of the Chicano novel in both traditional scholarly journals and Chicano journals. Recent anthologies of Chicano criticism have reflected the same pattern by including important articles on the Chicano novel. However, no anthology has yet appeared dealing solely with this genre.

This volume is a recognition of both the quality of criticism on the Chicano novel and the need to gather together for easy access some of the best of this criticism. Therefore, my first principle of selection has been to gather the best essays on the Chicano novel. Secondly, I have attempted to represent broadly the various Chicano novelists as well as numerous Chicano critics. Thirdly, I have attempted to avoid duplication with the volume *The Identification and Analysis of Chicano Literature* (Bilingual Press, 1979). In fact, my collection can be seen as its companion volume; together the two will give the reader a significant vision of the Chicano novel and its place within the tradition of Chicano literature.

Even with the above criteria, obviously, I found many essays that deserved inclusion, but which, because of space limitations, I have had to leave out. Such is the nature of any anthology.

Ramón Saldívar's essay, "A Dialectic of Difference: Toward a Theory of the Chicano Novel," is a good introduction to the Chicano novel because of its importance in helping to develop Chicano literary theory. His approach, a "critique of narrative structures," is based on the "poststructuralist" methodology and yields some good readings of four important Chicano novels.

José Armas' "Chicano Writing: The New Mexico Narrative" is important because it reminds us of the lineage of Chicano fiction as well as of the differences between Chicanos from the various areas of the United States. Armas' interest in culture and in themes reflects what have been the two most often-used critical approaches: the formalist and the cultural/historical.

The last essay of the first section, "The Urban Experience in Selected Chicano Fiction," reminds the reader that 85% of the Chicanos are urbanites and that Chicano fiction reflects this important reality. Lewis, one of the most prolific of the Chicano critics, leaves the reader with a complete sense of Chicano fiction.

The second section of the volume includes an essay on each of three significant early Chicano novels, all three written in English. *Pocho* (1959) is considered by the majority of Chicano critics to be the first in the new wave of contemporary Chicano novels, although some critics have refused to recognize *Pocho* as either "Chicano" or as a "novel." I have not included any essays on Richard Vásquez' *Chicano* (1970) because of the novel's inferior quality. Tomás Rivera's "... *y no se lo tragó la tierra*" (1971) is presented later as the first Spanish-language Chicano novel. *Bless Me, Ultima* (1972) is reserved for section four because Anaya, having published two other novels, needs to be considered as one of the novelists in the "Accomplished Voices" section.

Luedtke's article is included both because I think it is a good reading of *Pocho* and because it deals with the issues of assimilation, different cultural values, and that strange but recurring theme of the "American Dream." Smith's article treats both of Acosta's novels while also dealing with the often-discussed issue of the relationship of art to propaganda and social protest. Smith appreciates the novel's technique more than I do, but he does a good job of explaining the significance of Acosta's work. Alurista's reading of Acosta is a good companion to Smith's study and together the two articles give the reader a broad awareness of Acosta as a novelist. My article is a formalist approach to Barrio's novel and the only decent critical interpretation of a familiar Chicano novel. Quite clearly, Barrio's novel deserves more critical attention.

The third section of the volume is devoted to Tomás Rivera's "... *y no se lo tragó la tierra.*" Grajeda sees Chicano literature in terms of its ability to render the Chicano experience "authentically." Thus, for Grajeda, Rivera's novel is the first truly "Chicano" novel. Juan Rodríguez, one of the major Chicano critics, has written several essays on Rivera's seminal novel. Of these essays, I have chosen "The Problematic in Tomás Rivera's *And the Earth Did Not Part*" because I felt it important enough for readers to realize that Chicano critics are not simply "gushing" over anything written by a Chicano. Rodríguez recognizes both the strengths and weaknesses of Rivera's novel. I should mention in passing that I disagree with both of these essays but that here, as elsewhere, I have not used my agreement or disagreement with the critics as a criterion of selection. Alfonso Rodríguez, a critic of growing importance, allows us to see the totality of the diverse stories in the novel, using time as structure. One of the truly needed studies is that of time and history in Chicano fiction. Perhaps Dr. Rodríguez' essay will stimulate a more extensive study. Finally, Rascón's essay reminds us of the importance of the female in Chicano literature and of the significant failure of Rivera in presenting fully developed women characters.

The fourth section attempts to collect some of the best essays on the major Chicano novelists: Hinojosa, Méndez, Anaya, Brito, Portillo Trambley, Candelaria, Morales, and Romero. Perhaps some readers' favorite novelists or favorite critical essays have been omitted. However, by reading these essays one will get a good sense of the available critical understanding of the contemporary Chicano novel. The essays in this section, written in both Spanish and English, approach the major Chicano novelists through various critical methodologies. For example, Juan Bruce Novoa's approach to Méndez reflects his knowledge of poststructuralist methodologies; Eliud Martínez reads *The Road to Tamazunchale* from a postmodern and "magical realism" point of view; Marvin Lewis uses a basic formalist critical method; and Vallejos' reading of *Rain of Scorpions* is strongly influenced by myth criticism and ancient Nahua cosmology. These various approaches reflect not only the richness of the Chicano novel but also the maturity of Chicano criticism. Chicano critics are no longer limited to discussions of whether a novel reflects a cultural revolutionary/protest tradition, although portions of this approach also appear in a number of essays.

As reflected in this collection, Chicano criticism has also reached a stage of maturity that allows for serious discussion of a writer's weaknesses. The critics Guerrero and Juan Rodríguez see two of the leading Chicano novelists, Hinojosa and Rivera, as lacking in certain areas of accomplishment. Rodríguez finds Rivera's portrayal of the Chicano to be passive, "problematic," and Guerrero criticizes Hinojosa for failing to account properly for historical conflicts, economic conditions, and Tejano customs. One may agree or disagree with these critics, but either way the reader is forced to re-examine the novels with these objections in mind.

In the long run, the reader will come away from reading this collection with a new appreciation and understanding of the Chicano novels and a desire to return to the texts and re-read them.

Finally, for the reader whose appetite has been whetted, the last section provides information on additional critical essays on the Chicano novel. Because the bibliography had to be selective, many fine unpublished essays and reviews are not listed. Yet enough is presented for the reader to spend many valuable hours continuing his or her reading of the Chicano critics. If the reader both re-reads the novels and searches out more criticism, this volume has been a success.

VERNON E. LATTIN
THE UNIVERSITY OF WISCONSIN

# 1. Critical Overviews

A Dialectic of Difference:
Toward a Theory of
the Chicano Novel

*Ramón Saldívar*

In a widely acclaimed essay, Joseph Sommers issued a challenge to all literary scholars, but especially to Chicano scholars, to justify the theoretical suppositions of their work.[1] Sommers argued that the students of Chicano literature were, if not wrong, at least partially misguided in our critical efforts. He implied that a move could be made toward the proper path of criticism. As proof of his own critical self-awareness, he revealed the critical presuppositions of his work, which were to serve as models for our own future critical acts.

Sommers's reasoning was clear and the distinctions he offered between the "formalist" and "culturist" criticism on the one hand and his own "historical dialectical" method on the other, were basically correct.[2] One could quibble with his admittedly partisan interpretations of formalist methodology, but such is not my intention. Of greater moment, both for literary studies in general and for Chicano literary studies in particular, is the urgent need for a reassessment of the critical act. Sommers, to his great credit, knew this. What his essay was not in a position to recognize, however, was that this reassessment is already taking place in Chicano studies, through what has been inelegantly termed "post-structuralist" criticism.[3] I do not necessarily align myself within that revisionist criticism; nor am I one to take up challenges indiscriminately. But Sommers's challenge, as his legacy to Chicano literary criticism, is one which cannot be easily ignored. In what follows, I would like to respond to Sommers by outlining what I take to be the possibility for a new, revolutionary critique of narrative structures, and by attempting a partial survey of the Chicano novel, based on a "post-structuralist" methodology. At the outset I will admit that I side with Sommers, at least to an extent. I too believe that a confrontation with the sociological, historical, and cultural conditions under which the Chicano novel has been created is virtually indispensable to an informed "ethnic student" in our time of legal, fiscal, and moral retrenchment.

## I. The Dialectics of History

In the second chapter of José Antonio Villarreal's germinal novel, *Pocho* (1959), Juan Rubio, paradigmatic hero, patriarch, and warrior, having participated in the "world-historical" event of Mexican history, the Revolution of 1910, finds that he must flee in defeat from Mexico to the United States.[4] For Chicanos, Juan Rubio's flight dramatizes an equally historical event: it marks the beginning of the rapid growth of Mexican communities in the American Southwest. And it is, of course, not accidental that here, at the beginning of the Chicano novel,[5] we find the events of fiction firmly rooted in the events of history. The novel, more so than any other literary genre, insists on this tie to the real. In respecting the necessity of this tie, Villarreal offers us not so much a slice of reality, as he does a representation of the cultural rules and conventions by which the fictional character Juan Rubio, and real men like him, dealt with that reality.

For all its sociohistorical significance, the Revolution is mainly important in this novel for the tremendous personal meaning Rubio has attributed to it—as a result of its shattering events, the world of Juan Rubio's values has been radically polarized. The rules of personal conduct personified in his character sharply specify that one must live and die with dignity, or existence has no value at all. Juan Rubio is therefore represented as an independent and autonomous source of absolute value, which value he holds even against life. But already from the beginning of the novel, when confronted first with a pimping *gachupín*, whom he kills, and then with an old friend now a general in the army of the institutionalized revolution, whom he mocks, Juan Rubio begins to suspect that the passing of the revolution will mean more than political defeat. He realizes that with the death of Pancho Villa, the grand dream of social and individual dignity will be subverted.

From this subversion will emerge a new class of men, like René Soto, a political intriguer, whom Juan sees as worthless: "He was *nothing*," Rubio says to one of them, "and you are *nothing*."[6] This is Juan's vision of the world: one is either *something*, dignified and real, or one is *nothing*. In this formulation, Villarreal seems less concerned with portraying "abstract stereotypes drawn from the popular Mexican collective unconscious" as Tino Villanueva suggests,[7] than with representing the thematics of the patriarchal will to power. What is to be willed here is the power of absolute value over and against any other formulation concerning human action. From the perspective of narrative stratagem, not only is Villarreal's ploy of skirting with stereotypes dramatically effective, it is also essential for the intended analysis of *value* which is now to follow. Life, as action, manifests itself in Juan's view in a continuing resistance to that which would negate it. For Juan there can be no middle ground, no reconciliation between the poles of being and nothing, which have become ethical as well as ontological terms. The result of this irreconcilability is, as various readers have pointed out, a narrative about "the menace of chaotic discontinuity."[8] What has not been pointed out, however, is the dramatic effect of this discontinuity in Juan Rubio's life.

But the novel is, of course, not about Juan Rubio. It is rather about his son, Richard, the *pocho* born in a melon field of the Imperial Valley in California. In the remainder of the novel, the cataclysmic Revolution freezes into a past of intractable and alien value. The United States is not Mexico, and the old values do not seem to apply. This does not mean that the novel idealizes the remote past of the Mexican Revolution in order to explain the present disintegration of Chicano cultural life. Nor does it mean that the novel offers the conventions of Anglo-American culture as a positive model. Instead, it offers us a difference. Among the various options of absolute value posed for Richard Rubio by Anglo-American culture, by the Roman Catholic Church, by his father's demands, and by his mother's wishes, Richard consistently chooses *not* to choose. Herein lies Richard's special and generic difference.

The young Richard early reasons that since, as the Church teaches, there is only good and evil in the world, and that since the differences between good and evil are inherently ambiguous, then it is possible that these differences cannot be known. "He was frightened," the narrator tells us, "because he could not know [the differences]" and because "somehow God was in the middle of the whole thing. To do 'bad' things had something to do with being alive, but really what were bad things?" (*Pocho* p. 37). This naive conflation of "life" and "bad things" is later expressed in more exact terms: "I was scared," says Richard, "because if He willed it so, I knew that the earth would open and it would swallow me up because I dared to demand explanations from Him.... Then, one day, I knew that ... if He could do the best thing in the world, He could also do the most evil thing in the world" (*Pocho* p. 65). If after this recognition the two concepts of good and evil are still to be differentiated, then the difference must be based on a perception of something other than a pure meaning or idea to serve as the substance of good or evil. Richard's question of the nature of good and evil is posed, therefore, not to eliminate their opposition, but to show that the terms appear as the *différance*[9] of the other: in Richard's view, "good" constitutes itself by its very relation to what it absolutely is not. Good is *not* evil; but it *is* evil that has not yet happened, and vice versa. The significance of Richard's elementary intuition into the differential structure of moral codes is that it removes value, and therefore meaning, from the realm of a static, transcendent sphere and places it instead within the active domain of history and culture.

By the same token, this recognition of the differential structure of moral codes leads to Richard's later rejection of all "codes of honor," in so far as they are founded upon falsely absolute standards. He does so because he sees that moral codes, as cultural artifacts, are contingent upon time, and therefore not to be arrested into static presences by human knowledge. This inability to know absolutely characterizes the development of Richard's character and culminates in his portentous response to his mother's insistence that he be *something* when he grows up: "I do not want to be something; *I am*" (*Pocho* p. 64).

The melodrama of adolescence aside, Richard's affirmation of being indicates that for him the world is not a source of value as it is for his father. Richard wishes rather to appropriate the world to himself, and to subjugate it by shaping it with his understanding, in the commanding mode of divine self-reference, "*I am*." The real world is thus not to be seen as a determinant of action, but more accurately, as the scene of action. Socioeconomic conditions of rural California in the 1930s preclude, however, that Richard's action can be anything more than a spiritual rebellion against the various imposed forms of cultural reality. Yet, by resisting the imposition of cultural norms, Richard wishes subversively to devalue reality: "Everything does not have to be real," he claims (*Pocho* p. 65).

If everything is not real, then what is it? Richard Rubio, at the source of contemporary Chicano narrative, is not afraid of the un real, the *nothing*, which his father rejects. But at this point, as his mother realizes when she says to him, "I have really lost you, my son!" (*Pocho* p. 66), Richard is indeed no longer with us. It may be instructive to find out where he is.

The novel *Pocho* has always been somewhat of an embarrassment to Chicanos. Even the preface to the Anchor paperback edition seems to show the need to apologize for the novel. Richard's rejection of his father's values, his statements that "codes of honor are stupid" (*Pocho* p. 108), his rejection of the Catholic faith, and, of course, his departure at the novel's end to join the United States armed forces in the months just prior to Pearl Harbor are seen as assimilationist tendencies. But given the fact that Richard has always been a tolerant person among social, religious, sexual, and moral intolerants, and given the fact that he sees the coming war as an event spawned by wrong and bound only to create further wrongs (*Pocho* p. 158), Richard's decision to enlist can be seen either as a supreme contradiction, or as a positive step in a dialectic of developing understanding.

As an indication that we may pursue this second option, it should be noted that at the conclusion of the novel, Richard is in fact closer in spirit to his father than he has been at any other time in their relationship. He realizes that within that other world of value, "Father had won his battle" because he "had never been unaware of what his fight was" (*Pocho* p. 187). "What about me?," asks Richard, for he enters a battleground where definitive distinctions between right and wrong are not as apparent as he imagines they must have been for his father. Richard's decision to fight for his country is made with the clear recognition that his is a country that refuses him his own measure of justice, that imprisons his friends, and that makes economic serfs of his family. As soldiers and as men, Juan and Richard thus symmetrically oppose and reflect one another, with history serving as the mirror of their reflection.

For both men, life constitutes itself on the basis of concerted human action. Life does not happen to men and women; they happen to life. The first and foremost moment of this consituted life is that which is presently in action against anything which would restrict it. But the dialectics between fathers and sons are such that while for Juan it is the "nothing" that would restrict life, for Richard it is the codification of life that would destroy it. In dramatic terms, Juan's and Richard's opposed different lives and values might thus be seen as Villarreal's artistic intuition of the differential structure of human values as revealed by a Marxist transformational criticism.[10] Juan projects personal power into separate spheres—codes of honor and traditions of action—which dominate him. Richard's desire for an authentic existence within a new historical reality requires him to turn his father's values around, making codes of honor valid only as they arise from the actual movement of personal history. The interaction between these two ways of perceiving the value of human action creates the novel's complex dialectical force. Since this dialectic of values is inherent in the reality the novelist describes, it makes little difference whether the novelist intends to reveal it or not; the economy of opposed forces which he dramatizes reveals it for him.

When Richard claims at the novel's end that for him "there would be no coming back," we cannot be certain that his earlier confrontations with death, "the infinite nonentity" (*Pocho* p. 180), have not been foreshadowings of his own real death in war. But even if Richard does not here embrace a literal death, he welcomes a figural one: the death of the child he was, at the mercy of random historical events and of determinant social codes. Now he begins to seem capable of overcoming the opposition between the real and the unreal, between the options of the absolute value and the nothing, by plunging directly into the dynamics of history. He does so not so much to validate either the world or the self in isolation, as to validate the actions of the self in the world. Richard's acceptance of the unreal allows him to transform his father's idealist concept of history as the realization of Value through Man, into the materialist concept of history as the self-realization of men and women, through the detour of alienation in the spheres of society and culture.[11] As Marx points out in the Eleventh Thesis on Feuerbach, the necessary logical step after this *interpretation* of the world is to *change* the world.[12] That Richard does turn to the politics of change is apparent, I think, if only by the fact that the book he has always hoped to write *is* written, as semi-autobiographical fiction, in the form of the novel *Pocho*.

In contrast to the imposed word of cultural and ethical law, the "traditions which could take a body and soul . . . and mold it to fit a pattern," (*Pocho* p. 63), Richard sees the possibility of creating his own world, in the difference between absolute value and nothing, which might serve as the foundation for a revitalized personal and cultural identity. But the price of this emancipation is the security of the known, lamentable reality in favor of "the unknown" (*Pocho* p. 144). In effect, *Pocho* might well be thought of as the narrative equivalent of that earlier declaration of independence, "I don't want to be something; *I am*." The force of both his singular utterance and of the novel itself is such that it brings about an alteration in Richard's subjective condition, solely by virtue of the fact that the declaration and the novel have been performed. His words, embodied as narrative, testify to the power of language to constitute a state of subjective integrity, even if it is an integrity founded upon an initial act of renunciation. Thus, the writing of this text does initiate a substantial change; it changes the world of literature by opening a place for Chicano literature, a place from which future Chicano authors might open up the vistas of the genre of the novel to their own significant culture. From the perspective of literary history, therefore, the historical phenomenon of cultural consciousness expressed by later Chicano novels can become a reality only after Richard Rubio postulates his own identity as a new and different source of personal consciousness. At least this recognition is due Villarreal's first novel.

After *Pocho*, the question concerning the Chicano novel is no longer one of where it exists but of how it exists. The question is a proper one because the Chicano novel, individually and as a genre, constitutes itself by posing this question in explicit and concerted terms. In effect, the problematic of generic form, in both the real and fictional worlds, becomes the substance of its content. The preceding description of Villarreal's novel attempts to emphasize this fact: Richard's story is an operation of rectification, of ontological restitution, of values which have ceased to be effective in a new cultural, historical, and psychological space. It emphasizes the novel's own operation of interpretation as it moves in narrative time from Juan's to Richard's life; and within Richard's story, from belief to doubt and back again, as he attempts to pass from a surface to an underlying reality and finds a measure of certainty only in the opposition of their difference. That Richard has failed to locate that reality absolutely in either personal or cultural terms by the novel's end does not negate the procedure. The failure simply indicates that the closure of interpretation, by characters within fiction or by readers outside of it, cannot be established in this or perhaps any linguistic text. What a linguistic text can do, however, is activate the components of our concrete social life—words, ideas, desires, intentions—by revaluing, or even devaluing, them. This *foregrounding* of value[13] can neither create a meaning which was not already present in the words of the text, nor can it cause the end of interpretation. But *Pocho* succeeds as a novel, and more significantly as the paradigmatic Chicano novel, precisely because in bringing to the fore the question of value it both violates and subverts our received ideas of value, and forces us to define in real historical terms what has not been defined within the text.

Given the strength of the model text, *Pocho*, it should not be surprising that subsequent Chicano novels have looked to it, consciously or not, for inspiration. I am not here making a case for a Chicano "anxiety of influence,"[14] but I am suggesting that in its isolation of the differential structure of meaning, of the dialectic between history and art, and of the roles played by these issues in the protagonist's creation of a new cultural and personal consciousness, *Pocho* is the central Chicano novel. Like all progenitors, it has had its good and its bad offspring. I neither intend to discuss *Macho*, nor *Chicano*, nor the unfortunate *Fifth Horseman*.[15] I would like to sketch a brief history of its impact on Tomás Rivera's ... *y no se lo tragó la tierra*, Oscar Zeta Acosta's *The Revolt of the Cockroach People*, and Ron Arias's *The Road to Tamazunchale*. I caution that I offer here simply a tentative model of a possible Chicano literary history.

## II. The Dialectics of Difference

At the outset of such a history, we have Villarreal's novel. Tomás Rivera's magisterial work, ... *y no se lo tragó la tierra* (1971), however, takes the formal and thematic issues raised by Villarreal's novel to their limits. The twelve sections of Rivera's novel, preceded and concluded by a frame story, relate the seasonal events in a year of the life of an unnamed migrant child. As is the case in the major Chicano novels after *Pocho*, Rivera faithfully situates his story in the day to day life of present social reality. The poverty, hardships, and exploitation which his characters experience is no more than that which he himself might have experienced. But apart from the reality of economic exploitation, Rivera's novel also represents the anguish of a transcendently spiritual exploitation: his anonymous narrator, born of absence and loss, seeks to recover "un año perdido."[16]

Without a name, initially without a sense of specific geographical space or real time, unable to decide whether he wakes or dreams, the child calls out and turns, not realizing he himself has spoken: "oía que alguien le llamaba por su nombre pero cuando volteaba la cabeza a ver quién era el que le llamaba, daba una vuelta entera y así quedaba donde mismo" (Rivera p. 1). Thus situated between madness and chaos, the child reacts by beginning immediately to construct a context for order: "Se dio cuenta de que siempre pensaba que pensaba y de allí no podía salir.... Pero antes de dormirse veía y oía muchas cosas" (Rivera p. 1). In terms more grandly absolute than any imagined by Villarreal, Rivera thus sets the scene for his own portrayal of a radical revaluation of values.

Through a series of wire-tight chapters, which amount to no more than an interior monologue repeating snatches of half-heard conversations, Rivera portrays *la raza's* indomitable will to survive. With the two core episodes of the novel, "La noche estaba plateada" and the title piece "... y no se lo tragó la tierra," Rivera now chronicles the rise of an even more intractable will to power. But it must occur by degrees. First, one silvery night, the child walks into a wood to summon the devil because: "Lo del diablo le había fascinado desde cuando no se acordaba" (Rivera p. 55). Flashing back to another time, the child offers us a possible motive for this inexplicable summons of the devil when he recalls overhearing that "con el diablo no se juega. Hay muchos que le han llamado y después les ha pesado. La mayoría casi se vuelve loca.... Hay unos que se mueren de susto, otros no, nomás empiezan a entristecer, y luego ni hablan. Como que se les va el alma del cuerpo" (Rivera p. 55).

But the child is of a mind to summon the devil: "Nomás quisiera saber si hay o no hay," he says in innocent simplicity, and adding with a line of logic we have seen before, "Si no hay diablo a lo mejor no hay tampoco ... No, más vale no decirlo" (Rivera p. 56). He calls repeatedly but nothing happens: "No se apareció nada ni nadie ni cambió nada" (Rivera p. 56). Returning home, relieved and proud of himself, it occurs to him that the devil has not appeared because "no había diablo" (Rivera p. 56). And since in the rhetoric of the Church evil is inseparable from good, the absence of the devil leads him to the partial conclusion: "si no hay diablo tampoco hay ..." (Rivera p. 56). The binary pattern of what I have termed the Chicano novel's "differential structure" necessarily brings into question the complement of evil and the supreme origin of value, God Himself. At this point, however, the child's inability to separate himself from the ultimate of imposed value systems, especially from an apparently beneficent one, is designated by the inconclusive ellipse. It is curious, moreover, that his intimation of the world as a place without devils or gods, "No hay diablo, no hay nada," does not lead him into existential despair. On the contrary, the child senses the possibility of freedom in their absence. He now understands that "Los que le llamaban al diablo y se volvían locos, no se volvían locos porque se les aparecía sino al contrario, porque no se les aparecía" (Rivera p. 56). In an impressive rhetorical move, the narrator signals the sublimity of this partial recognition by transferring metaphorically the joyful serenity of the child's insight to the moon hovering over his head, "contentísima de algo" (Rivera p. 56).

The protagonist's reticence before the annihilation of traditional value schemes in "La noche estaba plateada" is overcome in the climactic conclusion to the following section, " . . . y no se lo tragó la tierra." There, haunted by his inability to understand why a beneficent God would allow disaster to strike unremittingly a good and innocent people, the protagonist finally brings himself to curse God. This ultimate rejection of an ideology of acceptance and submission allows him to elevate his own creative will into a higher sphere of existence and thus to produce his own history. Here too, as in *Pocho*, the act of rejection isolates a systematic distrust of any pre-existent, transcendental rule of value because such systems contribute to the enslavement of the individual will. It is only in the context of present historical conditions and under the influence of its own productive intellect that the individual can create a personal and cultural identity. With " . . . *y no se lo tragó la tierra*," the Chicano novel moves from a possible to an actual state of being.

Rivera's story places us in the full misery of a South Texas field, parched by the noonday sun, as a small group of Chicanos weed a crop. The previous day, the young boy's father, working under these same conditions, has suffered a sunstroke. Trapped as much by his mother's passive faith as by the exploitative economic system, he screams, "¿Qué se gana, mamá, con andar . . . [clamando] por la misercordia de Dios? . . . si Dios no se acuerda de uno . . . N'ombre a Dios le importa poco de uno de los pobres. . . . Dígame usted ¿por qué? ¿Por qué nosotros nomás enterrados en la tierra como animales sin ningunas esperanzas?" (Rivera pp. 67–68). But his previous day's anger and despair of their bondage to the earth are nothing compared to this day's, as his youngest brother also falls now from the sun's devouring rays: "¿Por qué a papá y luego a mi hermanito? . . . ¿Por qué?" (Rivera p. 70).

Rushing home with his brother in his arms, the protagonist brings himself to do openly what he had done previously by indirection: "Maldijo a Dios" (Rivera p. 70). At this instant, he imagines that the earth might indeed open to swallow him up; but it does not. Instead, he continues homeward with the solidity of the material earth beneath his feet. With his acceptance of his own universal isolation comes "una paz que nunca había sentido antes" (Rivera p. 70). This almost Nietzschean serenity, a liberating joyful wisdom, is the direct result of his appropriation of the site of God's former existence as the place for his own self-determined presence: "por primera vez se sentía capaz de hacer y deshacer cualquier cosa que él quisiera" (Rivera p. 70). The religion of Job reconciled or of Christ crucified here has not diminished but rather added to man's burden of suffering. By rejecting that religion, the protagonist implies that in this life *understanding*, the source of humanistic power, is salvation; it survives and replaces the decay of faith in the divine. Freed now of transcendental myths, he knows that the earth cannot "swallow" and the sun cannot "devour." He saves himself to act within the bounds of history by realizing that those anthropomorphic projections of human will onto unfeeling nature are, like the myth of God Himself, only the fraudulent means by which the force of the individual human will can be diminished and enslaved. Authentic life is constituted by the will's interpretive act, the determination of its own fate. Having attained this level of dialectical insight, the child's recovery of his "lost year" cannot be far off:

> Se dio cuenta de que en realidad no había perdido nada. Había encontrado. Encontrar y reencontrar y juntar. Relacionar esto con esto, eso con aquello, todo con todo. Eso era. Eso era todo. Y le dio más gusto (Rivera p. 169).

If in Rivera's view life can be stabilized only after we have experienced its instability, in Oscar Zeta Acosta's representation, life is constituted only as instability, as chaos. Around the chaos, order can be momentarily constructed, but precisely because this order is a human construct, it cannot be made permanent. In the tragicomic antics of his fictional persona, Buffalo Zeta Brown, lawyer, writer, and would-be revolutionary, Zeta Acosta attempts to transform the debilitating effects of psychic doubt into political action, to fashion out of the absence of absolute value, a new hypothetical order. In the process, he creates one of the most outrageous and iconoclastic novels of recent years. *The Revolt of the Cockroach People* (1973) is, as the stinging irony of its double-edged title suggests, a profane, ambiguous attempt to reconstruct the traditional values of an ostensibly rural people in a modern urban society.

Despite the narrator's overt sexism, his blatant anti-clericism, and his heavy-handed egoism, no single feature of this novel offends the common reader more than Buffalo Zeta Brown's assessment of the American legal system as an arbitrary weaving of semantic threads created to hide the empty forms of notions such as "justice" and "natural rights." Whereas we would expect Law, at least in its ideal form, to permit us an approximation of the state of transcendental right, Buffalo Zeta Brown shows us, in a series of increasingly allegorical trial scenes, that the truth of justice is intimately tied to its differential opposite, the lie of justice: "*All of them*," he tells us in the climactic scene of the novel's closing trial,

> ... *every single witness, both prosecution and defense ... is lying.* Or not telling the whole truth. The bastards know exactly what we have done and what we have not done.... But they have all told their own version of things as they would like them to be.[17]

Brown's version of the law offers us two correlative qualities: Law is *arbitrary* because it is constituted by a systematic difference between truth and lies and not by its own individual, *de jure*, fullness. It is *differential* because law does not function from the compact force of meaning at the core of "truth" and "lies" but by the *de facto* network of oppositions that distinguish them and relate them to one another. The major consequence to be drawn from this double recognition, as Brown realizes, is that an objective truth, sufficient unto itself and available for all to see, can never be made present, either in the courtroom or elsewhere. Brown does not mean that there are not statements that we can judge "true" or "false." He does suggest, however, that every attempt to specify "truth" forces us to define it in terms of an abstract entity which is only a cultural convention: All speak "their own version of things as they would like them to be." From Brown's point of view, truth and falsehood are not by-products of the direct adhesion between a word and some actual state of the world but functions of coincidences or discrepancies between multiple versions of the same event. This recognition is at once frightening and exhilarating for Brown, for it allows him to fashion, if only temporarily, the unity of his earlier schizophrenic desires, to counsel at law and to write "THE BOOK" of his life (*RCP* p. 14).

This reconciliation is possible because Brown comes to see living, like lawyering and authoring, as a play of stylistics. The play allows the fashioning of a formal context into a thematic content. And all three activities finally entail a play with "lies" so that "truth" might be revealed. But all also entail the possibility that in the play with form, the form itself can become an end and seduce one away from the hard-won recognition of its foundation upon *arbitrary difference*. The flow of judicial, as well as fictional, language points to no meaning other than its own pleasurable self-reproduction. In other words, legal and artistic truth depend not on a direct relation between a linguistic expression and a real object or state of affairs, but rather on the process of continuously displaced sign functions, which attempt to name the truth. The arbitrariness of truth statements, however, does not lead Brown either to nihilism or to a sense of powerlessness. On the contrary, his understanding of the arbitrary difference of truth statements permits him to establish meanings as cultural units *materially* accessible to the individual will itself. He comes to realize that forms of law, political, philosophical, religious, and even artistic ideologies are products of the concrete social relations into which people enter at a particular time and place. As products, they can also be reproduced. Reality thus becomes a shocking montage of dissimilar qualities which the revolutionary artist can help transform. Buffalo Zeta Brown accepts this fact and uses it to convert chaos into a palatable anarchy of both forensic and poetic form.

Oscar Zeta Acosta's novel, in tandem with his earlier *Autobiography of a Brown Buffalo* (1972), is probably the most concerted attempt by a Chicano novelist to create a truly "radical" art. But as we have seen in both Villarreal's and Rivera's novels, the general impulse of the Chicano novel leads it to examine root concepts. Thus its radical tendency can emerge in various ways.

With Ron Arias's *The Road to Tamazunchale* (1975), the Chicano novel begins to exploit its privileged position at the juncture of the North and South American novel, and to perform the deconstruction of value in yet another way.[18] Fausto, the hero of Arias's novel, wanders imaginatively from the *barrios* of East Los Angeles to the rain forests and mountain clearings of Peru, as he attempts to track down the scene of his own death. In this novel, the realism of American literature is mixed with the "magical realism" of Latin American literature to create a super-natural Chicano realism. As Pablo Neruda has shown, the super-natural musings of the solitary poet at Macchu Picchu can have significant impact on the course of events in the mundane communal world. It is just such a synthesis of poetry and life that Arias seeks to effect through the figure of his dying protagonist, Fausto.

While the texts we have previously examined begin with a moment of spiritual decay, Arias's novel begins with a dream of material decay:

> Fausto lifted his left arm and examined the purple blotches.... He tugged at the largest one, near the wrist.... Slowly it began to rip, peeling from the muscle. No blood. The operation would be clean, like slipping off nylon hose.[19]

A life of smog, poverty, and emptiness behind him, Fausto amuses himself now "waiting for the end" (*RT* p. 14), by metaphorically stripping the shreds of life from his skeletal frame. But of late, he has begun to hear again what he calls "the song of life . . . somewhere beyond the house" (*RT* p. 14). Seized with a sudden "monstrous dread of dying," Fausto begins the most unlikely quest man has ever undertaken. Pursued by the death of life, Fausto decides to find, in present real terms, a life within the bounds of death. But the life within death he seeks is not that of traditional Christian theology; Fausto's life-in-death is to be one of his own making.

Once the old man sets out on his wanderings through the surrealized landscape of East L.A., accompanied only by Mario, a weird "goateed teenager . . . dressed all in black" (*RT* p. 25), we cannot be certain when "real" events end and hallucinatory Faustian or Quixotic ones begin. In fact, in scenes such as that of Fausto's self-excoriation at the beginning of the novel, of his escape from the police by hiding and later emerging from an occupied coffin (chapter 3), of the appearance of a singular snow-cloud over Los Angeles (chapter 5), of the figurative rebirth of David, the drowned illegal alien (chapter 7), or of Fausto's attempted wholesale smuggling of hundreds of "mojados" across the U.S. border (chapter 8), the normal lines between the real and the imaginary have totally disappeared. Fausto's masque, "The Road to Tamazunchale," which is enacted on the stage of his imagination in Chapter 11, sums up the fact that what persists is a metaphor of reality.

In Fausto's play-within-the-novel we are, as in Rivera's novel, on the road in search of a lost or never fully present plenitude of being. "Tamazunchale" is a real Mexican village, but more significantly, it becomes a metaphor of the inaccessibility of that plenitude. In fact, the road to Tamazunchale may be, as one character tells us, the road to no place at all: "You see," says the stage-director of Fausto's play, "whenever things go bad, whenever we don't like someone, whoever it is . . . we simply send them to Tamazunchale. We've never really seen this place, but it sounds better than saying the other, if you know what I mean" (*RT* p. 84). The director thus sees the name of Tamazunchale as signifying, without actually denoting, "the other" unnameable resting place. In contrast, Fausto's personified self-presence, the "Tío" in the play, makes Tamazunchale significant in its own right. Responding to a child's question, "What's [Tamazunchale] like?", Fausto's alter ego claims:

> Like any other place. Oh a few things are different . . . if you want them to be. . . . [If] you see a bird, you can talk to it, and it'll talk back. . . . If you want to be an apple, think about it and you might be hanging from a tree. . . . You can be the sun. . . . You can be the stars. . . . No one dies in Tamazunchale. . . . Tamazunchale *is* our home. Once we're there, we're free, we can be everything and everyone. If you want, you can even be *nothing* (*RT* pp. 89–90).

Before he too vanishes "between the horizon and the stars," Fausto

thus succeeds in doing something he has never before accomplished—
he isolates a place of free and absolute self-presence. He does not need
someone to die for him to bring him everlasting life because he is perfectly willing to die, and to live, his own death. Through the various
transformations Fausto experiences in the moments before his death,
he realizes that death is the ultimate mirror against which life is reflected
and in the face of which life's only values exist. By sheer force of will,
he manages to carve from the give and take between life and death,
from the difference between being and nothing, a fleeting point of eternal space, unaffected by the decaying effects of time.

Thus, even in this most fantastic and abstract representation of Chicano life, we find the dialectics of differences at work, reevaluating,
restructuring, and reinterpreting the nature of human experience.[20]
The novel's abstractions and ambiguous time relations are precisely intended to be read in situation, as neither fantasy nor reality, against
the reader's urge to reduce their complexity. In fact, the complexity
of the interaction between life and death as Fausto envisions it not only provides the novel's aesthetic base, but it also serves as a clue to its
ideological direction. The novel's complexity demands a descent on the
reader's part into what one writer has called "the materiality of language and the consent to time itself in the form of the sentence."[21] The
reader's descent into the materiality and temporality of the text is thus
the concomitant of Fausto's production of life from out of the tightly
woven fabric of life's interaction with death. By making us work through
the concrete details of this interaction in the form and content of the
text, Arias removes his work from the simple bounds of either reality
or abstraction in isolation. Through the very act of reading, Arias forces
the dialectical method upon us. Far from bearing no relation to the
real world, Arias's text registers in its very structural and thematic forms
the phenomenological fact of the *density* of contemporary life.

In contrast to this density, the simplicity of Fausto's death becomes
an act of revolutionary art: it allows the ground of life, which is death,
to become visible and manageable. And it makes the gap between subjective experience and the empirical world collapse in a moment of pure
insight. Fausto's creation of "Tamazunchale" as the symbolic place of
life-in-death forces upon us the view that reality is a changing, discontinuous process, produced by men and so transformable by them. It
demonstrates how character and action can be different and need not
be conceived of as historically fixed. Writing about how the storyteller
"borrows his authority from death," Walter Benjamin notes the "The
novel is significant ... not because it presents someone else's fate to
us, perhaps didactically, but because this stranger's fate by virtue of
the flame which consumes it yields us the warmth which we never draw
from our own fate. What draws the reader to the novel is the hope

of warming his shivering life with a death he reads about."[22] Seen as the storyteller who can let the wick of his life be consumed by the flame of his story, Fausto thus joins the ranks of philosophers and poets who produce their own valid reality. In effect, Fausto transforms his death into the triumphant life of art, which is the difference between life and death.

## III. History as Dialectics

The subversive edge of each of the novels we have examined effects destruction. But this destruction always implies the reconstruction of what has been undone at the site of its former presence.[23] This reconstruction is not simply the ordering of the chaos of reality. The Chicano novel's ideology of difference emerges from a more complex unity of at least two formal elements: its paradoxical impulse toward revolutionary deconstruction and toward the production of meaning. A unified theory of the Chicano novel must be able to handle this duality. The general notion of "difference" I have proposed allows us to consider this dual tendency of the Chicano novel faithfully, for it uses a dialectical concept that determines the *semantic* "space of Chicano literature" as that intersection of the cultural-historical reality appropriated by the text to produce itself, and of the esthetic reality produced by the text.[24] Opting for conflict rather than resolution, for difference over similarity, the Chicano novel is thus not so much the *expression* of this ideology of difference as it is a *production* of that ideology.

To be true to the principles of the text and the world which conditions it, criticism must, as a consequence, take the text's deconstructive pattern as its analytical model. We must remember, moreover, that a true dialectic necessarily involves us in negation. In a relationship between opposed terms, one annuls the other and lifts it up into a higher sphere of existence: development through opposition and conflict— neither Mexican, nor American, nor yet a naive Mexican-American, but something else. This something else is the *difference* of contemporary Chicano literature, which allows it to retain its special relation to both its Mexican and American contexts, while also letting it be marked by its relation to its own still unconditioned future. It should be clear that in pointing out this differential structure of the Chicano novel, I have not intended to reduce the significant differences among Chicano novels. The rich and varied profundity of these texts would frustrate any critic's attempt to squeeze them into any kind of reductive schema. What I have intended is to provide a theoretical context within which a practical literary history and criticism of the Chicano novel's difference might be elaborated.

As a genealogy of significant inter-textual relationships, such a history would not provide a *tool* for revealing immediate and essential truths, for the novels consistently show us that such truths are never unambiguously present, either in the text or elsewhere. It would provide us rather with a *theory* of the Chicano novel, with a framework of analysis, which, while remaining alive to the social and historical forces present in the artistic word, would allow the word to free itself from the enslaving myth of absolute and universal truths. It would place "truth," as does the Chicano novel itself, in brackets and consider the analytic process as an ongoing operation, rather than as a static event in historical time and cultural space. And it would permit, I believe, perhaps for the first time, the development of a truly "new" American "criticism." The primary value of this "new criticism" and its dialectics of difference is that it allows us to examine the formal and thematic dynamics *within* the literary text and to account for the nature of its special interaction with both the Mexican and American social and literary history that *surrounds* it with a clarity which other critical methods do not allow. In short, this prospective literary history situates Chicano criticism where it properly belongs, as part of the history of dialectics in general and of the dialectics of difference in particular. As Joseph Sommers suggested, to the extent that the Chicano novel accurately represents in rhetorical terms the dynamics and economy of social forces, it challenges the reader to become aware of the nature of the critical act.[25] It is a challenge well worth accepting.

THE UNIVERSITY OF TEXAS AT AUSTIN

# Notes

[1] Joseph Sommers' calling into question of Chicano literary criticism first appeared as "Critical Approaches to Chicano Literature" in the special issue, "Chicano Literature and Criticism," of *De Colores: Journal of Chicano Expression and Thought*, Vol. 3, no. 4, 1977, pp. 15–21. The essay later appeared in revised and expanded form as "From the Critical Premise to the Product: Critical Modes and Their Applications to a Chicano Literary Text," *New Directions in Chicano Scholarship*, ed. Ricardo Romo and Raymund Paredes (San Diego, California: University of California Press, 1978), pp. 51–80. I refer to this later version. See also a similar call by Gustavo Segade in the note entitled "Toward a Dialectic of Chicano Literature," *Mester* 4 (November 1973), pp. 4–5.

[2] Sommers, see especially pp. 55–62, where these distinctions are specified.

³ Sommers was correct in noting that, as of the time of his essay, semiological, structuralist, and post-structuralist methodologies were not yet being widely applied to Chicano texts. This is still the case. Recent studies, however, begin to apply these critical theories, if not wholly, at least in part. See, for instance, the review article by José David Saldívar, "Rhetoric and Ideology," *Mango* (Los Angeles) and his dissertation of the same title at Stanford University. See also the work of Juan Bruce-Novoa, "Miguel Méndez: Voices of Silence," *De Colores*, Vol. 3, no. 4, 1977, pp. 63-69. Cf. the renewed version of Marxist criticism offered by Juan Rodríguez in his essay, "Acercamiento a cuatro relatos de Y no se lo tragó la tierra," *Mester* 5 (November 1974), pp. 16-24. Another excellent study, more traditional at base, but equally aware of the viability of a neo-formalist, interdisciplinary approach to Chicano literature, is that of Raymund A. Paredes, "The Evolution of Chicano Literature," *MELUS* Vol. 5, no. 2 (Summer 1978).

⁴ The term "world-historical" event (or fact) is Marx's and is defined in Sections 1 and 2 of *The German Ideology* (1888) as the process by which local individuals, facts, or events become empirically significant on a wider scale: "World-historical existence of individuals, i.e., existence of individuals which is directly linked up with world history." I use the text edited by Robert C. Tucker in the anthology, *The Marx-Engels Reader*, 2nd ed. (New York: Norton, 1978), pp. 161, 162, 163, and 172. See also Terry Eagleton, *Marxism and Literary Criticism* (London: Methuen, 1976), pp. 28-29.

⁵ The purported "awakening" of Chicano letters in the 1960s was, of course, not an absolute beginning. Various studies have shown recently the extent and quality of works by Mexican-American authors in non-traditional formats prior to the flowering which did take place in the early '60s. See, for instance, the essay by Raymund Paredes, "The Evolution of Chicano Literature." See also, Tomás Rivera's discussion of the importance of Mexican-American newspapers of the nineteenth century, "Into the Labyrinth: The Chicano in Literature," in *New Voices in Literature: The Mexican American. A Symposium* (Edinburg, Texas: Department of English, Pan American University, 1971); Doris Meyer's study of a rediscovered nineteenth century Mexican-American novelist, "Felipe Maximiliano Chacón: A Forgotten Mexican American Author," *New Directions in Chicano Scholarship*, pp. 111-126; and Luis Leal's essay on the early interactions between Mexican and Mexican-American literature, "Mexican American Literature: A Historical Perspective," *Revista Chicano-Riqueña* 1 (Spring 1973), pp. 32-44. The question of "origins" is itself an important issue in contemporary critical theory.

⁶ José Antonio Villarreal, *Pocho* (1959; rpt. New York: Anchor, 1970), p. 19. I cite this edition of the novel throughout my discussion.

⁷ Tino Villanueva, "Tres aspectos de la narrativa chicana," forthcoming, *Cuadernos hispanoamericanos*.

⁸ Juan Bruce-Novoa, "The Space of Chicano Literature," *De Colores*, Vol. 1 (1975), pp. 22-42. This essay remains one of the more influential of theoretical discussions of Chicano literature.

⁹ In formulating my case for a theory of the "differential structure" of the Chicano novel, I have been influenced by a number of texts, including Paul de Man's essay on "The Rhetoric of Blindness: Jacques Derrida's Reading of Rousseau," in *Blindness and Insight* (New York: Oxford Univ. Press, 1971), pp.

102–141; Jacques Derrida's discussion of *differance* (with an *a*) in "Differance," *Speech and Phenomena*, tr. David Allison (Evanston, Illinois: Northwestern Univ. Press, 1973), pp. 129–160, and in *Of Grammatology*, tr. Gayatri C. Spivak (Baltimore: Johns Hopkins Univ. Press, 1976). "We shall designate by the term *differance*," writes Derrida, "the movement by which language, or any code, any system of reference becomes 'historically' constituted as a fabric of differences.... Differance is what makes the movement of signification possible only if each element that is said to be 'present,' appearing on the stage of presence, is related to something other than itself but retains the mark of a past element and already lets itself be hollowed out by the mark of its relation to a future element" ("Differance," pp. 141, 142). From Derrida's concept I wish to retain the two ideas of differance as a *differing* (in kind) and as a *deferring* (in time). Cf. Fredric Jameson's discussion of the notion in *The Prison-House of Language* (Princeton: Princeton Univ. Press, 1972), pp. 173–186, and his more general discussion of "structuralism" in *Marxism and Form* (Princeton: Princeton Univ. Press, 1971), and his recent essay on the possibilities of an "ethnopoetics," "Collective Art in the Age of Cultural Imperialism," in *Alcheringa*, Vol. 2, no. 2 (1976), pp. 108–112. The most incisive original works using the dialectical method are Walter Benjamin's *The Origin of German Tragic Drama* (London: New Left Books, 1977), and "The Work of Art in the Age of Mechanical Reproduction," in *Illuminations*, tr. H. Zohn (1959; New York: Schoken Books, 1968), pp. 217–251.

[10] See Robert Tucker's "Introduction" to his *Marx-Engels Reader*, pp. xix–xxxviii, for a discussion of Marx's development of a "transformational criticism" from Hegel's theory of history.

[11] Tucker, "Introduction," pp. xxiii–xxv, makes this distinction between idealist and materialist views of history. See also Karl Marx, *The German Ideology*, Part I, "Feuerbach: Opposition of the Materialist and Idealist Outlook," pp. 147–148.

[12] Marx, "Theses on Feuerbach," published in 1888 as an appendix to his essay *Ludwig Feuerbach and the End of Classical German Philosophy*, in Tucker, p. 145.

[13] I borrow the term from the Russian Formalist School to designate the narrative stratagem by which the Chicano novel focuses on and revises the concept of value. See the essay by Boris Eichenbaum, "The Theory of the 'Formal Method,'" in Lee T. Lemon and Marion Reis, *Russian Formalist Criticism* (Lincoln, Nebraska: Univ. of Nebraska Press, 1965), pp. 99–140, and the valuable discussion by Victor Erlich, *Russian Formalism: History and Doctrine* (The Hague: Mouton, 1955).

[14] The phrase is of course Harold Bloom's in *The Anxiety of Influence* (New York: Oxford Univ. Press, 1973); it refers to the intertextual debts incurred and remissed among "weak" and "strong" poets.

[15] Richard Villaseñor, *Macho!* (New York: Bantam Books, 1973); Richard Vásquez, *Chicano* (New York: Doubleday, 1970); José Antonio Villarreal, *The Fifth Horseman* (New York: Doubleday, 1974).

[16] Tomás Rivera, *Y no se lo tragó la tierra* (Berkeley: Quinto Sol Publications, 1971; reissued by Justa Publications, 1976), p. 1. All quotations are from the Quinto Sol, bilingual, first edition of Rivera's prize-winning novel.

[17] Oscar Zeta Acosta, *The Revolt of the Cockroach People* (New York: Bantam Books, 1974), p. 272. Hereafter referred to as *RCP*.

[18] On the possibilities of a comparative study of the Chicano and Latin American novel, see Charles Tatum, "Contemporary Chicano Prose Fiction: Its Ties to Mexican Literature," *Books Abroad* 49 (Summer 1975), pp. 432–438; and Carlos Monsiváis, "Literatura comparada: Literatura chicana," *Fomento Literario* 1 (invierno 1973), pp. 42–48.

[19] Ron Arias, *The Road to Tamazunchale* (Reno, Nevada: West Coast Poetry Review, 1975), p. 13. All subsequent citations are to this edition of the novel. Hereafter referred to as *RT*.

[20] The "fantastic" quality of Arias's novel has led some readers to ignore its substantial critique of both Mexican and American ideologies of death. See, for instance, the strident misreading and false question posed by Mariana Marín in "The Road to Tamazunchale: Fantasy or Reality?" *De Colores*, Vol. 3, no. 4, pp. 34–38. Bernice Zamora offers a more perceptive reading of the novel in her forthcoming review essay in *Mester*.

[21] Jameson, *Marxism and Form*, p. xiii.

[22] Walter Benjamin, "The Storyteller," in *Illuminations*, pp. 94 and 101.

[23] The pattern I have been describing is also evident, in different ways, in other major Chicano novels. A complete history would specify how Raymond Barrio's *The Plum Plum Pickers*; Rudolfo Anaya's *Bless Me, Ultima*; Miguel Méndez's *Peregrinos de Aztlán*; Alejandro Morales' *Caras viejas y vino nuevo*; and Rolando Hinojosa's *Estampas del Valle* and *Generaciones y semblanzas* adhere to the structure of *différance*.

[24] On the possibility of a Marxist "theoretical space of the referent"—a conciliation of semiotic and dialectical methodologies—see the fine essay by Thomas E. Lewis, "Notes Toward a Theory of the Referent," *PMLA* 94 (1979), pp. 459–475. See also Terry Eagleton, *Criticism and Ideology* (London: New Left Books, 1976).

[25] Sommers, p. 62: "The role of the critic is to challenge both writer and reader to question the text for meaning and values (which are inseparable from its formal disposition), and to situate this meaning and these values in a broad cultural framework of social and historical analysis." The status of the concepts "meaning" and "values" are of course also implicated in the analysis.

# Chicano Writing:
# The New Mexico Narrative

*José Armas*

Chicano literature in New Mexico shows a direct relationship to the historical, cultural and geographical landscape.[1] Therefore, to get some understanding about the writers and their work, it may be helpful to have some background about this "magical," "mystical" "Land of Enchantment" that has attracted so many people—tourists and artists—from every part of the globe.

New Mexico, admitted into the Union 66 years ago as the 47th state, is a land of many paradoxes and extremes. Probably no other state in the United States has such variety of landscape, natural color, scenic beauty and contrasting cultures existing side by side. It has some of the flattest land (the Great Plains) and some of the most spectacular natural formations (Carlsbad Caverns) in the world. The Rocky Mountains split the state almost in half, East and West. Lava flows have shaped many areas, and volcanic peaks still stand as sentinels overlooking the valley where Albuquerque, its largest city, rests. Rich and fertile lands are offset by rugged terrain, canyons and desert where even the cactus must struggle to survive. New Mexico can be described as a land of vibrant and dramatic color which leaves few untouched.

Dr. Sabine Ulibarrí, one of the major Chicano writers, speaks for many when he says:

> Our culture is based on the soil. We have a running and ancient dialogue with the mountains and the mesas, the sunsets and the deserts, the paisano (roadrunner) and the ponderosa, the wail of the coyote and the lament of *La Llorona* (mystical wailing woman) that no one has been able to interpret.[2]

New Mexico is a blend of old and modern worlds. Sandia Man and family lived here 25,000 years ago. It has some of the oldest settlements in North America. For example, Santa Fe, its capital, which was founded in 1610, predates the European capitals of Germany and Russia. New

Mexico also ushered in the era of modern world technology and science in the 1940s with its nuclear research.

New Mexico also belongs to the Old West era of cowboys and Indians, of cattlemen and sheepmen wars, and of outlaws. It is the adopted home of Billy the Kid, killer of many men; native home of Elfego Baca, killer of many men; frontier home of Kit Carson, U.S. hero, killer of many men; territory of Geronimo and Cochise, Native Americans, killers of many men; land of Los Alamos Scientific Laboratory, creator of the Atomic Bomb, killer of many, many men.

The natural beauty of the land contrasts with its dismal poverty. It is one of the poorest states in the Union. The per capita income of many of its one million people is lower than that of the American Colonists in 1776 when the country was founded.

The land is visibly marked by various cultures; their art, their music, their architecture, their food and language. Numerous Native American tribes peopled New Mexico for more than 10,000 years; then in the 1500s Spanish adventurers looking for the fabled Seven Cities of Cíbola became the first Europeans to set foot on the land. In 1680 the Pueblos successfully managed to drive them out for ten years, but the Spanish returned. Then came the Mexican government period in 1821, followed by the United States government in 1864. Conflict has marked every epoch, and the evidence of these conflicts is still being felt today. The noted historian Dr. George I. Sánchez writes in his important book, *Forgotten People*:

> There has never been a reform administration for New Mexico—Spanish colony, Mexican province, United States territory and state. To the New Mexican, change in administration has meant only change in office holders and not change in his status.[3]

Native American children are confronted daily with the evidence of their conquest in the form of the ruins of their homes which cover the state. Although New Mexico attracts tourists by advertising its Spanish traditions, as late as the 1970s Chicanos who spoke their native language in school were physically punished. Land ownership is a bitter issue. In 1967 Reies López Tijerina led what became a world-renowned episode to recapture some of the Chicanos' lost land grants in the Tierra Amarilla Courthouse Raid. He declared the Alianza de Pueblos Libres a free and independent republic. Land grant heirs are still active in the courts, in the streets and on the international political scene trying to get redress from the aftermath of the Mexican-American war.

Resolving the conflicts and ongoing struggle of the cultures is one of the major challenges of the state for the future. It will not be easy; there are major principles involved. The concept that "might makes right" is countered by proud people who refuse to succumb to the efforts of conquest and colonization. Even conservative and establishment individuals such as Dr. Ulibarrí are strong when it comes to maintaining pride in their distinctive cultural identity: "We make damn good Americans, but we make lousy Anglos."[4]

The Chicano culture itself is not homogenous. There are important distinctions even within the state. The Northern New Mexican is different from the Southern New Mexican. The profound differences are found in their speech as well as in some of the lifestyles. The literature also reflects the distinctions as will be shown later. The Northern New Mexicans consider themselves Hispanos or Spanish and can show historically how they have maintained that tradition. The Chicano in Southern New Mexico, on the other hand, has a marked *Mexicano* influence in the culture, and most are "recent" arrivals to the area. The proximity of the Mexican border has influenced the culture on a daily basis from the start. The Chicanos here are most likely to identify themselves as Mexican American or *Mexicano*.

## The Chicano Writers and Their Works

When talking about the writers we must note that there are native New Mexican writers and non-native Chicano writers who currently live and write in New Mexico.

For example, José Montoya, possibly the best Chicano poet in the country today, lives in California but grew up in New Mexico. His use of language, cadence and themes of the *barrio* Chicano are among the most penetrating and sensitive. His poem "El Louie" is now considered a classic. It has been dramatized by *teatros* and records have been made of this work which eulogizes the passing of Louie, a street dude who lived the hard life. Montoya is originally from the mountain villages of Torrance County and has lived in Albuquerque, the urban center of the state. Montoya still considers himself a New Mexican and surely his New Mexico beginnings have influenced his writing.

Fernando Gómez is also a New Mexican living outside the state, "exiled" because of lack of job opportunities. Fernando is Assistant Professor at Michigan State University and is editor of a journal called *Voces de Norte*. New Mexico is evident in Gómez. His personal writing still deals with themes of native traditions, rituals and scenes in the form of short stories.

Dr. Sergio Elizondo, Chairman of the Department of Foreign Languages at New Mexico State University in Las Cruces, is a recent immigrant to New Mexico. Since being here he has published his second book of poetry, *Libro Para Batos y Chavalas Chicanas*.

This book of poetry is a dialogue that attempts to turn the Chicano's head toward contemporary times. Elizondo represents the more traditional approach to literature, and at the same time manages to deal with the Chicano experience with keen introspection, playfully satirizing the Chicano and using some street language in his art. (He is originally from Mexico, although he has lived, studied and worked in various places around the United States.)

A native New Mexican from Las Cruces is Rudy Apodaca, author of *The Waxen Image*. This novel, published in 1977, has received favorable critical attention in the state. Apodaca is an attorney by profession. This first novel, primarily a commercial effort, is billed as the first Chicano mystery-suspense novel. Chicanos and New Mexico are only incidentally a part of the plot and setting, but he is currently at work on another book whose focus is on a "Mexican American" family.

Also from Las Cruces is Dr. Frances Hernández who recently published a translation of stories called *Only The Wind: Legends of the Onas of Tierra del Fuego*. *Only the Wind* is of special significance today, not only for the fine oral legends which are captured but also because of the area; Tierra del Fuego is currently disputed land over which Chile and Argentina are on the verge of going to war. This war could split the Western Hemisphere politically. The book received Honorable Mention in the Premio Pajarito in 1977.

Moving to the extreme Northern part of the state, close to the Colorado border, we find San Cristobal, a picture card village of adobe houses, fertile farmland, meadows and fish-laden mountain streams. This is the home of Cleofas Vigil, farmer, sculptor, philosopher, poet, and musician. Cleofas first gained fame throughout the Southwest as a singer of old ballads and *alabados*. *Alabados* are songs and chants of the Penitentes, a religious sect which was also active in the social-political arena during the American occupation. Cleofas, who was a member of the Penitentes at one time, represents the utopian blend of adherence to the concrete world, in the form of the land, and the intellectual and creative dimension which fuses the spiritual, physical and mental domains. Master storyteller in the oral tradition, he has begun to write more in volume in the past seven years. His sculptures have been on exhibit in a number of universities, and his poetry is anthologized in books and published in various newspapers. He continues to lecture in colleges across the country when he is not tending to his crops.

It's often been noted that much of Chicano literature is oral. One group that tried to capture this oral literature in print has been La Academia de La Nueva Raza. This group was most active in the early seventies. They attempted to show that oral literature and tradition which they called "El Oro Del Barrio/Barrio Gold" is much more than a means of aesthetic expression. ("While this is our literature, it is also our soul").[5] They wanted to make use of the "barrio gold:" "... La meta última que surge con más importancia es aquella de conservar nuestra sabiduría y utilizarla en la educación de nuestro pueblo."[6]

Their efforts to utilize the oral literature in the social development of the pueblo produced an important publication called *Entre verde y seco*.

Aside from *Entre verde y seco*, La Academia de la Nueva Raza also published a journal called *El Cuaderno* which came out sporadically. Although the group and publications are now defunct, the efforts of such Academia members as Tomás Atencio, Estevan Arellano, and Alberto Lovato to forge the people's oral literature into something much more functional has been partially fulfilled. Their works are an excellent source of study for a contemporary and dynamic picture of the Northern New Mexican.

Novelist Orlando Romero, author of *Nambé-Year One*, is another native whose family roots lie deep in New Mexico. Romero's work springs from a different perspective than La Academia and adds another dimension to the oral literature. While La Academia attempted to make use of the accumulation of the oral literature and tradition in contemporary life, Romero has managed to release his literature from time and space, moving fluidly and sanguinely from the past to the present, to the future. In *Nambé-Year One*, ghosts and souls still roam the land, inhabit the houses and invite themselves into the lives of the new generations that follow them like meddling in-laws. A skillfully handled work of magical realism in which the protagonist, Mateo Romero, "a stumbler into the world of dreams and illusions creates ... the intrahistory of the people of Nambé, a rural community in the Sangre de Cristo Mountains...."[7]

Romero is also a sculptor of *santos*. This religious folk art found only in New Mexico comes from a "culture vastly different from European-American tradition."[8] It is the native tradition of things such as the sculpting of *santos* which adds to the elements which make the New Mexico experience unique. The roots of this uniqueness lie in the history of the New Mexican development, identified by Cary McWilliams when he says, "Isolation is the key to the New Mexico cultural complex."[9]

Dr. Sabine Ulibarrí is the Laureate of New Mexico. His books, especially *Mi Abuela Fumaba Puros/My Grandma Smoked Cigars* and *Tierra Amarilla: Cuentos de Nuevo México* are poetic paintings of the Hispanic (as he prefers to identify them) community. Long before it became fashionable, Ulibarrí was actively promoting the language and the culture. Despite the limitations of writing in Spanish in this country, he has persisted. He has published five books, all in Spanish, although the latest publications are in bilingual form. He is aware of the dangers and consequences of adherence to his language and also of the status which the Hispano and his culture has in the dominant society:

> We never left our native land. New Mexico is our native land, our father, and mother land. We never set out in search of the American Dream. The American Dream came to us unannounced and uninvited. For most of my people the American Dream remains just that, a dream, unfulfilled and unrealized. The mainstream has marginized us.[10]

Ulibarrí has traveled and worked nationally and internationally but his first love is still Northern New Mexico.

## Influences of Development

The Chicano is historically a *mestizo*, a blood and cultural mixture of the European Spanish (and the mixture that made up that Spanish) and Native American, but also of Anglo American. The influences of this development must and do show up in the literature. As Reies Tijerina states, "This is where the East and West meet." Chicano culture is the result of the East and West liaison, which cumulates into a holistic philosophy of the universe. To one understanding the history, the resulting product is not difficult to follow, as Guillermo Fuenfrío writes:

> For the Chicano, Indian forms and symbols are no affectation. They are in his blood, his religion and his culture. Who but the Chicano is better suited to bridge the gap between Western rationalism and non-Western symbolism? To translate technology into poetry?[11]

Besides Ulibarrí and Romero, no other writer has captured the essence of this holistic relationship in the cycle of the universe more effectively than novelist Rudolfo A. Anaya. His best-selling novel, *Bless Me, Ultima*, has sold close to 90,000 copies since it was published in 1972. It is the story of young Antonio Marez who is initiated into the world of adulthood. Antonio's idyllic journey is shaped by forces of the land, the spirits, and the tangible realities of family, life, death. In terms of artistic achievement *Bless Me, Ultima* holds its own among the best in modern literature. In his second novel, *Heart of Aztlán*, his "political" novel, the theme of the spiritual blending with the material world continues. Clemente Chávez strives to save himself and his family after leaving the land because of lack of work and goes to the city only to find that the new environment also brings other destabilizing factors of the intercity's *barrio* life. This work integrates the collective unconscious of the cultural traditions of the past with the present.

## Major Themes of the New Mexico Narrative

What makes Chicano literature fundamentally different from other literature is the fact that this community has developed from a completely different set of circumstances from the rest of Anglo America. Its different history, different blood origin, different language, different philosophies of life have been a part of what has shaped the Chicano experience. The Chicano experience is a story of a culture in struggle for economic and cultural survival. This quest for survival as well as its celebration of life are fundamental elements which color and texture all facets of human experience. This is reflected in the literature because true literature cannot be written independent of the realities of the world to which it is tied. This conflict may not always be the theme of the literature, but it is the "paper" on which its stories are told.

In New Mexico the historic isolation of the people left the community to practice its cultural attributes without a great deal of interference. In the *barrio* there was security. The disorienting forces that kept the community from developing its full human potential happened when the people came in contact with the dominant society that has not yet accepted the notion of cultural democracy. Lifestyles, religion and specific customs are important in this narrative, but there is much more which elevates the literature from being merely "quaint" and "romantic" or folklorish to truly universal experiences.

We can see some of these by examining themes of the Land and the Family, the Language, the "Invisible realities" and the Pueblo.

### *The Land and the Family*

Perhaps it was only an extreme manifestation of romanticism that proposed as a literary and philosophical theory that the individual is at the center of all life. However, this concept has continued to influence the "democratic" world in all realms. We see it in America where the dominant society has dictated that the individual is the center of the universe (the *me* syndrome) and that the land must work and produce and accommodate the individual.

This contrasts with the relationship that Chicanos have to the land in which the philosophy is that the individual is merely one element in a much larger picture, a cyclical universe; and that the land is a sustaining force for the individual, the family, the world. Cleofas Vigil, who has raised his family on the land and continues to make his living from what the land gives forth, writes of it as "The mother of all life."

> The poor man's heart rejoices
> when the fields are green . . .

> If anyone takes her from you
> you will be an orphan.[12]

Most people understand that relationship instinctively. It is no accident that Reies Tijerina was able to touch a responsive chord and arouse an armed insurrection in 1967 over the issue of the land. It was much more than the dirt, or their homes they were dealing with. Sabine Ulibarrí also knows this when he writes: "Anglo culture has come between him and his past ... uprooting him from the soil, cutting him off from his ancestors, separating him from his own culture."[13]

Orlando Romero's *Nambé-Year One* centers on the land and people's relationship to it. The profound impact of the land is clear to him. He states, "*Nambé-Year One* could never have been written in Los Angeles or San Antonio or Denver." Of *Nambé-Year One* he says:

> It was the beginning of real-realization, more precisely an autobiographical way to state the Hispano's relationship to the earth ... Ritual motivates me. Ritual as in the seasons, the menstrual cycle of streams and all life therein.[14]

Rudolfo Anaya similarly is affected in a major way by the environment. Two of the pulling forces in *Bless Me, Ultima* are the *llano*, the open ranges, and the farming valley. The pull of the forces on Antonio are symbolically represented within his own family: his father's name Marez (representing the ocean) and his mother's maiden name, Luna (the moon). Antonio's discoveries and growth are a process of the relationship with these kinds of cycles.

In *Heart of Aztlán*, the land also plays an important role in stability (or lack of it) for the family of Clemente Chávez.

Anaya makes no secret about the impact of the land on him as an individual and on his art. In his essay "The Writer's Landscape: Epiphany in Landscape" (the religious connotation is worth noting) he writes:

> In speaking about landscape, I would prefer to use the Spanish word *la tierra*, simply because it conveys a deeper relationship between man and his place, and it is this kinship to the environment which creates the metaphor and the epiphany in landscape. On one pole of the metaphor stands man, on the other is the raw majestic and awe-inspiring landscape of the Southwest; the epiphany is the natural response to that landscape, a coming together of these two forces ... I don't believe a person can be born and raised in the Southwest and not be affected by the land. The landscape changes man, and the man becomes his landscape ... my vision was limited until I was taught to see the stark beauty which surrounded me. I was fortunate to meet a few old *ancianos* who taught me to respond to my landscape and to acquire the harmony which is inherent between man and his place.[15]

There is a reverent, even religious attachment to the land in the culture of the Chicano. It is held sacred and even influences comparisons with individuals:

> It seems to be the stabilizing element for the family, that in turn provides the stabilizing force for the people. People often talk of their *"pedazo de tierrita."* They speak of the land with gentleness, and the land is referred to as *"La Tierra Sagrada,"* the sacred earth, and on this *tierrita*, the roots of the family drops its seed and grows, expands and takes nourishment from the *tierra* and the plant of life, the family. This is where the family grows ... If a son exhibits qualities of respect he is said to be from *"buena mata"* (a good plant). The land is worked when possible, and the harvest of the land rewards the *familia* spiritually as well as psychologically.[16]

The family is at the core of the culture. Through a complex network which encompasses the immediate blood relatives and out to an extended family which includes *compadres, padrinos, concuños* on down to the "family" of the community. It is impossible to understand the Chicano without understanding the importance of the family. This is obvious in both novels of Rudy Anaya. In *Bless Me, Ultima*, the family is the security and shelter for Antonio. Ultima is an integral extension of that family. In *Heart of Aztlán*, it is the potential disintegration of the family and how it is dealt with which causes the crises. Ulibarrí's stories are filled with relationships and actions that take place through, because of, or with *"parientes."* Even the title of his book *Mi Abuela Fumaba Puros/My Grandma Smoked Cigars* gives an indication of the place of the family.

Romero's novel is an identity search in which Mateo is guided by family and ancestors. Ancestors who, even though their bodies are gone, their presences are very much alive and still teach and affect the development of their descendants. Mateo's grandfather explains this when he counsels Mateo to have faith and be open to life:

> And if, after that, Mateo, the ugliness of men's limited imagination keeps you from soaring like your beloved eagles and hawks, then all you can say is that you've lived as we have been taught by the wisdom of your forefathers who came to this land and mixed their blood with the rhythm of the universe.[17]

## The Language

Sabine Ulibarrí has persisted in using Spanish as his first language both in speech and in his literature. He is quite rightly concerned that "... as his language fades the Hispano's identity ... becomes more nebulous."[18] Sergio Elizondo, who also writes primarily in Spanish, is also convinced that the maintaining of the language is prerequisite to keeping the culture alive.

Anaya writes in English because he has a firmer grasp of the mechanics. But he is well aware of the nuances of the language, as when he says "... I prefer to use the Spanish word *la tierra*, simply because it conveys a deeper relationship between man and his place." Spanish is called a romantic language and at the very least is a much more personal language than English. Its special qualities are not lost on the writers of New Mexico.

The people of La Academia de la Nueva Raza were not only aware of the language but consciously built on it. Tomás Atencio elaborates in his introduction in *Entre verde y seco* that the language is the living language of the people and not of traditional Spanish class students:

> Reflejamos el idioma de una gente viva ... sabemos que muchas de las palabras en el español nuevo mejicano son antiguas y arcaicas por el aislamiento de nuestro pueblo de lo demás del mundo de habla español.[19]

Atencio also acknowledges that the language of the Northern New Mexican was in recent times influenced by the Indian, Anglo and the mixture of languages: "Otras palabras reflejan el influjo de dialectos indios y otras sufren cambios. El caló y anglicismos son parte del vocabulario utilizado por nuestro pueblo ..."[20]

A flavor of some of the language is captured by Alberto Lovato in the following poem:

> Agusa'o Con La Vida
> Porque No Retona
> Hay mucho que decir del compañero pero la friega siempre es pa' empezar—
> o como luego dicen los viejos de cuanto hay—si yo no le temo a la muerte—
> si lo que le temo es a la cruzada;
> Chu, calle la boca y no sea malcria'o
> Hijue las hijas, cómo ando cansa'o, ¿que no traen nada güeno?
> Hijue las hijas, cómo ando cansa'o
> Chu, calle la boca y no sea malcria'o
> Con Fama (O infamia, depende a quién y 'ónde le ajuste el zapato) de muy hombrecito no sólo entre los mayores sino también entre la plebe porque se prestaba pa' todo y cuando alguien le tiraba de borracho les decía—Borracho pero güen muchacho. ¡Hay Dios si en la peda te ofendo, en la cruda me sales debiendo!
> Chu, calle la boca y no sea malcria'o.[21]

Spanish is only one dimension of the language. Some write in English and still others use a mixture. Since the innovative work of Alurista and Ricardo Sánchez in the Chicano (also known as Caló) language (the interchanging from English to Spanish in the same sentence, phrase, or work), a great many writers have taken to using this form. This is the language that most Chicanos use in their everyday speech, although few writers have been willing to use this pattern of communication because of the obvious limiting effects for people who don't speak or read one language or the other. But as with Ulibarrí, the feeling is getting to be that if people are truly interested in the literature of the Chicano which reflects a dual experience in this country, they must make the effort to study the language. After all, one does not give up on a poem or a story simply because they don't understand some of the words used. The lack of understanding is not necessarily the fault of the writer. That's what dictionaries are for. I. B. Singer, this year's Nobel Prize winner in literature, has written all his life in Yiddish, considered a "dead" language.

The writings of people such as Jenny Montoya, Rómulo García, Beverly Sánchez Padilla, Virginia Granado, Jim Sagel, and the other up-and-coming New Mexican Chicano writers are comfortably using this mode. (A great deal of time could be given to the "medium as the message" but this is not the space for that discussion.)

## Invisible Realities

If there is an area which is distinctive to Chicano literature in general and in particular to New Mexican writing, it is the naturalness and "easiness" in which the mystical, spiritual, magical world is interwoven with the literature. It is much more than a style. It is form, a dimension of literature which captures an underground manifestation in the culture of Chicanos in *Nuevo México*. Anaya was the first to do it with such craft and skill. In *Bless Me, Ultima*, Ultima, the *curandera/bruja*, is an integral part of Antonio's life. In *Heart of Aztlán* the same mystical, supernatural qualities are the forces which move Clemente Chávez to act. There is magic and there is witchcraft. Both are unexplainable and unacceptable in rational terms to Western thinking or religious doctrine, yet they are very much alive, very real. In *Bless Me, Ultima* Tony's father talks about the powers of Ultima:

> "Ultima had sympathy for people, and it is so complete that with it she can touch their souls and cure them—"
> "That is her magic—"
> "Ay, and no greater magic can exist," my father nodded. "But in the end, magic is magic, and one does not explain it so easily."[22]

The same invisible realities are at work in Romero's *Nambé-Year One* as noted by Lomelí and Urioste: "Voices from the past are resurrected to give meaning to the here-and-now, thereby creating an atmosphere of legendary timelessness."[23]

Romero is convinced that there is much more to real life than the things which we can see and prove. In the novel, the protagonist, Mateo, thinks: "But it is in our magic, in our auras and in our souls that we constantly find the beauty of truth and peace."[24]

Superstition, witchcraft and spirits are alive and active in the lives of the New Mexico writers. They are not so outrageous to accept. I. B. Singer has made a career of writing of these ghosts and spirits and recently stated to an interviewer for a national magazine in all seriousness, "I would give half of my prize if I could get to see and talk to one."

Herminio Ríos of Justa Publications writes, "For those people still totally with the strait jacket of Western concepts of objective reality, a reading of the works of Carl G. Jung and the works of Carlos Castaneda may best be useful."

## The Pueblo

There is a consciousness of the Chicano as a *pueblo* in the writers of New Mexico. Often this is not a political awareness but it is an understanding that the Chicano experience is different from the Anglo or the Black reality. Recognition of the *pueblo* Chicano can be found in the dedications of the books published by most of the major writers. Anaya, Ulibarrí, and the writers of La Academia de la Nueva Raza all acknowledged and dedicated books to *La Raza, el pueblo, la gente*, etc. This may not seem to be too significant until one tries to find out how many of the one billion books published in this country last year were dedicated to the Anglo community.

Perhaps this consciousness should come as no surprise. "*La Familia de La Raza*" has been fairly tightknit due to historical circumstances in the American experience. The cultural attributes of the language, the values, beliefs, are all things which have bound Chicanos (even with the differences within the culture). Despite the fact that they are a large community and that it is predicted to be the largest minority before the year 2000, they are still an "invisible people." There is little evidence that this will change dramatically in the immediate future. This can be seen in the publication of the literature.

Although the first press was brought to New Mexico in 1835, the major presses have yet to recognize Chicano writers in any serious way. None of the Chicanos spoken about in New Mexico narrative have been published by major publishing houses. All have been published by Chicano presses, small presses, self-published or published in foreign countries. Ulibarrí was first published in Spain, then Ecuador, then by a Chicano publisher. UNM Press reprinted the English translation of *Tierra Amarilla* in 1971. Hernández Apodaca, Anaya, La Academia de La Nueva Raza, Orlando Romero—these as well as other Chicanos publishing in other fields have been virtually ignored by the major publishers.

This paper is a brief and broad overview of the New Mexico narrative. A closing statement on the status of the literature should be made. Despite the geographical, cultural and historical landscape from which the writers and their literature stem, it must be pointed out that the literature is not nationalistic by design. Indeed, most of the Chicano writers talked about would simply identify themselves as writers, period. Writers whose themes are universal. Some have chosen to write about the Chicano experience in relationship to the Anglo society specifically, but this is not the case of most. It is the basis of the socialization process; that the writers themselves grew from that shows up in the literature. Those who tell their story well cannot help but return to the source of that unique experience. There are enough distinctions in the culture and there is enough talent to assure that the New Mexico narrative does add a new dimension to Chicano literature and will leave its mark in the world of American letters.

ALBUQUERQUE, NEW MEXICO

## Notes

[1] The term Chicano will be used in this paper to identify the pueblo *mestizo* also known as La Raza, Spanish, Spanish American, Spanish surnamed, mexicano, Mexican American, Hispanic, Hispano Americano, Indio Hispano. While the term Chicano does not hold universal acceptance, the social and political connotations that it denotes are important especially when talking about the characteristics of the literature.

[2] Sabine R. Ulibarrí, *La Fragua Sin Fuego/No Fire For the Forge* (San Marcos Press, 1971), p. 5.

[3] George I. Sánchez, *Forgotten People, A Study of New Mexicans* (Calvin Horn, 1967), pp. 10-11.

[4] Sabine R. Ulibarrí, *La Fragua Sin Fuego/No Fire For the Forge* (San Marcos Press, 1971), p. 8.

[5] Tomás Atencio, "La Academia de La Nueva Raza: Sus Obras," *El Cuaderno*, Vol. 2, No. 1, 1972, pp. 10-11.

[6] Tomás Atencio, "Introducción," *Entre verde y seco* (Academia de La Nueva Raza, 1972), p. 7.

[7] Francisco A. Lomelí and Donaldo W. Urioste, *Chicano Perspectives in Literature* (Pajarito Publications, 1976), p. 47.
[8] Thomas J. Steele, S.E., *Santos and Saints* (Calvin Horn, 1974), p. 1.
[9] Cary McWilliams, *North From Mexico* (J. B. Lippincott, 1949), p. 63.
[10] Sabine R. Ulibarrí, *La Fragua Sin Fuego/No Fire For the Forge* (San Marcos Press, 1971), p. 5.
[11] Guillermo Fuenfrío, "The Emerging of the New Chicano," *Aztlán* (Vintage Books, 1972), p. 228.
[12] Cleofas Vigil, "Mother of All Life–The Earth," *Aztlán* (Vintage Books, 1972), pp. 227-228.
[13] Sabine Ulibarrí, "Cultural Heritage of the Southwest," *We Are Chicanos* (Washington Square Press, 1973), p. 14.
[14] Orlando Romero statements for *Contemporary Authors*.
[15] Rudolfo A. Anaya, "The Writer's Landscape: Epiphany in Landscape," *Latin American Literary Review*, Vol. V, No. 10, Spring-Summer, 1977, pp. 98-99.
[16] José Armas, "La Familia de La Raza," *De Colores*, Vol. 3, No. 2, 1976, pp. 44-46.
[17] Orlando Romero, *Nambé-Year One* (Tonatiuh, 1976), p. 169.
[18] Sabine R. Ulibarrí, *La Fragua Sin Fuego/No Fire For the Forge* (San Marcos Press, 1971), p. 7.
[19] Tomás Atencio, "Introducción," *Entre verde y seco* (Academia de La Nueva Raza, 1972), p. 6.
[20] Ibid., p. 6.
[21] Alberto Lovato, "Agusa'o Con La Vida/Porque No Retona," *El Cuaderno*, Vol. 3, No. 1, Winter 1973, p. 50.
[22] Rudolfo A. Anaya, *Bless Me, Ultima* (Quinto Sol, 1972), p. 237.
[23] Francisco A. Lomelí and Donaldo W. Urioste, *Chicano Perspectives in Literature* (Pajarito Publications, 1976), p. 47.
[24] Orlando Romero, *Nambé-Year One* (Tonatiuh, 1976), p. 112.

# The Urban Experience in Selected Chicano Fiction

*Marvin A. Lewis*

## I

### Introduction

In their landmark sociological study of Mexican Americans, Leo Grebler and his co-authors make the following pertinent observations concerning settlement patterns:

> A population once dependent largely on agriculture is now so greatly linked with city life that many of its problems mirror the problems of urban America. And although on balance the group has benefited from the rural-urban shift, the transition has been associated with the usual stress of adjustment to the city, and compounded by the problems of minority status and often by language handicaps. Formal and impersonal controls enforced by an anonymous urban officialdom have replaced the informal and person-to-person contacts with authority in rural areas. There is a world of perplexing and ego-wounding forms and documents. City living compounds the problems of transportation and schooling. The new urban milieu often has a disruptive influence on family life.[1]

Historically, Mexican Americans have always formed a part of the urban environment. In a not-too-dated issue of *Newsweek*, a related assessment of this population is made:

> Contrary to popular perception, only 8.5 percent of Chicanos are farm workers. Four out of five live in cities, and many of them are poor ... East Los Angeles is the nation's biggest barrio. It is a community of 700,000 where a full third of the people speak only Spanish.[2]

The purpose of this study is to determine to what extent, if any, urban problems such as adjustment to the city, minority status, language handicaps, formal and impersonal controls, transportation and schooling, disruptive influence on family life, and the environment itself are artistically dramatized in selected Chicano fiction. The Los Angeles context is the preferred location for a majority of artists in their interpretations of Chicano urban conditions. Therefore, the primary focus of this paper will be on works treating aspects of the Los Angeles scene.

The period between 1970 and 1980 has witnessed some interesting developments in Chicano fiction. There was a concentrated effort, spearheaded by Quinto Sol, Tonatiuh, Justa, Mortiz, Peregrinos, and others, to have Chicano writers published and read. These efforts have resulted in a variety of literary forms of divergent degrees of depth and sophistication.

In this paper I will analyze five stylistically different works of art that are thematically linked by Chicano experience. They are: *Blue Day on Main Street* (1973), stories by J. L. Navarro; *The Gypsy Wagon* (1974), a collection of short stories edited by Armando Rafael Rodríguez; *The Road to Tamazunchale* (1975), a novel by Ron Arias; *Memories of the Alhambra* (1977), a novel by Nash Candelaria; and "Estilio" (1980), a short story by Miguel Méndez. In the first part of my discussion the critical thrust is the literary progression in different interpretations of the urban experience from social realism to fantasy and magical realism. In the second section I return to the more traditional narrative perspective of the authors of *Memories of the Alhambra* and "Estilio." Exemplary short stories from the two volumes will be used since it is impossible to treat each one individually.

## *The Gypsy Wagon*

From *The Gypsy Wagon*, "Ellipses," "A Story," and "The Proletarian" will be briefly examined.[3] *The Gypsy Wagon* is a collection of short stories concerned with human experience. Life, death, and survival is the stuff that forms the essence of the work. Since each *cuento* has a different author, there is no uniformity of style or narrative technique. Thematically, most of the works are connected by their assessment of the urban experience.

"Ellipses" by Yolanda A. García is one of the more cleverly written stories in the book, although more of the interpretation should be left to the reader. The narration begins with the following observation:

> If, in the dawning of a person's life, he encounters circumstances and situations which cause that same dawn to turn suddenly and fiercely to noonday sun, sooner than expected, he may find himself in a state of perpetual futile revenge against those forces which have caused him to prematurely struggle with himself. (p. 5)

This sets the tone of the story as Roberto and Miriam's romantic high school love affair turns into a nightmarish confrontaion with daily reality in the adult world of Los Angeles. After marriage, the two are engaged in a struggle for survival. He maintains two jobs in an effort to support Miriam, the baby, and himself. The persistence of the never-ending *cucarachas* serves to lend a depressing note to the narrative.

The author uses both overt narration and subtle ways to dramatize her characters' plight. The reader is told that: "Roberto unconsciously pushed at Miriam's back in their *twin* bed, causing her to face him and protest in turn . . ." (p. 5). "He sprang out of bed and slowly pulled back a *thin, worn* curtain at the window" (pp. 7, 9; emphasis added). Their physical position also mirrors their mental state. A constant air of depression causes them to bicker continually between themselves.

Perhaps the most important element in "Ellipses" is the examination of the troubled psyche of Roberto, caused for the most part by everyday pressures. The central dream/nightmare in the story revolves around the shooting of Roberto's brother by the police and the resulting feeling of impotency Roberto experiences. At the end of his dream, Roberto is in bed choking his wife instead of the policeman who was supposed to have killed his brother. Thus "Ellipses" is concerned with the effect of real or imagined situations upon life. The ending is such that we can imagine Roberto ". . . in a state of perpetual futile revenge against those forces which have caused him to prematurely struggle with himself." Roberto cannot change these forces, just as he cannot lift his family from their poverty. The result is utter frustration and despair caused by both internal and external strife.

"A Story" by Francisco Martínez explores the middle-class Mexican-American world of Frank, Sally, and their children, who have been successful. Once again the setting is Los Angeles, where the unrest of 1970 serves as a backdrop for the assessment of bourgeois attitudes:

> Frank in a rather cool voice tried to amuse his guests by pointing out that they were in a quiet community. Of course, his statement was directed to the several whites, supervisors of his, in the group. Immediately though, as if without any real suggestion from any source, the talk, of a buzzing nature, turned to the protest march that had passed by earlier in the day. Again Frank in a reassuring manner voiced that things are peaceful in East Los Angeles. In his slip of the tongue he blurted, "There is no need for another Watts." (p. 51)

The story, narrated in a sarcastic manner, draws an analogy between a protest march and a birthday party. The two separate events are brought together when the police order everybody off the streets while breaking up the demonstration. The party participants comply with only a meek "Why?" Obedience to the law is primary. Frank, who has killed his son-in-law for beating Frank's daughter, is characterized as not having the guts to stand up to the police. Throughout, Frank is portrayed as a hard-working individual who has earned his place and now knows how to play by the rules. Frank's "story" is typical of people who struggle to achieve material progress and then forget quickly their backgrounds. Class and status do not erase the pressure of minority status, but rather make it more bearable.

David J. González' "The Proletarian" deals with two barbers: one, José Navarro, beginning his career, and the other, Ernesto López, at the end. Both are looking for security—the former in life, the latter in death: "Ernesto had decided it was time to buy a piece of ground, a place to be buried. Just one more job and everything would be okay. He had worked all his life and had nothing to show for it" (p. 60). Ernesto is presented as dying both a mental and physical death. In his agony, he raises pertinent quesions concerning the oppressed working classes: "If we all die, why not do something besides work and produce workers by having children? Unless we can free them from the same suffering why bring them here?" (p. 62). The inability to break class lines is the issue here since Ernesto sees perpetual suffering for his people. On the other hand, José can only think of the two dollars he advanced the man. Money, it seems, does cause a great deal of insensitivity, regardless of ethnic background.

In a sense, the three stories assess survival in the urban environment. The setting seems to increase the amount of tension experienced by the characters since the emphasis is on making it on society's terms. Although the artists are young, they show a keen awareness of the difficulties faced in the urban milieu.

## Blue Day on Main Street

Whereas the three stories from *The Gypsy Wagon* present family situations, *Blue Day on Main Street* switches, for the most part, to the promiscuous world of the streets of Los Angeles.

*Blue Day on Main Street* by J. L. Navarro[4] contains twelve stories and a play that treat both rural and urban aspects of the Chicano experience. Six of the selections—"Weekend," "Cutting Mirrors," "Blue Day on Main Street," "Tamale Leopard," "Frankie's Last Wish," and "Eddie's Number"—are thematically linked by their treatment of urban problems such as drug abuse, prostitution, and violence, which of course are not limited to the Chicano.

"Weekend" probes the adolescent world of Teddy and his relations with his girl, Tina, and friends, Peanuts and Little Man. The action takes place in the Elysian Park area where Teddy moves in a maze of marijuana, reds, wine, sex, and death. The friends' efforts to burglarize a liquor store end in utter frustration when they are unable to open the safe. Their escapade turns into an absurd orgy before Teddy is shot when they flee the cops. Teddy is quickly forgotten by his friends and his death rapidly becomes everyday conversation. What is distinctly Chicano about this story is the appearance of certain types such as the *vatos locos* and lowriders as well as the intertwining of graffiti into the novelistic structure.

The storyline is fairly simple. What does seem to be lacking is a sense of purpose among the characters, who appear to be moving blindly toward nothing. The need for control and direction is of primary importance and is emphasized by the absence of responsible grown-ups in the story. In "Weekend," just as in the aforementioned stories of *The Gypsy Wagon*, a hostile attitude toward the police, who represent anonymous urban officialdom, is manifested. This posture is maintained throughout most of the collection.

"Cutting Mirrors" concerns the middle-class world of Anthony Alonzo, an advertising copywriter, and his reaction to his milieu. As Anthony sits in the country contemplating nature, the narrator surmises:

> As far as Anthony was concerned, the ads could wait. At this point in the day he didn't care whether he lost his job or not. The moment, this moment was enough for him. The mere thought of feeling cleansed from the city ways, and the ways he functioned in the city, had him at ease in a way he could not have felt in L.A. The air was clean and fresh; away from smog, he felt alive. All thought that came his way was welcomed. This mood was felt by every sense and cell, giving him knowledge of being Man rather than counterfeit Homo Sapien. In this and in many other thoughts he drenched his mind, gliding from mood to mood, not caring for answers, just for a moment of wholeness. (p. 59)

During his self-analysis, Anthony reacts negatively to the institution of marriage and his economic situation. The urban experience weighs upon Anthony as he escapes into a fantasy world and dreams of a type of utopia. His desire is to escape from the ritualistic world of nine-to-five and to return to a more simple existence. Anthony seeks spiritual as well as physical release. In his mind he is attacked by the mechanized world as he is unable to cope with daily existence. Alienation is the key issue since Anthony experiences estrangement from self, institutions, and his fellow man.

"Tamale Leopard" is a story of night life and prostitution told in a tongue-in-cheek manner as two lonely people, Alfred and Esther, seduce each other under false pretenses after meeting in a cantina.

"Eddie's Number" treats the old triad of dope, prostitution, and death. Johnny, the pusher, betrays Eddie, the hype, who is supported by Carmen, the hooker. Eddie is shot and killed by the police while resisting arrest.

"Blue Day on Main Street" is concerned with urban degradation as seen through the eyes of a man recently released from a mental institution. His focal point is Sixth and Main in downtown Los Angeles where he experiences some abnormal delusions. He assesses the situation: "As I look around me, I can't help thinking that what I see is just an extension of the place I left behind" (p. 65). The entire story is a sequence of disjointed images that represent a protest against the absurdity of the urban scene.

"Frankie's Last Wish," one of the more artistically appealing selections, relates the confrontation between pachucos and sailors in 1943 to the situation in Los Angeles in 1970. Payaso, one of the pachuco participants, introduces the reader to the action:

> ... singing in the village square: the señoritas are passing by with roses in their hands. Mando. The shotgun. He has a .22 in his pocket. Use it. The rifle poised. The horse fell. A bullet in the head. Closer. Hector. Shined his shoes all day for the fight. Spit. He could see himself in them. The bleeding heart throbbing in the light of the flaming Sun. He won't die. The people waiting, watching, watching. Can see them through the corner of my eyes. Across the street. A cross. He won't die. Drink the wine that will kill him for three days. Somewhere else; elsewhere again. Alive again. Closer. Heart beating in anticipation of the knife. Closer. Alive. In México. The desert heat. The sticky juice of the cactus. In L.A. In México. On Main Street. The people shouting. Wanting blood. Anybody's blood. Crowds of hungry flesh eaters. Eating with their eyes. Feeding what they feel with what they see. Virgins. The pace is slow. Bleeding hands of blood. Hector's shiny shoes. She won't die. Sweat gathering on my brow. Damp climate. The spear, the fish, the spear and the miss and the warm damp climate. Closer. They keep coming. Sailing. What did they want? Why this? The gold. Plumed headdress. The dance last night at Cuco's house. The feathers and the paint and the brown dancers dancing for the harvest. Slow numbers got me hard against Virgie. Wooden ships. Closer. Tall waves. She was fine. Did it good. Won't go back. Fear. I feel fear. He's dead. Loco. Closer. Won't die. Got my gun. The earth is quaking and the thunder of its anger devours. Man. He called me a man. Then. The sailor the night last week said punk, greaser, dirty Mex. The man of bronze called me a man. Closer. The sailor. Told him to suck it. Fuck him. All the same. Killed Loco. The furs and the cold and the meat and the rawness of it and the taste of blood. Wine. Had wine before coming down. Warm now. Pato and his machete. Chop some head, Pato. Yesca was good too. Two of them. Ripped out. I watched. Red flowers off a bush of flesh. Richard said they raped his sister. For survival. I watch them coming. Closer. Coming and we going to meet them. To fight them. Warm and not afraid because it's too late to fear what is coming closer.... (p. 81)

There is a juxtapositioning of time and space as the situation in Los Angeles is related to an Aztec sacrifical ceremony in Tenochtitlán and, vaguely, to the Mexican Revolution of 1910. Payaso's primary thoughts are of his Aztec heritage which he hopes will help sustain him during the confrontation. At the same time ruminations about more immediate physical pleasures are also evident.

These two primary incidents lend historical perspective to Chicanismo as the author draws an analogy between the Aztec past and 20th-century attempts at self-definition, embodied in the pachucos. Blood and sacrifice are foremost in both epochs.

When the scene shifts to the present, the atmosphere reflects a dramatic change to the world of Frankie and his lowriding friends, concerned more with escape from, rather than confrontation with, daily reality. A link between past and present is maintained through the presence of Stella, Payaso's sister, who is now an alcoholic and aunt of Martha, one of the gang. There is a similar effort to present Aron as a reincarnation of Payaso through physical similarities:

> Payaso reached up to scratch at his left ear. There was a mole just behind the lobe of the ear. (p. 80)

> Aron rubbed the mole behind his left ear and, to Stella, said, "Who's the guy in the picture?"
> "That's my brother."
> "Oh yeah. Where's he at now?"
> "Dead. He got killed during the riots of '43."
> "I heard about them," Frankie said. "My uncle told me. He said them were some bad days."
> Aron looked at the boy's face in the photograph. He somehow felt that he knew whoever it was very well. (p. 89)

In the ensuing argument between Aron and Frankie over who is going to possess Stella, Frankie is shot and killed. Events of 1970 are in ironic contrast to the sacrifices made in 1943. Aron, Payaso's counterpart, and his friends are bent on self-destruction and the annihilation of their fellow Chicanos instead of being united against a common enemy. This is true because of the heavy use of drugs and the need to play a role.

A brief examination of these stories, which set the tone of *Blue Day on Main Street*, reveals that Navarro's focus is not on traditional rural problems of Chicano existence but on the confrontation between new aspects of the urban milieu. True, the police, drugs, sex, violence, and alienation have always been there, but the author's concern is the toll they take on the younger generation. Society is partially to blame for the new promiscuity that reaches down into the barrio and destroys.

The urban scene has prompted a rash of drug use and crime that often ends tragically.[5]

## The Road to Tamazunchale

The Chicano novel, too, has been concerned with the urban environment, ranging from the surface treatment of the topic by Richard Vásquez in *Chicano* (1970) to the agonizing border experience portrayed in Miguel Méndez's *Peregrinos de Aztlán* (1974), where the city literally destroys its inhabitants. More recently, however, the Chicano novel has gone beyond social realism in treating the urban scene to enter into the realm of fantasy. Such a work is *The Road to Tamazunchale* by Ron Arias.[6] The approach here will involve examining the themes of the *mojado* or wetback (undocumented worker) and the search for paradise. These themes are inextricably bound together in the novel. Although the novel is also concerned with some of the urban problems pointed out at the beginning of the study, Arias treats them on a different literary plane.

*The Road to Tamazunchale* explores the world of the aging Fausto Tejeda as he confronts the fact that he is dying. For the past six years Fausto has been ill and under the care of his niece, Carmela, who serves to maintain a balance between reality and fantasy. Fausto's dead wife, Evangelina, his alter ego, also functions in this capacity. Fausto's mental processes oscillate between the reality of Los Angeles smog and freeways, from which he wishes to escape, and the fantasy of real or imagined heroic incidents in the past. He spends most of his time in a darkened bedroom in a dream world.

Chapter 1 introduces us to the family situation and closes on the following note: "In silence the old man listened carefully for the song of life. Curled in the darkness somewhere beyond the house, it beckoned with the faint, soft sound of a flute. Then it was gone" (p. 14). The flute, a central image of life and death, recurs throughout the novel and is related to the Peruvian motif personified by Marcelino Huanca, the shepherd, and his alpacas.[7] Early in the second chapter, Fausto embarks on an imaginary voyage to Peru, which provides the opportunity for him to make a comparison between the great American civilizations of Tenochtitlán and Cuzco.

Humor is a key ingredient in the novel. Most of the incidents in which Fausto could have actually participated are presented in an absurdly hilarious manner. During a bus trip downtown, he is ridiculously dressed, encounters a herd of alpacas on the freeway, meets Mario, an aspiring *vato loco*, disrupts a funeral procession, and evades capture by the police. After Mario steals Carmela's boyfriend's car, the odd couple, Mario and Fausto, goes joyriding in Elysian Park where images of the past surface. These recollections serve to maintain Fausto's contact with reality:

> Fausto remembered his neighbor's face behind the tall, chain-linked fence. Tiburcio had been mistakenly corraled in an Eastside round-up of Mexican illegals and was in a terrible mood. The academy tennis courts were covered with men. (p. 34)

The incident recalls indiscriminate acts of deportation, perhaps of the 1930s, which form a part of collective Chicano history and memory.

The theme of undocumented workers is quite prevalent in *The Road to Tamazunchale*. The *mojado* incident is prompted by the appearance of David's corpse; he has apparently drowned while attempting to swim across the river.[8] David's corpse is cared for by the people in Fausto's barrio, especially Mrs. Rentería, a lonely woman who uses him for positive psychological reasons. In the past, Fausto may have actively engaged in the illegal human traffic. Fausto now imagines a situation in which he provides services for the workers and gives them dignity. Thus he conceives of himself as a maker of history rather than as a mere participant. Arias' magical treatment of the episode assures a certain amount of distance that minimizes overt social protest.

Fausto's grand plan to bring the undocumented workers across in ships is not realized in life. However, in his fantasy world, he leads them across the border, up through Southern California, and into Los Angeles. Eventually the *mojados* and the barrio residents act out scenes from a play, "The Road to Tamazunchale," which gives the novel its title.

The central place image of the novel, Tamazunchale, represents Paradise, a place where there are no problems or worries.[9] This is what Fausto envisions both for himself and for the workers. This idea is reinforced throughout the novel in several places. For instance, in Chapter 2, Fausto's dreams place him in the unspoiled world of the Incas, but in reality he is on the floor of his bedroom. The presence of the young Inca shepherd, Marcelino Huanca, and his alpacas, who have lost their way, also suggests a simpler world. It is worth noting that it may be possible to extend the paradise image to the very Elysian Park in which Fausto and his friends congregate, although we know that this park really exists.[10] The park is presented as a *locus amoenus* and is, symbolically, Fausto's final resting place.

> Except for the cars, the park was deserted. The streets were gone, some trees had shriveled, others had grown. Squirrels poked their heads out of the leaves on the ground, a bank of snow lay gleaming on the ridge below the blue, richly blue sky. A fantailed pigeon escaped the jaws of a snake by swooping up as a hawk, losing itself among

> the uppermost pines. And there was silence, then the sounds of other birds, of crickets, of frogs by the eddies of a stream. A rabbit moved among the ferns, a twig cracked under the weight of age and a bobcat's paw. The grasses grew high, and the flowers bent with the breeze then sprang back and curled their heads to the sun. The scent of pine and sage mingled with the smells of moist earth, tiny onion shoots and the tangled fountains of wild strawberries. (p. 104)

Obviously the accent here is on the natural world and serves to demonstrate that, in the end, Fausto has truly arrived at his destination, a friendly coalescence of man, other animals, and nature. Marcelino Huanca, the flute, and the alpacas all form a part of this peaceful union. The novel closes with the Tejedas contemplating an absurd world from their heavenly vantage point.

The preoccupation with nature is in direct juxtaposition to the freeways, cars, smog, and other aspects of Los Angeles civilization. Fausto is characterized as always looking for the simpler things in life. A snowstorm, which appears briefly and causes a stir in the barrio, represents a purifying element in the dirty environment. Through suggestive imagery and subtle dramatization, Arias is able to accomplish by suggestion what other artists, Navarro for instance, present overtly.

Fausto's barrio is populated by such types as Mrs. Rentería, the spinster; Smaldino, the fisherman; and Cuca, the *curandera*—all of whose presence helps convey a sense of community. However, since Fausto is the primary literary focus, these characters move in and out of his world without any great impact on events.

Unlike most other Chicano novels, *The Road to Tamazunchale* is not basically concerned with Chicano social problems. At times allusions are made to the problems in the past in an effort to place the present in its proper perspective. The work's primary concern is with a dying man who happens to be Chicano. On the other hand, certain customs, modes of behavior, and attitudes toward life make us realize that we are dealing with a work which is distinctly Chicano.

## II

### Memories of the Alhambra

Since the publication of *The Road to Tamazunchale*, there have been both significant progress and stagnation in Chicano fiction. The most sucessful authors still write from a strong culturalist perspective while those who delve into fantasy and magical realism often receive negative criticism for writing escapist literature (Arias included).

Of recent fiction published, the majority of authors continue to interpret the rural experience. For example, four major novels were published in 1976: *Nambé-Year One* by Orlando Romero, *Below the Summit* by Joseph Torres Metzgar, *Heart of Aztlán* by Rudolfo Anaya, and *El diablo en Texas* by Aristeo Brito. Of these works, only *Heart of Aztlán* is urban, an assessment of the mythic dimension of a people's struggle within the Albuquerque barrio of Barelas. *Heart of Aztlán* is similar to *The Road to Tamazunchale* in the author's attempt to use an adverse environment as a point of departure for a mythic evaluation of culture.

The Chicano short story, too, is experiencing a resurgence, in terms of both quantity and quality as evidenced by several major recent publications. These include: *Requisa treinta y dos* (1979), edited by Rosaura Sánchez; *Rosa, la flauta* by Sergio Elizondo; and *Cuentos para niños traviesos* (1979) and *Tata Casehua y otros cuentos* (1980) by Miguel Méndez. Of the several dozen selections included in these volumes, only one concentrates entirely, in a penetrating fashion, on the urban environment—"Estilio" from *Tata Casehua*.

*Memories of the Alhambra* by Nash Candelaria[11] was published in 1977, the same year as *Generaciones y semblanzas* by Rolando Hinojosa, a work which assesses Chicano life in the Río Grande Valley of Texas. Although most of the action in Candelaria's novel takes place in Los Angeles, the dislocation associated with the move from New Mexico to California is of prime importance. The novel takes place within a forty-year time span in Los Angeles.

*Memories of the Alhambra* is one of the most fervently promoted works of Chicano fiction. It has been acclaimed as a major Hispanic American novel reflecting a man's search for his roots. At the heart of *Memories of the Alhambra*, however, one finds the same themes that have preoccupied Chicano writers for several decades. The primary difference is the manner in which Candelaria's protagonist attempts to resolve the dilemma of who he is and where he is going. Candelaria explores the Chicano/Hispano heritage myth (in its true significance) within the urban environment of Los Angeles.

The novel begins with the funeral of José Rafa's father and ends with the funeral of José. In between these two events the narrator traces two generations of Rafas from Albuquerque to Los Angeles, concentrating upon José and his son Joe. Not to be overlooked is the fine characterization of Theresa Trujillo, José's wife. For some time José has been concerned with the origins of the Rafa family, who have been part of the New Mexico Hispano community since before 1706, the year in which Albuquerque was founded. From California, José suddenly embarks upon a trip which takes him to Mexico and to Spain, the mother country, in search of his roots. The quest is unfruitful, however, since José belatedly discovers that man must be judged by what he is in the present not by what he might have been in the past.

*Memories of the Alhambra* thematically assesses the personal and ethnic identity crises brought on by social pressures experienced in the United States. Although the Rafa family considers itself Spanish rather than Mexican, they find that in Anglo society the terms are synonymous and denote inferiority. José contemplates the possibility of a United States cultural amalgamation of Spanish, Indian, and Anglo but promptly rejects the Indian component. He reacts similarly toward Mexicans, as exemplified by his rejection of Joe's Mexican-looking girlfriend Isabel and his acceptance of Joe's Anglo wife Margaret.

The historical irony here is that José does not take into account the many cultural and genetic exchanges that occurred in Spain over the centuries, a process analogous to what happened in Mexico and throughout the Americas. The novel's central ironic thread is woven around these circumstances, which do not allow José to rise above his bigotry. Coupled with the pressures exerted upon him in Los Angeles, José is forced to respond irrationally.

José both hates and admires Anglo society since there is a dichotomy between his material and his spiritual approach to the United States, where so much value is placed on physical appearance. His reaction after being rounded up with a group of illegals in Los Angeles is typical:

> Those damn police, treating me like a Mexican. It's time these Anglos dropped this Mexican crap about us. We're Americans. The same as every Goddamned Anglo who looks down his snotty nose at brown skin. (p. 127)

José is intent upon securing his share of the American Dream on his own social and economic terms. He is unable to forgive Anglo society for rejecting him or to forgive himself for denying who he is. José raises questions of identity that are left for subsequent generations to resolve.

His son Joe carries the idea of being American to its extreme. He is "college educated in spite of his father's reservations, middle class and un-Spanish in a sense that was both pride and despair to José" (p. 141). Opting for assimilation, Joe marries Margaret and fathers Terry, Joe, and Bill.

A balanced presentation of José's wife Theresa is one of the positive features of *Memories of the Alhambra*. In Los Angeles she immediately assumes control of the family although José thinks he is in charge. In addition to being level-headed and assertive in day-to-day situations, Theresa is often contemplative. At one point she wonders: "Was there a gene linked to brown skin, contaminating the behavior of their young men?" In her brief assessment of the biological basis of human behavior, Theresa concludes that, genetically, Chicanos are not predisposed to crime and violence, but that at times social circumstances can cause individuals to react violently.

The Rafa family is middle class in background, outlook, and behavior. Their material success is due to the fact that they have money, education, and excercise a certain amount of control over their destiny. However, these values do not insulate them from the bigotry and discrimination inherent in United States society. Although the Rafas do not experience prejudice within the same socioeconomic context as many other Chicano protagonists, its impact on them is comparable.

## Estilio

In "Estilio" Miguel Méndez presents a profound assessment of urban life.[12] It is the tragic story of Estilio, an outcast, a victim of broken dreams, a lack of love, and the absence of communication and communion with other human beings. He is, in the end, a dehumanized object. Unlike most of Méndez's stories, which mirror the rural ambience, or his novel, which oscillates between the rural and urban extremes, "Estilio" focuses entirely upon the city. It is a retrospective view of the process of individual alienation and degradation.

The story begins in an anonymous city, where the protagonist is spying on his ex-wife and her lover intending to murder them, but he cannot do it. After temporarily disrupting their activities, he flees into the city but not before he experiences a metamorphosis, reflected in his catlike activities and accentuated by the frog he carries in his pocket. Before returning to his lair, Estilio provides the reader with justification for his total estrangement. He perceives the city in the following manner:

> From the hundreds of cell boxes of the skyscrapers off key honking of neurasthenic women escaped; in the streets automobiles, paralyzed with urgency, yelled in desperation. The cries of ill-behaved kids bounced off the towers in chain-linked echoes. Cabroronn, cabrorronn puta puta puta roared a scooter with the air of a trained leopard, an ape man astride its back. The T.V. sets, pregnant with fetuses of victims and assassins, flashed their strident alarm. (p. 38)

The absurdity of the urban environment is dramatized by the narrator/protagonist in this meshing of humans, animals, and objects in a surreal description.

Estilio is a product of the very culture he is in the process of rejecting. An accident, he is conceived in a moment of weakness when his parents, "Mr. and Mrs. T.V.," turn away from the fantasy world of television. The question of abortion is raised and as an infant

Estilio suffers from a lack of love and from psychological child abuse. Since television has such a profound impact on his upbringing, Estilio experiences from the beginning the impact of mass commercialization. In fact, he becomes a media zombie suffering from a degree of commercial imprinting: "Not even he could explain years later, why the sight of certain products or known brands aroused in him an intense carnal desire" (p. 50).

In its satirical dimension, "Estilio" is a critique of middle-class cultural values. Even the deaths of his parents are narrated in mechanical terms: "... a bulb in her brain went out" and "... due to a failure in the carburetor because he hadn't had the motor tuned on time." Subsequent denunciations are made against sex/the pill/abortion, television/mass popular culture, and marriage/separation/divorce.

Estilio has become a rootless, dehumanized being because of his experiences with modern life. His search throughout life has been for human love and warmth. Yet when he returns to his paternal home Estilio encounters the opposite:

> Anxious and hopeful he took a look at the kitchen and found pyramids of empty cans that had contained soups and other metalized foods. He looked in the cupboards; they displayed an assortment of containers that used to hold vitamin pills. He ran towards a mysterious door, opened it violently and hundreds of capsules that contained antibiotics and other miracle drugs broke at his feet. Crying like a frightened child he went to the closets, nothing; the diapers they had pinned on him were disposable. (pp. 53-54)

Estilio is seeking an archetypal return to the womb in search of meaning and a better existence. Instead, he finds the superficial trappings of modern society in a city where even the stars are blotted out by pollution. In despair and frustration, "he became one more deserter of the great society," preferring to exist as a beast in his lair.

Méndez has written a classic case study of alienation, the estrangement of individual from self, others, and society. Of the many manifestations of alienation discussed by contemporary social scientists, Melvin Seeman has enumerated five that are applicable to Estilio: "powerlessness, meaninglessness, social isolation, normlessness, and self-estrangement."[13] Not only does the protagonist experience total disassociation from himself and his surroundings, he is also controlled by imposed superficial cultural norms. Consequently, he loses his sense of self in confronting the material aspects of urban culture.

## Conclusion

In light of the central question posed in this paper—the extent of the fictional representation of common urban themes in Chicano fiction — it is safe to say that Chicano artists are not concerned with merely stating the obvious. The urban situation has created an environment in which the old problems of discrimination, police brutality, inequality, and family unity have been compounded immensely by the addition of new ones such as drugs, inflation, crime, and alienation, which all transcend ethnic and cultural lines. As pointed out in the initial citation concerning the Chicano population, "... many of its problems mirror the problems of urban America." In *The Road to Tamazunchale* and "Estilio" these preoccupations are handled on a symbolic rather than a literal level.

In treating the aforementioned motifs, the authors also supersede cultural limitations in terms of audience. For the most part, the young writers of *The Gypsy Wagon*, J. L. Navarro, Ron Arias, Nash Candelaria, and Miguel Méndez all write for a general public as far as a surface interpretation of their work allows. However, an understanding of the Chicano substructure greatly enriches the reader's experience. To a degree, the artists reflect some dual aspects of their culture. There is a need to interpret common urban problems while maintaining a strong sense of Chicanismo.

UNIVERSITY OF ILLINOIS-URBANA

# Notes

[1] Leo Grebler, et al., *The Mexican American People: The Nation's Second Largest Minority* (New York: The Free Press, 1970), p. 112.

[2] "Chicanos on the Move," *Newsweek*, January 1, 1979, p. 23.

[3] Armondo Rafael Rodríguez, ed., *The Gypsy Wagon* (Los Angeles: Aztlán Publications, 1974).

[4] J. L. Navarro, *Blue Day on Main Street* (Berkeley: Quinto Sol, 1973).

[5] Commenting on the relationship between poverty and crime in the cities, Joan W. Moore, *Mexican Americans*, 2nd ed. (Englewood Cliffs: Prentice Hall, 1976), pp. 76-77, observes: "Chicanos share disproportionately in two types of arrest and convictions — in youth crime, particularly in activities related to the traditional Mexican urban gangs, and in narcotics. An exceptionally high proportion of the Mexican American individuals incarcerated in California state institutions are persons involved with narcotics, either directly or indirectly, and who have a history of juvenile offenses."

[6] Ron Arias, *The Road to Tamazunchale* (Reno: West Coast Poetry Review, 1975).

⁷ It is necessary to clarify possible symbolic levels of the novel since we are not limited to the artist's literal world at all times. In J. E. Cirlot, *A Dictionary of Symbols* (New York: The Philosophical Library, 1962), are the following explanations: "The basic meaning of the flute corresponds to erotic or *funereal* anguish" (p. 105); and "The *shepherd* is also the conductor of souls to the Land of the Dead—the psychopomp, and a symbol of supreme powers since flocks are representative of the cosmic forces" (p. 280). (Emphasis added.) These motifs are directly related to my interpretation of the novel's archetypal thrust.

⁸ This incident resembles a story by Gabriel García Márquez, "The Handsomest Drowned Man in the World," in *Leaf Storm and Other Stories* (New York: Avon Books, 1973), pp. 145-54.

⁹ From the editor's postscript: "A naturalists' and sportsmen's Eden—river fishing from dugouts, mountain game" (p. 108).

¹⁰ The name association is apparent in its mythological context where the name Elysian is synonymous with Paradise: "On the western margin of the earth, by the stream of Ocean, lay a happy place named the Elysian Plain, whither mortals favoured by the gods were transported without tasting of death to enjoy an immortality of bliss." In Edmund Fuller, ed., *Bulfinch's Mythology* (New York: Dell, 1967), p. 14.

¹¹ Nash Candelaria, *Memories of the Alhambra* (Palo Alto: Cibola Press, 1977).

¹² *Tata Casehua y otros cuentos*, trans. Leo Barrow (Berkeley: Justa, 1980).

¹³ *The Encyclopedia of Philosophy*, Vol. 1 (New York: Macmillan, 1967), p. 78.

# 2. The Early Writers in English: Villarreal, Acosta, Barrio

## Pocho and the American Dream

*Luther S. Luedtke*

More than twenty years have passed since José Antonio Villarreal became the first man of Mexican parents to produce a novel about the experience of his people in the United States. In that time have appeared Raymond Barrio's *The Plum Plum Pickers* (1969), Richard Vásquez' *Chicano* (1970), Tomás Rivera's "... y no se lo tragó la tierra" (1971), Rudolfo Anaya's *Bless Me, Ultima* (1972), Oscar Zeta Acosta's *The Autobiography of a Brown Buffalo* (1972) and *The Revolt of the Cockroach People* (1973), Rolando Hinojosa-Smith's *Estampas del Valle* (1973), Ron Arias' *The Road to Tamazunchale* (1975), and a wealth of stories, poems, *actos* and anthologies.[1] Scholars interested in the origins of Chicano literature have begun cataloging newspapers, journals, diaries, ballads and other literary prototypes of the Southwest,[2] even while poets and critics concerned for the future of Chicano literature still are issuing its aesthetic manifestoes. In the midst of the burgeoning literature, Villarreal's novel *Pocho*, published in 1959, holds a secure position not only as the first Mexican-American novel, but also as a powerful statement on the enigmas of coming-of-age in the United States.[3] My concern in this essay is a thematic analysis of the novel and its confrontation with the cluster of ideas provocatively, if diffusely, known as the American Dream.[4]

Despite its historical importance and dramatic force, Villarreal's novel is not well known even among specialists in American literature, nor has it received more than cursory critical mention. This initial essay on the novel, therefore, will begin with a narrative overview of *Pocho* and the development of its young protagonist, Richard Rubio. For all its latent political significance, *Pocho* is a novel of initiation and, true to its genre, intensely personal. Understanding young Richard's character as it unfolds is fundamental to measuring the social ideology of *Pocho* and its contribution to an emergent Chicano literature.

The scene of the novel is the Santa Clara Valley of California during the late 1920s and 1930s. There Richard, the only son of Juan and

Consuelo Rubio, searches for his identity while pulled between the old country ways of his parents and the mercurial new world south of San Francisco. The first chapter actually begins a generation earlier in Ciudad Juárez, Mexico, during the early 1920s, with a heroic depiction of Juan Manuel Rubio—a one-time cavalry officer in the army of Pancho Villa that liberated Juárez from the Díaz regime in 1911 and assaulted Columbus, New Mexico, in 1916—who dreams of returning with his deposed leader to again purge the *gachupín* (Spanish) stain from the land. A virile country warrior in huaraches and sombrero and the lover of many women, Juan Rubio symbolizes the Mexican past in the days of the Revolution. After casually killing the city-bred lover of a cantina dancer, Rubio is forced to cross the border into El Paso, where he stays until cut adrift by the assassination of Villa in 1923. "Thus Juan Rubio became a part of the great exodus that came of the Mexican Revolution.... It was the ancient quest for El Dorado, and so they moved onward, west to New Mexico and Arizona and California ..." (pp. 15–16). In Los Angeles Rubio's tirelessly faithful wife finds him once more. The birth of a son, Richard, two months later on a melon farm in the Imperial Valley stirs a new family pride in him and a love for his wife that is intensified by their exile. He stops drinking and gambling, becomes discreet in love affairs and eventually surrenders the nomadic life of the migrant laborer for a home in the prune country of Santa Clara to the north. There, rubbing his sore knees, this man of the gun thinks: *"Next year we will have enough money and we will return to our country.* But deep within he knew he was one of the lost ones" (p. 31).

With the second chapter, the novel shifts from the father to the son, from the Mexican past to the California present. The abruptness of the transition caused one reviewer to complain that "the story begins unnecessarily with Richard's father in Mexico."[5] Thematically, however, the transition establishes important generational conflicts, the loss of the old world values and the suspension of Richard between the cultures. The first chapter of *Pocho*, like the documentary interchapters of *The Grapes of Wrath*, portrays for an unaware audience the backgrounds of immigration to the Southwest, both the causes of uprooting and the subsequent erosion of the elder generations. It is more properly an historical introduction than the first chapter of Richard's life. Yet this is his legacy—a lost world refracted through prisms of memory and nostalgia.

Chapter 2 depicts Richard, nine years old, in an early stage of consciousness. Although labor strikes, violence and Communist rallies in the Depression year 1931 provide a context of social turmoil, the locus of this chapter is Richard's inner world. From the outset he shows the characteristic introspection and distance that make him more a spectator of the world than a participant. Reading the scenes of his spiritual awakening, one is immediately reminded of *A Portrait of the Artist as a Young Man*; in fact, Joyce's novel of initiation may be the most appropriate literary comparison for this similarly episodic work. Like Stephen Daedalus, young Richard agonizes over the immensity of God, suffers the guilt of childhood sexuality, mistakes the laughter of his teachers for ridicule, flees abusive adolescents, fears the dark, and strives to unriddle the natural universe through language and sign. Richard's troubled soliloquy on creation, time and sin, as he makes his way home from his first confession—the first of his age group to learn the catechism—has a distinctly Joycean cadence and imagery;

> *God made the world. Who is God?* But if He was good and kind, why did He make darkness? Night was the scariest time of the day, because a day is twenty-four hours and night is a day. But not daytime. He was scared at night because he could not see and he was frightened now because he could not know, and somehow God was in the middle of the whole thing. To do "bad" things had something to do with being alive, but really what were "bad" things? (p. 37)

Richard's spirit wilts at the thought of hell and damnation but flowers again before the textures and pulse of the natural world. "His every sense responded to life around him": to the "mild, almost tangible wind [that] caressed his face and hair like a mother's hands, washing him clean as it fondled him and passed to who knows where"; to the sadness of "the wake of trampled grass he created"; to the bounding jack rabbit, and the green bugs, and the multicolored birds that lend "their opulence to the scene" (p. 32). He is certain that someday he will learn to ask the questions that unlock the mysteries of creation and empty sky.

At the center of Richard's life stand his protective, superstitious mother, part of the mystery of birth and priesthoods, and his authoritative father, whose smell "the boy ... associated with his happiness" (p. 43). Often, Richard finds a refuge from the raucous world with Marla Jamison, the teenage daughter of a small farmer who opens to him her home and its world of books. Immured by family, social class, religion, and his own sexuality, Richard nevertheless readies himself even as a small child to fly from the labyrinth on the wings of art.

The theme of imprisonment and flight continues in Chapter 3, but as Richard matures, the sheltering arms of his family begin to fall back, exposing him to a harsher cultural orphanhood. Painfully the parents watch their child grow away from them. "We cannot teach you the things that you want us to teach you," Consuelo grieves, "—we cannot guide you, we cannot select your reading for you, we cannot even talk to you in your own language" (p. 61). Juan Rubio refuses to take his son out of school for work, sacrificing himself for the next generation. Undirected, Richard vacillates between the English and Spanish languages, between independence and family responsibility, between his father's proud hope that he will return to Mexico as a doctor or lawyer and his mother's plaintive warning that he, the only son, must go to work after secondary school and begin his own family. "Angry that traditions could take a body and a soul—for he had a soul; of that he was certain—and mold it to fit a pattern" (p. 63), Richard shuns both the fatalism of his mother and the materialism of his father. "Ah Mamá!" he cries. "Try to understand me.... I do not want to be something—I *am*." When she admonishes him for "that kind of feeling against the family and the custom"—"It is as if you were speaking against the church"—Richard flees deeper into a realm where his parents can neither lead nor follow him:

> "Mamá, do you know what happens to me when I read? All those hours that I sit, as you sometimes say, 'ruining my eyes'? If I do ruin them, it would be worth it, for I do not need eyes where I go then. I travel, Mamá. I travel all over the world, and sometimes out of this whole universe, and I go back in time and again forward. I do not know I am here, and I do not care. I am always thinking of you and my father except when I read. Nothing is important to me then, and I even forget that I am going to die sometime." (p. 64)

Someday he might even talk with God. Only with Mary, his slender Anglo-Protestant confidante, can he share the world of imagination; and to her he reveals his secret ambition to write books when he grows up.

Shackled by language and tradition, Richard's mother and father fall by the wayside along his pilgrimage toward self-realization. True to the second-generation immigrant experience, he begins to look for mentors and models outside the family. The first of these is the agnostic Portuguese cowherd, João Pedro (Joe Pete) Manõel Alves, whose story is told in Chapter 4. Because of homosexual incidents as a university student in Lisbon, Joe Pete was banished by his aristocratic father, a marquis, and after years of teaching philosophy in São Miquel, the Madeiras and Africa, took up a reclusive life in the Santa Clara Valley. Pan-like, he enthralls young Richard with his erudition and wondrous tales of Iberiam royalty. The lad becomes a devotee to his poetic vision and Whitmanic compassion. "There was an innate communicableness in the small, honest face that made the man speak out and say things he had withheld even from himself" (p. 81). Finally, however, in loneliness and sexual distress, Joe Pete gets young Genevieve Frietas pregnant and then goes mad. He too fails Richard. Nevertheless, like George

Willard in *Winesburg, Ohio*, the boy has shared an "adventure" of his people that he can later tell the world.[6]

The destruction of Joe Pete drives Richard further inward, hardening his resolve to rise above the mysterious force "of tradition, of culture, of the social structure of an individual" (p. 95). He feels more and more alienated from his decaying family, and in Chapters 5 and 6 he turns instinctively toward the popular heroes, icons and formulas which the dominant culture offers. In the midst of domestic chaos, "He sat at the table with his chin in his hands and said aloud, *in English*, 'I am Buck Jones and Ken Maynard and Fred Thompson, all rolled into one—I'm not Tom Mix, too, because I don't like brown horses'" (p. 96, italics added). Like every twelve-year-old American boy, he idolizes the man on the *white* horse, not the *brown*. In his search for fathers, Richard turns to the mythos of the culture for the guidance his parents are unable to give.

Traditional guides to life fail the young Mexican-American. At an early age he learns, first, "that one should never discuss matters of sex with one's parents. Second, one should not, on penalty of going to Hell, discuss religion with the priests. And, last, one should not ask questions on history of the teachers" (pp. 85–86). It is expected that Richard's mother cannot select readings for him; more crushing, however, is the failure of the public educators to provide the standards of belief and behavior he hungers for. Teachers encourage his reading, but do not direct it. The only works prescribed are the novels of Horatio Alger, given him by a dear old librarian. "Funny about her, how the Horatio Alger books meant as much to her as the Bible meant to Protestants" (p. 108). Richard follows the adventures of Alger's trusting young heroes in his tangled desire to learn the rules of his world, yet he rejects the ethos of dutiful service to one's superiors. He does not aspire to become the gardener on a rich man's estate, as the well-meaning librarian recommends. Nor does he wish to study automechanics or welding because these are good trades for Mexicans, as his high school counselors advise. He spurns all efforts to reconcile him to the "Mexican" role in the social-economic pattern of America. In a scene echoing the "battle royal" in *Invisible Man*, Richard is coaxed to join the boxing game and fight his friend Thomas Nakano. "'How about it, kid?' asked the man. 'I'm giving ya the chance of your life—it's the only way people of your nationality can get ahead'" (p. 106). Richard walks away laughing at the absurdity. Even as a twelve-year-old, he is less trusting than Ralph Ellison's high school valedictorian and more emancipated from the stereotypes of ethnicity. One by one, he abandons the potential mentors who fail to perceive his *self*.

As Richard grows into adolescence, the foundations of family and church continue to erode beneath him. The last link with Mexico is cut when Juan Rubio buys a house. Outwardly the family prospers and assimilates to its new culture, but the "strange metamorphosis" that takes away tradition without imposing new controls is fatal to its integrity. Richard's mother changes completely. She learns from her neighbors that in the United States women are individuals and have rights. While this releases her sexually, it also transforms the once submissive and fastidious woman into an unhappy termagant who challenges her husband's discipline of the children, gossips, argues and keeps a dirty house as "a symbol of her emancipation." As authority and happiness slip through his hands, Juan Rubio turns to other women once more, his "raucous, infectious laugh" gone, his once solid body become flabby. All discipline disappears, "and even the smallest child screamed at either parent, and came and went as she pleased." But "no one could be blamed," the author adds, "for the transition from the culture of the old world to that of the new should never have been attempted in one generation" (pp. 134-135). (The same breakup of the male dominated family and the rise of a trenchant matriarchy is seen in other uprooted ethnic groups, e.g., the "Jewish Mother" syndrome and the disproportionate number of Black female heads of households.)

In the latter chapters of *Pocho* the conflict between Richard's inner and outer realities intensifies. As he grows towards manhood, he confronts both the significance of his social acts and disturbing new currents in the community. In Chapter 8 he becomes intimate with the scrappy hoyden of his boyhood clique, Zelda, and agrees to take her for his "girl" on the condition she will stop "laying pipe" with the other fellows. With Zelda he loses some of his restlessness. The mating ritual they enact seems to establish the traditional authority of the male and the sexual fidelity of the female. Yet Richard maintains his customary distance, even as Zelda becomes wholly obedient. This friendship, like that with Mary, is destined to be outgrown and left behind.

At the same time, the town of Santa Clara also is changing. While soldiers walk the streets following the Conscription Act of 1940, the main change in Richard's life, told in Chapter 9, is his confrontation with "the race." His home in town and childhood gang of Anglo, Japanese and Italian friends had sheltered him from much association with other Mexicans. When large numbers of migrants from Southern California now settle in the valley, he begins "to attend their dances and fiestas" and to seek out their company. Ever uncertain of his own identity, Richard is "obsessed with a hunger to learn" about the new breed of young men and women he meets:

> They had a burning contempt for people of different ancestry, whom they called Americans, and had a marked hauteur toward Mexico

and toward their parents for their old-country ways. The former feeling came from a sense of inferiority that is a prominent characteristic in any Mexican reared in southern California; and the latter was an inexplicable compensation for that feeling.... The result was that they attempted to segregate themselves from both their cultures, and became truly a lost race. (p. 149)

Richard considered his identity a personal matter, to be nurtured both in family traditions and in the values of American culture—until someday it should burst from its dark chrysalis. His angry friends, to the contrary, seek a group identity through repudiating both their parents' customs and the new society.

The *pachucos*—or zoot-suiters, as they were called after their billowing pegged pants and fingertip black coats—were rebels without a cause, the raw seeds from which the Chicano would later emerge. After first finding them ludicrous and brutal, Richard comes to appreciate that "in spite of their behavior, which was sensational at times and violent at others, they were simply a portion of a confused humanity, employing their self-segregation as a means of expression." He learns their polyglot of "English and Spanish syllables, words, and sounds"—"unintelligible to anyone but themselves"—and disparages "whites" in their presence (pp. 149–150). For a time he hangs suspended between the friends of his youth and the angry pachucos, dressing and acting in such a way as to offend neither. As community tensions increase, Richard is mistaken for a pachuco hoodlum and beaten by the San Jose police. A militant strain enters his character as he is ground by conflicting loyalties; nonetheless, he sustains his brittle affirmation: "Never—no, never—will I allow myself to become a part of a group—to become classified, to lose my individuality" (p. 152). A "protective shell of cynicism" grows over his innate idealism (p. 164).

In Chapter 10 Juan Rubio leaves his family for good. Richard, torn by personal affection for both his mother and father and for the values that had once been theirs, rejoices at his father's renewed manhood. In their tearful departure, Juan Rubio exhorts his son to be true to himself and let nothing stand in the way of his determination to be a writer, "be it women, money, or—what people talk about today—position" (p. 169).

In the last chapter of the novel, the legacy of the father threatens to fall upon the son. From picking fruit, following his graduation from high school, Richard moves on to lucrative wartime work in a steel mill. Inexorably, it seems, he yields to his mother's will that he should take responsibility for the family and, as the eldest son, provide for his sisters. "Slowly the temporary aspect of the situation was giving way to permanency" (p. 174). His dreams for writing, like his father's visions of return to Mexico, begin to fade. Finally he does start spending time in the library once more, and even enrolls in a night course in creative writing. But the course teaches him little, and it pains him that his liberal classmates want him to "dedicate his life to the Mexican cause" (p. 175).[7] Unprotected by family, church or school, he can no longer mistake the spectre of his own existence: "He was now a part of the infinite nonentity—the worker, the family man. He had slowly dropped into oblivion even in his mind, the one place where once he had soared above the multitude" (p. 180). His only flight is the war, and impulsively he enlists in the Navy. What lies on the other side he does not know; he only knows, like Stephen Daedalus from Dublin, George Willard from Winesburg and Ellison's Invisible Man, that "for him there would never be a coming back" (p. 187).

This simple narrative critique should awaken in readers of American literature a sense of déjà vu, for *Pocho* is a typical American story. We are ready now to take a systematic look at the ideas surrounding the novel and its place in the history of the American Dream.

Mexican-Americans are one of the last great folk migrations to the United States. At the turn of the century the number of residents of Mexican background in the Southwest did not far exceed 100,000; however, the upheaval of the Mexican Revolution—combined with the poverty of the Mexican states, the birth of the Southwest as an economic empire and, after 1942, the government subsidized *bracero* program—opened floodgates from the south through which poured nearly 10 percent of Mexico's total population.[8] Even while the immigration restriction acts of the 1920s stemmed the transoceanic flow, this new tide surged. Today more than five million Mexican-Americans form the nation's second largest minority,[9] and the Mexican dream of the El Dorado to the north remains a major challenge to social planning in the border states.

Immigrant families like the Rubios, who joined the great wave of the 1920s, now have reached their third generation in the United States. Their experience, therefore, might be compared to patterns of acculturation in other immigrant groups, fomulated tersely in "Hansen's law" that "what the son wishes to forget, the grandson wishes to remember." This theorem refers to the phenomenon observed by historians and sociologists that the *first* generation (grandparents), uprooted from their ancestral culture, remain fundamentally estranged from the new society regardless of economic attainment; the *second* generation (parents), embarrassed by their forebearers' backwardness and eager to prove themselves "American," pursue the goals and behavior of the majority culture in an exaggerated way; the *third* generation (children), sensing their parents' rootlessness, look again to the grandparents for clues to their moral identity and seek a synthesis of old and new values. (The transition from second to third generation attitudes is evident today in the unfashionableness of the Melting Pot concept and the emergence of Pluralism and the Mosaic as rival national symbols.) In the Mexican-American community, the *pelado* of the first generation looks forward to the *Chicano* of the third.[10] Between stands the American son of Mexican parents, the hyphenated Mexican-American called *pocho*.[11]

The setting of Villarreal's novel in the 1930s and its actual writing in the 1950s bracket an extended second generation of assimilation when the Mexican-American community, with such exceptions as the pachucos, accepted the public attitudes of conformity and patriotism. The agonies Richard suffers are those both of a novice seeking his cultural birthright and of a generation suspended between two cultures. Richard dramatizes dialectics of:

| | | |
|---|---|---|
| Self-determination | and | Tradition, Filial Piety |
| The Individual | | The Community |
| Personal Freedom | | Social Responsibility |
| Teachers, Schools, Libraries | | Parents, Home |
| Father | | Mother |
| English Language | | Spanish Language |
| Free Thought | | Catholic Creeds, Confession |
| Dreaming, Reading, Writing | | Working |
| Childhood Friends | | Pachucos |
| United States | | Mexico |
| Flight | | Acceptance |

Their synthesis awaits a third generation.

In important respects, however, the Mexican American has proven an exception to the rule of intergenerational change. Sociologists have discovered that Mexican-Americans hold onto their language and cultural habits more tenaciously than other immigrant ethnic groups; in general they have been the slowest to assimilate. On the basis of the 1950 census data, Mexican-Americans "constituted the only major ethnic group with no substantial intergenerational rise in socio-economic status."[12] Among the factors retarding acculturation are the proximity of the fatherland and the continual nature of Mexican immigration and repatriation, which have prevented the ultimate cutting of ties, physical and psychological, that propelled other immigrant groups into the Melting Pot. Absence of an educational tradition has been another important deterrent. The group's perception of opportunity has been further limited by the concentration of Mexican-Americans in rural areas and agricultural jobs, in contrast to the predominantly metropolitan and industrial thrust of European immigration.[13] Richard Rubio, given his urban setting in the most liberal state of the Southwest, was exceptionally well exposed to ideas of mobility and change.

The root cause for the culture lag, finally, may be a fundamental difference in world view between dominant America and the Mexican-American people. While comparing the value orientations of the two cultures, Florence Kluckhohn identified the following differences of approach to five basic human problems:[14]

| Problem | Mexican-American Response | American Response |
|---|---|---|
| Man's relation to nature | Subjugation-to-Nature | Mastery-over-Nature |
| Essence of human nature | Mutable Good-and-Evil | Evil-but-Perfectible |
| Man's relation to man | Lineality (group, family) | Individualism |
| Preferable activities | Being | Doing |
| Time orientation | Present-Time | Future-Time |

The progressive orientation and success ethos of American core culture contradict the traditional world view of the Mexican-Americans, with its emphasis on continuity, community and the obligation of one's assigned role.

By the late 1960s, however, there were signs that a "take-off stage" had been reached. In her study of the attitudes of Mexican-American high school seniors in Los Angeles, Celia Heller found expectations of high "relative" mobility.[15] Subsequent work has demonstrated not only that the education gap narrowed between 1950 and 1960, but also that median income and home ownership "of Mexican-American individuals in the Southwest rose at a substantially higher rate than that of Anglos," and that moderate occupational upgrading also occurred.[16] In *New Converts to the American Dream?* Professor Heller asked what effect the militant Chicano rhetoric of the late sixties might have on the incipient drive towards individual success.

> At a time when the climate of opinion is not conducive to the traditional rhetoric of the American dream, making it sound old-fashioned and dated, many Mexican-American youths are laying claim to that dream.... The process of responding to the American ideology of advancement, observed in all other immigrant groups is being similarly reenacted here, although it took longer to get underway. What typically took place in immigrant groups in the second generation is now occurring among third- and fourth-generation Mexican Americans. As a phenomenon of noticeable proportions, it is new among Mexican Americans. Also, these third- and fourth-generation Americans are facing the problems of marginality and assimilation which other ethnic groups met in the second generation.

She went on to speculate:

> By focusing attention on the incipient Mexican-American militancy and not bringing to light the beginning "success story," the mass media may play a part . . . in the extinguishment of the embryonic achievement orientation.[17]

*Pocho* issued from a period when the ideology of personal advancement was still much alive. A tributary from the pre-militant fifties, it fed into the mainstream of American literature just above the gulf of sixties and seventies revisionism. From its origins America has been a nation of immigrants, and, as if to satisfy Thomas Jefferson's call for a revolution each generation, continual social and political change has kept the crucible churning. At heart, our imaginative writing has been a "second-generation" literature, preoccupied with the struggles of rebirth, identity and acculturation. The typical protagonist is a stalwart, introspective young man like Richard Rubio, stripped of his past, who leaves home to seek his destiny in the new world lying open before him. When his parents are not entirely absent, they are ineffectual guides on new frontiers; at best they offer a memory of unrecoverable harmony. The young man, actually or metaphorically, is an orphan.

Chicano critics who discuss Villarreal's book approach Richard's ambivalence as part of "the alien[ation] in both worlds that many social scientists speak of when they portray the Mexican American."[18] Such an attitude enables scholars to mark stages in the evolution of Chicano literary consciousness; however, it threatens to narrow the interest and achievement of the work by tying it too closely to a particular ethnic strain. The same motifs of ambivalence, alienation and brooding introspection on personal freedom run through Henry Roth's *Call It Sleep*, Budd Shulberg's *What Makes Sammy Run?*, Saul Bellow's *Dangling Man*, and other "second-generation" novels. They are the core of the novel of initiation, and in one form or another they constitute the classic tradition of American literature since the time of Hawthorne and Melville. The greatness of American ethnic and regional literature has been its ability to dramatize the universal dilemmas of self-awareness in a specific social context. Richard Rubio joins a long line of novices who have sought their spiritual birthright in America.

Bereft of the past, the young American must seek a new "father." When Richard finds he cannot discuss sex with his parents, religion with his priest or history with his teachers, he stands naked before the symbolic abstractions of the culture itself. The story of American literature has been just this initiation of expectant youths into the corporate myths of America and the psychological and metaphysical mysteries they conceal. A culture as idealistically conceived and committed to personal progress as the United States particularly needs a unifying myth to direct its energies. Since *Father Abraham's Speech* (1759), such a mythology has appeared.[19] Its Old Testament is *The Autobiography of Benjamin Franklin*; its New Testament the synoptic writings of Horatio Alger; and its Book of Revelations the apocalyptic visions of Arthur Miller's *Death of a Salesman*, Norman Mailer's *An American Dream* and Edward Albee's *The American Dream*.[20] Compulsively they tell the story of fatherless youths pursuing the chimerical patrimony of the culture and honoring its abundant opportunities — or not — through their discipline and success.

"The American Dream" is a particularly appropriate image for Richard Rubio's experience, because *Pocho* is pervaded by the same air of unreality and half-sleep that surrounds every effort to lay hold on the substance of America. The structure of the novel is fragmentary; Richard's glimpses of reality are fleeting and unconsummated. By nature dream is not a negative state; it is a psychological bridge from sleep to reality and back, during which passion and will weigh the demands of the waking world. *Pocho* enacts this dreamlike ritual of segregation from the past, transition and awakening to a new reality — except that Richard never fully awakes.

Like Jay Gatsby, Richard builds his identity as best he can from the cultural debris around him. Young James Gatz of North Dakota, before he became "The Great Gatsby," forged his life models from the ragged ends of the Benjamin Franklin legend and Hopalong Cassidy books. Richard Rubio of Santa Clara, through his omnivorous reading and reverie, also imagines truths unseen by the human eye. His lodestones are artifacts of the culture: at first limp books cast off by teachers, *Toby Tyler, or Ten Weeks with the Circus*, or rescued from the city dump and smelling of garbage; later the popular culture of small town library shelves and radio programs, *Tom Swift* and *The Rover Boys*, stories of Buck Jones, Ken Maynard and Fred Thompson; all culminating in the adventures of Horatio Alger. Such stuff dreams are made of in America. Because Richard's parents cannot instruct his reading and imagination, teachers and librarians become his cultural mentors. But they fail in their appointed task to educate the boy because of their own ignorance of his spiritual needs and the duplicity of their culture. The heroes and images of success they offer do not lead him out of sleep into action. Celia Heller put this phenomenon in sociological terms when she reported:

> Thus we have found that the schools have managed to instill the goals and values of success. But they have failed drastically in developing behavior conducive to advancement. The result is a rising appetite for socio-economic success without a corresponding development of the capacity to satisfy it.[21]

Books are one means of bridging the gulf between individual dreams and collective realities. Unfortunately, the books given to Richard by his teachers and librarians are from the wrong phase of the American Dream to suit either the contemporary milieu or Richard's special temperament.

The author seems to have had the success dream of Franklin and Alger in mind when writing his book. The historical formula requires leaving one's father, journeying to a new city, learning the dictates of life from a series of mentors, seeking education, seizing opportunity, rising to middle-class substance through luck and pluck, and perhaps sealing the achievement through marriage. Richard breaks the formula of course at crucial points: he's hampered throughout by uncertain will, vague opportunities, careless mentors, and his own sensual impulses; nor does he leave home until the end. But sufficient vestiges of the pattern remain to identify the dream that has defaulted. Villarreal's protagonist bears the name of both Richard Saunders (Franklin's persona in *Poor Richard's Almanac*) and Richard Hunter (the hero of Alger's most famous novels, *Ragged Dick* and *Mark the Match Boy*). He is a shrewd and detached lad, "not showing his impatience, quietly calculating until he saw what he wanted" (p. 51). Like Ragged Dick, he learns manners and behavior from daughters of the Protestant gentry: first the courageous Marla Jamison and then ethereal Mary who announces her intention to marry him. Furthermore, Richard looks for a mentor outside the family and finds him for a time in Joe Pete Manōel.

The most interesting images of the dream of material success appear in the episode of Mat Madeiros' drayage barn in Chapter 2. Madeiros rose from poverty to moderate wealth by cashing in on the booming hauling business during the 1920s. Confident of the future of the machine, he bought a Reo truck and soon "had visions of a fleet of trucks and an important position in the community." When the Depression struck, he was forced to "put his rig up on blocks" and go to work in a cannery. But he regarded this as only a temporary setback, even while his savings disappeared. The Madeiros barn was next used as a meeting place for the Unemployed Council of Santa Clara County. When Communist organizers from the city took over, "the wall behind the table was bedecked with bunting, of which a red flag with hammer and sickle was the centerpiece," and "Mat's truck was once more on the road. Working parties forayed the bakeries for stale bread, the dairies for skim milk, and any place where they might find something to help feed the people" (p. 48). Ostensibly, Mat's truck and drayage barn were transformed from symbols of private enterprise into a badge of communal action. The author's imagery, however, discloses the material dream that continued to run through the people's thought. The "red flag with hammer and sickle . . . always reminded the child [Richard] of the picture on the box that held his father's indigestion medicine" (p. 48). Thus, the symbol of communal action becomes Arm and Hammer Baking Soda, a mark of dyspeptic middle-class America. Likewise, one of the most popular musical settings for lyrics of protest was the bourgeois "Stanford Fight Song." At heart the people were still buying the dream.

Whatever might be the validity of the entrepreneurial dream of Mat Madeiros, it was the wrong dream for Richard. Richard's soul was attuned, even as a child, not to the American Dream of material self-advancement that characterized the nation during the age of Alger, but rather to a more profound American Dream of spiritual self-realization that preceded and outlives its narrower economic expression. When Consuelo Rubio warns her son, "I know that we cannot live in a dream, because everything around us is real," he declares: " 'I do not care about making a lot of money and about what people think and about the family in the way you speak. I have to learn as much as I can, so that I can live ... learn for *me*, for *myself*—' " (p. 64). Richard is an Emersonian. His repeated assertions of the importance of the individual soul, like the following passage—

> I can be a part of everything, he thought, because I am the only one capable of controlling my destiny.... I will not become a follower, nor will I allow myself to become a leader, because I must be myself and accept for myself only that which I value and not what is being valued by everyone else these days.... (pp. 152-153)

—echo Ralph Waldo Emerson's proclamations on self-reliance, individualism, friendship, and unity with the Over-Soul. Compare, for example, this passage from the essay on "Self-Reliance":

> Live no longer to the expectation of these deceived and deceiving people with whom we converse. Say to them, 'O father, O mother, O wife, O brother, O friend. I have lived with you after appearances hitherto. Henceforward I am the truth's.... I appeal from your customs. I must be myself. I cannot break myself any longer for you, or you.'[22]

The importance of the *self* requires that Richard transcend the hereditary bonds of family, church, school and society until he can express his own intuitions. When the church forbids him from reading the scriptures, he steals away to study the Bible. From Catholic dogma to the inquiry of Protestantism to free thought is a natural spiritual evolution. Likewise, he successively outgrows his parents, his duty to dependent sisters, his childhood gang and adolescent girl friends in the course of personal emancipation. At the end of the novel the process of liberation is still underway. In his introduction to the 1970 paperback edition of *Pocho*, Ramón Ruiz spoke of "that sense of inferiority that settled down upon Richard in his lonely battle with reality" (p. xii). There is no indication in the novel itself, however, that the author wished Richard not to have asserted his spiritual independence. His liberation from tradition is a painful but fundamental process.

In their essay "The Militant Challenge to the American Ethos," Armando Gutiérrez and Herbert Hirsch assailed American ideas for "destruction of the culture [of Mexican-Americans] coupled with the concomitant destruction of individual identity."[23] The central questions are, first, whether the American Dream retains its power to unify diverse peoples around new cultural symbols and loyalties and, second, whether it enables individual self-discovery or is merely imperious, prescriptive and culturally appetitive. The family, ethnic community or social brotherhood is potentially just as tyrannous towards individual freedom as the dominant culture. This is the theme of works like *A Portrait of the Artist as a Young Man*, *Winesburg, Ohio*, and *Invisible Man*. The tragedy of the American Dream for Richard Rubio is *not* that it frees his mind from old ties and sends it exploring the possibilties of *self*; this is its excellence. The tragedy of the Dream is that it has not simultaneously given ethical norms by which this freedom might be embodied in action; thus, Richard's *anomie*.

It is no doubt because the normative standards for belief and behavior are less certain in complex modern America than they were in the expansive nineteenth century, that the countermythos of Aztlán has such appeal for Chicano polemicists. The myth of Aztlán calls forth the romantic vision of a great *indígena* culture in the Southwest before the coming of the Spanish and the Anglo-Americans. In the mind of Chicano poets and critics like Luis Valdez, originator of the Teatro Campesino, the mestizo who crosses the border today from Mexico into the occupied ancestral lands of the Southwest may suffer a "spiritual regression," but the European remains "the eternal foreigner, suffering from the immigrant complex.... His culture, like his name for this continent, is imported."[24] Chicanos did not come to America, the poets claim: America came to them. The poetry of Aztlán calls to mind the blood-consiousness of D. H. Lawrence and William Carlos Williams, who mythologized redskins and the spirit of the Southwest as a counterpoise to a mechanistic paleface culture. The cultural traits which Florence Kluckhohn identified as retarding Mexican-American assimilation in the United States—communalism, a circular view of time, emphasis on Being rather than Doing—have become the basis for a mystagogic religion aimed at recreating the "universal man." The Chicano, writes Guillermo Fuenfríos,

> is by nature a pluralistic man, a universal man, combining the racial strains and cultures of the entire world in his own person. José Vas-

> concelos coined the term "La Raza Cósmica" to describe him. The term is apt.... It is no wonder that he has successfully resisted the best efforts of the North American to melt him down into a mere American.[25]

At first this manifesto may sound like the cosmic decrees of Walt Whitman. But where Whitman chanted his song to the Self, the future and the new American, the poets of Aztlán extol an ancient race that preceded America. Luis Valdez asserts with fervor:

> Now the gringo is trying to impose the immigrant complex on the Chicano, pretending that we "Mexican-Americans" are the most recent arrivals. It will not work. His melting pot concept is a sham: it is a crucible that scientifically disintegrates the human spirit, melting down entire cultures into a thin white residue the average gabacho can harmlessly absorb. That is why the Anglo cannot conceive of the Chicano, the Mexican Mestizo, in all his ancient human fullness.[26]

Can this mythos, this merging of "Indio mysticism ... with modern technology to create *un nuevo hombre*,"[27] sustain itself? Or will the Cinco de Mayo celebrations, like St. Patrick's Day and Oktoberfest, be absorbed by dominant America as one more bright color in the fabric of national life? To affect the lifeways of its people, a myth must *emerge* with primitive strength. Efforts to create new myths have not been very successful as cultural amalgamation continues to take place. The demise of Yiddish Theatre in our time stands as a challenge to the prophets of Teatro Chicano.

In a provocative essay, "National Development and Ethnic Poetics: The Function of Literature in the Liberation of Peoples," Jay Martin has weighed the relation of national aesthetics to cultural development by comparing American literary nationalism between the 1770s and the mid-1840s to the contemporary Black Aesthetic and the Americanidad Aesthetic of Latin America. The impulse of literary nationalism, he has decided,

> originates when a formerly colonized people begin to achieve political equality with their former oppressors. Its function resembles magical thinking—it is to persuade the newly liberated group that the former oppressor is decadent and powerless and that the new nation has replaced the old on the historic stage—that a new race of men has appeared to redeem the world. It is, in short, an expression of the new nation's sense of its own value while it is still vulnerable.[28]

Once economic independence and social equality are achieved, the aesthetic loses "its force as an instrument of liberation" and disappears. If, on the other hand, the progress towards social and economic equality with neighboring cultures is arrested, then the aesthetic eventually will turn upon itself through private mythologies, surreal images and racial memories that dismiss the importance of economic achievement. The function of Chicano poetics in the liberation of its people has been only partially revealed; however, recent works like Ron Arias's *The Road to Tamazunchale* show an inclination to escape from the novelistic world of man and society into the imaginary dramas and private language of myth.[29]

When introducing the novel, Ramón Ruiz warned the reader to keep in mind, "lest he misunderstand and misinterpret its major premise," that the ambivalence in *Pocho* reflects "the ambiguities and ideological confusions inherent in Mexican-American thinking" during the assimilationist phase in which Villarreal was writing (p. viii). Today the Chicano's "commitment to unity of 'race' places loyalty to the community above all else"; a generation earlier, "in rebellion against his dual heritage, Richard [stood] defenseless, an insecure and beaten young man" (p. xii).[30] The point of this essay has been to suggest that Richard Rubio is not so time-locked as Professor Ruiz and many others may believe. He is a universal man. As such he suffers an existential insecurity against which no community can protect him but which has been brilliantly dramatized during a century and a half of American literature. We do not know that Richard has been beaten; however, we also do not know at what point along the social and metaphysical frontier of America he will emerge from his rites of passage. That story still has not been told.

University of Southern California

# Notes

[1] Readily available anthologies include: *Mexican American Authors*, ed. Américo Paredes and Raymond Paredes (Boston: Houghton Mifflin, 1972); *Voices of Aztlán: Chicano Literature of Today*, ed. Dorothy E. Harth and Lewis M. Baldwin (New York: New American Library, 1974); *Chicano Voices*, ed. Carlota Cárdenas de Dwyer (Boston: Houghton Mifflin, 1975); *Festival de flor y canto: An Anthology of Chicano Literature*, ed. F. A. Cervantes et al. (Los Angeles: University of Southern California Press, 1976). A still useful bibliographical essay is Raymond J. Rodrigues' "A Few Directions in Chicano Literature," *English Journal*, 62 (May 1973), pp. 724–729.

[2] See, for example, folklorist Américo Paredes' seminal analysis of the *corrido* (border ballad): *With His Pistol in His Hand: The Ballad of Gregorio Cortez*

(Austin: University of Texas Press, 1970); and the work of the University of Texas (Austin) Mexican-American Library Project.

[3] *Pocho* (Garden City, New York: Doubleday & Company, 1959). All passages from *Pocho* quoted in this essay are taken from the Anchor Books paperback edition (1970), introduced by Ramón Eduardo Ruiz. In addition to freelance journalism in Southern California, José Villarreal has written one other novel, *The Fifth Horseman* (Doubleday, 1974), the story of a passionate and rebellious young peon who joined Pancho Villa's army and later rode north to California. *The Fifth Horseman* is a conventional, lusty, action-packed romance, in contrast to the introspective *Pocho*. Its hero, Heraclio, may have been inspired by Juan Rubio, the protagonist's father in *Pocho*.

[4] The rhetoric of The American Dream spans some half dozen interlocking sets of ideas and postulates. As background to a formal analysis of The Dream in American literature, I am now preparing a historical bibliography of publications, addresses and media presentations that have used the label "The American Dream" since 1931.

[5] Frank L. Cinquemani, *Library Journal*, 84 (Nov. 15, 1959), p. 3587. I shall not discuss the author's novelistic accomplishments, except to say that like much of America's myth-making literature, *Pocho*'s strength resides in its dramatic portrayal of a young male learning the rules of the national game, while narrative finish is subordinated to the depiction of significant moments in his social and moral growth.

[6] Like the "grotesques" of Sherwood Anderson, Joe Pete saw "in a boy a reflected justification for his own misspent life"; and he hoped aloud to Richard: "Because you are young enough and as yet unspoiled enough, . . . perhaps you *can* understand. Else why would I be telling you all this?" (pp. 84–85, 87). The parallel between Joe Pete and Anderson's misunderstood schoolteacher, Wing Biddlebaum, is especially striking. As in the story "Hands," the children in *Pocho*, "encouraged by their parents and by the importance that was suddenly thrust upon them, 'confessed' in detail to the horrible things" the older man "had done, or attempted to do, with them" (p. 90).

[7] The manipulation of Richard by the Marxist intellectual coterie presents another analog to *Invisible Man*. Both Richard and Ellison's protagonists are used simultaneously as political symbols and bed partners for the liberal wives.

[8] Carey McWilliams, *North from Mexico: The Spanish–Speaking People of the United States* (Philadelphia and New York: J. B. Lippincott, 1948), p. 163.

[9] Leo Grebler, Joan W. Moore, and Ralph C. Guzman, *The Mexican-American People: The Nation's Second Largest Minority* (New York: Free Press, 1970), p. 14.

[10] "The Chicano is the grandson, or perhaps even the son, of the Mexican *pelado*. Who is the *pelado*? He is the Mestizo, the colonized man of Mexico, literally, the 'stripped one.'" Luis Valdez, "Introduction" to *Aztlán: An Anthology of Mexican American Literature*, ed. Luis Valdez and Stan Steiner (New York: Alfred A. Knopf, 1972), p. xxix.

[11] Pocho is also a linguistic term designating "a mixture of Spanish, English, and some unique elements." In a call for bilingual, bicultural education Ysidro Ramón Macías explains: "Chicano and Latino artists have now recognized Pocho, with its Pochismos (idioms of Pocho), as a truly artistic and expressive bastard tongue. Moreover, it expresses the Chicanos better than either Spanish

or English and should be preserved and expanded. Accordingly, throughout the great Aztlán (U. S. Southwest), Chicanos express themselves daily in their native tongue, Pocho, and continually seek new ways of reviving, maintaining, and enriching the Chicano culture." "The Chicano Movement," *Wilson Library Bulletin*, 44 (Mar. 1970), p. 732. While adopting Pocho as a literary tongue, Chicanos repudiate the pocho as a historical figure. The moment he *affirms* his biculturalism, it would seem, the pocho becomes a Chicano and learns to synthesize customs and speech of the two cultures that hitherto had been the Charybdis and Scylla of his rudderless existence. Villarreal's novel, unlike much contemporary Chicano writing, does not use the pocho argot.

[12] Celia Heller, *New Converts to the American Dream? Mobility Aspirations of Young Mexican Americans* (New Haven, Conn.: College & University Press, 1971), p. 225

[13] Grebler, et al., p. 95

[14] Florence R. Kluckhohn and Fred Strodtbeck, *Variations in Value Orientations* (Evanston, IL: Row, Peterson, 1961), p. 353; cited in Heller, pp. 86–87.

[15] Heller, pp. 85, 160.

[16] Grebler, et al., p. 27. See all of Chapter 14, "Social Class and Social Mobility," in this work. These conclusions are further borne out by Armando Gutiérrez and Herbert Hirsch in their article, "The Militant Challenge to the American Ethos: 'Chicanos' and 'Mexican Americans,'" *Social Science Quarterly*, 53 (Mar. 1973), pp. 830–845. While the authors protested the supremacy of the melting pot and the "identity crisis forced upon a subcultural people by the Anglo dominated state," their survey of 786 high school students in Crystal City, Texas (May 1971), showed a consensus that education is valuable and accessible, success can be achieved through hard work and the United States is a land of opportunity for all men regardless of origin.

[17] Heller, pp. 14–15. For a more detailed comparison of Mexican-American assimilation patterns vis-a-vis other immigrant groups, see Heller, pp. 244–246.

[18] Inez Tovar, "'One Can Decipher a Well-Articulated Cry': The Emergence of Chicano Literature" (unpublished paper, University of Texas, Austin), p. 10

[19] As used here, *myth* (*mythos, mythology*) obviously does not connote fictions and untruths. Rather, it refers to the deeply structured memories, beliefs, and stories shared by a culture and responsible for its *ethos*.

[20] F. Scott Fitzgerald's *The Great Gatsby*, Nathanael West's *Cool Million* and Ralph Ellison's *Invisible Man* should also be counted among the main literary statements of the American Dream.

[21] Heller, p. 251.

[22] Ralph Waldo Emerson, "Self-Reliance," in *Essays First Series*, Autograph Centenary Edition (Cambridge, Mass.: The Riverside Press, 1903), II, pp. 72–73.

[23] Gutiérrez and Hirsch, p. 87.

[24] Valdez, "Introduction" to *Aztlán: An Anthology of Mexican American Literature*, pp. xxix, xxxii.

[25] Guillermo Fuenfríos, "The Emergence of the New Chicano," in *Aztlán: An Anthology of Mexican American Literature*, p. 284.

[26] Valdez, pp. xxxii–xxxiii.

[27] *Ibid.*, p. xxx.

[28] Jay Martin, "National Development and Ethnic Poetics: The Function of

Literature in the Liberation of Peoples," in *The Study of American Culture*, ed. Luther S. Luedtke (DeLand, Fla.: Everett/Edwards, 1977), p. 225.

[29] The social intent of Chicano aesthetics is candidly acknowledged. "Like the modern art of Mexico, the new Chicano art is essentially an art of social protest," writes Manuel J. Martínez ("The Art of the Chicano Movement, and the Movement of Chicano Art," in *Aztlán: An Anthology of Mexican American Literature*, p. 352). "Nowadays it tends toward 'secular religiosity' " (editor's note, *ibid.*, p. 349).

[30] Professor Ruiz's introductory remarks are themselves ambiguous at times. Awakened Chicanos, he states, "demand their share of the good life in the United States" (p. viii). How the essence, or details, of this "good life" are to be lifted out of a total cultural-ideological context is unexplained. That, of course, is the issue.

# Buffalos and Cockroaches: Acosta's Siege at Aztlán

*Norman D. Smith*

> Mexico is such a poor country, and I could never understand how, after the Revolution, they could produce all that beautiful art. But now I see it in our own strikes, it's a very small revolution, but we see this art beginning to come forth. When people discover themselves like this, they begin to appreciate some of the other things in life.[1]

The complex question, "Is Chicano art literature or propaganda," is entertaining. However, these either/or critics generally affirm that propaganda and social protest are prevalent in Chicano artistic expression. And art is the vehicle conveying the message. But César Chávez' observation that revolution produces both social change and art synthesizes an aesthetic point of view helpful in the explication of Chicano writings.[2] Chávez' notion that the adrenalin spent in the heat of struggle produces art concurs with the aesthetic statement found in Oscar Zeta Acosta's novels, *The Autobiography of a Brown Buffalo* (1972) and *The Revolt of the Cockroach People* (1973).

The narrator of Acosta's autobiographical fictions views his writing as a "dump" on his buddies, a dislike of the truth, and "death as a world of art." A point-blank telegraphic style enables him to conjure up a pastiche of images that repulse each other while they interlock: fragments of historical struggles are reflected in the Chicano's immediate revolution for cultural, social, and economic identity in an environment controlled largely by an unspecific, unyielding Anglo-Saxon establishment.

In a rapid series of short sentences Acosta's images indicate that his hero-victim of *The Autobiography of a Brown Buffalo* cannot identify with his environment. Shedding the last vestiges of his innocent youth, Oscar asks, "Christ, what happened to the culture of the fifties."[3] He says, "I speak as a historian, a recorder of events with a sour stomach. I have no love for memories of the past. Ginsberg and those coffee houses with hungry-looking guitar players never did mean shit to me. *They* never took their drinking seriously. And the fact of the matter is they got what was coming to them. It's their tough luck if they ran out and got on the road with bums like Kerouac, then came back a few years later with their hair longer and fucking marijuana up their asses, shouting Love and Peace and Pot. And still as broke as ever."[4] Hypocritically, Oscar Buffalo Brown becomes a spaced-out "fucking buffalo on the lam. *Dropping out with Timothy Leary*."[5] Acosta has his protagonist running not from the law but from the limbo of living—merely surviving—between the Anglo culture and counter culture and his half-forgotten Mexican birthright. He is what Enrique Hank López calls "a schizo-cultural Mexican or a Cultured schizoid American."[6] Acosta sums up his antihero's cultural equivocation in the sequel novel, *The Revolt of the Cockroach People*. Gilbert recognizes the Buffalo as a type and says, "The *vato's* a flower child!"[7]

The tumultuous conflict that gives *The Autobiography* its form is marked by Buffalo Brown's inability to reconcile his Anglo conditioning with his being "an innocent, brown-eyed child of the sun ... a peach-picker's boy from the West Side. Riverbank."[8] Sick—psychosomatically suffering from bleeding ulcers—Buffalo Brown, Oscar Zeta Acosta, protagonist, departs on a spiritual quest searching for both personal identity and a place within two countries, Mexico and the United States, where he might belong. His picaresque and episodic adventure has been interpreted:

> Acosta, in *The Brown Buffalo*, runs away from the hapless world of an Oakland welfare-lawyer, a so-called "lily-livered Legal Aid communist," and takes a left turn toward malaise. Oscar then roams throughout the west, from the Oakland-San Francisco Bay Area, to Aspen, Sun Valley, El Paso, etc., always, though haphazardly, in search of meaning and an identity, a place in the sun he finally does find in Ciudad Juárez. But not before paying his obligatory fee, struggling through and enduring a harrowing psychedelic American nightmare, typical of the late 60's, mixing drugs, booze, drifters, and numbness. Acosta's quest takes over six months, from his escape on July 1, 1967, to January, 1968. It is then that he finds solace, a budding desire to both affirm his Chicano identity and to write.[9]

The protagonist views himself as a man of the future, a popular culture advocate. The historian who has "no love for the past" insanely tries to break out of his asylum; he says:

> It is all madness, I think to myself. Five years of madness in this hideout. No wonder I'm cracking up. I take the green death into my hands and see my reflection on waves on the mirror behind the bar. I am

the son of Lorca, I remind myself. The only poet of this century worth reading. Did he suffer with those black eyes? That smooth, long greaser hair; did it make him hurt?

Who are these strange people, these foreigners that don't understand me? Friends all, yet they bring me memories of pain and long suffering. I definitely must run. I've got to go hide, to seek my fortune in the desert, in the mountains. Anywhere but here.[10]

Oscar, "thirty-three, the same age as Jesus when he died," dissipates, debauches himself, moving toward his own crucifixion. His Christ-like resurrection is foreshadowed in the pit of *gabacho* deprivation.

Ketchum, Idaho: Spaced out on bennies and booze, high on Hemingway, the Brown Buffalo takes on the guise of Henry Hawk, a Blackfoot and Samoan Chief. With Karen Wilmington's family and friends, he drinks spiked Koolaid and eats a Frito covered with guacamole and peyote—placed for effect on an American flag. It is as much to say that Mexico and Mexicans are little more than Acapulco beach boys and grass. The irony is that Henry Hawk outgringos the gringos, saying of the guacamole: "Foul scum, green turd with arsenic is what it tasted like. But I am a macho who eats hot chili for a penny a bite, remember?"[11] Acosta carefully develops obvious contradictions for his hero. The macho who eats hot chili is a reference to his Mexican cultural heritage when as a boy in Riverbank he took his father's dare. In retrospect, Oscar says of his childhood, "The sole purpose of childhood was to train boys how to be men. Not men of the future, but *now*."[12] The peyote-guacamole experience violates Oscar. In this sense *Brown Buffalo* may be likened to Hemingway's Nick Adams tales of maturation. The violence that Oscar Zeta Acosta experiences is the catharsis which will bring him into manhood.

The catharsis, however, is more than merely allowing Buffalo Brown to come of age. His suffering, his loss of dignity, and his self-vilification is a means of survival, survival as a mythical son of Malinche. Mexican novelist Carlos Fuentes poetically restates the original betrayal:

> Your father will never recognize you, my dark-skinned son; he will never see you as an heir, but rather as a slave; you will have to make your way as an orphan, with the help only of the thorny fingers of your outcast mother. Get drunk, son of sadness, fornicate, sing, dance, dress in all the colors of the earth, my orphan son of the earth, so that the earth may be reborn in the clay of your hungry body; turn our land into a great secret celebration, underground and invisible . . . a fiesta; you shall have no other communion in your loneliness; no other riches in your poverty; no other voice in your silence, except those of the great fiestas of death, dreaming, rebellion, and love; dreaming, loving, rebelling and dying will all be the same for you — the delirious fiesta in which you rebel in order to love and you love

in order to dream and you will dream in order to die; cover your body well with earth, son of mine, until the earth becomes your mask, and the masters are unable to recognize, behind it, your dreams, your love, your revolt or your death. Cover yourself with dust, my son, so that even when you are dead, you will seem alive and they will fear you, pícaro, thief, drunk, rapist, rebel armed with firecrackers and razors and shrill shrieks, threatening even in your stubborn, silent submission. You will know how to wait and wait, as our ancestors awaited the arrival of the god Quetzalcoatl, the god who fled in fright from his own face, so that your own face, easily frightened, my son, would have the feathers of mist and jade, with a mask of dust and weeping. Someday, my son, your wait will be rewarded, and the god of good and happiness will reappear behind a church or a pyramid on the mirage of the vast Mexican plateau; but he will only appear to you if from now on you prepare to reincarnate him, you yourself, my little hijito de la chingada; you must be the feathered, the winged earth, the clay bird, the screwed and doubly screwed son of Mexico and Spain: you are my only legacy, the legacy of Malintzín, the goddess; Marina, the whore; of Malinche, the mother.[13]

Acosta's Buffalo Brown, bumbler that he is, is similar to Ixca Cienfuegos, Fuentes' sad inheritor of Aztec myth and Mexican history in *La región más transparente*. Teodula Moctezuma, the omniscient priestess, passes her metaphysics on to Ixca, the journalist-observer in the shadows. Unlike Cienfuegos, Oscar's innocence must be defiled before he is allowed to visualize the truth of his quest. This truth, as interpreted by Octavio Paz, is: "In every man there is the possibility of being—or to be more exact, of his becoming once again—another man."[14]

After Oscar leaves Alpine and continues on his terrestrial *trip* to what he believes to be the land of his ancestral inheritance, El Paso and Juárez, he finds rejection and symbolic death. The Brown Buffalo agonizes, "Again the challenge! Just when I'd thought I'd become a Mexican in a bed of whores some pimply faced old man with a white brooch under a cracked, long nose questions my identity once again."[15] Insulting the hotel clerk he is thrown in jail. It is significant that Acosta appears before a female judge, a Malinche figure. She satirically asks in parting, "Why don't you go home and learn the language of your father."[16] The barb of her directive is, of course, Oscar's father allowed his children to speak only English, the language of his adopted country. And home? Oscar says in a telephone conversation to his brother: "I've checked it all out and have failed to find the answer to my search. One sonofabitch tells me that I'm not a Mexican and the other one says I'm not an American. I got no roots anywhere."[17]

Flash—in the pathos of failure—Buffalo Brown sees what the gods have in store for him. He reincarnates himself Quetzalcoatl and buffalo, a new man to lead a new people. Naively, he rehearses a speech, daydreaming that he rallies the Brown Berets to create a new nation. He states his identity as another man: "I am neither a Mexican or an American. I am neither a Catholic nor a Protestant. I am a Chicano by ancestry and a Brown Buffalo by choice."[18] In the resolution his incarnation of Zeta, "the world-famous Chicano Lawyer who helped to start the last revolution" is incomplete; however, his commitment as a revolutionary and as a writer of *truth* redirects him ... giving him a transcendental view of the larger struggle of Chicanos.

In the mainstream of American fictional heroes, Zeta of *The Revolt of the Cockroach People* compares with Preacher Casey of John Steinbeck's *Grapes of Wrath* and medical student/journalist Luis Cervantes of Mexican novelist Mariano Azuela's *Los de Abajo*. Like Preacher Casey, Acosta develops a proletariat orientation—mixing ideology with broads. "Who in the shit ever said that revolution has to be a drag?"[19], Buffalo asks. And diametrically, he, like Luis Cervantes, is in the revolution to get the story, the money for personal aggrandizement. This conflict of interests keeps Acosta from becoming a romantic hero of epic proportions. The protagonist, then, becomes the Revolution itself. Revolution is bigger than the little people whose sordid lives have little to do with the momentum of the soul-lifting ramifications of the revolutionary spirit. Therefore, Acosta *dumps* on his buddies, developing a string of character types involved in the revolution. The *truth* of the matter is that the majority possess all of the weaknesses of people who have been deprived success and alienated racially, economically, and socially. In the struggle for social change—revolution and death—Acosta's characters achieve a dignified status. Or as he says, "Some of the men look at me strangely. They know that I'm no wimp, but here I am, running around the world, talking of writing and revolution and women and death. But my commitment to death is different, larger than theirs."[20] Seeking death—not suicide—anticipating death— "determined to go out in a blaze of glory when the time arrives"[21]— Acosta accepts death as the catalyst needed to produce revolution and art: "find your death before you can find your life."[22]

Zeta's buddies, Pelón, Gilbert, and Black Eagle, are much like the deceased—murdered—Robert Fernández. They are *vatos locos*. As a type: "He wears a white T-shirt and a blue beanie, the traditional garb ... the Chicano street freak who lives on a steady diet of pills, dope, and wine.... You learn about life from the toughest guy in the neighborhood. You smoke your first joint in the alley at the age of ten; you take your first hit of *carga* before you get laid; and you learn to make your mark on the wall before you learn to write. Your friends know you to be a *vato loco*, a crazy guy, and they call you '*oso*,' or '*vato*,' or '*man*.' "[23] Reared on the violence in barrios like Tooner Flats, "a neighborhood of shacks and clotheslines and dirty back yards,"[24] the militant Chicanos bring to their revolution a knowledge of hard, dirty fighting, jails, and death. An army of *vatos locos* organizes against a common enemy, and like the Buffalo's transformation, they quit rumbling with each other and rally to *la causa*. Setting the rhetoric of the revolution aside, Acosta's truth and art depend upon the integrity of his cockroach descriptions. He calls them, "a new breed of savages ... the Cockroach People ... the little beasts that everyone steps on."[25] The primordial roach, symbol of Pancho Villa's marching song *La Cucaracha*, Acosta's characters are offensive, expendable, and nearly indestructable.

One of the interesting features of Acosta's descriptions—of his style—is the manner in which he sets the tone and mood of an episode by striving for a cinematic quality. Setting descriptions are minimal. The focus is on character action designed to affect film literate readers. Stereotyped settings, such as the one of Robert Fernández' second autopsy, provides a visual construct that doesn't compete with the action. For example: "In front of us, the casket is on a cart with small wheels. On a clean table we have scales and a bottle of clear liquid. There are razor-sharp tools, tweezers, clips, scissors, hacksaws, needles and plenty of yellow gloves. The white flourescent light shines down upon us."[26] The mind's eye becomes the camera, and in this particular shot reads like a shooting script for a proposed film production. The Bogart movie fantasies in *The Autobiography of a Brown Buffalo* and Oscar's confession, "I am the world's only living *T.V. Guide*,"[27] hint that a knowledge of filmmaking may enhance one's appreciation of Acosta's work.

Certainly the affectively grotesque autopsy may be visualized as a montage. An illustrating definition: "Among commercial filmmakers, montage is a term often used to describe a sequence using rapid superimpositions, jump-cuts, and dissolves in order to create a kind of kaleidoscopic effect to leave audiences with a particular emotional experience."[28] The autopsy sequence begins with the narrative voice solemn with respect for the dead. "The body is intact, dressed in fine linen. Clearly, Robert was a bull of a man. He had big arms and a thick neck now gone purple."[29] Concluding this paragraph, the author's tone becomes flippant and the atmosphere becomes grotesquely comic and absurd. He writes: "The chest has been sewn together. Now the orderly unstitches it. Snip, snip, snip. Holding open the rib cage, he carefully pulls out plastic packages from inside the chest cavity. I hold my breath."[30]

A jumbled visual record follows: "Cut here. Slice there. Here. There. Cut, cut, cut! Slice, slice, slice! And into a jar. Soon we have a whole row of jars with little pieces of meat." And:

> The face is a mask. The mouth is where the brain ... The nose is at the back of the neck. The hair is in the ears. The brown nose is hanging where the neck ... Get your goddamn hand out of there.
> My hand?
> That is the doctor's hand. It is inside the fucking face.
> I mean the head.
> His hand is inside. It is pulling at something. What did he find in there. What is it?
> ............................................................
> God! With hammer and chisel in hand, the Chinese doctor goes to town. Chomp, chomp, chomp ... Hack, hack, chuck, chuck, chud, chomp!
> Ah! Got it!
> Out it comes. Long, gizzard-looking. Twelve inches of red muscle and nerve dropping sawdust. Yes, we'll dissect this old buzzard, too.
> How about those ribs? You want some bar-b-que ribs, mister?
> Sure, *ese*. Cut those fucking ribs up. Chomp 'em up right now![31]

Superimposed on Robert Fernández' butchery is the reminder that this was once a man: "I see the tattoo on his right arm ... God Almighty! A red heart with blue arrows of love and the word 'Mother.' And I see the little black cross between the thumb and the trigger finger. A regular *vato loco*. A real *pachuco, ese*."[32]

The emotional experience triggered by this montage vivifies Acosta's view of death. Death gives life. Robert's autopsy both arouses indignation over the events that caused his death and makes a Chicano proletariat martyr of Fernández. With Robert's death Acosta foreshadows the death of Ronald Zanzibar. The police and the court cover up of the Fernández murder mirrors the corruption of the legal system that vindicated Sergeant Tom Wilson who killed Zanzibar with a bazooka. Because there is no justice for the Chicano, the dead must be desecrated to enlighten the public. Concluding the autopsy, Zeta prays: "Forgive me Robert, for the sake of the living brown ... I am no worse off than you. For the rest of my born days, I will suffer the knowledge of your death and your second death and your ashes to my ashes, your dust to my dust ... Goodbye, *ese*. Viva la Raza!"[33]

As revolutionary types Acosta's zealous *vatos* are a disorganized *palomilla*: "The *palomilla* ... is essentially a peer group or association of Chicano males who interact, informally, with some frequency. The associations are highly personal and voluntary in character.... The principal group activity ... was purely recreation in company of other men."[34] Their *pelado* antics are humorous, and events before and after revolutionary death struggles are comically dissipating: i.e., the orgy that followed the Safeway bombing. The relationship of caricatures like Pelón and Gilbert to the revolutionary cadre, Ronald Zanzibar, César Chávez, and Rodolfo "Corky" Gonzales, is the dignity they share risking their lives as "soldiers of Aztlán."³⁵ Zeta sums it up by twice quoting the aphorism read in César Chávez's chapel:

> LA VIDA NO ES LA QUE VIVIMOS
> LA VIDA ES EL HONOR Y EL RECUERDO
> POR ESO MAS VALE MORIR
> CON EL PUEBLO VIVO
> Y NO VIVIR
> CON EL PUEBLO MUERTO
>
> Lopitos
> Acapulco, Guererro, 1960.³⁶

Calculated to arouse empathy and benevolence, Acosta's tone becomes chauvinistic and patriotic, underscored by a vision of Aztlán.

With the respect that a son reserves for his spiritual father, Acosta describes César Chávez: "I know that for twenty-five days now, César has not tasted a morsel of solid food. He has starved himself like Ghandi. He believes that physical resistance to oppression only produces lesser men. Self-defense by design only creates violent characters. A revolution accompanied by brute force generates but another bruted society. By way of example of his followers, he gives up flesh and strength to their cause. The height of manhood, César believes, is to give of one's self."³⁷ As César and Corky Gonzales "are number one and two in the Nation of Aztlán,"³⁸ Acosta does not "fun" with them as character types. Corky Gonzales is pictured:

> Corky has on his usual red shirt and black pants. He comes in cagey like the top professional boxer he used to be. He knows the men are here to run him through some tough questions. He knows he is still considered an *outsider* to the *vatos* on the street. Tonight, here in L.A., he knows the mistrust one Chicano has for another. He understands the fear in the room toward a leader from another barrio, suspicion of a strange leader because . . . because Santa Anna sold us out to the gringos . . . because Juárez did nothing about it . . . because Montezuma was a fag and a mystic who had the fear of the Lord for Cortez or for Malinche . . . because anybody who has so little is afraid to lose what he just barely has got.³⁹

Juxtaposing portraits of *vatos*, spiritual and militant leaders, and martyrs gives Acosta's work a sense of immediacy in the dynamic present. Historical reference to Villa and Zapata, journalism and film accounts of the Moratorium, and futuristic promises of a continuing revolution generically establishes that *The Autobiography of a Brown Buffalo* and *The Revolt of the Cockroach People* is a literary compilation documentary.

It is possible to view these two novels as a film script rebutting the shot record of the film Sheriff Peter Peaches entered as evidence in the trial of the Tooner Flats Seven. Peaches' film is a distortion of what happened in Laguna Park. The establishing shot pictures Laguna Park as a happy, clean place for picnics, sports activities, and cultural awareness programs. The film cuts violently to helmeted policemen with riot weapons. Acosta narrates:

> And now you see people suddenly coming out. Now you see a cop lunge for a kid with long black hair.
> Cut to the sidewalk.
> A kid is winging at a cop. He has a red headband. The cops are pushing the people on the sidewalk. The people are being struck with clubs.[40]

The sheriff's film depicts contrasting scenes, purposefully emphasizing that the police and the sheriff's department were preserving both order and the good life.

As a script for a potential documentary film *The Revolt of the Cockroach People* fits what appear to be unrelated scenes, episodes, and eyewitness reports together creatively reconstructing the truth of the Moratorium riots, of Rubén Salazar's assassination, and of the Chicano's right to the mythical homeland of the Aztecs, Aztlán. Had Salazar lived—called Ronald Zanzibar in the novel—Acosta probably would not have had to assemble this document. Zanzibar was murdered, he writes, because "He talked too much. And specifically because they knew he had photographs of what really happened that day back at the park. He had those films with him at the moment he was killed. They were never recovered."[41] A non-fiction reference to Acosta's accusation has been restated by Albert Herrera: "Attorney Oscar Acosta charged that the deputies, knowing Rubén Salazar to be inside the tavern and fearing him as a spokesman for the Mexican American community, committed 'political murder, plain and simple.'"[42] After the death of columnist and T.V. news reporter Rubén Salazar there was no one left objective enough to tell the truth. Except Acosta. He says:

> The book offer has made me enemies. That I would think to make money off the struggle for freedom of the Cockroaches has made some people whisper traitor, *vendido*, *tío taco*, uncle tom and a capitalist pig to boot....
> I have explained it a thousand times. I have no desire to make a martyr out of Zanzibar. I know he has been murdered.... But now there is no Zanzibar to tell our story, no way for us to use the media to get us back our land.... we need writers, just like we need lawyers. Why not me? I *want* to write.[43]

Why not Acosta? The argument for the defense was clear and eloquent; however, the Chicanos and causes he had been defending put him in the unique position of knowing too much. Perhaps this was the reason Acosta chose to give some of the characters pseudonyms based on real people. To tell the truth of the violence precipitated by both gringos and Chicanos, he could hardly avoid being labeled a *vendido* or sell out. However, since the truth had to be told, Acosta "was qualified and had a grasp of the situation."[44] A Moses figure, Zeta was a tool of the revolution, a reluctant lawyer. Unable to participate, except for two conciliation bombings, he was always on the periphery of revolution and the Chicano promised land, Aztlán. As the Chicano lawyer he enjoyed special treatment—an untouchable status that kept him from being fully trusted by his clients. As Zeta says, "They just need me."[45] But when the truce was signed, he is given the opportunity to write his "memoirs": "my swan song about all my friends and our many problems."[46]

Revolution lifted the oppressed up—somewhat—and gave Oscar Zeta Acosta his identity as a man and writer. It produced the revolutionist and his art. *The Autobiography of a Brown Buffalo* belongs to the north from Mexico migrant genre of Chicano fiction celebrated by such able writers as José Antonio Villarreal, Tomás Rivera, Edmund Villaseñor, Raymond Barrio, Ernesto Galarza and others. What makes *Brown Buffalo* a novelty is Acosta's experiments with time and point of view. Neither of his novels are narrated chronologically. Time is implied, and the reader sorts and separates stream-of-consciousness recountings. Like James Joyce, J. P. Donleavy, and Vladimir Nabokov, Acosta provides the reader with specific reference points whereby violent impression, afterthoughts, drug reveries, and daydreams may be associated. The impressions of Acosta's montages, particularly in *The Revolt of the Cockroach People*, give far more insight into the frustrations of the oppressed than could a straightforward narrative of the Chicano search for identity and ensuing revolt against the gringo establishment. Ultimately, *The Autobiography of a Brown Buffalo* and *The Revolt of the Cockroach People* possess an artistic integrity debunking "holy cows" of religion, of romantic revolutionary ideology, and of the supposedly innate nobility of the majority committed to *La Causa*. The nobility of La Raza is collective; but individually, Acosta's *vatos locos* are in his own words "a bunch of goddamn outlaws."[47]

# Notes

[1] Peter Matthiessen, *Sal Si Puedes: César Chávez and the New American Revolution* (New York: Random House, 1969), p. 185.

² See Guadalupe Valdés Fallis, "Metaphysical Anxiety and the Existence of God in Contemporary Chicano Fiction," *Revista Chicano-Riqueña* (Winter 1975), p. 33. Valdés concludes that the summary treatment of Chicano literature as propaganda supporting the *gritos* of the outraged oppressed is too limiting. She writes: "The modern Chicano novel, like all important contemporary fiction, is deeply rooted in man and man's predicament in the alien and inhospitable universe of our times. This concern for values that transcends the propagandistic is an indication that the Chicano novel has indeed come of age."

³ Oscar Zeta Acosta, *The Autobiography of a Brown Buffalo* (San Francisco: Straight Arrow Books, 1972), pp. 17-18.

⁴ Ibid.

⁵ Ibid., p. 99.

⁶ Enrique Hank López, "Back to Bachimba," *The Chicanos: Mexican American Voices*, eds. Ed Ludwig and James Santibáñez (Baltimore: Penguin, 1971), 261.

⁷ Oscar Zeta Acosta, *The Revolt of the Cockroach People* (New York: Bantam, 1974). p. 28.

⁸ *Brown Buffalo*, p. 54.

⁹ Arthur Ramírez, "*The Autobiography of a Brown Buffalo, The Revolt of the Cockroach People*: A Review." *Revista Chicano-Riqueña* (Summer, 1975), pp. 47-48.

¹⁰ *Brown Buffalo*, p. 67.

¹¹ Ibid., p. 124.

¹² Ibid., p. 75.

¹³ Carlos Fuentes, "La Herencia de la Malinche," from *Todos los Gatos Son Pardos*, reprinted in *Chicano Literature: Text and Context*, eds. Antonia Castañeda Shular, Tomás Ybarra-Frausto, and Joseph Sommers (Englewood Cliffs, N.J.: Prentice-Hall, 1972), 304-305.

¹⁴ Octavio Paz, *The Labyrinth of Solitude: Life and Thought in Mexico*, trans. Lysander Kemp (New York: Grove Press, 1961), p. 28.

¹⁵ *Brown Buffalo*, p. 191.

¹⁶ Ibid., p. 194.

¹⁷ Ibid., p. 196.

¹⁸ Ibid., p. 199.

¹⁹ *Cockroach People*, p. 85.

²⁰ Ibid., p. 227.

²¹ Ibid., p. 233.

²² Ibid., p. 202.

²³ Ibid., pp. 90-91.

²⁴ Ibid.

²⁵ Ibid., pp. 36, 142.

²⁶ Ibid., p. 101.

²⁷ *Brown Buffalo*, p. 24.

²⁸ Harry M. Geduld and Ronald Gottesman, *An Illustrated Glossary of Film Terms* (New York: Holt, Rinehart and Winston, 1973), p. 107.

²⁹ *Cockroach People*, p. 101-102.

³⁰ Ibid.

³¹ Ibid., pp. 105-106.

³² Ibid.

³³ Ibid., p. 167.

³⁴ Joseph Spielberg, "Humor in a Mexican-American Palomilla: Some His-

torical, Social and Psychological Implications," *Revista Chicano-Riqueña* (Summer, 1974), p. 41.

[35] *Cockroach People*, p. 136.
[36] *Ibid.*, pp. 41-42.
[37] *Ibid.*, p. 38.
[38] *Ibid.*, p. 270.
[39] *Ibid.*, pp. 227-228.
[40] *Ibid.*, p. 215.
[41] *Ibid.*, p. 267.
[42] Albert Herrera, "The National Chicano Moratorium and the Death of Rubén Salazar," *The Chicanos: Mexican American Voices*, eds. Ed Ludwig and James Santibáñez (Baltimore: Penguin, 1972), p. 240.
[43] *Cockroach People*, p. 249.
[44] *Ibid.*
[45] *Ibid.*
[46] *Ibid.*, p. 281.
[47] *Ibid.*, p. 131.

# Acosta's *The Revolt of the Cockroach People:* The Case, the Novel, and History

*Alurista*

The notion of the novel as literary mediation of historical events is as old as the genre itself, being, as it is, that "without letters the memory of arms perishes." In this brief essay I shall examine a contemporary Chicano novel, *The Revolt of the Cockroach People*, through which Oscar Zeta Acosta, its author, narrates the events of the Chicano revolt in Los Angeles in 1968–70. Upon asserting that the novel focuses its narrative on events of a historical nature, events that can be verified through other documents, two central problems emerge immediately: selectiveness and subjectivity.

The process of selecting representative events that reveal the fundamental contradictions of the period as well as those experienced by the participants is an essential and problematic task. In Acosta's narrative one is confronted with a judicial focus; the historical events of the popular Chicano revolt are revealed through three court cases, two coroner's inquests, and a political candidacy for sheriff, historical events that peak with the political campaign. Acosta chooses these three structural elements as the backbone of his literary production, given the fact that his own role, in real life as well as fictionally, is that of defense lawyer and narrator of the events or cases.

Even though Acosta's selective process is founded on verifiable documents such as court cases, the narrative, far from maintaining an objective posture, suffers from a deliberately unrestrained subjectivity. Subjectivity in Acosta's narrative is manifested at three levels: genre, narrator, and tone. As a genre, the novel is a bourgeois literary form that tends to glorify the individual. Whether this glorification is one that negates the persona or one that affirms it, the novel remains an individual product to be consumed and appreciated by other individ uals. Moreover, the modern novel examines the individuality of being, with all the anxieties a capitalist culture produces by alienating the self from the persona.

Acosta magnifies the subjectivity of the genre by narrating his novel in the first person: he acts as the protagonist who triggers the plot and ends up as its antihero. As if both genre and first-person narration were not enough to subjectivize the telling of real events, Acosta saturates his novel with an ironic tone that grotesquely caricatures the historical setting and the characters within it.

With these narrative strategies, Acosta attempts to place the reader before a historical codification of real events. Even though the greater portion of this reality is highly subjectivized, the concrete and objective nature of the narrated events surrounding the Chicano revolt in Los Angeles during 1968–70 is preserved with some veracity:

> "Come on, Brown, come on! ... I'm trying to tell you ... I'm telling you, that picketing thing is over. ... All you're doing is getting your own people in trouble. Now look ..." he leans over toward me and lowers his voice, "the blacks picketed for years ... for years. They marched and they did the very things you people are doing now ... but you know something, and this is the honest-to-God truth ... they didn't get a thing until they had Watts! That is a fact! And I'm telling you, until your people riot, they're probably not going to get a thing either! That's my opinion."[1]

This is, summarily, the world view of the politician, the highest executive power in the City of Los Angeles, Mayor Yorty. He and his accomplices and witnesses—Chief of Police Redding and the Mexican-American banker Dr. Bravo—established a consensus with the cynical edict that violence is equivalent to the public recognition of the historical presence of the Chicano people. Irony of ironies: Institutional "law and order" instigates massive criminality in order to obtain legitimacy and social justice! Within this ideological framework and consciousness the "revolt of the cockroach people" will manifest itself.

The two years 1968–1970, more so than the first eight years of the decade, were characterized by mass movements at an international level. The intention of these movements was to dramatize the fundamental contradictions of U.S. militarism as manifested in the Vietnam War. U.S. youth acquired consciousness from the world denunciation of the imperialism crystallized in the universal draft of the United States. Simultaneously, the privileged classes within the very belly of the U.S. empire organized themselves to launch an anti-Communist campaign in the name of Christ:

> A consensus of the most powerful middle-aged and elderly Wasps in America—statesmen, corporation executives, generals, admirals, news-

paper editors, and legislators had pledged an intellectual troth: they had sworn with a faith worthy of medieval knights that Communism was the deadly foe of Christian culture. If it were not resisted in the postwar world, Christianity itself would perish. So had begun a Cold War with intervals of overt war, mixed with periods of modest collaboration. As Communist China grew in strength, and her antagonisms with the Soviet Union quickened their pace, the old troth of the Wasp knights had grown sophisticated and abstract. It was now a part of the technology of foreign affairs, a thesis to be called upon when needed. The latest focus of this thesis was of course to be found in Vietnam.[2]

This war, far from being a lucrative and stable investment, far from opening the markets of Asia to American salesmanship, in fact devoured 30 billion dollars a year and stained the reputation of the United States and its "noble" war to propagate American democracy with napalm, premeditation, and economic advantage. American boys were being killed by the thousands. The options open to more than half of the Chicano population between 16 and 25, particularly those that made it as far as the eighth grade, consisted of Vietnam, underpaid/unskilled labor, high school/university, anomie/jail!

A disproportionate number of Chicanos, Blacks, and poor whites were dying in the front lines of Vietnam. A very small number of Chicanos graduated from high school to go on to college, and that was the half that made it past the eighth grade! The army, the farm fields, the factories, the schools, jails, stores, and offices had become, in the history of the United States, veritable nests of institutional racism.[3]

By the beginning of the two years in question, César Chávez had already run out of patience trying to organize in East Los Angeles through the Community Service Organization. Chávez was convinced, as early as 1962, that the California farmworker was at the bottom of the U.S. labor totem pole. In 1965, he organized a march under the United Farmworkers Organizing Committee banner. This pilgrimage from Delano to Sacramento was mobilized for the purpose of dialoguing with California Governor Pat Brown regarding the working and living conditions of one of the essential labor forces in California and the nation: the farmworker. After all, food and military weaponry remained the principal United States exports during the Vietnam years.

Reies López Tijerina captured the attention of the Chicano in general, particularly the youth, and some of the national mass media with his cry for "land, culture, language and religion" in New Mexico as affirmed by the Treaty of Guadalupe-Hidalgo's protocol. The Tijerina Courthouse Raid was the subject of numerous articles in the state and the nation in 1968. "Corky" Gonzales from Denver, Colorado, severed his ties with the Colorado Democratic Party after the "Viva Kennedy" campaign, opting by 1965 for an independent initiative with his founding of the Crusade for Justice. José Angel Gutiérrez mobilized the MAYO organization of Texas University students into political action as early as 1969, moving toward the formation of La Raza Unida Party in 1971.

The United Farmworkers Organizing Committee led by César Chávez, Tijerina's Federal Alliance of Free Pueblos, Gonzales' Crusade for Justice, and La Raza Unida Party of Texas led by Gutiérrez welcomed with open arms the new generation of Chicano students willing and eager to struggle for social change. Their mature leadership was welded to the ardent fervor of Chicano youth, a relationship that began to forge a nationalist consciousness and a concrete awareness of class, cultural, racial, and sexual struggle. The "Chicano Movement," more specifically the "Chicano Student Movement," was at its mobilized best when Acosta appeared on the scene.

*The Revolt of the Cockroach People* opens its third chapter with the "East Los Angeles School Blow Outs" in the spring of 1968:

> I feel right at home. So now a frog asks me to a Blow Out? It may be something or nothing, but why not? I am a free buffalo in a horrible place, looking for a little excitement. I still don't believe a damn thing. (p. 37)

Zeta Brown has just resigned from his job as a lawyer with the Legal Aid Society in Oakland.[4] He is in Los Angeles "searching for material to write an article for the *New York Times* . . . and nobody is impressed." He is on the verge of resuming the profession that alienates him so: law practice. Zeta Brown accepts an offer to work with *La Voz*, a popular Chicano newspaper of progressive tendencies (which, in reality, was called *La Raza*) and its directors, ". . . a toothy Cuban and his white chick." His formal role will be that of a legal observer during the L.A. Blow Outs.

> All around me is a new breed of savages, brown-eyed devils who shout defiantly to the heavens. And what am I to do? Is all this just to write some story? Do up-and-coming great men march at the command of a wretched voice over a bullhorn? Is this the place for a lone buffalo? Will they bust me for passing out Camels? I am divided against myself, torn in two. (p. 42)

The buffalo, Zeta Brown, is, in fact, divided against himself since he is thoroughly aware that in order to write the story of the Blow Outs he will end up acting the part of a lawyer, a role which he abhors to the point of nausea. Moreover, he is not the only "buffalo" who, after some soul-searching and confrontation with social institutions, desires to join the "cockroach people" in their struggle to humanize their lives through "revolutionary" acts. Thousands of Mexican Americans confront the recurring dichotomy: Mexican or American? Can one be both or either in the United States?

The economic border is clear between farmworkers and growers. Identity and its redefinition is the key to the self-affirmation and self-determination of Chicano people in East Los Angeles. Zeta Brown searches for his own self-affirmation. During the spring of 1968 he visits César Chávez, who has been fasting for 25 days in order to bring an end to violence in the farm fields of Delano. César is waiting for him since Risco (the "toothy Cuban") and Ruth ("his white chick") have spoken to him about the Chicano lawyer in Los Angeles. Zeta Brown complains to César:

> "Buffalo?"
> "Yeah, I'm here César."
> "So how are things in L.A.?"
> "All right, I guess."
> "Are you guys trying to get the *viejitos* to join you, too?"
> "Well, you know how old people are. Besides, I'm not doing much organizing myself. I'm kinda confused."
> "Look," he says, a little stronger. "I *know* LA is a graveyard for organizers. You, personally, Brown Buffalo, a Chicano lawyer, have got to help those kids. Nobody else is going to do it. The militants are doing a terrific job. Aren't you satisfied?"
> "Oh, yeah." I think about his philosophy of non-violence. "I didn't know if you would approve," I say lamely. I don't know how to explain to him where I'm at.
> "Listen *viejo* . . . It doesn't matter if I approve or if anyone approves. You are doing what has to be done. ¿*Qué más vamos a hacer?*"
> "It's not exactly what you do . . ."
> "So what? I'm a man, just like you, no? Each of us has a different role, but we both want the same, don't we?"
> Role? Want the same? "I guess . . ."
> "Come on, *viejo*! Don't be so . . . They tell me you are one hell of a lawyer. Don't give up so easy, hombre."
> "But I don't want to be a lawyer!" Finally I get out a part of it.
> "So?" he says, leaning up again. "Who in his right mind would *want* to be a lawyer, eh?" (pp. 45–46)

From Chapter 5 on, we begin to see Acosta/Brown's novelistic production unfold as the history of judicial cases that climax in rhetorical debates in the halls of justice of Los Angeles or in collective acts of protest that confront the militaristic L.A. police force and the sheriff's department. Zeta Brown Buffalo is the defense lawyer in some minor cases in the Garfield Blow Out when the Los Angeles County Grand Jury expedites warrants for the arrest of thirteen "conspirators" in the school strikes of East Los Angeles: The "East L.A. Thirteen" case has begun and Zeta Brown reacts immediately:

"The East LA Thirteen are behind those bars up there. Are they in jail because they rose to speak out against the educational system in this country? Do you think they have been rousted from their offices and their homes like a bunch of criminals simply because they got thousands of Chicanos to walk away from their schools for a few days? Is this government to fall because a small group of men and women have demanded an end to the racist system in the schools? Would the government go to this extreme simply because we want better schools, better teachers, better administrators, because we want the books, the teachers and the materials to reflect our own culture? Are we such a threat just because we have demanded a compliance with the Treaty of Guadalupe Hidalgo, which provided for a bilingual society? Is there something wrong with speaking Spanish in our schools? But when you stop and think about it, that is *exactly* why they are in jail on this monstrous prosecution.

"Imagine, forty-five years behind bars because of an idea. A life sentence for disturbing the minds of people in power. For that is all they have done. They have only *said* things. They are not being prosecuted because of any violence. They are not charged with throwing eggs or bottles or setting fires. They are charged with having planned, organized and executed a *demonstration*. The DA isn't saying that they incited anybody to riot. He doesn't claim that they told anyone to throw anything. And he doesn't say that they threw anything themselves. Only that they *conspired* to tell people to walk away from their schools. Period.

"We most emphatically agree with the prosecution. We did, in fact, plan, and we did, in fact, execute a demonstration at five Chicano High Schools in March of 1968. So what?

"If that makes us criminals, then criminals we are. Outlaws and rebels against any government of men that would make it a crime to speak out against injustice? We are definitely that.

"I represent the East LA Thirteen. I am the chief counsel for these men. I will be needing a lot of help in the days to come. We will need lawyers, law students, leg men, secretaries, and the support of anyone who is in agreement with our position. And to be honest, even if you aren't in agreement, but you simply want to help out of the milk of human kindness, then join up with us.

"Unless we all band together and fight against this type of political persecution, we are all doomed. If Evelle Younger can throw you in jail for speaking out against racism, he can just as easily throw you in jail for speaking out against the regime presently in power. (pp. 59–61)

It is important to note, as Acosta does, that the indictment coincides with the Presidential campaign and that both Robert Kennedy and Senator McCarthy have pledged their support to the Chicano Legal Defense Fund, promising to contribute funds. The California primary is impending, and the state does not want any problems but rather some scapegoats to justify the law and order proposed by Nixon. The picketing in front of the "Glass House" (Los Angeles County Jail) is at its peak.

Zeta Brown tells us that "The Blow Outs were buried in the back pages. We were nothing but a bunch of outside agitators, radicals, communists and racists. But now that the racist-agitators are in jail, charged with conspiracy, now it is news" (p. 57).

The social contradictions manifested in the schools and in their structure had existed for over a hundred years. Nonetheless, they had never been the focus of public concern, and it took a high school student strike in six institutions to dramatize the case in point: institutional racism in American education.

Robert Kennedy is murdered at the Ambassador Hotel in Los Angeles one day after Zeta Brown is able to free the East L.A. Thirteen on bail. Zeta Brown's worst fears materialize over the political future of the United States: "It doesn't matter who killed him; liberals choke at violence. You watch and see. This will insure the election of that motherfucker Nixon" (p. 64).

Regional and statewide conferences are organized at USC and Loyola University in Los Angeles with the purpose of organizing Chicano students who are willing to struggle for justice in the schools, against institutional racism at their universities, and to form support committees for the farmworkers' boycott of non-union grapes. Brown Beret chapters spring up throughout California with the purpose of keeping an alert eye on the law enforcement abuses that often border on brutality and have become a daily occurrence throughout the state. The *L.A. Times* writes of "Chicano Militants," and Rubén Salazar starts his column, his last act as social critic and respected Chicano journalist. After raising antiracist consciousness to the level of institutional confrontation (the schools), it was only a matter of time and obvious necessity before the movement extended its activities to similar fronts such as the Roman Catholic Church.

The Chicano Law Students Association begins its efforts to have a dialogue/confrontation with Cardinal McIntyre, a visible member of the Los Angeles round table of city fathers. McIntyre cancels his meeting with the Chicano militants, who in turn organize to denounce the corruption of the Church and its irresponsible behavior toward the real needs of the Chicano laity.

> It is Christmas Eve in the year of Huitzilopochtli, 1969. Three hundred Chicanos have gathered in front of St. Basil's Roman Catholic Church. Three hundred brown-eyed children of the sun have come to drive the money-changers out of the richest temple in Los Angeles. It is a dark moonless night and ice-cold wind meets us at the doorstep. We carry little white candles as weapons. In pairs on the sidewalk, we trickle and bump and sing with the candles in our hands, like a bunch of cockroaches gone crazy. I am walking around giving orders like a drill sergeant. (p. 11)

Thus begins the second case: "St. Basil's Twenty-One." This candle-lit vigil becomes a battleground when the ushers turn out to be law enforcement officers, who shut the main doors of the temple on the noses of the "cockroach people." Twenty-one persons are arrested:

> The media turn out in full force. Chicanos have not fought inside a temple since the Spanish conquistadores invaded the shrines of Huitzilopochtli in the Valley of Mexico. We make headlines without the assistance of Stonewall and his liberal white connections. McIntyre heaps it on us. We are the rabble at the foot of the cross, calling for the death of Christ. We are agents of the devil and communists to boot. (p. 78)

Zeta Brown tells the reporters that the Chicanos are the Jews of "Nazi America" and that the government and the Church have combined their efforts to exterminate a people. These days witness the militaristic formations that threaten a neo-fascist show of force. The Los Angeles Tactical Squad begins the training and practice of mass control strategies, including the paradigmatic wedge formations designed to disperse and isolate small groups and ringleaders.

The Mexican community in the barrios of Los Angeles disagrees with the tactics used by the Chicano militants against the Catholic Church. The militants dramatize their case with a collective fast at St. Basil's in protest of McIntyre as principal administrator of the Los Angeles Church. The fast takes place at the Jewish synagogue across from St. Basil's. While the Chicano consensus remains divided over tactics, Pope Paul removes Cardinal McIntyre as head of the Los Angeles Diocese.

The separation of conservative Mexican Americans accelerates the consciousness-raising of the Chicano militants. The relentless focus on public activism by the more progressive elements in the urban forums of the nation ensures the FBI and CIA an opportunity to infiltrate the Movement. Police brutality against Chicanos in the barrios of California escalates wantonly. Acosta narrates the case of "Robert Fernández" who, after being taken to jail to "check the marks he had on his arms," is later found hanging in his cell after being brutalized. The autopsy report from the Coroner's Office declares his death a suicide. Robert's family insists that he died at the hands of another. After exhaustive inquiry, Brown Buffalo is convinced that Fernández has been murdered either by the officer who arrested him or by the son of a known drug-dealing family who shared his cell at the time Robert died.[5]

Frustrated by the silence of the cellmate, the arresting police officer, and the inquest proceedings, Zeta Brown firebombs a Safeway store, central urban target of the nonviolent farmworkers' committee organized by César Chávez. A boycott protesting Safeway's conspiracy to stop the unionization of farmworkers in the United States was the national strategy of the United Farmworkers. That same week, Zeta Acosta/Zeta

Brown launches his candidacy for Los Angeles County Sheriff under the banner of La Raza Unida Party:

> The publicity from the trials and my numerous contempt of court charges have brought hordes into my camp. Cockroaches from Hollywood and Venice, *vatos* from car clubs, elderly churchgoers. Cockroaches from the barrios and beaches have begun to pass out bumper stickers. Posters drawn by nuns and hippies, statements of my single-issue platform are stuck under windshield wipers. Lawyers from the National Lawyers Guild, from the ACLU and from the Legal Aid Societies have joined up to elect the radical Chicano lawyer. (p. 168)

Zeta Brown finds himself in the middle of the most grotesque U.S. transnational play ever. The trials of the East L.A. Thirteen and the St. Basil's Twenty-One, as well as his candidacy, Zeta for Sheriff, are all under way at the same time that B-52 bombers are sent into Cambodia during the "Looking Glass" operation. On May 4, 1970, Ohio State troopers murder four Anglo-American students at Kent State University during a protest to stop the Asian war, a murder which triggers mass demonstrations throughout the land. At UCLA, Zeta Brown ridicules the antiwar movement and himself:

> Hell yes, a little dope, a little love, a cheer here and there. Let's march around the block, let's go on up to the pigs at the skirmish line and give them hell.... We'll kill them with our buttons and beads.... We'll slaughter them with our Rolling Stones albums, right. (pp. 179–180)

Objective conditions of struggle are subjected to constant contradictions and oscillations at future-shock speeds. Zeta Brown's vision gazes beyond the radicalism of the antiwar movement. As soon as the universal draft is abolished in the seventies, the student movement subsides. Bringing the boys home and stopping the bombing do not, in any way, shape, or form, change the social, economic, or political relations of United States transnational monopoly interests in Asia or at home.

"Chicano Moratoriums," or protests against the war in Vietnam and the disproportionate number of Chicanos on the lists of military casualties, are organized during the summer of 1970. The war against injustice is a "war at home not in Vietnam." August 29th is designated for the first National Chicano Moratorium mass rally in Los Angeles' Laguna Park. It is on this date that Zeta Brown falsely claims he is in Acapulco[6] while 20,000 men and women—Chicanitos and Chicanitas of all ages and walks of life—march through the streets of Tooner Flats, down Whittier Boulevard, to demonstrate against the local and international genocidal strategies dictated by U.S. transnational monopoly capitalism:

It seemed that twenty-five thousand Chicanos had marched down Whittier Boulevard. But what had started as a protest against the burning of peasants in Vietnam turned into a massive public declaration by fire of their own existence. Even before the first speech, a fight broke out between the pigs and the *vatos*. An hour later, Tooner Flats was in flames. An hour later, Zanzibar and two other young Chicanos were dead, killed by agents of the SOC Squad. An hour later, Corky, Gilbert, Elena and four other CMs were behind bars, facing life sentences. The Tooner Flats Seven were indicted by the Grand Jury on felony charges of Arson, Firebombing, Inciting to Riot and Conspiracy. (p. 209)

Zeta Brown is furious and immediately leaps at the throat of the California legal system: "The Grand Jury which indicted my clients is a racist institution . . . and I'm going after the judges that selected those jurors" (p. 209).[7] The remainder of the novel moves toward its closure with an innocent verdict and liberty for the East L.A. Thirteen and St. Basil's Twenty-One. The Coroner's Inquests of Fernández and Zanzibar turn into grotesque official parodies. Zeta Brown's candidacy for sheriff, as expected, is lost, but by an unexpectedly close margin. Nonetheless, as planned, a significant portion of the L.A. voters are turned on to the plight of Chicanos in the United States. Only the trial of the Tooner Flats Seven is unresolved, and its legal motions remain active for almost another year before charges are dropped because of insufficient evidence. "Corky" Gonzales, however, is sentenced to 40 days for carrying a 22-caliber handgun. A few anarchic acts of violence remain to be told. Zeta Brown claims to have committed them, even though:

> No, they didn't catch me for any of the shit I've pulled. But the fact of the matter is, they *know* exactly what I've done. That is the frightening thing. Those bastards know every single act of violence I ever pulled off with the lunatics from Tooner Flats. (p. 257)

In three collective trials—The East L.A. Thirteen, The St. Basil's Twenty-One, and The Tooner Flats Seven; two individual inquests— those of Robert Fernández and Roland Zanzibar; and one political campaign—Zeta for Sheriff, Acosta has dramatized the populist contradictions that characterized the sixties. He produces his text from a militant point of view, dramatizing ironically and exaggerating the historical events of the epoch. Acosta's vision turns grotesque when he portrays the creation of a revolutionary movement through narrative parody. Even though his literary objective is signified as a historical concern, it is really the unveiling of his own alienated labor and that of the "cockroach people" that commands his attention. His novelistic "gonzo" production calls for an imperative humanizing praxis capable of demystifying the real object of his grotesque narrative: the Yankee militarist empire and its "democratic" gymnastics: "It's in the blood now ... just like a slave is chained to his master" (p. 258).

THE COLORADO COLLEGE

## Notes

[1] Oscar Zeta Acosta, *The Revolt of the Cockroach People*. San Francisco: Straight Arrow Press, 1973, p. 74. All further references to the text will be incorporated within the article.
[2] Norman Mailer, *Armies of the Night*. New York: Signet Books, 1968, p. 204.
[3] President's Commission on Civil Disorders. *Report, 1968*. New York: Bantam Books, 1968. This report confirms the practice and history of institutional racism in the United States.
[4] In Acosta's autobiographical novel, *The Autobiography of a Brown Buffalo*, we find a narration of his odyssey with the Legal Aid Society of Oakland, California.
[5] In Chapters 8 and 9 of the novel we find superb examples of Acosta's grotesque, ironic, and morbid novelistic techniques.
[6] In Chapter 14, Zeta Brown claims he was with his brother in Acapulco, where they surrounded themselves with a decadent atmosphere of drugs and prostitution. This is false, at least on the date mentioned.
[7] In Chapter 17, Zeta Brown interrogates California judges on their racist practices in the selection of grand juries.

Paradise and Plums:
Appearance and Reality in
Barrio's *The Plum Plum Pickers*

*Vernon E. Lattin*

The setting for most of the action in Raymond Barrio's *The Plum Plum Pickers* is the Western Grande Migrant Compound owned by Mr. Frederick C. Turner. Mr. "friendly adroit Turner," known to the Mexican American fruit pickers as "el Gusano Verde," the green worm, has worked his way up in the good old American way; once a poor boy doing odd jobs from house to house, he is now one of the richest orchard owners in California. Hard work, greed, unscrupulous business ethics, and his wife's inheritance made his success story possible. His earlier career included jobs as a cowboy extra for Hollywood, where his favorite image of himself was that of Black Bart, the outlaw. Now that he is wealthy, he has become more and more concerned with creating a favorable public image. He has allowed himself certain eccentric hobbies, one of which is turning the Western Grande Compound into a "real" western town by giving all the migrant shacks false fronts. These "pseudo shops"[1] are an appropriate symbol, for they hide the reality of Turner's greed, Quill's self pity, and the misery and hopes of the Gutiérrezes, Delgados, and other migrant workers living behind this fantasy with their own dreams, nightmares, broken lives, and hopes for a better future. One of the few reminders of reality in this bizarre world of make-believe created by the pseudo-actor Turner is the hangem oak behind No. 12, the Bar-Noon Saloon; hanging from this authentic hangman's tree is a straw effigy of Black Bart.

The tree with its effigy swaying in the wind reminds the reader of its true history and the reality of death and unhappiness, however camouflaged, behind the appearance of the Western Grande Compound, called a "pickers' paradise" (2). Raymond Barrio has created a novel structured around the appearance of paradise and the reality of plums ripening to death or fulfillment. The novel is a web of appearances, facades, dreams, hopes, fantasies, and aspirations that constantly contrast with reality, facts, living nightmares, disappointments, and death—all revealing the greed and injustice existing in the agricultural United States. The rhetoric of paradise, the false image of equality, the facade of the "Horatio Alger" story, the cunning appearance of capitalism and good business practices, and the fantasy of a horticultural paradise create the world of harsh realities of the migrant workers' day-to-day existence. The theme can be most clearly seen by examining the major characters in the novel, all caught somewhere between the appearance of paradise and the reality of misery and death.

The novel opens with a loud "Bang bang. Crash," disturbing the troubled dreams of Morton J. Quill, manager and overseer of the Western Grande. He has been dreaming, as usual, about driving a hearse. The noise of reality brings him back not only from sleep but from a kind of life-in-death where he was listening to "all the underworld noises infiltrating his tender sleep" (1). Ironically, his return to real life from the underworld is not an escape with an Aeneas/Odysseus-like vision of truth; it is a return to the reality of his own hell and the hell that he manages for Turner. He is the "blubbery majesty" of this hell who is awakened by the sounds of protest and rebellion against his rule. He is blind to both the protest and the reality of its meaning—as well as to the meaning of his recurring dream. Quill cannot understand either his life nor his dreams. As he gets up and stares into the darkness, he seems to be "testing his prescient powers, as though foreshadowing his own death, as though plums could be prevented from ripening relentlessly" (1). He is forever unable to see into the darkness of which he is a part and which he has helped create; he cannot see his individual fate nor the fate of all men—he must surely die unprepared. Pepe Delgado, standing out in the dark after a night of drinking and wenching, asks, "Whatsa matter, el miserable pal?" (1). Quill can only refer ignorantly to the crash and noise that awakened him and to the note signed Joaquín M. A wiser man than this "giant gaseous burp" might have realized that the "pickers' paradise" which he considers his own private domain has a logic of its own. The reality of that logic is that plums must ripen, that the oppressed must fight back somehow to gain dignity and identity, that blubbery tyrannical majesty must fall, and that in the life cycle death is real.

Quill is only a pseudo-logician, fooling himself with arguments and cliches learned from Turner, Rat Barfy, Governor Howlin Mad Nolan, and all the other defenders of the faith. The logic and rhetoric of paradise are simple and foolproof, for they are blind to the deception involved: the logic argues that the greed of the capitalist is necessary for the prosperity of the worker and that those "who have to meet payrolls" are really the saviors of the world. Such logic claims to help the worker yet despises him as lazy and ungrateful. Quill spouts the logic as he defends the run-down shacks of the migrant workers against housing inspectors and housing codes:

> What in hades did they want them to do. Crap outside. Die. Great scott, what the devil was wrong with a few leaky pipes. Those deranged inspectors. Just because they had running water. Blind. No heart. Yap yap yapping. They really did not care. Weren't these migrants much better off precisely because of Mr. Turner's limitless benevolence. The Western Grande . . . was a godsend to most of the riffraff coming by here from Texas. . . . weren't these workers human beings too. . . . What was the good of raising good, fat, healthy, plump prune trees next to the garbage pits if you didn't also raise enough prune pickers? . . . And wasn't it good for them to go out into all that fresh natural air and free sunshine, though. (4–5)

Rat Barfy, the radio commentator Quill helps support with his weekly dime, is the public voice of this "profound logic" (26). He is able to prove that equality does not exist because he says it does not exist; he refutes Abe Lincoln, the U.S. Constitution, and the Supreme Court justices by linking them with "pinko freakybop nincompoops" and their social reforming schemes that will destroy the workers' cornucopian paradise (26). Of course, Barfy is correct: equality does not exist. His message, however, is that it should not exist, for equality is equated with socialism and all the other dangerous "isms." The acceptance of this logic creates the appearance of truth and ensures that equality will never exist.

Turner, of course, is king of the pseudo-logicians, "non disputatum" (48). He is the master of a free enterprise system based on the logic of slavery where the rich get richer, all for the benefit of America and the workers. He protects the pickers from their own greed, from social reforming intellectuals, from education, from everything that might harm their happy-go-lucky existence. And he protects his psyche with "somersaults" and "crooked leaps" of his mind:

> The pickers are perfectly happy with the way things are. I never met a picker who didn't say he was happy working for me. They all say they'd be happy to be my slave. And believe me I've asked hundreds of them. Thousands. They are the happiest people on the face of the earth. That's why I like going to Acapulco. (48)

The author's irony, of course, is obvious, but it is not obvious to the Turners and Quills as they deceive the world. What is even less obvious to Turner is that he is sterile, cut off from reality—symbolized by his mansion among acres of fruit trees, its eighteen rooms without children, hidden from view by "rapacious" bushes (46), and guarded by wild dogs. Here Turner lives with his wife, Jean Angelica Turner, who also wanted a career on stage. Her stage is now her mansion where she acts the angelic part her name suggests, doing good works and living a tormented neurotic inner life. The Turners' tragedy is that they are trapped in their own cage of self-deception.

Barrio is aware that the trap of the free enterprise system springs both ways. Behind the appearance of *free* enterprise lives the slave worker who must "stoop and pull and pluck and spoon./Again and again./And bay at the moon" (158). The workers become trapped animals; their dreams turn to nightmares, and their hopes turn into fantasies. They are forced to accept the logic of the Turners like Serafina Delgado, to rebel like Ramiro Sánchez, or to dream, fantasy, and search for identity like Manuel and Lupe Gutiérrez.

Pepe and Serafina Delgado are better off than most of the workers, for Pepe has a regular job in the cannery, they own a home, and their children attend Drawbridge High School. Prune picking is relatively easy, and the entire famiy (except Danny) earns extra money this way. Apparently, these Chicano workers have escaped the trap and attained the good life; in reality, however, it is too late for Pepe and Serafina: they have lost contact with the earth and the processes of life, and they have been twisted by the Anglo image of success and the fear of poverty. Pepe has accepted the image of the lazy drunken Mexican, running crews for the bandito, Roberto Morales, and beating his children. He is lost between two cultures, and the juices and joy of life have been squeezed out of him. Serafina, who is constantly protecting Danny's *machismo*, expresses her acceptance of the logic of the workers' paradise; she seeks only to exist, to continue the status quo:

> She didn't like all that radical talk among her compañeros about how the rich ought to be stripped of every dollar and every hectare of land. That was terrible. The rich had earned what they got.... And without them, where would she, and all other poor families be?... They should be grateful, not critical, her compadres. How ungrateful they were!! (72)

More typical of the pickers' existence are the lives of Manuel and Lupe Gutiérrez, the main characters in the novel. Both are trapped in a dream world of fantasies and hopes as they try to provide for their three children and maintain human dignity and worth. Both are able to defy their animal existence, to assert their humanity at least once in the novel, and to continue to some extent a genuine search for identity and meaning. Lupe exists almost entirely in a world of appearances and dreams; her life is "un sueño loco" (15), a series of "dreams with memories" (13), desires for a "clean dream" (13), visions of freedom from hunger and terror, "strange inner images," living nightmares (10), "happy dreams," "twisted dreams" (37), dreams that are "constantly chipped away" (90), and even dream-like prayers in the midst of furious picking that seem only a part of the entire "bad dream" (156).

This dream world, forced upon her by frustration and fear, is part of her trapped existence. Her "living nightmare" consists of a constant fear of being arrested, of her children being taken from her, of Manuel's death, of deportation, of pregnancy, and of filth and rot. In her "Drawbridge dreamshack" (159), Lupe is constantly mopping, always fighting the dirt and bugs, forced to exist in memories and fantasies. Living fears constantly intrude in the day-to-day reality as in the daytime nightmare in which she believes her two children, Manuelito and Mariquita, have been plowed underground by a tractor working outside their shack. In her frantic search for her children we have a good image of the agricombine, "the big monster machine" that devours and plows under the innocent lives of the migrant workers. The machine cannot, will not, understand what it is doing. Lupe, over the roar of the tractor driven by "one of Mr. Turner's regular hands," attempts to find out if the driver has seen her children. The driver is watching her, unaware of what she is saying, unaware of her terror and panic. The business/machine age has been separated from the earth and the people; it remains blind to the emotions of life and to the reality of human love, fear, and death.

Although Lupe finds her children "safe," neither she nor they can escape their paradisaical existence. They are, as Lupe realizes, like "helpless fish trapped in tanks, writhing and helpless, like trapped turtles in a rocky pool, screaming brotherhood, gulping for air" (157). No wonder Lupe at times feels that "all nature was so filthy rotten" (159) and that she has recurring nightmares of being overwhelmed by the bugs and filth of her day-to-day life. Manuel often has to awaken her, screaming and moaning from dreams that merely repeat the reality of her daytime fears: "Ants and roaches and earwigs and hundreds of mice scurrying around her, from under the house, cockroaches getting inside the coffee pot, fighting small wars over luscious scraps of fresh ripe garbage.... fattening on the poison, and her children kept getting smaller as though they weren't getting enough food" (160).

Paradoxically, Lupe is not only trapped by her dreams, which repeat the terrors of her life, but she also uses dreams to escape her daily existence. Symbolic of their real, shoddy world is the flea market they attend one hot July day. Here among useless wares, among the appearance of values and bargains, they seek some kind of value, some kind of happiness for the moment. The children are still easy to deceive—a "sad rag doll" for Mariquita and a harmonica for Manuelito are enough (74). For Lupe, trapped in the cage of necessities, such a solution is impossible. She can only watch as everything is bought: a mixer, a lamp, a huge pewter tureen. In this carnival of values Lupe is lost until she comes to the ceramic stand, where she can momentarily fulfill her dreams of a better world, a paradise represented by the statues of Greek maidens suggesting innocence and angelic purity. As she looks at these "white goddesses" she is tantalized by all the things the Anglo world represents and by all she has missed. She "dreamed of a paradise where she might hold herself slim and erect and virginal all over again" (77). However, her love and longing are mixed with hate, for the reality is that she is dark skinned and that she will never be slim and virginal again. In her confusion she revolts against the white world, the statues, wishing to "grind them back to dust" (77). Finally, she buys only an urn for the life and certain death of her avocado plant. On the way home, ironically, the urn is used to carry life-giving water to their over-heated car; in the process the urn is cracked, and this "monstrous vessel of their conscience" (84) becomes another piece of junk for the poor to accumulate. The paradise of Lupe's dreams is cracked by the serpent of necessity. Finally, a comic-devil of a service station attendant with a snake-like hissing, slithering air hose cons them out of their last few bucks; Lupe, in tears, returns to her dreamshack without her Venus.

Generally unable to understand Lupe's frustrations and dreams, Manuel, in contrast with his wife, is the innocent man of labor and the earth. He seeks his existence in the joy of working and, like his forebear, Gaspar de Portolá, in the simple mystery of life (59). Working in the field, he is "a living model for da Vinci's outstretched man. Adam heeding God's moving finger" (59). Occasionally Manuel also dreams, but his dreams are primarily practical ones of physical comforts, of cool drinks and soft, tender music. However, even this simple Adamic man of innocence cannot escape the destroying reality of his punishing work. His existence is "locked to hunger," and he finds himself unable to escape his bestial imprisonment. In this paradise he becomes a beast, a brute; in a terrifying image Barrio turns the neat row of apricot trees into the bars of a hellish jail (60).

As difficult as it is for Manuel and Lupe to find dignity, they continue to seek it; they refuse to abandon their quest for reality and truth as they struggle against the uneven odds. Manuel defies the attempt of crew boss Roberto Morales to cheat the workers and experiences a feeling of honor and pride at being more than a dumb beast. He is able to recognize his trap and continues to question what he is: "Am I not a man?" (129). When, following the death of his friends, he goes drunk to a pet shop and looks at the other animals, the only thing he is able to do with any dignity is to throw up. In an act of defiance which gains for her a moment of being real and alive, Lupe refuses to use Mrs. Turner's hand-me-down clothes. Symbolically, she continues to water her avocado plant, suggesting life and its possibilities among the snares and death-like sterility of the Western Grande Compound.

In spite of his recognition of overwhelming oppression in the world, Barrio believes that love and revolution can challenge society's oppressors. Paradise may never exist in the relentlessly ripening plum orchards, but a real possibility for change is represented in the characters of Margarita Delgado and Ramiro Sánchez. Margarita is a dream-like child of seventeen who learns to love Ramiro, the rebel, who rejects the appearance of the Western Grande paradise and its false dream-life. Early in the novel Ramiro refuses a life built on deceptions, appearances, and false dreams. He "had already invested all the dream life he'd ever want. What he wanted now was to live, to really live" (18). By the age of twenty-four he has learned of brutality and oppression (Texas Ranger style), and he has neither illusions nor a false vision of possibilities. He knows his current life and the life of his people are not paradise; his is not a perfect existence. The "grito" of Padre Hidalgo still echoes in his soul (19), and he plans to change things. He has his desires and "dreams of warmth" (99), but his search for home is founded on an idea and a true vision, not just a glittering mirage.

Ramiro is, probably, Barrio's spokesman; he is willing to fulfill his dreams through revolution if necessary. His mestizo heritage is his strength; he is Tenochtitlán, "a god again" (103). Ramiro is not blinded by "isms"; he sees his future based on human values, hating anything that detracts from his manhood (186). However, the heritage of Zapata, Murrieta, and Padre Hidalgo seems to reduce itself to a restatement of the worn-out American dream after Ramiro declares himself to Margarita. With perhaps unintentional irony, Ramiro speaks of a future in which he can make the "American system a human system, to grow, to save, to plan, to plant, to buy, to invest. Invest in futures" (193). However, Ramiro still knows that a revolution is necessary against the Turners and Quills who have built the plum paradise. Their greed has enslaved his people.

In the final chapter we return for a last view of Quill. He has finally received a raise of $1.50 a week, which has given him the courage to confiscate some of the migrant workers' belongings for debts. His exuberance in his new sense of power has him fantasying his future as the "Santa Claus of Santa Clara County ... Captain Q. Q. Quill ... Mayor of Drawbridge" (199–200). When he comes down from his vision, he manages to get into bed, and, as in Chapter One, he is startled by crashing and smashing sounds. Getting up to investigate, he is captured by his fate in the form of unknown tormentors. Throughout the novel Quill has been unable to hear or see his fate relentlessly pursuing him because he has only listened to his self-pity and to the logic of paradise. "El Grito" is everywhere, but Quill cannot hear it. Thus his dream of death becomes a reality, and the hangem tree becomes his destiny. Quill, who so envied Turner's role as Black Bart, now replaces the hanging dummy; his grinning, slowly twisting corpse rotates there to remind us, although Turner is still blind to this reality, that the natural process goes on: slavery leads to revolt, and life ends in death. Even in the Western Grande paradise the plums go "right on ripening. Relentlessly" (201).

In his presentation of the appearance of paradise opposed to the reality of misery and death, Barrio has revealed more than just the physical miseries involved. He has peeled off the mask of benevolent capitalism; behind the mask he has discovered a twisted world where the orchard owners, accepting appearance as their reality, have lost contact with the higher reality of man's dignity and human worth and of man's place in the cycle of life and death. He has also discovered that the workers are forced into reacting as they struggle for identity and existence.

Barrio uses an important symbol to summarize his theme: the summer sun. Margarita, looking at the sun, imagines it an orange topaz or the jewel of an engagement ring her princely love is bringing across the heavens as he comes to rescue her from her misery and longing. But "the yolk burst," and her dream turns into burning reality. She cannot continue to look at the sun: it is too bright, too searing (70). Manuel, likewise, gets up one morning to breathe the sweet air and to hope, but the "hot orange ball" of a sun rules again, and his reality is to toil in the burning heat (153). The summer sun has risen many times with its appearance of hope and a new life, but it has brought to the worker merely the hot day of a reality which is too harsh to be admitted but which cannot be escaped.

THE UNIVERSITY OF WISCONSIN

# Note

[1] Raymond Barrio, *The Plum Plum Pickers* (New York: Harper & Row, 1969), p. 163. Subsequent references are to this edition.

# 3. Tomás Rivera and the Spanish Language Novel

## Tomás Rivera's Appropriation of the Chicano Past

*Ralph F. Grajeda*

Like two other Chicano novels—*Pocho* by José Antonio Villarreal and *Chicano* by Richard Vásquez[1]—Tomás Rivera's "*. . . and the earth did not part*" is the author's first published book. Unlike *Pocho* and *Chicano*, however, Rivera's book was originally written in Spanish, and it was published by a Chicano publishing house, Quinto Sol Publications[2]—two extraliterary facts that only upon reflection acquire significance. If Villarreal's and Vásquez' work can be said to mark the first attempts by Mexican American writers to give literary expression to the experience of La Raza, Rivera's book marks a progression from those initial efforts toward a literature that—in authentically rendering the Chicano experience—can be considered a literature of liberation.

"*. . . and the earth did not part*" is difficult to describe structurally. It is not a novel in the conventional sense, but then neither is it a mere collection of stories and sketches. The book contains a set of twelve thematically unified pieces—symbolic of the twelve months of the year—framed at the beginning by an introductory selection titled "The Lost Year" and at the end by a summarizing selection titled "Under the House." Preceding each of the stories except "The Lost Year" is a brief anecdote, now directed backward (echoing or commenting on the thematic concerns of the preceding story), now pointed forward (prefacing the story that follows). Sometimes the anecdote does not relate directly either to what immediately precedes or to what follows, but instead echoes or re-echoes values, motifs, themes or judgments found elsewhere in the book. The effect is incremental. Through the reinforcement, variation, and amplification provided by the twelve stories and the thirteen anecdotes, a picture of the community is gradually filled. At the end, the entire experience is synthesized and brought to a thematic conclusion through the consciousness of the central character.

This central figure—presumably the author's alter ego—is the unnamed hero of the two frame-pieces: the one for whom, at the beginning, "that year was lost," and who at the end discovers "that he hadn't lost anything." Though it may be conjectured that this central figure is the same one who moves through some of the other selections in the book, direct and explicit identification between the characters in the stories and the central figure is of minor importance, for the overall impression created by the book is not of an individual but a communal experience. The various persons of the stories, the experiences and the landscape of these lives, belong unmistakably to the hero's past. The emphasis, however, remains on the general experience, communal and social rather than individual and personal.

In his introduction to the book, Herminio Ríos observes that "*el pueblo* becomes the central character. It is the anonymous and collective voice of the people we hear" (p. xvi). He is correct. The voice of the people rings as clear for the reader as it does for the central figure. Structurally this figure has importance as an individual; thematically, however, this importance is de-emphasized (it is no accident that he remains nameless). The experience of the book is finally a general one. Many of the selections have an uncanny emblematic tone to them; some of them — particularly the frame-pieces — emphatically invite an allegorical or symbolic interpretation. Even in the two frame selections, at the beginning and end, the protagonist's voice is not that of an individual hero intent on discovering and expressing his own subjective reality, but that of a Mexican American in the significant process of discovering and embracing representatively his community's experience and culture. The end towards which the narrative is directed is a social identity.

The hero of the frame-pieces plays no explicitly active part in the book. He serves merely as the "rememberer," the central figure — however unrealized he may appear as a rounded character — around whom Rivera weaves his thematic tapestry. At the beginning he is confused, alone, frightened and disoriented. He is the one for whom the year is lost. The succeeding twelve stories and thirteen anecdotes compose his effort to reclaim a past. At the end of the book he has become the synthesizer and commentator, the one who discovers his lost year and who would like to have "long enough arms," so that he "could hug them all at the same time" (p. 176).

The form of the book is thus cyclical. Though there is no attempt to shape a strict correspondence between specific months and particular stories, the twelve stories in a general sense represent the year that the protagonist seeks to recapture. The first story is set in early April; the last anecdote is set in December. This cyclical movement functions effectively to delineate the cyclical and repetitive nature of the migrant farmworkers' lives as they yearly retrace the same roads to the same fields, from Texas and cotton in the winter months to Utah, Minnesota, Iowa, and Michigan in the spring and summer. It is, therefore, appropriate that the first story treats a family working in the Texas fields, the twelfth story a truckful of workers journeying north to the beet-fields of Minnesota.

Throughout the book tension is created between the opposing values of resignation and rebellion as the people are shown enduring the repetitive hardships of the present, and as they anticipate their future. Usually, but not always, these differing values break down along generational lines. The older people—parents and grandparents—are usually resigned. Theirs is a stoical position learned after years of suffering and variously expressed by the grandfather who tells his twenty-year-old grandson that he is "very stupid" for wanting "the next ten years of his life to pass instantly so that he would know what had happened in his life" (p. 87); by the older speaker who advises the young student not to even bother with going to school, for "the downtrodden will always be downtrodden" (p. 45); by the worker in the fields who, in fear of being fired by the *patrón*, urges his children time after time to endure their thirst "a little longer" (p. 10); and by the father, knowing little English and fearful of the schools, who is incapable of responding to his son's plea that he accompany him to the principal's office the first day of school (pp. 30–31). These are parents who through years of deprivation and colonialism have learned to stay in their place. Again and again in Rivera's book we see them encouraging their children to stay in school, in hopes that they will escape the treadmill of migratory field labor.

The children are in many instances the victims. But they are also the rebels. There is the boy in "It Was a Silvery Night" who tests the superstitions of his parents and learns that the devil does not exist. There is the boy in " . . . and the earth did not part" who in anger at the suffering of his family curses an uncaring God and learns, in contradiction to what his parents have taught him, that the earth does not swallow up a blasphemer. And characteristically it is the young man in "When We Arrive," who—in the middle of the night in a broken-down truck loaded with people on their way north—with assertive vehemence cries out in his heart: "This goddamn fuckin' life. This goddamn son-of-a-bitch's life. This is the last time I travel like a goddamn animal standing up all the way. Just as soon as we arrive I'm going to Minneapolis, surely I'll find something to do there where I don't have to work like a goddamn animal" (pp. 158–159). In the privacy of his anxiety, he then utters a threat ("One of these days I'll screw 'em all") which, however idle it may actually be, gains its full force from its juxtaposition with the mild thoughts of a concerned wife and mother with a child in her arms, who thinks only of helping her husband in the fields when they arrive.

The affirmation in this book, however, is not dependent on any final resolution of the tension created by the two differing stances of resignation and rebellion. Rivera's work, after all, is not a transient book of protest, but an enduring *book of discovery*. The question of "proper" or "improper" responses to social conditions is a false one, inappropriate to the premises upon which the work is created. The substantial affirmation of this book rests on the reality discovered and depicted by the author. And this process of discovery is given artistic form through the use of the central character within the frame-structure of the book and the cyclical movement of the narrative.

The overall scheme is laid out in the four brief paragraphs comprising the introductory selection, "The Lost Year." There Rivera uses the language of the dream—or at least a language suggestive of a deeper reality than what is ordinarily accepted as objective fact—to suggest the sense of psychological and social disorientation in which the hero lives. The impetus is to discover the self. The origin and cause of that impetus is perhaps outside the concern of Rivera's book; it is enough to state the truism that personal and social identity is never a "problem" until it is threatened. As Frantz Fanon writes: the native's affirmation of his own culture, and his attempts at recovering a usable past, are symptomatic of the "realization of the danger that he is running in cutting his last moorings and of breaking adrift from his people." Unless the native moves culturally in the direction of his true self, "there will be serious psycho-affective injuries and the result will be individuals without an anchor, without a horizon, colorless, stateless—a race of angels."[3]

Tomás Rivera's metaphor for this felt sense of breaking adrift is "the lost year." The confusion and general disorientation brought on by the sense of "that year [that] was lost to him" began for the protagonist "when he would hear someone call him by name. He would turn around to see who was calling, always making a complete turn, always ending in the same position and facing the same way. And that was why he could never find out who it was that was calling him, nor the reason why he was being called. He would even forget the name that he had heard.

"Once he stopped himself before completing the turn, and he became afraid. He found out that he had been calling himself. That was the way the lost year began" (p. 3).

His confusion and fear have their source in the realization that it is he himself who has been "calling." The full implications of that realization, however, are not clearly understood until the end of the book. In his beginning confusion he thinks that he thinks, and determines not to think, but does nevertheless. It is the content of this "thinking" — what Rivera describes as the hero's *seeing* and *hearing* — that the twelve stories and sketches and the thirteen anecdotes reveal. The cumulative effect is a felt sense of struggle.

"Why is it that we are here on earth as though buried alive?" asks that young protagonist of the title story, upon hearing the moans of his father, who has suffered a sunstroke in the suffocating heat of the fields. This sets the tone of the book. The full-length stories, the impressionistic sketches, and the brief anecdotes that fall within the two frame pieces are quick but lasting glimpses into the lives of the characters. There is no attempt to relate them realistically and explicitly. That they are related only in time by the metaphor of "the lost year," and in space by the fields and *colonias* in Texas and the unspecified north suggests, again, Rivera's interest in the general and social, not the specific and individual reality. The same spirit informs all of the "framed" selections: a desperate clinging to life in the midst of deprivation and suffering, and the seemingly ever-present hope that if not for themselves, at least for their children, life will not exact such a heavy toll.

The suffering begins with childhood. In "The Children Were Victims," a child is accidentally shot and killed by a boss who, because he is paying the workers by the hour, does not want them "wasting" time drinking from the water tanks that he keeps for his cattle. The story is told from an objective and detached point of view, a technique common to many of the other stories and sketches. Rarely does Rivera-as-author intrude; the understanding, the judgments, and the emotions are generated out of the narrative situation itself, which is quite brief. It consists of an introductory paragraph, some dramatic dialogue between father and child; two brief paragraphs matter-of-factly describing the child drinking water and being killed; and at the end, another fragment of dialogue, between two unidentified fieldworkers, inhabitants of the barrio, members of what, through the book, quickly assumes the form of a *colonia* chorus — a collective Chicano voice that, standing at times at a distance, describes and judges the actions that are being enacted on the stage.

In this story the chorus discusses the fate of the boss after the killing. One speaker affirms the consequences of human guilt feelings; he wants to believe that the boss almost went insane, that he is drinking heavily now and that he tried to commit suicide. The other voice denies the boss even the dignity of remorse. He wants to say: "they are such brutes that with absolute impunity they can kill us and our children." The first speaker says: "I really think he went crazy. You've seen the state he's in nowadays. He looks like a beggar." The other voice answers, "Sure, but it's only because he doesn't have money any more." And his *compadre* says "I guess you're right."

At the end, the story refuses to affirm either position. The chorus's function is to articulate them both as part of the book's reality. Part of that reality—in all of its harshness and brutality—is expressed through the routinely dispassionate manner of presentation. The child is shot and "he didn't even jump like the deer; he just fell into the water like a dirty rag and the water became saturated with blood . . ." (p. 11). Such a matter-of-fact tone outweighs paragraphs of "concerned" and "committed" prose describing "the lot of the underdogs." In this selection it succinctly intensifies the horror of the situation. In other selections it works similarly to bring out the stark quality of the lives of these people.

Equally bleak and despairing is the lot of the parents and children in "Little Children Burned." In hopes that one of his children will become a boxing champion and earn thousands of dollars, a father buys boxing gloves for his children and teaches them to rub alcohol on their bodies the way he saw boxers do in a movie. Alone in their shack while the parents are working in the fields, the children accidentally start a fire while playing with the boxing gloves and two of the three children are burned to death in the shack. The chorus that enters at the end provides necessary information, and dispassionately comments on the cruel irony of everything having burned—even the children—except for the boxing gloves: one speaker, in respect if not in awe of Yankee ingenuity, says "the fact is that those people know how to make things so well that not even fire will touch them" (p. 102).

In this story, the chorus speaks with convincing authority. Responding to a question about the parents' reaction, one of the speakers expresses an essentially tragic point of view, one that acknowledges the uncertainty of human existence and the profound sense in which one has little control over what will be: "They're getting over their tragedy, but I doubt if they will ever forget it. What else can one do? You never know when death will come, nor in what manner. What a tragedy. But one never knows" (p. 102). The reticent "I guess not" that ends the sketch affirms that point of view as a community reality.

"The Night of the Blackout" is a love tragedy about two young people who are temporarily separated by their families' journeys in the migrant stream and vow to be true to one another until they return to Texas where they plan to marry. Rumors reach Ramón about Juanita's "cheating" in Minnesota, and when they meet again, they quarrel; heart-broken and in despair Ramón kills himself by grabbing onto a transformer at the electric power station. Distance and objectivity are achieved here by Rivera's focus on one tangible effect of Ramón's suicide at the power station: The lights go out all over the community! And it is in reference to this manifestation that the community thereafter speaks of Ramón and Juanita: "They were very much in love, wouldn't you say?" "Yes. Of course" (p. 116).

The attempt to hide from a harsh reality becomes frantic among people who are continually forced to struggle for their self-hood and dignity. That attempt—as it is lived by a youth—is the subject of "It is Painful." A young man is expelled from school for defending himself against the physical attack of an Anglo student and now faces the painful duty of telling his parents. The youth's experience is intensified by the shame, anger, and hatred he is made to feel by a school nurse who forces him to undress and stand naked in her presence while being inspected, and by an Anglo American student who tells him that he doesn't like Mexicans "because they steal." The main part of this story is told by a first-person narrator thinking in the present as he walks home from school the day of his expulsion. On his way home he wrestles with the problem of telling his parents—who have high hopes that he will remain in school and become a telephone operator like the one they saw as the leading character in a movie. Brief flashbacks fill in the context of the narrator's shame and anger and provide ironic point to his desperate desire to disbelieve the reality of his situation. "What if they didn't expel me? What if they didn't?" he thinks repeatedly throughout his walk home. Reality, however, is too severe and too sharply insistent to be denied. Ultimately he must accept it: "Sure they did" (p. 35).

The children in Rivera's book, like the adults, are victimized by what exists outside them—the often invisible social and economic forces that govern their lives, the institutions, and the physical environment in which they live and work. But their victimization does not stop there. For they are also prey to what lies within. As the narrator of the title story says, "either the germs eat us from the inside or the sun from the outside. Always some illness" (p. 75). Rivera traces not only the "Chicano" and the "farmworker" contours of his characters' lives, but the universally human as well. In the fields, in the barrios, in their shacks or in the trucks moving north for the summer, the young people, particularly, are shown struggling with the "problems" always inherent in the move into adulthood. Of the twelve selections, four—"His Hand in his Pocket"; "First Holy Communion"; "It Was a Silvery Night"; and " ... and the earth did not part"—are "initiation stories."

Guilt and the curious mixture of good and evil in the same person are major themes in "His Hand in his Pocket," a story about a young man who suffers a debilitating guilt from his innocent role in a macabre crime. The naive first-person narrator is sent by his parents to live with don Laito and doña Boni, an elderly couple in the barrio who steal in order to sell or give away: "when they couldn't sell it to the neighbors they gave it away. They gave almost everything away" (p. 48). Understandably, the couple are well liked by the people, and have a good reputation in the community, even among the *americanos*. The narrator, however, notices the rotten teeth that surround the gold in don Laito's mouth and begins to wonder about his hosts' goodness, for not only do they admit their stealing to him, they try to persuade him to join in it. During the boy's visit, they murder a Mexican drifter for his money and possessions and force the boy to help them bury the body and keep their secret. At the end of the story he is given a ring that belonged to the victim and the ring becomes a symbol of his guilt. He tries to throw it away but can't. He wears it, "and the worst of it was that for a long time, whenever I saw a stranger, I put my hand in my pocket." Time compassionately repeals his "guilt," but the habit of putting his hand in his pocket, he says, "stayed with me for a long time" (p. 50).

Guilt is again a major theme of "First Holy Communion." On the morning of his first communion—after spending a restless night memorizing all his sins—the narrator, while walking to church, looks through a tailor shop window to see what is causing the noises he hears, and sees a naked man and woman having sexual intercourse. Torn between fear and the strange attraction to see more, he intently remains until discovered by the couple and told to go away. He cannot forget what he has seen, but neither is he willing to share his experience with his friends. He is bothered by the feeling of himself having "committed that sin of the flesh." He keeps his "sin," even from the confessional priest, and when, after his communion, he arrives home with his godfather for the traditional sweet bread and chocolate, "everything seemed different." He imagines his father and mother—and even the priest and the nun—naked on the floor. "I almost wasn't able to eat the sweetbread or drink the chocolate," he says, "and I remember that as soon as I finished I ran out of the house. I felt all choked up" (p. 91). Alone outside, he recalls the scene at the tailor shop and soon begins to derive some pleasure from his memory, and even forgets that he lied to the priest. Then, he says, "I felt the same way I did when I heard the missionary talk about the Grace of God." The ambiguity at the end of the story enriches its meaning. When the boy says "I had a strong desire to learn more about everything. But then I started to think that perhaps everything was the same," he expresses both the resiliency that will enable him to take his experience in stride and a propensity to put aside what is "bothersome."

Two pieces in the book that represent, on one level at least, youth's metaphysical rebellion and its testing of religious and superstitious notions that its elders accept are "It Was a Silvery Night," and " . . . and the earth did not part."

In "It Was a Silvery Night," after hearing his parents tell of people for whom the devil has appeared, the protagonist becomes curious and decides to see for himself. Carefully he plans his invocation and, according to the traditional formula learned from his parents and others in the community, issues his summons. Nothing happens. "No one appeared. Everything looked the same. Everything was the same. Everything paceful. He then thought that the best thing to do would be to curse the devil. He did. He used every cuss word he knew and in varying tones of voice. He even cursed the devil's mother. But nothing happened. Absolutely nothing appeared and absolutely nothing changed" (p. 62). The devil does not exist, he thinks; but if the devil does not exist, then neither does . . . , and at that moment he cannot follow through with the inexorable logic of his discovery. Later on, however, as he reconsiders his experience of the evening, he accepts the implication of his discovery: "There is no devil" he thinks, "There is nothing. The only thing he had heard in the field had been his own voice" (p. 63). This brings him to the conviction that people who went insane after summoning the devil did so not because the devil appeared, but because he didn't. There is nothing but one's own voice in the dark. His logic thus forces on him a realization of his own existential solitariness, with an empty sky as premise.

The hero-narrator of " . . . and the earth did not part" correspondingly tests God's existence. Not in the deliberate manner in which the protagonist of the preceding story attempts to verify the devil's existence but in the full passion of hatred, he protests against and curses a God who would allow the illness and death of his aunt and uncle, the suffering of their children, the illness of his own father, and the fate of his small brothers and sisters, who seem destined to feed the earth and sun "without any hope of any kind." In the frustration he feels at his own powerlessness "to do anything," he refuses to take solace in his mother's religion, refuses to resign himself to God's will, refuses to accept the notion that there is no rest until death. He finds his humanity in the very weariness, despair, and hatred which he feels. Having been conditioned by historical and cultural forces, however, he is at first incapable of seriously accepting the absence of a transcendent and determinant final cause. After his father suffers a sunstroke in the fields, he reviles his mother for clamoring for God's mercy. "What do you gain by doing that, mother? Don't tell me you believe that sort of thing helped my uncle and my aunt? . . . God doesn't even remember us. . . . God doesn't give a damn about us poor people" (pp. 75–76).

But at this point his subservience and dependence—wrought out of fear—prohibit him from cursing God, let alone imagining His absence. "There must not be a God . . ." he begins, but cannot go on with this thought: "No, better not say it, what if father should worsen?"

The next day his nine-year-old brother has a sunstroke, and as the protagonist carries him home from the fields he cries in anger and hatred. Yet at every moment of the emotion that he feels, he draws from it a new integrity. Without knowing when, he starts to swear; and "what he said he had been wanting to say for a long time." Unthinkingly he curses God and immediately "upon doing it he felt the fear instilled in him by time and by his parents." He imagines the earth opening and swallowing him—but nothing happens! Instead, he begins to feel the solidity of the ground: "He then felt himself walking on very solid ground; it was harder than he had ever felt it" (p. 78). His discovery—in the context of his former despair, dependence, and sense of powerlessness—is affirmative. Recognizing the emptiness of the heavens he does not fall into the self-pity of the existential anti-hero who finds himself in the midst of a meaningless and absurd universe. Instead he embraces his freedom, and that very evening experiences a sense of peace—and detachment—"that he had never known before." The following day, as he leaves for work, he feels himself, for the first time in his life, "capable of doing and undoing whatever he chose."

Rivera has a clear eye for the cruel ironies of life. In the world his characters inhabit, people are often victimized by the very hopes they nurture, hopes that spring from the positions in life which they endure. In such a world, attempts at alleviating one's situation often serve merely to reinforce one's deprivation. In such a world even anger is preempted. This is the theme of "The Portrait," one of the better stories in Rivera's book. The door-to-door salesmen from San Antonio—those who thrive on the innocence and misfortune of the powerless—converge on the barrio like vultures when the people arrive from the north with a few dollars in their pockets. In this story it is the portrait salesman who promises Don Mateo that "for just thirty dollars" they can enlarge—and, in color, inlay—the photograph of his son, who is missing in action in the war, so that he looks "lifelike, as though he were alive."

Don Mateo and the others in the barrio who have been "sold" wait week-after-week for their portraits. As they wait, they hopefully rationalize the delay that gives them intimations of having been duped. The photographs are finally found dissolving in a tunnel leading to the dump, and Don Mateo, in full anger, goes to San Antonio to search out the salesman who took the only picture he had of his son. He finds the salesman and forces him, upon threat of violence, to do the inlaid enlargement of his son. "He had to do it all from memory," Don Mateo tells his neighbors afterwards. "I think a person is capable of doing anything out of fear," he explains as he shows off the finished portrait of his son. Justice is done. Don Mateo receives what he paid for. "What do you think? How does my son look?" he asks the admiring *compadre*: "Well, quite frankly I don't remember what Chuy looked like anymore. But more and more he was beginning to resemble you, right?" Complacently and with some pride, Don Mateo says "Yes. I think so. That's what everyone tells me now. That Chuy resembled me more and more, and that he was beginnning to look like me. There's the portrait. One might say we're one and the same" (p. 145).

In their simplicity and powerlessness, Rivera's characters live by illusions that acquire the force of necessity. "I guess it's always best to have hope," one of Rivera's characters says halfheartedly, and—in its various forms—that is the attitude informing their lives. In "When We Arrive" these hopes are emphatically represented in the thoughts of some migrants who find themselves stranded in the middle of the night in a broken-down truck going north for the season. Privately, each is encouraged by the hope that when they arrive things will be "better." There is the pathetic anticipation of the experienced, which reality has distilled down to a modest longing for "a good bed for my wife; her kidneys are really bothering her. I hope we don't wind up in a chicken coop with a cement floor as we did last year" (p. 160). And there is the radical resolve of youth to escape altogether the rat-trap of the dispossessed.

The impact of the book finally is cumulative. Though the sketches and stories can be read individually and out of context, it is as particular parts of a whole which is greater than the sum of its parts that Rivera's work can best be understood and appreciated. All of the experiences, the themes, and judgments contained in the twelve selections and the thirteen anecdotes are finally summarized and "fixed" into a context by the consciousness of the central character of the book, who reappears in the concluding selection, "Under the House"—the piece that in combination with the introductory selection, "The Lost Year," constitutes the frame.

In "Under the House" the collective voice of the community is predominant, but now it speaks explicitly to and through the central character. Till now the voices have been the developing expression of what the protagonist brings up out of the depths of his memory; but so readily do the stories and sketches acquire an independent life of their own that the fact that they constitute mere elements of the protagonist's "lost year" is obscured. Here at the end the reader is reminded of the literary device being used and, like the main character, is brought full circle to the beginning—but now with the layers of experience rendered by the successive voices. There is, in other words, an analogy between the reader's experience and the protagonist's.

For the latter, the total experience is regenerative, capped by his realization that instead of losing anything, "he had discovered something. To discover and to rediscover and synthesize. To relate this entity with that entity, and that entity with still another, and finally relating everything with everything else. That was what he had to do, that was all. And he became even happier" (p. 177).

As a "book of discovery," "... *and the earth did not part*" is a variation of the *bildungsroman,* for the focus of Rivera's work is not on the forging of the individual subjective identity; it is informed by a concern for social and collective identity. The characters in the protagonist's recoverable past—the field-worker father, the Mexican revolutionary grandfather, the devout mother, the *gachupín* priest, the kindly Cuquita who is everyone's grandmother, the quarreling lovers, the exploitative *patrón,* as well as all the *comadres, compadres,* and *padrinos*—all are recognizable not through personal quirks in their particular character, but rather because they assume—at least within the context of the Chicano experience—archetypal dimensions.

In including "the names of the people in town," Rivera's book—like Bartolo's poems—performs the significant function of discovering and ultimately appropriating and embracing the past in all of its sometimes-painful authenticity. The importance of looking closely and hard at the colonial experience of the Chicano protagonist is assumed. The first step in his liberation must begin with an understanding of his position. Presumably it is the kind of understanding—however felt or perceived—that leads the protagonist of Rivera's book, as well as the author himself, toward re-identification with that which is his own, i.e., with his people. The movement in the book is inward collectively toward an understanding of the barrio experience as it is—in its pain and in all of its suffering, assuredly, but also in its essential strength, vitality and sense of human celebration.

Besides being a significant work of art, "... *and the earth did not part*" performs a valuable function in using "the past with the intention of opening the future, as an invitation to action and a basis for hope."[4] Criticism of the work because it does not more directly perform the function of social protest is short-sighted. The reality discovered and depicted by this author contributes to the Chicano art of self-discovery in a manner more profoundly effective, aesthetically as well as socially, than much of the explicit literature of protest that is being written. The vitality of the Chicano social movement depends on the development of a deep understanding of Chicano reality. Rivera contributes notably to this end.

UNIVERSITY OF NEBRASKA-LINCOLN

## Notes

[1] *Pocho* (New York: Doubleday, 1959); *Chicano* (New York: Doubleday, 1970).

[2] Tomás Rivera, "... y no se lo tragó la tierra"/"... and the earth did not part" (Berkeley: Quinto Sol Publications, 1971). Rivera's book was awarded the Quinto Sol National Chicano Literary Award for 1969–70. English translation by Hermino Ríos C., "in collaboration with the author, with assistance by Octavio I. Romano-V."

[3] Frantz Fanon, *The Wretched of the Earth* (New York: Grove Press, 1968), pp. 217–218.

[4] Ibid., p. 232.

# Time As a Structural Device in Tomás Rivera's "... y no se lo tragó la tierra"

*Alfonso Rodríguez*

"... *y no se lo tragó la tierra*" is one of the first major works of contemporary Chicano fiction to show a marked separation from the traditional linear narrative of social protest. In the attempt at creating a modern art form, Rivera elaborates a complex of aesthetic elements; one of these elements is time, which appears simultaneously as a major theme and as a structural device. "... *y no se lo tragó la tierra*" is structured on three temporal modalities: present, past, and future, each represented by a cycle. Furthermore, there are various manifestations of time as a structuring technique in the novel: circular time, psychological time, a distortion of linear time by a shuttling of events, and a fusion of separate temporal sequences through a dislocation of space.

Rivera's treatment of time places him among a rather large group of contemporary writers whose works exhibit a preoccupation with the relationship between temporal succession and man's search for identity. Rivera structures his novel on the premise that human experience is made up, among other things, of memory and expectation, both past and future operating in the present. In this sense, time is inseparable from the concept of the self, for the quest for existential identity leads to a search of the past and a look into the future. This is precisely the experience of the protagonist in the novel.

Before we proceed to analyze the text, however, a word about its genre is in order. Rivera's work is considered a novel by some and rightly so, for it traces the development of the protagonist. Thus, it can be classified as a novel of character. On the other hand, it exhibits the characteristics of a compendium of framework tales, that is, stories within a narrative setting. The introductory story, "The Lost Year," and the concluding one, "Under The House," provide the general setting. The other twelve stories, which form the central column of the work, are stories within the general framework.

The essential meaning of the novel can be arrived at by making a series of associations between the framework and the framework stories, thus detecting the internal logic of the novel. It is worth noting that the diverse settings in the framework stories are part of the protagonist's personal history, pieces of direct and indirect experience that trace the hero's process of individuation. Thus, the three major temporal cycles are manifested as follows: "The Lost Year" represents the present circumstances of the boy-hero, the next twelve stories (which symbolize the months of the year) are his search of the past, and in the concluding story, "Under The House," past and present merge and a new cycle opens up into the future.

Objective or historical time—the time of calendars and watches—is an indispensable convention in practical human affairs. It can be conceived in one of two ways, either as linear or as circular. Rivera treats it as circular. In the first story, "The Lost Year," the protagonist is trapped in the labyrinth of chronological time. He feels the anguish produced by a sense of disorientation. In the very title of this story, Rivera's use of time as a rhetorical device is apparent. The word "year" is repeated seven times until it becomes "the lost year," thus alluding to the circular aspect of objective time and also suggesting the recurrence of the same patterns until the cycle is broken.

The cycle represents a prison in the life of the boy-hero, a no-exit situation. The first sentence in "The Lost Year" is: "That year was lost to him."[1] That is, chronologically, he is one year older, but inwardly he has seen no progress; he feels overwhelmed by present circumstances because of his sense of alienation. However, in order to recuperate the loss, the protagonist must break the cycle in which he is trapped. He can only do so by responding to the voice that keeps calling him. After several unsuccessful attempts, everything ends in bewilderment as the cycle continues:

> He would always turn around to see who was calling, always making a complete turn, always ending in the same position and facing the same way. And that was why he could never find out who it was that was calling him, nor the reason why he was being called. (p. 3)

The physical motions of the boy-hero making a complete turn provide a symbol of contemporary man lost in the labyrinth of chronological time. The cycle breaks the moment the protagonist responds to the calling of his inner voice: "Once he stopped himself before completing the turn, and he became afraid. He found out that he had been calling himself. That was the way the lost year began" (p. 3).

In "The Lost Year" the narrator goes beyond the surface; he gazes deeply into the impulses of the unconscious of the boy-hero, who initiates a search into his past through an oneiric process in an attempt to find meaning for his own existence:

> Then he would force himself into thinking that he had never thought anything at all, and that was when everything finally would go blank and he was able to go to sleep. But before falling asleep he would see and hear many things. (p. 3)

At this point, objective (measurable) time comes to a complete stop for the protagonist and subjective (psychological) time takes over. The first cycle ends and the second one begins. The author takes us back to the lost year, which in symbolic terms could represent a whole epoch, as the title of the story suggests and as the narrator implies: "He tried to figure out when it was that he had started to refer to that period as a year" (p. 3).

Objective time, which implies order and direction, is completely distorted in the second cycle. The twelve stories give us twelve different situations as they occurred in the past. But these situations are shuffled around in such a way that they appear as unrelated fragments of the protagonist's direct and indirect experiences. They manifest themselves as a succession of distinct, discontinuous fragments of time due to the disintegration of chronology.

The twelve vignettes are part of what the boy-hero sees and hears in his visions. However, they are presented as independent narrative units, each with its particular structure, rather than as a series of recollections. It is not until the conclusion of the second cycle that the protagonist sorts out in his mind his past experiences and places everything in proper perspective.

A disordering of significant events is the basis for the structure of the second cycle, which as we have indicated is a return to the past. This shattering of chronology is carried even further in individual stories within the cycle. The most evident examples of this technique are seen in such stories as "It Is Painful," "The Night of the Blackout," and "When We Arrive."

Once more, in the title of the concluding story, there is an allusion to circular time. The words "the house" are repeated seven times until they become the title words "Under The House," signifying the conclusion of the second cycle and the consequent return to the present.

In the human psyche, time becomes elastic; it can either be condensed or extended. The introductory story, "The Lost Year," ends as the boy-hero is about to fall asleep. During that night he searches for the lost year, or perhaps for the totality of his life experiences and even beyond.

This is entirely possible, which is another way of saying that psychological time is timeless.

The beginning of "Under The House" indicates a return to the historical flow of time (the present). We find the protagonist making an important decision. Rather than attending school that day he chooses to hide under the neighbor's house: "That morning on the way to school he felt the urge not to go" (p. 172). This "urge not to go" is motivated by the dream experiences of the previous night. Now, under the circumstances, he makes a better choice. For him, school is a return to the monotony of practical, everyday affairs, to objective time, from which he tries to flee because it has become oppressive. Thus, he chooses to isolate himself in the dark under the house. The house, in Freudian logic, can be taken as the symbol of the mother's womb, which offers protection and security: "He was lying face down and every time he moved he felt the floor touching his back. This even made him feel secure" (pp. 172-73). It is as though he were escaping to a mythical time, a time of beginnings.

As the boy-hero begins to think in the dark, he resumes his search for identity by reliving the past once again. This time everything is reproduced in his mind in such a way that persons and events appear vested with new significance; what was once a patchwork of pieces without a pattern becomes a meaningful synthesis through psychological time. However, the recapture of time in experience alone is not enough to produce new meanings. In addition to this there has to be the right association of events that happened only once in an individual's life and can never be repeated. The subconscious has a logic of its own. This is why in the protagonist's stream of consciousness, although events flow chaotically, harmony is achieved.

The protagonist's "thoughts returned to the present." His reverie is interrupted by the commotion of the children and the lady of the house, who have discovered his hiding place. When he emerges from the dark he is a new individual because he has found something he never had before. He has gained a new perspective that can never be understood nor appreciated by those who have not gone through a similar experience. The boy hears the woman's remark as he walks away: "Poor family. First the mother, and now him. Maybe he is going crazy. I think he's losing his mind. He has lost his sense of time. He's lost track of the years" (p. 177). But the boy has a different reaction:

> Suddenly he felt very happy because, when he thought about what the lady had said, he realized that he hadn't lost anything. He had discovered something. To discover and to rediscover and to synthesize. To relate this entity with that entity, and that entity with still another, and finally relating everything with everything else.

> That was what he had to do, that was all. And he became even happier. (p. 177)

This point marks the beginning of the third and last cycle. It is a vision of the future, produced by the boy's hope and optimism. This is expressed through a symbol:

> Later, when he arrived at home, he went to the tree that was in the yard. He climbed it. On the horizon he saw a palm tree and he imagined that someone was on top looking at him. He even raised his arm and waved it back and forth so that the other person could see that he knew that he was there. (p. 177)

The other person is actually the protagonist himself, projected forward in time. What we mean when we assert that the element of time is inextricably fused to the problem of the self can be seen in the experience of the boy-hero in the novel. The anguish caused by an existential vacuum launches him into the past. But the new hope engendered by a deeper sense of self-awareness projects him into the future, which opens up countless possibilities.

UNIVERSITY OF NORTHERN COLORADO

# Note

[1] Tomás Rivera, "... y no se lo tragó la tierra" (Berkeley, Calif.: Quinto Sol, 1971), p. 3. All further references to this novel will be incorporated in the body of the paper.

# The Problematic in Tomás Rivera's "... and the earth did not part"

Juan Rodríguez

Soundless Words

Words without sound
how terribly deaf.
What if I were to remain
here in the words
forever?

Tomás Rivera[1]

No one can deny the importance of Tomás Rivera's novel[2] "... y no se lo tragó la tierra" ("... and the earth did not part")[3] to the development of contemporary Chicano literature and to its exposure to a wide readership after a long period of neglect. *Earth*, published in 1971 as the 1970 winner of the first Quinto Sol prize (awarded by Quinto Sol Publications of Berkeley, California, whose contribution to the public recognition of this literature has been equally important), and the *Actos*[4] of the Teatro Campesino represent the opening of a new stage in the evolution of Chicano literature, a revitalized, conscious stage which some have inaccurately labeled the Chicano Renaissance,[5] but which can be described more precisely as the flowering of Chicano literature.

Partly because of its role as inaugurator, partly because the historical moment demanded that the flowering literature be protected and cultivated, and mostly because *Earth* was and remains a work of art whose fourteen tightly-knit stories and complementary anecdotes gather around themselves an impression of totality, "wholeness," and self-sufficiency in style, technique, and theme[6] – elements that are on a par with the best of the world's literatures, thus making it defendable – many critics, this writer included,[7] stressed the progressive nature of the novel. Here was a work, we stated at the time, that realistically presented the Chicano migrant workers' condition and profoundly questioned the enslaving belief in the existence of a static, unalterable world in which immense powers, such as those of God, the devil, the boss, etc., are enthroned forever. It was precisely *Earth*'s questioning posture that seemed most progressive to us, for it synthesized a modernization of thought much in tune with the times in which it was written and published, times that witnessed the manifestation of this questioning attitude in the very streets of this country.

And yet, even as the progressive aspects of the work were affirmed and analyzed, there surfaced, on a closer reading of the novel, elements which were problematical and lent themselves to a false, non-progressive interpretation of Chicanos and Chicano reality. For example, one critic, somewhat removed from the immediacy of the Chicano situation at the time and thus not recognizing the need to emphasize the positive elements of the novel, writes:

> Held as mentally inferior, therefore relegated to the hardest and lowest paid jobs, Rivera's farm workers might be expected to rebel. But among these little people there is not the slightest hint of a rebellion, at most, a lonely timid protest here and there. They have not yet matured to political consciousness and independence and Rivera seems to doubt they ever will as he lovingly portrays the world of touching simplicity, religiosity and tradition in which he grew up and they still live.[8]

Even Grajeda in his excellent analysis of *Earth* refers to the "simplicity" of Rivera's characters.[9] Needless to say, such simplicity does not in fact characterize the Chicano people, migrant farmworker or urban dweller; and when a Chicano writer who doubtless knows this to be true presents such an image of his people, questions of much import arise. These, then, are the questions with which this essay is concerned.

In order to begin to comprehend the problematic, one must first examine the element that gives the work cohesiveness and which in essence makes *Earth* more a novel than a mere collection of short stories. I refer to the structuring element of the work, the child protagonist[10] who is introduced in the first selection, "The Lost Year," and who rather deliberately is used to end the novel in the last selection, "Under the House." In fact, the child becomes much more than a protagonist, for all of the novel's action ultimately takes place in his mind, as if in a dream: "Then he would force himself into thinking that he had never thought anything at all, and that was when everything finally would go blank and he was able to go to sleep. But before falling asleep he would see and hear many things . . ." (p. 2). Obviously, what he "sees" and "hears" forms the body of the novel, i.e., all of the selections between the first and last story. Thus he becomes a center of consciousness that controls and colors—structures—the action to serve his particular need; as expressed in the introductory selection, that need is to find himself, to find his identity. Consequently, *Earth* turns out to be a novel of initiation and education in life, an *Erziehungsroman*.

By means of this particular relationship between the body of the novel and the center of consciousness, Rivera presents two distinct yet related worlds: the Chicano migrant workers' world of physical struggle against oppression, where the problem is survival, and the child protagonist's world of reflection, where the main concern is a search for identity. While the former represents a concrete struggle for survival and the latter a mental struggle for personal identification, the two are intimately related, for the child protagonist is obviously a member of the migrant workers' community and as such must participate in their struggle also. Interestingly enough, the dynamic of this relationship is clearly evident in the novel's title, which emphasizes this outer struggle insofar as it apparently refers to the general, workers' struggle (the characters of the title story are farmworkers in a farmworker situation). Since the presentation of this theme, however, is subjected to the exigencies of the center of consciousness and is in truth subordinate to the child protagonist's personal struggle, the novel's title could well have been *The Lost Year* and still made perfect sense. This thematic ambiguity can easily mislead the reader into accepting at face value the child protagonist's view of the Chicanos in the body of the novel.

But what is the basis of this ambiguity? For an answer one must return to the child protagonist and his quest for self-identification. "The Lost Year" nicely presents his quest as the dilemma of discovering "who it was that was calling him" (p. 2). In the end he realizes that he had called himself, thereby discovering the power of the word, the power "to call himself," as the means to his identity. In fact, as one learns in the last selection, "Under the House," what initiates the child protagonist's quest and the action of the novel itself is his lack of words: "That morning on the way to school he felt an urge not to go. He thought that the teacher would surely spank him because he didn't know the vocabulary words. That was why he thought of crawling under the house" (p. 118). For the protagonist, then, words are the key to self-identity, to liberation.

This explains the importance of words in the novel. Words, for example, soothe the mother who wishes to know about her son at war in Korea ("A Prayer"); the inability to utter words worsens an already painful situation for the Chicano in school ("It is Painful"); spoken but not understood—even by her!—words climax the lost Chicana's dilemma in a store ("Christmas Eve"). But more importantly, words are the liberating weapons used by the protagonists of the two key and centrally located (in the middle of the novel) selections, "It Was a Silvery Night" and "... and the earth did not part." Nonetheless, it is Bartolo, the town poet whose efforts are identical to those of the center of consciousness (i.e., to mention and recall the people), who best expresses the importance of words:

> Bartolo always came through town around December, when he felt that most of the people had returned from work in other states. He always sold his poems. They were almost completely sold out by the end of the first day because they mentioned the names of the people in town. And when he read the poems out loud, it was a serious and an emotional experience. I remember once he told the people to read his poems out loud because the voice was the love seed in the dark. (p. 116)

This concern for words leads us to another related concern in the novel: school. School and education are *Earth*'s main reference points. They appear explicitly or implicitly in almost every story and in several of the anecdotes. Thus, words and the institution responsible for word acquisition and usage, school, are linked in such a way as to suggest the conclusion that "reformed schools," those that have been changed to meet the Chicanos' "true" needs, are the answer to the Chicano "problem," which, after all, is seen as an educational one. In suggesting such an incomplete/misguided answer to the Chicano condition, Rivera was in step with the statements and goals of *El Plan de Santa Bárbara*, a manifesto and program for school reform that in 1969 expressed the main thrust of the Chicano Movement at the time: "We recognize that without a strategic use of education, an education that places value on what we value, we will not realize our destiny. Chicanos recognize the central importance of institutions of higher learning to modern progress, in this case, to the development of our community."[11]

Having placed the protagonist physically and having specified his concerns, it is in order now to characterize him. He is a loner, into himself, highly sensitive and perceptive, obviously a thinker, a daydreamer one might say, and above all a person who sets himself apart (note his mania for hiding) from the community in which he lives, a community which is in fact hostile to him, for when he is discovered hiding under the house he is bombarded by rocks and a dog is even sicked on him. By now the contradiction is obvious: here we have a protagonist who, on the one hand, wants "to see all those people together," wishes he had "long enough arms" to "hug them all at the same time," and would like to "talk with all of them again, and have them all together" (p. 126); and on the other hand, has to hide from those very same people because he believes "that could happen only in a dream" (p. 126). In short, a protagonist who *"has to be alone in order to bring everyone together"* (p. 126, my emphasis).

This, I am sure, is the basic contradiction in the work, the element that explains the type of novel it is, its structure, and the ambiguity that invites false interpretations of Chicano reality. To explain, one of the most important characteristics of the hero of an *Erziehungsroman* is that in the process of initiation and education in life he must separate himself from his group, necessarily seen by him as an obstruction to his liberation;[12] and as an obstruction, the group from which he separates must of course be seen in a negative light. In *Earth*, therefore, the child protagonist must see the Chicano world as simple, backward, and static when viewed against the dynamic and complexity of his own world.[13] In other words, in the interaction of the two worlds the dynamic one—his—must appear to illuminate the static one of his people.

While this would certainly be a worthwhile effort, it does not in fact happen in the novel at all; in every instance in which a protagonist of a selection or an anecdote reaches a "liberated" level, he (it only happens to males!) keeps that knowledge to himself. The best two examples of this procedure are found in the first anecdote and in the title selection. In the former the protagonist discovers the falsity in his mother's superstition of offering a glass of water to the night spirits, "but once he was about to tell her ... he thought he would do it later when he had grown up" (p. 3). In the latter the protagonist has the opportunity to affect positively his family's oppressive fear of God, but "he decided to keep it a secret" (p. 56).[14] The same is true of the child protagonist himself. In the last selection, as he comes out of hiding enjoying his most illuminated stage, he "didn't say anything when he walked away from them [his people]" (p. 128).

This unwillingness to communicate his vision of the world around him underscores the child protagonist's separation from his community and paradoxically makes him wish he "had long enough arms [to] hug them [his people] all at the same time" (p. 126), a wish that implicitly attests to the distance between him and the community. Interestingly, his wish, which should have been realized through communication with his community, materializes only through the structure of the novel. That is to say, the first and last stories—those in which he is the key figure—are placed as "arms" that enclose/embrace the body of the novel, the part where the Chicano people are presented. In the end, however, the schism between the people and the child protagonist finally leads to the latter's becoming totally immersed in a world of reflection, where mental powers reign supreme and are even capable of creation. This is quite evident in the last paragraph of the novel:

> He had discovered something. To discover and to rediscover and synthesize. To relate this entity with that entity, and that entity with still another, and finally relating everything with everything else. That was what he had to do, *that was all*. And he became even happier.

> Later, when he arrived at home, he went to the tree that was in the yard. He climbed it. On the horizon he saw a palm tree and he *imagined* that someone was on top looking at him. He even raised his arm and waved it back and forth so that the other person could see that he knew that he was there. (p. 128, my emphasis)[15]

In essence, we have here the makings of an intellectual hero, one who gives birth to thoughts that generate further thoughts, which in turn lead to more thoughts, etc.; one who cherishes the illusion that thought, if properly applied, can solve all problems.[16] And in the isolated world he has created, thought can indeed do all of that and more. But a world where thought has such powers can only be conceived in the safety of a place away from the concrete social world that surrounds him. In this we discover the real reason for the child protagonist's hiding under the house, for, as we suspected all along, his lack of vocabulary words was "not the only reason" (p. 118) he wanted to hide. Ultimately, though, the people around him, those of the real world, interfere too much in his creation; they reach and disturb him even in his hiding place. Consequently, he has to create/imagine the first of many "illuminated" companions, friends who will understand him and replace the hostile and uncomprehending community who are so mentally immature that they mistake his liberated stage as a form of insanity (p. 128).

Thus, the child protagonist and the community from which he comes are made to see and experience two different worlds. The separation of the two leads to the perpetuation of an old and dangerous myth, namely, that despite oppression or any outside force, one is in complete control of one's destiny—which, by the way, is *Earth*'s principal message. If this is true, why are the people presented in the body of the novel not in control of their destiny? It must be because they have not learned to think, thereby remaining backward, superstitious, primitive, and simple. And since the child protagonist became "liberated" through his *own* efforts while living under the same conditions as the other people, these people must be in large measure to blame for their condition.

But let us go further, for the child protagonist of the introductory story becomes, in the concluding selection, the author/narrator. Like the child protagonist within the text, Rivera, in writing the novel, has himself used the word, the power of thought to bring together all the Chicanos and Chicano experiences that appear in the stories. Thus, the creative process of remembrance, of recalling—all thought processes—within the novel[17] is analogous to the concrete creation of a piece of art, "*... and the earth did not part*". Both child protagonist and author create a world with words. In view of this direct relationship between the author and his principal character, the contradiction we pinpointed above can be further elucidated by examining briefly the author's life.

Rivera was born (1935) in Crystal City, Texas, to migrant farmworkers. Following the migrant stream from Texas to the Midwest and back, he experienced the infamously oppressive conditions (portrayed in the body of the novel) imposed upon a work force completely subject to the merciless interests of business and agriculture alike. Despite these obstacles, Rivera managed to graduate from high school and enroll at a small state university in San Marcos, Texas, where he received a B.A. in English. For several years following his graduation, he taught English in a predominantly Chicano high school in San Antonio, Texas. A fellowship to the University of Oklahoma then took him to Norman as a Ph.D. student in Romance languages. Having completed his studies, and having held a couple of university teaching assignments, Rivera accepted one of the top positions in the administration of the newly established campus of the University of Texas at San Antonio. Later he became chancellor of the University of California-Riverside, a position he occupied at the time of his death in 1984.

For Rivera, then, it was his education that led him on an accelerated climb up the social class ladder. In a relatively short period of time he went from migrant worker to boss. Consequently, his emphasis on education as a remedy to the Chicano "problem" is absolutely logical. Moreover, his exorbitant belief in the power of words is also understandable since the university deals primarily in words, in ideas, in mental/abstract constructions; that is to say, it too attempts to build a world based on words. In view of these observations, it is quite obvious, I believe, why Rivera should place his novel within the realm of mental activity; why the Chicano liberation he proposes in *Earth* is ultimately a mental one, a liberation from tradition, from superstitions and beliefs; one which stems from the power of thought, not action.

But there is more: the seclusion and time for contemplation that the child protagonist finds under the house Rivera found within the walls of the university. Here Rivera could "relate everything to everything else" (p. 128). From the security and vantage point that the university provided, he observed and commented on the life of the Chicano community and gave it form: the novel. But, since throughout his career he maintained, as we have shown above, an intimate contact with the Chicano community, he was at the same time an outside observer and a part of the community that he observed, the same situation in which the child protagonist finds himself in the novel. This particular situation leads the "uncomprehending" community to hurl rocks and turn a dog upon the child protagonist in the text, and outside the text it led to accusations of Rivera's not "returning" to the community, an accusation which since the birth of the Chicano Movement (1965) has been at one time or another hurled—and not always unfounded—at each and every Chicano academician in this country.

While this writer believes that *Earth* provides the best answer yet to that accusation, it is also our belief that Rivera's accelerated ascension of the social-class ladder resulted in his having a false vision of the Chicano people and their struggle, a vision that is evident in his characterization of them as simple, helpless, and backward, timid in the face of oppression, etc., and in his suggesting that the Chicanos' main struggle for liberation must be against their own religiosity, that what Chicanos need to do is to learn to think, to use words in order to create a liberated world, and that all of this can be done in isolation and by ourselves alone. Ultimately, Rivera's false concept of the Chicano people—a concept in harmony with the one held by the social class to which he ascended—suggests that Chicanos themselves are to blame for much of their condition, an old idea which returns to haunt us in a new, more subtle form.[18]

TEXAS LUTHERAN COLLEGE

## Notes

[1] Tomás Rivera, "Soundless Words," *Café Solo*, 8 (Spring 1974), p. 32.

[2] Although published as a collection of short stories, "... *and the earth did not part*" was, according to a letter dated September 9, 1972, from the author to this writer, written as a novel. For proof of the book's novel structure, see Joseph Sommers' incisive essay, "From the Critical Premise to the Product: Critical Modes and Their Applications to a Chicano Literary Text," *The New Scholar*, 6 (1977), 51–80.

[3] *Earth*, as we shall refer to the novel, was written and published in Spanish under the title "... *y no se lo tragó la tierra*". The first edition, done in 1971 by Quinto Sol Publications of Berkeley, California, had a faulty English translation. Unfortunately, the same translation appears in the second edition, published in 1976 by Justa Publications of Berkeley. The quotations in our essay are taken from this second edition.

[4] Luis Valdez, *Actos* (Fresno, California: Cucaracha Press, 1971). It is important to note that the flowering of Chicano literature was actually begun six years before, in 1965, when the presentation of these *Actos* played a crucial role in keeping the fledgling United Farm Workers' Union alive during its first strike.

[5] Flowering, I believe, is the term that best describes the latest stage in the evolution of our literature, a literature that since the middle of the past century has produced literary works under the most severe limitations. (This writer has found hundreds of examples of these works in the superb Spanish language newspaper collection at the Chicano Studies Library at the University of California at Berkeley, among other places.) The term renaissance, in so much as it implies a previous static "dark age," ignores that production, and is therefore inadequate.

[6] These elements are studied in what is to date the best work of critical writing on Chicano literature: Rafael Francisco Grajeda, "The Figure of the Pocho in Contemporary Chicano Fiction," Diss. The University of Nebraska-Lincoln, 1974.

[7] See my "La embestida contra la religiosidad en . . y no se lo tragó la tierra," *PCCLA Proceedings: Changing Perspectives on Latin America*, 3 (1974), 83–86.

[8] Marcienne Rocard, "The Cycle of Chicano Experience in . . . and the earth did not part by Tomás Rivera," *Annales de l'Université de Toulouse-Le Mirail* (April–May 1976), p. 148.

[9] Ralph Grajeda, "Tomás Rivera's . . . y no se lo tragó la tierra: Discovery and Appropriation of the Chicano Past," to be published in forthcoming issues of *Hispania*.

[10] Hereafter I shall refer to the protagonist of the novel as the child protagonist, to distinguish him from the principal characters of the other stories, several of which also have children as protagonists.

[11] *El Plan de Santa Bárbara* (Santa Barbara, California: La Causa Publications, 1970), p. 10.

[12] Although *Erziehungsroman* and *Bildungsroman* are terms at times used interchangeably, I have chosen the former because *Erziehung* suggests upbringing or education, which I believe more accurately describes the process that the child protagonist undergoes. For a definition of the two terms and a discussion of their use, see Karl Beckson and Arthur Ganz, *Literary Terms: A Dictionary* (New York: Farrar, Straus and Giroux, 1975).

[13] This is a situation quite similar to the one where a social scientist undertakes a study of some "primitive" people without realizing that the whole approach from the very beginning requires certain visions and attitudes toward the group being studied and that the approach also establishes, *a priori*, certain conclusions without which his/her role as principal observer–controller of information–cannot be maintained.

[14] While the protagonists of *Earth*'s selections where a child is the principal character may or may not be the same child protagonist of the first and last story, the important thing to remember is that—as far as the reader is concerned—the latter does in fact control their action and being.

[15] The use of the imagination to project an individual upon a fabricated world happens quite often in Rivera's work. For a rather intriguing example of this, see the selection "La otra cara en el espejo" in *La casa grande del pueblo*, his second novel, soon to be published.

[16] See Victor Brombert, *The Intellectual Hero: Studies in the French Novel, 1880–1955* (Philadelphia and New York: J. B. Lippincott, 1960).

[17] For an extended discussion of the importance that Rivera gives to these processes, see his "Remembering, Discovery and Volition in the Literary Imag-

inative Process," *Atisbos: Journal of Chicano Research* (Summer 1975), pp. 66–77. This is an English translation by Gustavo Valdez of Rivera's lecture presented in Spanish before the Chicano Writers Workshop held June 2, 1973, on the Merrit College campus at Oakland, California.

[18] Rivera, of course, is not the only Chicano caught in the contradiction of wanting to do something for our people, who are basically working class, and subconsciously letting our new social position dictate a negative view of our own community. This is a problem with which we have only begun to deal.

# La caracterización de los personajes femeninos en "... y no se lo tragó la tierra"[1]

*Francisca Rascón*

Es importante notar cómo a través de la literatura surgen temas que se repiten en los distintos géneros literarios dentro de una misma década. Estos temas incumben sus problemas específicos. Pero observamos que, a medida que pasan las décadas y cambia el contexto y las condiciones históricas y sociales, el tratamiento literario del mismo tema varía de la misma manera que cambian aspectos del problema. La obra literaria, formada no sólo de expresión sino también de contenido, para poder reflejar el tema de una manera realista conforme al contexto sociohistórico del tema mismo, debe manifestar esos cambios en su propio contexto histórico, social y literario ya que de otra manera sería distorsionar esa realidad.

El tema del campesino chicano es buen ejemplo de este proceso ya que aquí se ve la continuidad y el cambio en el contexto histórico y social del campesino. Las condiciones de los campesinos en los veinte, cuando está en proceso una de las más grandes migraciones desde México, no son iguales a las de los treinta, cuando la depresión se ha venido encima. Tampoco las condiciones de los sesenta, cuando el paro del programa de braceros toma lugar son iguales a las de los cuarenta, cuando el énfasis está en fabricar armamento militar para la segunda guerra mundial y hay una rápida urbanización en el sudoeste. A medida que cambian las condiciones la conciencia del campesino también se agudiza y se calibra dando lugar a huelgas con diferentes demandas y con diversas perspectivas, según la época, como las huelgas que hubo durante los veinte y los treinta. Por lo tanto la literatura, tanto la novela y el cuento como la poesía, al tratar el tema del campesino reflejará estos cambios a distintos niveles, a nivel de expresión, de contenido, a nivel narrativo así como ideológico, tanto en el tratamiento de los personajes y su caracterización como en el reflejo de sus problemas. Pueden aparecer entonces diferentes tipos de un mismo personaje con distinto desarrollo, como por ejemplo: el campesino que de callado trabajador pasa a ser participante activo en la huelga; la familia del campo que luego vive en la ciudad; o el niño rural travieso y a la vez dócil y comportado que más tarde cuestiona las tradiciones que se le han enseñado. De la misma manera esperaríamos encontrar en la literatura distintas caracterizaciones de personajes femeninos que respondieran al contexto y momento socio-históricos.

A sabiendas de la pequeñísima cantidad de personajes femeninos en la literatura chicana hasta hoy día, me propongo ver hasta qué punto los tipos de personajes femeninos que aparecen en la distinguida obra "... y no se lo tragó la tierra," de Tomás Rivera, son coetáneos al contexto socio-histórico de la obra.

Algunos puntos claves que habría que destacar para aproximarnos al análisis de esta problemática son los siguientes aspectos textuales y contextuales. Lo primero sería ver el género de la obra. Se podría justificar que *Tierra* es novela, dados los patrones estructurales y narrativos del texto. Se identifican cuatro: la secuencialidad de relatos, por llamarlos así ya que no funcionan como capítulos, donde se asume que transcurre un año en la vida de una persona; el proceso progresivo de expresiones narradas que forman un *"rite de passage"* de un niño; los pequeños prefacios que le prestan profundidad y dimensión a cada relato, y finalmente el marco temático con el primer relato "El año perdido" como introducción y como final "Debajo de la casa," que otro crítico llamó "Año recuperado," así dando principio y fin a la obra.[2] Este texto novelístico, por lo tanto, permite un análisis de contenido y, a su vez, de la caracterización de los personajes femeninos a nivel novelístico.

Otro elemento textual que se tiene que examinar es el punto de vista que percibe el lector de la narración. Se distinguen dos: desde la desconocida tercera persona y desde la del niño, considerado protagonista-narrador. En gran parte la narración nos presenta los acontecimientos, las descripciones de personajes y las contradicciones socio-económicas desde el punto de vista de un niño. Es el niño que nos comunica una secuencia de acontecimientos y lo que siente, por ejemplo, al ver a su hermanito insolándose mientras trabaja en el campo bajo condiciones brutas. La escena de la madre llorando resignadamente y rezando por sus parientes y por el esposo, en el relato "... y no se lo tragó la tierra," es también interpretada por el niño. Las ambigüedades que surgen en identificar a un solo niño como narrador son clarificadas al final de la obra cuando el protagonista recuerda las escenas narradas.[3] Es pues importante especificar la voz narrativa ya que la mayoría de los personajes femeninos serán interpretados desde la perspectiva del niño.

Ya planteados estos puntos es necesario, para el análisis, identificar el contexto histórico en que toma lugar la obra, ya que los acontecimientos en el texto vienen a reflejar la vida del pueblo de origen méxicoamericano en determinadas situaciones socio-históricas. La narración establece que se trata de la década de fines de los cuarenta a principios de los cincuenta dándonos datos como la guerra de Korea en "El rezo" y en otros relatos. El contexto también se ve en las descripciones que se hacen de la gente chicana de clase socio-económica baja, casi todos campesinos migratorios, que vivía en Tejas durante ese período.

Por toda la novela se identifican más de treinta y cinco diferentes imágenes de personajes femeninos, desde personajes principales, como la "la Boni", hasta la simple mención de una figura femenina, como "la comadre." En la caracterización de ellas sobresale una constancia narrativa-descriptiva a través de toda la novela que podría deberse a la perspectiva narrativa infantil, ya que, como ya se observó, los personajes femeninos son presentados a través de las descripciones y los monólogos del niño. Consistentemente son personajes mudos; casi no hablan. No se sabe lo que piensan, o si están pensando, ya que su caracterización carece casi totalmente de monólogo interior. Las únicas que son descritas expresándose y compartiendo sus pensamientos son las tres madres: la que está rezando por su hijo que está en la guerra de Korea y que está dispuesta a sacrificar su corazón por el de él en "El rezo"; la que se puso nerviosa saliendo de su casa y se pierde en el centro comprando regalos de Navidad para sus niños; y la que cargando dos hijitos lleva más de veinticuatro horas en un troque con rumbo al norte a trabajar. Las circunstancias de estas tres imágenes son distintas y sus problemas son también diferentes pero el contenido de sus pensamientos refleja las mismas actitudes, reacciones y los mismos sentimientos y son éstos distintos sólo en su intensidad. En resumen, las tres sienten temor, acuden a Dios y piden ayuda. Es interesante que, siendo éstas las únicas que son mostradas por un instante desde una dimensión interior, sean tan similares en su forma ya que el contexto y el contenido de cada una es distinto en ciertos aspectos. Una está rezando y siente que la vida de su hijo está en peligro; la otra va caminando hacia el centro con la preocupación de ponerse enferma de los nervios por andar entre la gente y de perderse después; y la tercera tiene la preocupación de que por tener a dos niños pequeños no va a poder ayudarle al esposo en el trabajo. El instante que se escoge de esta dimensión interior refleja el mismo proceso mental, la misma interioridad. Da la presentación de un sólo mundo interior y no el de tres diferentes mujeres en diferentes relatos. Si se acepta la suposición de que esta constancia ocurre porque así percibe el niño a las mujeres, tendríamos que calificar su percepción de ellas como superficial. Por otra parte la obra en su totalidad crea una imagen simplificada de estas mujeres, un estereotipo de la dimensión, o falta de dimensión interior de estas imágenes, ya que deja de pintar un tipo femenino realista.

Para crear personajes que sean realistas, dentro de una sociedad particular, se necesita incorporar tanto lo personal-individual como lo social en la caracterización de los personajes. Georg Lukács así lo ha propuesto en su estudio sobre la características de los personajes de Balzac: "The realism of Balzac rests on a uniformly complete rendering of the particular individual traits of each of his characters on the one hand and the traits which are typical of them as representatives of a class on the other."[4] En el caso de la novela de Rivera se está pintando una visión inverosímil de la realidad ya que su representación se limita a ciertas características que sólo le permiten al lector una estrecha interpretación de la interioridad de estos personajes que carecen de particularidades individuales. Por lo tanto, la novela carece de una visión realista de la interioridad de las mujeres, ofreciendo más bien una representación estereotipada de la mujer.

Como punto técnico el elemento femenino generalmente sirve una doble función. Se emplea como personaje secundario para desarrollar los relatos y como objeto de interacción para el protagonista. Algunas de las muchas mujeres que caen en esta categoría de doble función son la maestra que manda al niño con la enfermera para fumigarlo contra piojos y las mujeres mexicanas que se espulgan frente a sus casas. El elemento femenino en este caso es empleado para mostrar las humillaciones que sufre un niño de escuela con personas—maestras, "principals" y enfermeras—que estereotipan a los chicanos.

Estos personajes femeninos no sólo sirven como vehículos para proyectar estos momentos desagradables sino también nos dan a conocer el complejo de culpabilidad que padece el chicano en la sociedad. El texto implica que los chicanos se sienten culpables por la clase de tratamiento que reciben, ya que causan y, por lo tanto, merecen esa clase de tratamiento. No negamos que la víctima llegue a culparse por su situación. Fanón dice que en una situación de opresión el opresor, en una forma sistemática, hace todo esfuerzo para hacer al oprimido creer en su inferioridad y en su imperfección; como resultado, el oprimido llega a criticar desfavorablemente su cultura nacional y a rechazarla y hasta a auto-odiarse.[5] No se discute el que las anécdotas puedan venir de condiciones existentes, como por ejemplo las mujeres espulgándose. Lo que importa ver es si el relato permite una forma de evaluación de ese mismo ambiente y de esa situación. Cuando solamente se dan ciertos rasgos que puedan reflejar la realidad parcialmente, sin indicios o análisis de lo que causa y determina esa realidad, fácilmente se puede caer en los estereotipos.

Siendo el papel de la madre el que surge con más frecuencia entre las imágenes femeninas, veamos más detenidamente los rasgos que las caracterizan. En un plano se nos pinta a la madre como mujer abnegada que piensa siempre en los demás, dispuesta a todo sacrificio, que en ningún instante demuestra la más mínima queja por su sufrimiento. En una obra literaria podría ocurrir que las características de un tipo de personaje se conviertan en constantes en la caracterización de otros personajes repitiéndose por el texto. Esa caracterización sería entonces una función mecánica con resultados estereotipantes. Veamos ahora estas imágenes bajo estos criterios. En la novela, dado el número de veces que aparecen las imágenes de la madre, es notable que jamás se queje alguna, ya sea de las condiciones en que viven, de su propio estado físico o de su trabajo. Esto cuaja muy bien con el estereotipo general de la madre mexicana de mucho aguante. Veamos a la madre que le dice al niñito, al reclamar éste el que no le haya planchado los pantalones la noche anterior, que ya no ve bien pero que de día puede hacerle todo, explicándole así su incapacidad de tener el pantalón listo. Al reclamo hay una aceptación de culpabilidad por no hacer un trabajo o cumplir con un deber. Esta constancia de no quejarse resulta mecánica, demasiado reiterada y por lo tanto estereotipada al darse como característica sin excepción en estos personajes.

Al observarlas en situaciones de alta tensión, como momentos trágicos o de crisis, vemos que las madres son descritas reaccionando invariablemente a nivel de emoción. Se les pone siempre en situaciones donde su reacción sólo puede ser descrita como la de loca o de pasiva aún cuando el contexto es distinto. Por ejemplo, se da el relato en el que el patrón mata al niño y se dice que la madre se volvió loca, o el de la madre que siente volverse loca al recibir la carta anunciándole que su hijo se perdió en acción. De la misma manera se ve la pasividad de la madre que dice que sólo la muerte trae descanso para gente como ellos, refiriéndose a gente pobre en el relato "... y no se lo tragó la tierra." Estas madres son caracterizadas con temor e inseguridad, dependientes y necesitadas de la protección de sus maridos o de Dios. Por lo tanto la caracterización de las madres es básicamente idéntica en todos los casos aun cuando el contexto y los problemas son distintos. Al no concederles rasgos individuales a estos personajes, se producen estereotipos.

A diferencia de las anteriormente discutidas y al contrario de lo que hasta ahora se ha observado, resaltan radicalmente dos personajes activos femeninos. Las dos juegan un papel importante, especialmente la Boni. Esta mujer gorda sin evidencia de tener hijos, según el niño, hace lo que puede para mantenerse. Roba, se prostituye y convence a su marido a que le ayude a matar a un mojado. La otra imagen femenina activa es Juanita, descrita como mujer que sale con otro muchacho no por romper con las cadenas de un sistema de valores masculinos sino, de acuerdo a las insinuaciones narrativas, por mentirosa, infiel y coqueta. La narración nos presenta en este caso, como en el de la Boni, que a consecuencia de sus acciones el novio se mata. Como vemos, lo que se sugiere es que estas dos mujeres inducen a los hombres a hacer el mal y a las malas consecuencias. Por lo visto, cuando la mujer asume un rol activo su función es negativa y las consecuencias son trágicas, especialmente para el hombre de acuerdo con la narración. Cuando la mujer es presentada como abnegada, considerada, religiosa y como madre su esfuerzo de acción lleva al fracaso. Esto se enfatiza cuando vemos a la única otra mujer en la novela que toma acción, la madre que trata de romper las barreras de su pasividad y de su cerca familiar protectora al tratar de ir a comprar regalos. Ella termina en el hospital en una situación todavía más pasiva y reducida que antes. Las implicaciones claramente podrían conducir a estereotipificación de las consecuencias de ser activa o pasiva. Pero si las mujeres que toman pasos para autodeterminarse son caracterizdas como individuos contraproducentes, los personajes masculinos que sí toman acción en sus manos son presentados por el narrador de una manera que provoca cierta simpatía de parte del lector. Esto sucede con el hombre que hace al muchacho que le fabrique la foto que había quedado en hacer, o el padre del niño que va a la barbería a confrontarse con el barbero por negarse a hacerle el pelo a su hijo.

Las imágenes de los personajes femeninos por estudiar con las que se presentan fuera de la cultura chicana. En este texto se nos presentan las maestras incomprensibles, la "principal" que saca al niño de la escuela, la americana que por ir borracha choca y mata a dieciséis campesinos, la esposa del ministro que se va con otro, la monja a quien le gusta escuchar los pecados del cuerpo, la enfermera que apena al niño cuando lo hace que se quite la ropa para examinarlo y la gabachita que vivía con el chicano que encarcelaron por ser ella menor de edad. La función de estos personajes femeninos distribuidos por toda la novela aparentemente es la de representar el nivel de interacción entre los dos grupos y por lo tanto, dado el número de veces que aparecen, aun cuando el personaje que se nos graba más en esta categoría es el patrón que mata al niño, nos detendremos a estudiarlas. Analizando su caracterización más a fondo sin dejar de tomar en cuenta sus distintos contextos, vemos que en realidad lo que se presenta es un conjunto de personajes femeninos que fracasan al desempeñar su papel ya sea a nivel profesional, doméstico o civil, cuyas acciones directa o indirectamente perjudican al chicano. La visión que el autor nos presenta de los personajes femeninos sólo permite una interpretación no más profunda ni más amplia de la que brevemente se esboza. Como este tratamiento de los personajes es constante nos lleva a una inconsciente y consciente estereotipificación de las mujeres no chicanas, ya que como se mencionó arriba el texto no nos da indicios que nos permitan otra interpretación.

Hemos visto que al analizar un texto se debe tomar en cuenta no sólo su significado literario sino la totalidad de sus significados, dentro de su contexto histórico y social. Al analizar la caracterización de los personajes femeninos en el texto encontramos que a primera vista el texto parece presentarnos una visión realista de la campesina chicana a nivel inmediato así como de los otros personajes femeninos. Una vez que nos adentramos más, vemos que hay una diferencia significativa entre las implicaciones de estos personajes que no cuaja con el contexto socio-histórico de la década en que son situados. Harto conocido es que poco importa lo que un autor diga sobre sus intenciones, lo que escribe es lo importante. Pero como referencia citaremos a Rivera quien nos asegura que el intento de la literatura chicana es entre otras cosas cambiar estereotipos y luchar contra la imagen que se ha creado del chicano.[6] Aquí vemos que el esfuerzo de este texto por presentar la realidad del chicano logra todo lo contrario en el plan de la mujer al presentarnos personajes femeninos estáticos, sin cambios o desarrollo individual, con características constantes sin profundidad o dimensión que carecen de rasgos particulares que permitan distinguir su individualidad a la vez que sirvan para reflejar lo real, lo dinámico de la misma cultura y para identificarlas como parte de la misma clase socio-económica.

Al analizar un texto donde se repiten mecánicamente las mismas características fundamentales sin variación ni distinción entre personajes supuestamente distintos, se crea un estereotipo y no un tipo de la realidad. Este texto, por lo tanto, tiene una probeza de tipos y un número de estereotipos.

UNIVERSITY OF CALIFORNIA, SAN DIEGO

## Notas

[1] Tomás Rivera, "... *y no se lo tragó la tierra*" (Berkeley: Quinto Sol Publications, Inc., 1971).
[2] Joseph Sommers, "From the Critical Premise to the Product: Critical Modes

and Their Applications to a Chicano Literary Text." *New Directions in Chicano Scholarship* (La Jolla, California: Chicano Studies Monograph Series, 1978), pág. 64.

[3] Ibid., pág. 70.

[4] Georg Lukács, *Studies in European Realism* (New York: Grosset & Dunlap, 1964), pág. 43.

[5] Franz Fanon, *The Wretched of the Earth* (New York: Grove Press, Inc., 1968), pág. 236.

[6] Tomás Rivera, "Literatura chicana: Vida en busca de forma" (New York: ERIC, 1972), pág. 11.

# 4. The Accomplished Voices
## A. Rolando Hinojosa

*Estampas del Valle:*
From *Costumbrismo* to
Self-Reflecting Literature

*Erlinda Gonzales-Berry*

In 1973, the leading publishing house of Chicano literature awarded the Third Annual Premio Quinto Sol to Rolando Hinojosa-S. for his work *Estampas del Valle y otras obras*. Consisting of a collection of sketches, the text appeared in a bilingual edition with a translation by Gustavo Valadez. Rolando Hinojosa, like most other Chicano writers using Spanish as a medium of communication, is a professor of Spanish. Born in Texas, he received his B.A. from the University of Texas, his M.S. from Highlands University in New Mexico, where he taught for a time, and his Ph.D. from the University of Illinois. Since the publication of *Estampas del Valle* he has written *Noticias de Klail City y sus alrededores*, which was awarded the 1976 prize for the best novel of the year by Casa de las Américas (Havana).

*Estampas del Valle y otras obras* consists of four parts, each bearing its own title. From the volume title we can suppose that each section was conceived as a separate entity and, in fact, each part can be read independently of the rest and hold its own as an integral unit. But despite the apparent dispersion in the various sections, as Luis María Brox has pointed out,[1] the work can justifiably be viewed as an organized whole with the following recurring elements acting as unifying motifs: (1) the presence of familiar characters in all four sections; (2) an intertwining of personal histories which becomes apparent as the work progresses; (3) a common spatial setting; (4) stylistic devices such as the stylization of popular speech and a strong preference for compact narrative. Additionally, the *pueblo*'s keen historical consciousness provides the important dimension of thematic unity.

The basic form of the text relies on a series of fragmented vignettes of varying length and the use of multiple perspectives, creating a color-

| Title | Narrator | Subject | Narrative Techniques |
|---|---|---|---|
| ESTAMPAS DEL VALLE | | | |
| 1. "Braulio Tapia" | first person identifiable: B. Tapia's son-in-law | Roque Malacara asks for B. Tapia's granddaughter's hand in marriage | Straight narrative |
| 2. "Tere Norriega" | first person identifiable: Tere Norriega | Talks about herself | Straight narrative |
| 3. "Roque Malacara" | first person identifiable: Roque Malacara | Talks about his wife Tere Norriega and son Jehú | Straight narrative |
| 4. "Huérfano y al pairo" | first person identifiable: Jehú Malacara | Tells his own story | Straight narrative |
| 5. "Mis primos" | first person identifiable: Jehú Malacara | The Briones family | Straight narrative |
| 6. "Contratiempos del oficio" | third person unidentifiable | Jehú Malacara and Don Victor Peláez | Dialogue and straight narrative |
| 7. "Aprendiendo el oficio" | third person unidentifiable | Jehú and Don Víctor | Dialogue, straight narrative, and long circus barker's call (Jehú) |
| 8. "Otra vez la muerte" | first person: Jehú Malacara | Don Victor, Mexican Revolution | Straight narrative and Don V.'s diary |
| 9. "Flora" | third person unidentifiable | Rufus Klail and daughter Flora | Straight narrative |
| 10. "Al pozo con Bruno Cano" | third person unidentifiable | Bruno Cano's death and funeral/fiesta | Dialogue, straight narrative |
| 11. "Don Javier" | first person identifiable: Don Javier | Don Javier's girlfriend Gela | Straight narrative |
| 12. "Emilio Támez" | third person unidentifiable | Emilio Támez | Straight narrative |
| 13. "La tía Panchita" | third person unidentifiable | Village *curandera* cures Rafa Buenrostro | Dialogue, straight narrative, prayers |
| 14. "Epigmenio Salazar" | third person unidentifiable | Don Epigmenio | Straight narrative |
| 15. "La Güera Fira" | third person unidentifiable | Fira, the village prostitute | Straight narrative |
| 16. "Arturo Leyva" | third person unidentifiable | Arturo Leyva and Tere Malacara | Straight narrative |
| 17. "Don Manuel Guzmán" | third person unidentifiable | Don Manuel, city sheriff | Straight narrative |
| 18. "El Maistro" | third person: could be Rafa Buenrostro, bartender | El maistro, housepainter | Straight narrative |

| | | | |
|---|---|---|---|
| 19. "Voces del barrio" | third person unidentifiable | El barrio at sunset | Dialogue, songs, games, straight narrative |
| 20. "Mesa redonda" | third person unidentifiable | Genealogy of residents of Klail City | Dialogue, straight narrative |//

## POR ESAS COSAS QUE PASAN

| | | | |
|---|---|---|---|
| 1. "Extract *Klail City Enterprise*" | third person journalist | Knifing of Arturo Támez by Baldemar Cordero | Newspaper extract |
| 2. "Por esas cosas que pasan" | first person: Baldemar Cordero | Events surrounding knifing | Tape recording of R. Hinojosa conversation |
| 3. "Marta cuenta lo suyo" | first person: Marta Cordero | Balde Cordero, brother | Tape recording of conversation with Hinojosa |
| 4. "Preface to legal statement" | | | Official statement |
| 5. "A deposition freely given" | first person: Beto Castañeda | Concerning the knifing | Record of official statement |
| 6. "Newspaper extract" | | Sentencing of Baldemar Cordero | Newspaper article |

## VIDAS Y MILAGROS

| | | | |
|---|---|---|---|
| 1. "Para empezar, una dedicatoria" | third person implied author | Concerning the art of creating fiction | Straight narrative |
| 2. "Así se cumple" | third person unidentifiable | Viola Barragán | Straight narrative |
| 3. "Los revolucionarios" | third person unidentifiable | Participation of Braulio Tapia, Evaristo Garrido, Don Manuel Guzmán in Mexican Revolution | Straight narrative |
| 4. "Un domingo en Klail" | third person unidentifiable | Arturo Leyva at baseball game | Straight narrative, dialogue |
| 5. "Los Leguizamón" | third person unidentifiable | The Leguizamón family | Straight dialogue |
| 6. "Beto Castañeda" | third person unidentifiable | Beto Castañeda's death | Straight narrative |
| 7. "Coyotes" | third person unidentifiable | Chicano opportunists who exploit their own people | Straight narrative, dialogue |
| 8. "Burnias" | third person unidentifiable | The tale and sale of a sick pig | Straight narrative, dialogue |

ful mosaic which contains the panoramic view of the human dimension of a Chicano *pueblo* in a manner reminiscent of Juan José Arreola's *La Feria*.[2] The first and longest section, "Estampas del Valle," includes twenty *costumbrista* sketches depicting a variety of characters who live in fictitious Klail City, Texas. Although the "Valle" of the title refers to the Valle del Río Bravo, the author consciously creates the fictional setting of Klail, whose literary antecedents are found in Faulkner's Yoknapatawpha County as well as in García Márquez' Macondo and Onetti's Santa María. In this first section Hinojosa creates some of the stock characters that will reappear in the subsequent parts and in his second novel[3] *Generaciones y semblanzas*. The second section contains a ten-page story called "Por esas cosas que pasan," in which the author exploits several points of view and supposed methods of documentation to describe the events surrounding the knifing of Arturo Támez by Baldemar Cordero of Klail City. A third section, "Vidas y Milagros," begins with a dedicatory note in which the author makes some oblique comments on the art of creating fiction and goes on to describe in detail more citizens of Belken County, some of whom have already appeared in the first series of sketches. The book ends with a series of twenty-four succinct "miniatures" collected under the title "Una vida de Rafa Buenrostro" which depict the narrator's experiences in two antagonistic realities. The outline in the table on pages 150 and 151 is designed to allow an overall perspective of the architecture of this work and delineates in particular the variety of identifiable and unidentifiable narrative voices, the various modes of narration, and the recurrence of characters.

With the exception of the second story, the remaining sections can be classified as a series of *costumbrista* sketches created with brushstrokes of sharp wit and humor which *in toto* constitute a colorful landscape of the inhabitants and cultural patterns of a specifically designated geographical area. The *costumbrista* trapping most obvious in *Estampas* is the use of stylized popular speech to vivify and transform popular culture into a literary topoi. The *costumbrista* tones of the sketches suggest initially a deceptively simple work. Upon examining the variety of narrative techniques, the deft manipulation of point of view, and the ironic humor created by the use of unreliable narrators, we realize that the work is far more complex than a superficial perusal would indicate. The basic *costumbrista* simplicity in the work is offset by modern techniques of fragmentation and multiple points of view which complicate the reading, requiring the reader's undivided attention. Hinojosa is a deeply reflective writer who handles with dexterity the tools of his craft and who has a profound understanding of the human values of his people. Regarding his use of the *costumbrista* mode, it is important to recognize that the author has not been satisfied merely to revive this form. In the process he has transformed it through his own unique creative powers and he has certainly enriched it with a consciousness that, beyond being a mere continuation of the Hispanic consciousness, has evolved and been modified by the particular *circunstancias* of the Chicano experience.

Because Hinojosa is dealing basically with a rural people whose world vision is rooted in the notion of a cyclical repetition of tradition and cultural patterns, his approach must of need depict their world view and do so on their terms. In an article examining the quality of southern United States literature, Marshall McLuhan expounds the difference between novels of agrarian societies and those of urban reality. Urbanites, with their sense of individualism, view themselves and the world in terms of their individual psyches. Every action must be analyzed in terms of interior motive. Thus, the nature of contemporary urban literature elaborates psychological development of character. The nature of traditional agrarian society, on the other hand, is such as to produce human beings who are primarily passionate in a strict sense. They understand the limits of mere human motives and habitually *feel* the fatality of the larger forces that are in them as well as outside them.[4] Such a world view, McLuhan concludes, could not withstand "elaborate character analysis."[5] Rather it prompts literature in which characters acquire their identities in relation to the clan or community from which they spring. In lieu of reflective characters, "the stress falls entirely on slight human gestures, external events which are obliquely slanted to flash light or shade on character."[6]

It is precisely this kind of vision that many Spanish American writers and particularly the Mexican writers Juan José Arreola, Elena Garro, and Sergio Galindo have created in their attempt to bring to life the *campesino* in their novels. Of the latter Joseph Sommers tells us that "Their distinctive feature is that they explain these dilemmas not through a detailed analysis of introverted individuals, but rather through their characters' interaction within the social framework provided by their fellow townsmen."[7] Much of Chicano literature shares this distinctive feature. Writers such as Hinojosa are seeking to capture and give expression to the world view of the Chicano who, by tradition, has been close to the earth; thus his kinship to the Mexican *campesino*. An obvious approach has been to document daily life patterns of the *pueblo*, providing an exterior view whose meaning is crystallized vis-à-vis a larger cultural and historical schema.

In his attempt to give fictional shape and form to the common folk of El Valle, Hinojosa captures the intrinsic humanness of his characters. That humanness is based on (1) the simple interrelationships of people; (2) a deep historical consciousness based on an awarenesss of the rhythm and cycle of human existence; (3) a keen sense of the need to preserve that consciousness through the oral shaping and reshaping of the *pueblo*'s generational cycle. In other words, what he has deemed important to include in his sketches of the life of the common Chicano folk is the need to create for themselves an oral history based on the simple repeated events which assure the continuity of the race, that is, the birth-death-birth cycle. When people are born, where they are born, to whom they are born, what their relationship is to others in the community, whom they marry, whom they sire, and when and how they die—those are the facts that life is made up of; at least, those are the essential facts that *la gente* is most aware of. If in the course of their lives they are touched by momentous historical events, these are absorbed in their oral history ever assuming the characteristics of the folk tale. McLuhan confirms this notion stating that "the tale is the form most natural to a people with a passionate historical sense of life. For in the tale, events march on, passing sometimes over and sometimes around human lives."[8]

Also important to the oral tradition are the customs which make up daily life, enabling humans to cope with illness and death, with good times and bad times, in effect, to endure and to ensure the continuity of race and culture. In the first section of Hinojosa's work there are three sketches which highlight the notion of cyclical regeneration. In the first *estampa* of the book, Roque Malacara appears before his girlfriend's father to ask for the girl's hand in marriage. Roque's presence sets off the father's memory. The latter begins to recall engaging in that very ritual as he approached Braulio Tapia to ask for Don Braulio's daughter's hand. The sketch closes with the question, "¿A quién vería don Braulio en el umbral cuando él pidió a su esposa?"[9] —emphasizing the cyclical nature of custom and tradition.

In the third sketch we learn that Roque and Tere married and had a son Jehú. We learn also that the father-in-law has since died but that he continues to live in the grandson, highlighting once again the idea of the continuity of the species: "Si la gente vuelve a renacer, yo diría que mi hijo y su abuelo son la misma persona" (p. 18).

The young son Jehú emerges as a main character in this mosaic of sketches, providing one of the unifying threads. On piecing together his biography, we discover him to be a picaresque type. In the sketch entitled "Huérfano y al pairo" we find that he lost both his parents at an early age. We also witness in this sketch one of those customs designed to ensure survival and endurance despite negative circumstances. At the insistence of his Tía Chedes young Jehú drinks a glass of water while she makes the sign of the cross on his forehead and utters a backward Lord's Prayer so that he might meet his new father that very day. As Jehú weaves in and out of the sketches we see the young orphan boy working at a variety of jobs with a variety of bosses much in the same way that Lazarillo de Tormes served a variety of masters. One of the more interesting jobs described is that of a barker in a travelling circus.

In the intermittent sketches we encounter a gallery of characters, all with nicknames as colorful as their backgrounds. The folk custom of assigning nicknames which correspond to one's personal appearance or some unfortunate episode in one's life adds the trimmings to oral history and shows once again the enduring force of custom. In one of the *estampas* Jehú's cousin returns from prison covered with tattoos. There is some confusion as to whether to continue calling him by the nickname acquired in childhood, Mión, or whether to call him Tatú:

> Con eso de llamarse Mión y ahora luciendo tanto tatuaje, la gente se despistó y no supo que llamarle: si Mión o Tatú. Parece que a la gente no le gusta que la despisten. Por fin, mi primo fue el que puso pare a la discusión diciendo que prefería que le llamaran Mión (pp. 21-22).

It is precisely this feeling of the sacredness of customs, though it may seem as ridiculous as the narrator in this sketch suggests, which allows the continuity of folk cultures.

The last sketch in the first section bears the ironic title "Mesa redonda." The participants of this seminar in a local barroom are four *viejitos* engaging in a lively exchange of genealogical information. In the course of the discussion they reconstruct in part the history of El Valle:

> ¿Quién es ese muchacho, Genaro?
> Se llama Rafa Buenrostro.
> ¿De cuáles Buenrostro?
> ¿De los de Julián?
> No, éste es de Jesús Buenrostro el que llamaban Don Jesús.
> Ah, sí; murió joven.
> ¿Ese fue el que trabajó con el viejo Burns?
> No. Ese fue Julián. Don Jesús tenía unas tierras cerca del Carmen.

And so forth. At one point one of the local historians is gently ostracized for misinterpreting history:

> ¿Dónde se echaron a los rinches?
> Ahí mero.
> Ya, ya. A don Jesús le decían El Quieto.
> ¿*El Quieto*?
> Sí; újule Leal tú ya no te acuerdas de nada (p. 50).

Thus, the first section ends as it began with a focus on the repetitive nature of life, pointing out that the individual is important only insofar as he relates to the rest of the community and his family line. The collective concept of *la gente* far outweighs the importance of the individual as we are reminded in a sketch called "Voces del barrio": "Lo importante, como siempre, es la gente" (p. 49).

Though folk culture keeps conscious of its past primarily through the creation of oral genealogical history, Hinojosa substantiates the Chicano's sense of historical past by including a sketch which ties him to Mexico and the Revolution. In "Otra vez la muerte" Jehú Malacara makes available to us passages from the journals kept by Don Víctor when he fought in the Mexican Revolution. In this sketch the author brings to life a piece of that historical event which for many Chicanos has acquired mythical dimensions, contributing in the process to their sense of historical identity. This theme will appear again in the third section of the book.

The title of the third section, "Vidas y milagros," reminds us once again of Hinojosa's formal exposure to Hispanic literature. The characters which he describes are not, however, fifteenth-century Spanish saints but rather more of the common folk of Belken County. If the word *milagros* leads us to expect descriptions of awe-inspiring, miraculous events we will indeed be disappointed. Perhaps the only *milagro* which Hinojosa would like to point out is that these people have survived at all despite the precarious nature of their existence—trapped between the Mexican Revolution on one side and unscrupulous Rangers and landgrabbers on the other. In these sketches Hinojosa seems to imply that the people remain ambivalent, in a theoretical sense, to the causal historical events which shape human existence and continue to live their lives as best they can:

> Como la tierra era igual para los méxico-americanos dada la proximidad a las fronteras y el bolón de parientes en ambos lados nunca distinguieron entre tierra y río, que el atravesar la una y cruzar el otro lo mismo era, fue y (aunque los de la inmigración—la migra—no lo crean) sigue siendo igual para muchos méxico-americanos; la raza pues, hacía lo que le daba la gana con su vida (p. 121).

Though their lives are overshadowed by the larger historical events, the prime motivating factor of these people is immediate survival rather than ideological compromise. What appears to be an ambivalent stance regarding history is the result of molding historical facts to fit into the framework of folk tales. In fact, within this framework, history is superceded by genealogy:

> Braulio Tapia, natural de El Esquilmo (ahora, Skidmore) Texas, nació agosto de 1883; a Braulio lo crearon Juan Nepamuceno Celaya y una

tía materna, Barbarita Farias de Celaya, ambos de Goliad, Texas, donde el que sustituyó al Gral. Urrea hizo pasar por las armas al coronel Fanin y a otros insurgentes durante la rebelión de Texas en 1835–36 (p. 122).

Braulio's life is then defined in terms of his procreative activities. Subordinated to the elaboration of a micro family tree we encounter some facts concerning the loss of land to the Anglos:

> Braulio apareció en lo que es ahora Belken County en 1905 y se casó dos años después con Sóstenes Calvillo, hija única de don Práxedis Calvillo y Albinta Buenrostro. De este matrimonio nació Matilde; ésta se casó con don Jehú Vilches y tuvieron una hija, María Teresa de Jesús, que se casó con Roque Malacara. Al llegar a este [sic] última generación, las tierras y propiedades que la raza sostenía en la región ya pertenecían, en muy gran parte, a los bolillos; la raza que llegó a quedarse con tierra se podía dividir casi en dos partes: en primer lugar los más viejos que se firmaron encontra de los bolillos en trámites de sí-y-no (aunque también corrió la sangre . . .) (p. 122).

The second *revolucionario* to appear in this sketch is Evaristo Garrido who "nunca se casó pero *dejó sucesión*" (p. 122, emphasis mine). Leaving descendants, as we see in this and in other sketches, is a key factor in estimating an individual's worth. In fact it plays such an important role in the world view of the Chicano *pueblo* that the individual, beyond being responsible for his or her own family tree, must also be familiar with the ascendancy pattern of *all* members of the village as is vividly illustrated in the sketch called "Mesa redonda."

Through the use of multiple narrators, Hinojosa has added an extra dimension to his work without interrupting the tone of folk tale. Whether the narrator be a first-person identifiable narrator or a third-person unidentifiable one, all speak with the voice and authority of a village chronicler. The language of these accounts is stylized to evoke the oral tradition. It is as if the reader were listening to some *viejito* spinning a yarn. What Hinojosa has done in these *estampas* is to capture the essence of the oral chronicler. He has reconstructed his vocabulary, his linguistic structures, and even his breath groups. But above all he has given us a clear vision of the relation between oral history and cultural continuity. The merit of this work lies in the fact that the author has succeeded in recording folk anecdote in a manner which remains vital and interesting for the reader. By creating narrators who function from within rather than narrators who observe and report omnisciently from the outside Hinojosa has produced a work riddled with irony and humor which allows us to recognize the human foibles of his characters and which in turn permit us to empathize with them. Through the use of folk idiom and unreliable narrators he has written a work with a genuine folk flavor and tone. Although the various narrators' perceptions of life, particularly the failure to grasp the causal significance of historical events, seem naive to the sophisticated reader—thus the irony—the knowledge that we are working within a framework of folk reference allows us to accept and value that perspective.

The most adept use of irony occurs in the final collection of vignettes, the disconnected series of moments from the life of Rafa Buenrostro. As a group they reveal a compact mosaic of Chicano culture in conflict with the suprastructure. In the first collection of sketches we had already encountered Rafa, first as the young boy who is cured by Doña Panchita the *curandera* and then in the last sketch of that section as bartender at the Aquí Me Quedo bar. In that particular sketch the dialogue between the old men is followed by some comments made by a third-person unidentified narrator who could well be Rafa Buenrostro. As bartender he certainly occupies a vantage point from which to gather the wealth of information contained in these sketches. The reader would not be misguided to assume at this point that the unidentified narrator throughout the first section may have been Rafa, who with his name and his role as observer stands in striking contrast to the *pícaro* Malacara. Rafa could, in fact, be viewed as a mask for the author's alter ego.

The sketches of the last section differ from the previous ones in that they are much shorter and their style is more compact. But the impact of their content, achieved primarily through the masterful use of irony, is to the point and amazingly forceful. What Hinojosa exploits in these vignettes is the cultural conflict experienced by Rafa and his generation. Those born in this country of parents who fled the Mexican Revolution formed the first generation to be fully exposed to Anglo culture through public schools and the armed forces. The various vignettes dedicated to the topic of war serve to remind us that war has always been an institution which draws men from their provincial existence and dumps them in the other extreme, the modern world. The clash experienced by Rafa is captured by juxtaposing or meshing these two incongruous realities within the same symbolic system.

Hinojosa's insistence on humor throughout his work, even when touching upon the more sensitive circumstances which in some Chicano writers have produced strident cries of protest, attest to his deep understanding of human nature. It is a fact that in the most miserable of conditions of human degradation people will seek the cathartic effect of humor. The humor works because it comes from within rather than from the exterior. Particularly in the last section, Hinojas employs humor as a device for highlighting the pathos of the Chicano experience. As such, he is able to elicit from the reader a sense of understanding and empathy for his characters.

Another interesting feature of this work is the dedicatory "Nota." Here Hinojosa elaborates on his approach to writing. The "Nota" is a typical example of the modern trend toward self-reflecting literature which emphasizes to its readers that they should not forget that the world they have entered is one of fiction. This world may, in fact, reflect the conditions of the real world; nonetheless, it is an invented relity. In the process of inventing that reality, Hinojosa assures us that he begs no one's permission but writes and invents as he well pleases. Though he often makes references to a non-fictitious setting, El Valle del Río Bravo, he warns us from the start that the characters and incidents related within the pages of his book may or may not be drawn from reality. As an artist he is conscious that he possesses the *audacia* of which the Greeks spoke, the freedom to tell, to withhold, to distort, or to elaborate the truth as he perceives it within his private creative psyche. He reveals this stance to us, not in a patronizing manner, but rather in that same vein of gentle ribbing and humor which permeate the entire work:

> La gente que aparece y desaparece en estas estampas, así como los sucesos que en ellas surgen, bien pudieron ocurrir o no. El escritor escribe y trata de hacer lo que puede; eso de explicar es oficio de otra gente. Uno cumple con escribir sin mostrar la oreja (p. 15).

Thus, he introduces us to his world with a very deliberate distancing device designed to remind us that we are in fact in a world of fiction. In the second story, "Por esas cosas que pasan," the distancing devices multiply and take on a Borgean tone. In the first place the story itself is framed between two newspaper extracts taken from the *Klail City Enterprise News* (March 15, 1970). A footnote serves to clarify the second entry of this *cuento álbum*:

> Nota del editor: La grabación en cinta magnetofónica que hizo Balde Cordero fue enmendada sólo en lo que va de ortografía. Ciertamente, lo que importa aquí es el contenido no la forma. Marzo 16, 1970. Klail City Workhouse (p. 93).

Just as Borges pulls the reader's leg by meshing "authentic facts" with invented realities, Hinojosa invents documentation with all the trappings of authenticity in an effort to destroy that deeply rooted notion in the reader of the distinct line separating reality and illusion. The question this technique invariably raises in the mind of the reader is "Did this event 'really' happen?" and Hinojosa is saying, "Of course it happened. It happened for me as creator and it happened for you as witness of my creation." And in the end we are left with the message that the function of writing is to create new realities that are as valid as empirically perceived realities. The author comments further on his aesthetic credo in the first entry of "Vidas y Milagros": "Hasta la fecha ha habido sólo un Napoleón (o un Romeo o un Raskolnikov); los tres, en diversos sentidos, se asemejan y dónde empieza y termina la ficción del primero y dónde la de los dos últimos?" (p. 16). Thus he questions where one draws the line between the reality of a historical figure and that of fictitious characters, just as he questions where the writer draws the line between people he knows and people he invents to fill his fictional world. In the end, his method is the following: "El escritor, sin permiso de nadie, se sale a la calle y escoge de todo un poco" (p. 116). With regard to the originality of this procedure he declares that "La originalidad, metal difícil de asir como el azogue, quizá no toque tampoco en los hombres por aquello de que de barro venimos, etc. A fin de cuentas, otra vez, somos y no somos iguales como han reconocido tantos otros" (p. 116). The point that Hinojosa makes is that what matters most is his daring to venture into the creative realm and that it is from the common folk that he has received the inspiration for the creation of his characters. Who is to say that they are not worthy creations? Just in case there is some critic who believes otherwise, Hinojosa directs the following message to him:

> De paso, esa gente curiosa que se divierte con datos científicos y que tiene el afán de explicarlo todo, tiene todo derecho de vivir y de decir lo que se le ocurra. De su parte, por supuesto, esa gente debe dejar de andar jodiendo al público por la muy buena razón de que tanto se lleva el cántaro al agua ... (pp. 116–17).

Just as writers must be conscious of their medium and able to defend and justify their work, so too must critics be held accountable. Hinojosa's censure of the literary critic stems from the commonly held belief by writers that the work of art is an autonomous entity that needs no explanation beyond its existence. Whether or not we agree with him, it remains clear that we are dealing with a writer who believes in himself and the value of his work. This attitude of reflection and consciousness of his craft places *Estampas del Valle y otras obras* in the mainstream of contemporary fiction, allowing it to transcend the limits of the local-color sketch. Hinojosa's revival of *costumbrismo*, nevertheless, is apropos and justifiable, for it is important that Chicano writers claim the traditional forms of their cultural patrimony if they are to bridge the gap created by their historical circumstances.

UNIVERSITY OF NEW MEXICO

## Notes

[1] Luis María Brox, "Los límites del costumbrismo en *Estampas del Valle y otras obras*," *Mester*, V, 2 (April 1975), p. 101.

[2] Juan José Arreola, *La Feria* (México: Joaquín Mortiz, 1963). This novel has been described by Joseph Sommers as "a version of the human dimensions of Zapotlán, a *pueblo* in Southern Jalisco, which is portrayed sensitively. Here society is viewed with a perceptive skepticism tempered by a compassionate understanding of man's foibles." *After the Storm* (Albuquerque: University of New Mexico Press, 1968), p. 172.

[3] *Klail City y sus alrededores* has recently been reprinted by Editorial Justa under a new title, *Generaciones y semblanzas*, with an accompanying translation by Rosaura Sánchez.

[4] "The Southern Quality," in *The Literary Criticism of Marshall McLuhan*, Eugene McNamara, ed.(New York: McGraw-Hill Book Co., 1969), p. 188.

[5] Ibid., p. 204.

[6] Ibid.

[7] Sommers, *After the Storm*, p. 174.

[8] McLuhan, "The Southern Quality," p. 204.

[9] Rolando Hinojosa, *Estampas del Valle y otras obras* (Berkeley: Quinto Sol Publications, 1973), p. 16. All subsequent quotations are from this edition and page numbers will be indicated in parentheses in the body of the text.

# Literatura y sociedad:
# Análisis de *Generaciones y semblanzas*

Yolanda Guerrero

Para hacer un estudio crítico de una obra literaria tenemos que tomar en cuenta la relación entre literatura y realidad, ya que, como producto de trabajo humano, la obra es un producto histórico y social y, como signo, presenta y comenta una interpretación de un momento determinado de la historia. Por lo tanto, la realidad que se presenta en la obra estará determinada por la elección de material y la visión y conciencia de clase, o sea la ideología del autor. Será importante a la vez ver si la realidad presentada encuadra de manera dialéctica los conflictos y contradicciones de la época, o si el autor se limita a presentar una situación estática. Esta interpretación de la realidad tendrá que verse estudiando el texto y su contexto. Utilizando este acercamiento pasaremos a analizar *Generaciones y semblanzas* de Rolando Hinojosa.

Para ver la realidad que presenta la obra estudiaremos los varios niveles de significación que se dan en el texto. Al examinar el contenido recordemos que se compone de forma y substancia. La substancia viene a ser el argumento en el cual encontramos elementos históricos, sociales y económicos que enmarcan la realidad chicana. La organización de estos elementos, o sea la estructura y el desarrollo de la substancia en el texto, constituye la forma del contenido. Dentro de la forma se incluyen el estilo narrativo, la fragmentación y la organización del tiempo y del espacio. Como nos dice Frederic Jameson: "... form is itself but the working out of the content in the realm of the superstructure."[1] De manera que la forma y la substancia van juntas, ya que una es expresión de la otra.

Al examinar el contenido de *Generaciones y semblanzas* debemos estar conscientes de que esta novela está directamente ligada a *Estampas del Valle*. Las dos se complementan ya que existe una continuación o suplemento de información que se establece entre ambas. Al igual que *Estampas*, *Generaciones y semblanzas* se narra a través de una serie de recuerdos transmitidos como si fueran transcripciones de la tradición oral. Esta forma breve y fragmentada sirve para los relatos costumbristas y bosquejos breves donde se describe esquemáticamente un tipo o se recuerda un momento o circunstancia de la vida cotidiana, utilizando un lenguaje popular. Debido a la estrecha relación de contenido y forma, los recuerdos y la narración corta hecha por distintos personajes, dentro de distintos planos temporales, aparecen desconectados temporal y espacialmente. Por lo tanto, harán que la realidad misma presentada en la obra aparezca fragmentada. Según Hegel:

> The insufficiency of a work of art is not at all to be seen as the results of individual clumsiness, rather the insufficiency of the form derives from the insufficiency of the content.[2]

Esta insuficiencia, como veremos, se debe a un enfoque particular de la realidad chicana.

*Generaciones y semblanzas* está centrada en la realidad histórica, económica y social del chicano del Valle de Tejas, y cubre la trayectoria comprendida aproximadamente entre 1914-1973. Hinojosa nos entrega una visión sincrónica de la historia, puesto que pinta momentos de ella en forma fragmentada sin conexión y relación entre sí más allá de una simple conexión cronológica. Como ya dijimos, utiliza el estilo de la tradición oral transmitido por medio de diálogos y monólogos. Esto no excluye la presencia de largas narraciones anecdóticas, que, a pesar de ser ampliamente descriptivas, no logran "neutralizar" la fragmentación del texto. Es interesante ver que, aunque el autor nos da una idea del tiempo y de la secuencia de los acontecimientos, no hay, sin embargo, evidencia en el texto de un análisis profundo y crítico de las contradicciones y conflictos del proceso histórico. Esta forma de presentar la historia en la obra literaria lleva a una mera acumulación de eventos. Balzac nos dice lo siguiente sobre este tipo de novelística al referirse a una obra en particular:

> The entire novel consists of 200 pages of which 200 events are dealt with; nothing betrays the incompetence of the author more than the reshaping-up of facts.[3]

Al contrario, Lukács afirma:

> What matters is that we should reexperience the social and human motives which led men to think, feel and act just as they did in historical reality.[4]

Sin tratar de restar valor a la obra y teniendo presente que trabajamos con ficción, creemos que Hinojosa introduce eventos históricos como mero trasfondo de sus cuadros costumbristas y como escenario pintoresco dentro de las anécdotas de varios personajes.

El uso de la historia como trasfondo pintoresco se podrá apreciar mejor si vemos que la novela gira alrededor de tres eventos importantes: la Revolución mexicana, la segunda guerra mundial y la guerra de Korea. Aunque se dice que la Revolución mexicana llevó a la inmigración de doña Sóstenes y su hermana y las familias Barragán e Imás, este acontecimiento histórico sirve meramente para introducir la anécdota del desafío de dos hombres que se matan por los amores de Sóstenes. En una carta vemos a don Manuel tomando parte activa en la revolución. Aquí se nos dan trozos de una batalla en Puebla, en mayo de 1920, donde don Manuel participa en el asalto de un tren en las filas del General Sánchez, aliado de Obregón. Es de notar que esta alusión a un acto específico y verídico en la historia de la Revolución mexicana, ataque a un tren donde iba Venustiano Carranza en los cerros de Puebla en mayo de 1920, dirigido por un General Guadalupe Sánchez aliado de Obregón, se ha presentado dentro de un contexto epistolar. Rolando Hinojosa confirmó esto en una conferencia que dio en San Diego:

> Son unos hombres de caballería que van atacando el tren. Ese tren es donde va Don Venustiano Carranza. Son partes que están ocurriendo en la misma historia donde tomaron parte los chicanos.[5]

Este incidente vale sólo para revelar la participación de chicanos en la revolución. Más allá de una exaltación de la valentía y capacidad de liderazgo de don Manuel, el relato no permite analizar ni la revolución misma ni la motivación de don Manuel.

Al relatar la vida de Viola Barragán surge el asunto de la segunda guerra mundial, como la razón por la cual ponen a Viola y su esposo alemán en un campo de concentración inglés. Continúa diciendo que el siguiente año los trasladaron junto con trescientos alemanes e italianos a otro campo de concentración en la república de Africa del Sur. Todo esto sirve de decoración para situar a Viola en un ambiente exótico e internacional.

En la sección de Aureliano Mora hay una referencia a la segunda guerra mundial; nos dice que Ambrosio y otros muchachos pertenecieron a la segunda división Indian Head durante la invasión de Francia. Hay dos referencias menores en las cuales la segunda guerra mundial se utiliza como punto de referencia. La primera es para situar a "la palomilla" que se da de alta en el ejército, porque ven regresar a los veteranos de la guerra. Aquí este detalle histórico no es más que un punto de referencia. El otro es para describirnos un período en la vida de Epigmenio Salazar.

> Hace mucho tiempo, en la política internacional figuraba entre los partidarios fijos del Eje: especialmente allá por 1940-1942 cuando a los aliados no les iba tan bien. Su fe en la suerte del Eje fue tanta que titubeó entre ponerle Rommel o Kesselring a su nietecito.[6]

Lejos de analizar el significado de la guerra y del impacto que ésta tuvo en la comunidad chicana, el autor se limita a indicar que hubo chicanos con ideas nazis. La relación entre esta ideología fascista y los acontecimientos y la presencia sinarquista en el sudoeste no se consideran para nada.

El último período histórico que aparece es la guerra de Korea. En la sección North Ward/Korea el autor nos describe "las chambas chingonas que les tocó" que fue "la pesca de los muertos de los ríos después de las batallas de artillería" (pág. 71). En esta sección incluye los nombres de algunos compañeros que no regresaron de la guerra. Esta escena grotesca también es mera decoración, ya que no sirve para profundizar en el análisis de los personajes ni de su situación socio-histórica.

Estamos, por lo tanto, conscientes de eventos históricos monumentales pero no de su significado en el desarrollo de la historia chicana ni de su efecto en las vidas de estos individuos. Por medio de estas referencias históricas y las generaciones de personajes es evidente el fluir del tiempo, aunque los eventos no estén en orden cronológico. Así se observa a Jehú Malacara crecer hasta llegar a adulto, mientras cambia de un trabajo a otro hasta llegar a la universidad. A través de las genealogías familiares, vemos también la marcha del tiempo; esto se ve concretamente en los relatos de la familia Támez: Jovita y Joaquín se casan, don Salvador y Ernesto mueren, Bertita se casa y Joaquín y Jovita tienen cinco hijos. A pesar de los indicios del paso del tiempo, no se muestra aquí el proceso histórico donde existen contradicciones y conflictos que son la fuerza interna de la historia. Esto sólo se ve muy esquemáticamente planteado en el desarrollo de Klail City. En la sección de doña Sóstenes, Echevarría nos dice que pavimentaron "allá por el '17 o el '18" (pág. 15). Sabemos que existe una vía de ferrocarril, porque en varias instancias menciona el tren que se usa para llevar los productos agrícolas de la región. También sabemos por la carta de Josefa Guzmán que en 1920 llegaron unos anglos tratando de sembrar toronjas y naranjas:

> Por aquí cayeron unos bolillos diciendo que van a sembrar naranjos y toronjos. Les dije que así que volvieras del otro lado que hablaran contigo. Uno de ellos se defiende bastante bien en español, y el otro, un chaparrito de pelo colorado, no hace más que sonreír y menear la cabeza. Te diré que como han vuelto dos otras veces y ellos con las mismas, pues yo también y de ahí no salimos.[7]

En *Estampas del Valle* nos damos cuenta que perdieron la tierra:

> Vuelva a Klail por un rato y se da cuenta que ha perdido el terreno que había comprado. Doña Josefa, a pesar de su fuerza, no le llegaba a la punta de los pies al papelaje que le encajaron los land developers.[8]

El autor nos ha dado los hechos esquemáticamente sin profundizar en las causas ni las contradicciones que causan tales hechos. Al ver la historia del Valle, encontramos que en 1902 el Reclamation Act permitió el uso de dineros federales para el riego. Esto, junto con la terminación del ferrocarril St. Louis-Brownsville-Mexican Rail line en 1904, atrajo a especuladores que formaron compañías para desplegar e irrigar la tierra para la agricultura comercial. Aquí es donde mucha gente perdió sus tierras por no tener sus papeles en orden o por el sistema burocrático de los anglos. El relato de Hinojosa plantea pues el problema de la tierra a un nivel superficial sin analizar a fondo las oposiciones socio-económicas que se dieron en el Valle de Tejas a principios del siglo.

Los cuadros costumbristas de Hinojosa también revelan una visión fragmentada y parcial de la realidad económica. En parte se limita a nombrar los empleos y oficios de la gente. Las personas no sólo se conocen por su nombre sino también por su oficio: Enedino Broca López, el locutor, y el tío Briones, el hielero. Por medio de esta descripción de empleos, podría establecerse una jerarquía ocupacional. Es interesante hacer notar que en la última sección el autor inserta unos párrafos dedicados a compañeros anglo-sajones de la escuela donde también nos da información socio-económica. Por ser los únicos párrafos dedicados a la presencia anglo-sajona, esta sección aparece inconexa y parece estar sobrante en el libro. El autor, al incluir una sección separada para ellos, hace una distinción étnico-cultural y después económica. Por esta razón obliga al lector a ver como separadas la jerarquía de los anglos y la de los chicanos cuando en realidad la economía del Valle es una. En la jerarquía de los bolillos aparecen, a nivel más alto, los ricos dueños de los modos de producción, como las compañías agrícolas y Suggs Manufacturing Co. Tenemos a los comerciantes, como el dueño del banco y los dueños de la tierra, en el siguiente nivel. Luego se presentan los profesionistas, como los doctores, dentistas y abogados. En el nivel más bajo incluye a los bolillos con menos tierra y a los bolillos urbanos "no tan ricos aunque tampoco pobretones como la raza" (pág. 171). Las implicaciones de esta estructura quedan en el aire sin conectarse al mundo donde en el nivel más alto encontramos a los dueños de las tierras que son las familias viejas Leguizamón, Buenrostro y Vilches y los comerciantes urbanos dueños de tiendas y la ladrillera. Los profesionistas como el doctor, farmacéutico y contador están en el siguiente nivel, pero es de importancia hacer notar que algunas de las personas en este nivel vinieron de y estudiaron en México estableciéndose al llegar a U.S.A. como la clase media. En el siguiente nivel, encontramos a los pequeños comerciantes, como los dueños de las cantinas, lechería, el circo y la barbería. En la parte más baja de este nivel, encontramos al hielero, dulcero y afilador de tijeras. El proletariado compone el siguiente nivel: los empleados en la fábrica de botones, cantinas y tiendas. Los trabajadores agrícolas migrantes también caben dentro de este grupo. La interaccíon de los dos mundos—el sajón y el chicano—y la dependencia económica chicana quedan así reducidos a brochazos pintorescos y casi insignificantes.

El autor ofrece una descripción larga de la situación del trabajador migrante, al narrar las muchas experiencias vividas por los campesinos. Vemos cómo se inicia el ciclo migratorio con el contratista de las compañías agrícolas. Las familias se ven en su rutina de constante migración donde tienen que cerrar con tablas las ventanas de sus casas y decidir con qué troquero van a salir. Vemos todo el ciclo de la cosecha de algodón que dura desde junio hasta agosto. De agosto a diciembre se van al norte a pizcar betabel, pepino u otras cosechas. En diciembre vuelven al sur a pizcar las naranjas y toronjas que "estiran de los árboles desde diciembre hasta marzo y si hay suerte y no hiela, hasta abril" (pág. 87). Se ve el viaje desde la perspectiva de los troqueros y de los trabajadores hasta la desgracia del accidente de los Múzquiz de Bascom. Vemos que los hijos de los campesinos también toman parte en este ciclo y que están acostumbrados a cambiar de escuela. La vida del campesino migrante es pues una de viajes, pláticas, escaseces y malas viviendas. Estos eventos objetivos, sin embargo, no conducen ni a un análisis de la situación ni a una profundización en la interioridad de los personajes. Son todos figuras pintorescas o meros esqueletos de personajes.

Al señalar el trato que recibe el trabajador, Hinojosa incluye no sólo el abuso de las compañías sino también el de los contratistas y el de la gente a los que se enfrenta el trabajador todos los días. Es interesante ver que aquí interviene el autor-narrador para señalar que también existe el anglo-sajón paternalista que ayuda a los chicanos: "una gente que no conocía y cuyo idioma ignoraba" (pág. 113). Aquí la intervención del autor-narrador le permite agradecer este apoyo, dando lugar así a un trozo adulón e irreal.

Hemos analizado el intento del autor de representar la realidad chicana a nivel histórico y económico y hemos llegado a la conclusión de que si bien capta algunos rasgos esenciales, la novela ofrece una visión bastante limitada. Hemos visto que la historia aparece como trasfondo pintoresco y que a pesar de la acumulación de anécdotas y episodios, el tiempo novelesco es estático puesto que el recuento fragmentado de costumbres y tradiciones impide elaborar la interconexión de estos eventos y revelar su importancia para los seres allí descritos. ¿Qué visión se ofrece entonces de la cultura chicana? Cabría entonces preguntarnos: ¿Qué es cultura? ¿Es la cultura el recuento de costumbres y tradiciones o es más que esto? Según Amilcar Cabral, cultura abarca la totalidad de experiencias y contradicciones de una sociedad. Dice así:

> Culture, the fruit of history, reflects at every moment the material, the spiritual reality of society, of man-the-individual and of man-the social-being, faced with conflicts which set him against nature and the exigencies of common life. From this we see that all culture is composed of essential and secondary elements, of strengths and weaknesses, of factors of progress and factors of stagnation or regression.[9]

De manera que la cultura no es sólo una mera serie de costumbres y tradiciones, sino que es un conjunto de elementos, algunos progresistas, dinámicos, creativos y sensibles a la experiencia dentro del proceso histórico y otros reaccionarios y regresivos. La cultura, por lo tanto, no se puede reducir a etnicidad o nacionalidad sino que es un producto social que se da dentro de determinado contexto socio-histórico; es síntesis de balances y soluciones en la cual la sociedad trata de resolver los conflictos; es una realidad social independiente del color de la piel y de la forma de los ojos.[10] La realidad cultural que presenta Hinojosa no pasa de ser una mezcla de rasgos superficiales así como la realidad histórica se limita a la acumulación de eventos.

La acumulación de costumbres descritas se podrá apreciar mejor si enfocamos en la presentación de algunos personajes e incidentes específicos. Lo distintivo de estas costumbres se da a conocer a través de la relación social bolillo-chicano, quedando contrapuestas la cultura anglo-sajona y la cultura chicana. Se observa esta contraposición al ver los entierros y cementerios de los chicanos y los de los anglos. Los entierros de los chicanos llegan a ser toda una exhibición y espectáculo para la gente curiosa, como vemos en los entierros de Bruno Cano, de Epigmenio Salazar y de Fidencio Anciso, "el que enterraron parado" (pág. 131). También se observa una diferencia marcada entre el entretenimiento del chicano y del bolillo que se establece en "Voces del Barrio" de *Estampas del Valle*, y se continúa en *Generaciones y semblanzas*.

> Los bolillos (como casi nunca salen de noche) no van al parque a andar o platicar. La raza, sí, y como el aire es libre, el que no se divierte es porque no quiere.[11]

Esta diferencia está relacionada con la situación socio-económica, porque la mayoría de los chicanos no tienen los recursos económicos para otro tipo de pasatiempo, pero en la novela aparece sólo como rasgo cultural sin que se haga la conexión social y económica. Estas costumbres funcionan como mero trasfondo pintoresco y vemos que el autor ve la cultura como equivalente a etnicidad sin tomar en cuenta que es producto de una sociedad dentro de determinado contexto socio-histórico.

Tenemos en la novela, por lo tanto, una variedad de costumbres unidas sólo por el hecho de que se le atribuyen a la misma población, pero fragmentadas en el sentido de que no tienen un papel importante para el desarrollo de una trama en la novela; tampoco se presentan como parte de conflictos y contradicciones que tienen causas y llevan a cambios mayores.

Dada la forma de relatos breves y fragmentados que el autor ha escogido, los personajes se desarrollan superficialmente, a través de pincelazos que aparecen y se borran. Al usar esta técnica, resulta imposible captar la esencia de la cultura dentro de la novela ya que estos personajes supuestamente típicos, no captan la unidad dialéctica entre tipo e individuo; o sea, que no aparecen como individuos y representantes de su clase a la misma vez. En la novela, la descripción costumbrista toma el lugar de una explicación de la motivación, que hace al personaje actuar de determinada manera. Los personajes aparecen entonces caracterizados por rasgos unilaterales, rasgos fijos, inmutables a través del tiempo, como si fuesen representantes de una cultura estática y sin cambio.

La novela documenta superficialmente la vida chicana del Valle de Tejas a través de una visión fragmentada de eventos históricos, condiciones económicas y costumbres por medio de un collage de anécdotas que dan cierta información sin contradicciones o conflictos. En la sección "Con el Rápido-Galindo" el autor-narrador interviene en la obra para aclarar el objetivo novelístico, diciendo que intenta "hacer memoria a cierta gente que figuró en una de las vidas del autor" (pág. 99). Continúa utilizando una metáfora para comprobar su propósito de documentar, al comparar el novelar con:

> ... la reconstrucción de una casa vieja que se quiera salvar, mejor, que se debe salvar; un poco aquí, un poco allá y todo hecho con aplicación ... El propósito es uno muy personal: el que escribe esto (así como los que escriben otras cosas) teme olvidar algo que en un tiempo fue muy importante para él ... El que esto escribe también cree mucho en eso de cambiar de dirección y, quizás por eso, también cree que al hacerlo ha recobrado algo que, impensable e insensiblemente iba gastando; el recuerdo de ser quién, qué y de dónde es.[12]

Es, en efecto, la novela un intento de reconstruir recuerdos donde el narrador se ha limitado sólo a recordar sin dar explicación ni reflejar un análisis de los hechos. En *Estampas del Valle* Hinojosa nos dice:

> El escritor escribe y trata de hacer lo que puede; eso de explicar es oficio de otra gente. Uno cumple con escribir sin mostrar la oreja.[13]

En un artículo sobre la obra, Luis María Brox nos dice que "el autor se autolimita al rechazar la explicación como algo ajeno a la función de escribir"[14]; esto es precisamente lo que ocurre en *Generaciones y semblanzas.* Como él mismo lo dice, no ha hecho más que incluir "lo bueno y lo malo o lo que salga" (pág. 99) y "un poco de aquí y un poco de allá" (pág. 101), produciendo así, un revoltijo de relatos, mecánicamente unidos, sin lograr crear una tensión novelística que refleje a fondo nuestras contradicciones y conflictos sociales y culturales.

UNIVERSITY OF CALIFORNIA, SAN DIEGO

# Notas

[1] Frederic Jameson, *Marxism and Form* (Princeton: Princeton University Press, 1971), pág. 329.
[2] Ibid.
[3] Cita de Balzac sobre la novela *Leo* de Latouche, en Georg Lukács, *The Historical Novel* (Atlantic Highlands, N.J.: Humanities Press, 1978), pág. 42.
[4] Ibid.
[5] Esta conferencia se llevó a cabo el 16 de mayo de 1978 en la Universidad de California, San Diego.
[6] Rolando Hinojosa, *Generaciones y semblanzas* (Berkeley: Editorial Justa Publications, 1977), págs. 77 & 79. Se cita siempre de esta edición.
[7] Ibid., pág. 85.
[8] Rolando Hinojosa, *Estampas del Valle* (Berkeley: Quinto Sol Publications, 1973), págs. 123-124.
[9] Amilcar Cabral, *Return to the Source: Selected Speeches* (New York: Monthly Review Press, 1973), págs. 50-51.
[10] Ibid., pág. 51.
[11] *Generaciones y semblanzas*, pág. 45.
[12] Ibid., pág. 101.
[13] *Estampas del Valle*, pág. 15.
[14] Luis María Brox, "Los límites del costumbrismo en *Estampas del Valle*," *Mester*, Vol. 5, No. 2, abril 1975, pág. 101.

## B. Rudolfo Anaya

## Ilusión y realidad en la obra de Rudolfo Anaya

*José Monleón*

Al hablar de literatura chicana se subentiende que existe una producción literaria particular, con características específicas que la diferencian de otras producciones literarias. La crítica ha llevado a cabo grandes esfuerzos por tratar de identificar o enmarcar el "espacio" chicano, con resultados no siempre convincentes. El problema parte de que lo chicano no contiene una unidad geopolítica que permita una fácil definición.

Una tendencia general ha consistido en hacer resaltar aquellos puntos que refuerzan el supuesto de una experiencia chicana homogénea. Esta actitud ha condicionado fuertemente tanto la metodología crítica como las conclusiones derivadas del análisis, pues no toma en consideración las connotaciones particulares de cada autor. Como es sabido, existen grandes diferencias sociales, políticas, económicas e incluso lingüísticas entre las distintas regiones del suroeste, entre, por ejemplo, California y Nuevo México, Los Angeles y San Antonio, el Valle Imperial y Tierra Amarilla.

No pretendo negar la existencia de una literatura chicana con ciertas características comunes, sino simplemente apuntar que el término chicano, en este sentido, es utilizado a un cierto nivel de abstracción, sin tener en cuenta una realidad más compleja y matizada. El resultado de esta simplificación ha sido, en muchas ocasiones, una excesiva esquematización o una dependencia analítica en los valores culturales, preocupados los críticos en hacer sobresalir verdades humanas esenciales o modelos arquetípicos.

El caso de Rudolfo Anaya no es una excepción. Su obra ha sido considerada, en general, como expresión mítica de valores culturales chicanos. Esta postura conduce a una encrucijada contradictoria un tanto difícil de resolver: la pretensión de que la literatura chicana es, al mismo tiempo, única y universal. Unica, en tanto que culturalmente posee unos signos propios. Universal, en la medida en que esos mismos signos se esquematizan, se despojan de su especificidad—es decir, de su chicanismo—para revelar la esencia universal.

Toda obra artística hace referencia a la experiencia humana, y en ese sentido se la puede considerar general. Pero si de lo que se trata es de analizar la producción chicana en particular, el crítico debe acudir, precisamente, a las connotaciones específicas de su producción. Es decir, a las coordenadas históricas concretas de donde surge un texto. De ahí la necesidad tanto de rescatar extensamente los antecedentes literarios históricos como de sistemáticamente emplazar cada obra en su correspondiente contexto.

I

Rudolfo Anaya ha publicado, hasta la fecha, tres novelas: *Bless Me, Ultima*,[1] *Heart of Aztlán*,[2] y *Tortuga*.[3] Para los propósitos de este análisis, voy a abordar las tres obras en conjunto, es decir como una unidad que presenta una evolución conceptual complementaria. Detalles concretos en los textos justifican esta decisión:

—La familia Chávez de *HOA* abandona, al principio de la novela, el pueblo de Guadalupe, lugar donde se desarrolla la acción de *BMU*. Al igual que la familia Márez, son propietarios de un pequeño terreno.

—La época narrativa de *BMU* es 1945; *HOA* transcurre aproximadamente entre 1955 y 1957.[4] Es decir, hay un lapso de 10 años. Benjie es unos diez años mayor que Antonio.

—Tortuga, el personaje, ha quedado paralizado como consecuencia de un accidente reciente. Al ingresar al hospital lleva su mano izquierda vendada. Benjie, al final de *HOA*, es herido en su mano izquierda, cae de la torre de agua y queda paralítico.

—Tortuga recibe la guitarra azul que le deja Crispín, personaje de *HOA* que efectivamente posee una guitarra azul.

Estos son algunos de los puntos de conexión que existen entre las tres novelas. No pretendo afirmar que son exactamente "continuaciones", sino simplemente señalar la presencia de un cierto nivel de complementación. Conforman, en cierta medida, una especie de trilogía donde problemas básicos planteados en una novela se desarrollan con posterioridad en otra. Así, una lectura global facilita la comprensión de aspectos particulares al mismo tiempo que permite observar la trayectoria ideológica de la producción de Anaya. Trayectoria ésta que, como vamos a ver, se caracteriza por una progresiva eliminación del contexto. Se trata de un proceso a través del cual un conflicto con claras connotaciones sociales propuesto en *BMU*, es desarrollado en *HOA* y resuelto, en última instancia, al nivel individual en *Tortuga*.

## II

Uno de los propósitos básicos de este trabajo es el de situar la obra de Anaya dentro de su contexto. Para ello me parece muy importante configurar el espacio narrativo, en el sentido de que éste va a determinar el tipo de obra que se está analizando. Para Elaine Johnson, por ejemplo, "the space which Antonio inhabits ... is a symbolic receptacle, the vessel wherein his cultural heritage is contained."[5] Esta premisa lleva a interpretar la novela alegórica o poéticamente, como la misma Johnson reconoce: "*Bless Me, Ultima* is to a great extent allegorical. . . . Thus the reader is constantly confronted with symbols." De ahí también que las deducciones e implicaciones, llevadas al terreno simbólico, despojen a la obra de la especificidad a la que antes me refería:

> Antonio Márez y Luna's odyssey is a search for his own identity, a spiritual journey which in the course of the narrative is developed into an *allegory for the whole Chicano experience*. Anaya is *forced by the demands of his symbolic structure to depict prostitution stereotypically without regard for its social context*.[6]

Toda obra conlleva, a un cierto nivel, un valor simbólico, por lo menos en tanto que ejemplifica situaciones. Pero, como se desprende de la cita anterior, la presunción de un carácter simbólico fuerza una determinada perspectiva analítica. ¿Es, en efecto, *BMU* una alegoría de la experiencia chicana? La omisión del contexto social, en el caso de la prostituta, ¿se debe a esa estructura simbólica? ¿O se trata, por el contrario, de una obra con marco realista?[7]

Anaya reconoce en varias ocasiones la importancia que para él tuvo la ubicación geográfica de su narrativa, el descubrimiento del marco contextual—aunque lo exprese en términos telúricos—: "The discovery of place was very important to me, and very crucial to the writing of *Bless Me, Ultima* and *Heart of Aztlán*."[8]

Obviamente, en *HOA* el marco físico no deja lugar a dudas: se trata de Barelas, barrio de Albuquerque, que si bien en ese nivel simbólico/ejemplar al que antes aludía, podría representar a cualquier barrio, el hecho es que se trata de uno en particular. En *Tortuga*, prácticamente toda la acción se desarrolla en el interior de un hospital, y en este caso sí se puede hablar de intento alegórico. Quedaría por determinar *BMU*, punto de partida de la "trilogía" y elemento clave para la comprensión de la evolución de la producción de Anaya. Roberto Cantú dice al respecto:

> Por otra parte, si estudiamos la estructura novelística en su conjun-

to, encontraremos que Anaya ha enmarcado su obra dentro de una dimensión tempo-espacial de carácter mítico. ¿En qué lugar o lugares se configuran los acontecimientos de la novela? En el pueblo de Guadalupe, en las Pasturas, o en el Puerto de los Luna (de obvia asociación con el Tepeyac, el Jardín del Edén, etc.). ¿Cuándo ocurre la acción? Se supone que durante la segunda gran guerra, o sea cerca de 1944. No obstante, esta guerra es el encasillamiento temporal que pone a la obra en nuestro tiempo, y sirve solamente para subrayar el mal que está acabando con el hombre; su función es meramente simbólica y subsidiaria al tema maniqueo de la obra, puesto que, en verdad, el pueblo de Guadalupe está al margen de la historia.... Lo curioso es que dentro de este mundo pastoril, encontramos también el vicio ... y el crimen.[9]

El punto de partida de Cantú es el de entender el pueblo de Guadalupe como un escenario puramente literario, como una invención mítica. Se trataría de un micro-cosmos cerrado, aislado y ajeno a toda realidad histórica. Sin embargo, una mirada al mapa de Nuevo México en seguida revela que los nombres que Anaya utiliza—salvo pequeñas variantes—no son inventados, sino que pertenecen a la realidad. Sin pretender establecer una relación de identidad absoluta, el hecho es que existe un pueblo de Guadalupe, no muy lejos de Pastura—donde nació Anaya—y de Puerto de Luna.[10] Me atrevería incluso a afirmar que el ficticio Guadalupe es en la realidad Santa Rosa, lugar donde se crió Anaya y que corresponde con bastante exactitud a la descripción narrativa.[11]

Así pues, debe ponerse en duda el valor puramente imaginativo—y, por tanto, simbólico—del marco novelístico. Cuando Johnson señala que "Antonio's community is surrounded by water, a detail that suggests that the world before us, on a figurative level, is isolated and closed," no toma en cuenta que Santa Rosa, en la realidad, se encuentra prácticamente rodeado de agua, pues lo contornan varios ríos y un lago. Su aislamiento no es sólo metafórico, sino que tiene su correspondencia real, y de contener algún valor figurativo éste habría que entenderlo como expresión de las condiciones peculiares del desarrollo histórico de Nuevo México. No hay que olvidar que, desde el asentamiento de los primeros colonos en el siglo XVII hasta bien entrado el siglo XX, partes del Estado mantuvieron infraestructuras bastante precarias. La aridez del terreno, grandes distancias, pobres medios de comunicación, etc., hicieron que florecieran pequeños y *aislados* pueblos autosuficientes allí donde había tierra irrigada. Para Clark Knowlton, "the feeling of sociopsychological distinctiveness and isolation still persists,"[12] y Alfredo Jiménez Núñez, en su investigación antropológica de Río Arriba, encuentra también en la actualidad residuos de ese aislamiento.[13]

## III

¿Se encuentra Guadalupe fuera de la historia? ¿Situar la novela en 1945 es acaso—como indica Cantú—simplemente una manera de "poner la obra en nuestro tiempo"? Todo lo contrario: el momento histórico es fundamental para la comprensión de la problemática que plantea Anaya.

A partir de la segunda guerra mundial, la fachada que Estados Unidos ofrece al mundo es una de prosperidad, con aumentos importantes del producto nacional bruto y del ingreso *per capita*. Es una etapa también de expansión de la industria norteamericana, con la formación de las grandes empresas transnacionales y el desarrollo de la política consumista. Sin embargo, frente a la imagen de abundancia difundida por los medios de comunicación, la realidad se ofrecía menos eufórica y más compleja. Si las grandes corporaciones representaron el esqueleto sustentador de la economía, su control descansó en las manos de un pequeño sector social: en 1956, por ejemplo, el 95% de la población no era propietaria de acciones. El rápido crecimiento de estas empresas no provocó una mayor distribución de la riqueza, sino, por el contrario, su concentración en las clases privilegiadas.[14] El dato es significativo, pues pone de relieve el desequilibrio existente en la estructura social, con una marcada desigualdad en la distribución de la riqueza.

Así, el país más rico del mundo esconde en sus entrañas la otra cara de la moneda. Mientras los autobuses de turistas recorren las mansiones de Beverly Hills, el 25% de la población califica como "pobre", según los estándares oficiales. La mayoría de esta población se encuentra recluida en ghettos urbanos o en áreas rurales, y comprende casi en su totalidad a las "minorías étnicas".

Es en esta situación de las estructuras socio-económicas del país donde hay que buscar el origen de los numerosos conflictos que poblaron los años posteriores a la segunda guerra mundial y que Anaya recoge en su producción.

El caso de Nuevo México—si bien inserto en las corrientes generales del país—tiene sus propias connotaciones particulares. De especial importancia es, en este sentido, el desarrollo de la industria militar. Este sector de la economía nacional se convirtió en uno de los elementos más influyentes en la configuración y dirección del país. Ya Eisenhower, en su discurso de despedida de la Presidencia, se vio obligado a reconocer la situación: "... he urged Americans to 'guard against the acquisition of unwarranted influence by the military-industrial complex."[15] El Pentágono se convirtió en el principal cliente de las industrias aeronáuticas, electrónicas y automovilísticas. Numerosos altos oficiales de las tres ramas del ejército pasaron a ocupar puestos ejecutivos en el sector privado, creándose así una poderosa élite industrial-militar que canalizó la orientación de la producción del país.

En la segunda mitad de nuestro siglo, Nuevo México va a ver radicalmente alterada su estructura socio-económica, debido principalmente a la influencia de ese sector industrial-militar que, desde la selección de Los Alamos como centro de investigación nuclear, va a expandirse notoriamente en todo el estado. Para todos los efectos, va a sufrir de golpe y con retraso los resultados de un rápido proceso de industrialización que incluye una modificación de la configuración de la población al nivel racial y ocupacional. Thomas R. López, Jr. señala, por ejemplo, que muchos pobladores mexicanos habían tenido muy poco contacto con anglos hasta la segunda guerra,[16] y Jiménez Núñez nota que "a partir de los años 40, Española y los pueblos y aldeas próximos han pasado de una economía agrícola a depender principalmente de un salario por trabajos no agrícolas."[17]

La época de la segunda guerra mundial, por tanto, no aparecería como algo casual, sino como reflejo de un momento histórico de transición, como expresión del origen de una serie de conflictos. A partir de los años 40, los pequeños pueblos agrícolas autosuficientes pasan a depender de unas nuevas fuerzas productoras, y sus viejos esquemas de relaciones sociales se ven amenazados. Las dos primeras novelas de Anaya van a seguir la evolución histórica de las capas rurales mexicanas de Nuevo México durante la década del 45 al 55: crisis en *BMU* y emigración a la ciudad en *HOA*. En *Tortuga*, como veremos, el planteamiento es distinto.

En cualquier caso, lo que sí hay que dejar establecido es que *BMU* tiene una concordancia con la realidad muy concreta, y que su espacio literario no ocupa lugares totalmente imaginarios sino que hace referencia a coordenadas precisas.

## IV

Para numerosos críticos, la literatura chicana debe ser aproximada desde una perspectiva arquetípica.[18] Ello se justificaría, por lo menos en parte, por la abundante presencia de elementos míticos y mitológicos en las obras. Sin embargo, los mitos, como cualquier otra estructura literaria, tienen una función y una historicidad, y es dentro de esa concreción que deben ser examinados. Cuando, por ejemplo, Vernon E. Lattin indica que "American literature has traditionally reflected what Annette Kolodny calls America's oldest and most cherished fantasy: a dream of the harmony between man and nature, a dream repeatedly betrayed as the land is exploited"[19] no toma en consideración que la idea de la armonía terrenal frustrada no es únicamente un sueño americano, sino precisamente uno de los mitos literarios más recurrentes y universales—véase sin más la Biblia—. El tópico de que existió un pasado mejor que el presente ha persistido en muchas obras o tendencias literarias, y en cada caso, por supuesto, ha venido a reflejar una ideología y unos problemas particulares. Así, por ejemplo, al indicar Egla Morales que el uso de la mitología india por parte de los autores chicanos significa "un intento deliberado de identificación con el pasado pre-hispánico en que el hombre vivía donde pertenecía y era parte armónica del ambiente",[20] lo que la autora de hecho revela es su propia ideología, al mitificar o idealizar a su vez la realidad conflictiva de la América precolombina. El resultado es un análisis un tanto tautológico.

En este mismo sentido, la crítica ha puesto demasiado énfasis, sobre todo en la que a *BMU* se refiere, en el concepto de "paraíso perdido". Se parte de la idea—véanse citas anteriores—de que esta novela es una recreación del jardín edénico. Roberto Cantú no tendrá más remedio que notar la presencia del "mal" en ese mundo armónico, pues, en efecto, el universo narrativo es conflictivo—ya antes señalé que Guadalupe se apoya en un marco realista y no en uno alegórico—. ¿Cuál es, pues, el elemento subyacente en la obra que alimenta este concepto que observa la crítica? ¿Qué sustenta la idea de paraíso perdido?

En una ocasión, Rudolfo Anaya indica que "in speaking about the landscape I would prefer to use the Spanish word *la tierra*, simply because it conveys a deeper relationship between man and his place."[21] La observación es muy indicativa del problema de base. La relación profunda del hombre, dice Anaya en su libre juego bilingüe, no es con el paisaje—palabra que mejor traduciría *landscape*—, sino con la tierra. Diferenciación ésta que vale la pena hacer resaltar, pues, quizás indirecta or simbólicamente, asume los términos del conflicto nuevomexicano de las últimas decadas. La tierra es fuente fundamental de riqueza y sustento para las sociedades rurales del Estado de donde se nutre el universo narrativo de Anaya.

Así, la relación epifánica refleja también unas condiciones socio-económicas. El poco de "tierra" que Clemente Chávez se lleva de Guadalupe a Albuquerque puede tener todo un valor metafórico, pero detrás del gesto se esconde también la verdadera tragedia: la pérdida real de esa tierra como factor causante de la diáspora.

Ya desde la conquista de Nuevo México en 1848, se puede observar una constante expropiación de tierras pertenecientes a mexicanos por parte de los norteamericanos. Aprovechando trucos legales, la falta de títulos de propiedad, el no reconocimiento de las mercedes, etc., la población mexicana es poco a poco despojada de sus posesiones.

*BMU* hace referencia a esta primera etapa. Gregorio Márez se ha visto obligado a abandonar su tierra, su llano y su vida de vaquero, para refugiarse en Guadalupe y trabajar en la construcción de una carretera.

> They were the first cowboys in a wild and desolate land which they took from the Indians. Then the railroad came. The barbed wire came.... The people were uprooted. They looked around one day and found themselves closed in. The freedom and land and sky they had known was gone. Those people could not live without freedom and so they packed up and moved west. They became migrants. (BMU p. 119)

> "Ay, but those were beautiful years," my father continued. "The llano was still virgin, there was grass as high as the stirrups of a grown horse, there was rain — and then the tejano came and built his fences, the railroad came, the roads..." (BMU p. 51)

HOA recoge el mismo tema:

> "Because we lost the land," one of the men answered, "A new way of life and a new set of laws pushed us out of the land grants. We lost las mercedes and the communal lands." (HOA p. 103)

> "Somehow we began to lose the land a long time ago. The tejano came, the barbed wire came, the new laws came." (HOA p. 5)

Conviene hacer notar que los elementos que se nos presentan como responsables de esa "tierra perdida" son típicos de una sociedad industrial: ferrocarril, alambre de púas, carreteras... Con ellos, y con las nuevas leyes, la tierra se convierte de expansión indefinida en parcelamiento. Es decir, en propiedad privada: es la primera señal de intrusión de la sociedad capitalista del XIX.

Este proceso, sin embargo, no se detiene ahí. Al contrario, como ya he señalado, se intensifica a partir de la segunda guerra:

> This retreat of the Spanish American from the plains still continues. It can be seen in the areas just south and east of Las Vegas, N.M., where a number of villages such as La Liendre, Chaparito and Trujillo are being squeezed by neighboring Anglo-Texan owned ranches.[22]

Son dos factores simultáneos los que dan origen, en Nuevo México, a las transformaciones fundamentales de su estructura. Por un lado, la ya indicada aparición del complejo industrial-militar, que sirve de atracción de mano de obra. Por otro lado, la progresiva presión que sobre las pequeñas comunidades rurales ejercen el Gobierno Federal y los grandes intereses agrícolas. En realidad, en todo el país se puede observar una concentración de la tierra en manos de corporaciones agrícolas ligadas al capital industrial.[23] En Nuevo México, el National Forest Service se convierte en uno de los mayores propietarios — junto a los intereses agrícolas tejanos — y con él se va a enfrentar directamente, por ejemplo, el movimiento de Reies Tijerina. Así, "from subsistance farmers they (Spanish Americans) are becoming unskilled industrial workers."[24]

Esta última problemática asoma en *BMU*: es el caso de los hermanos de Antonio, que emigran a Las Vegas. Pero es desarrollada en extensión en *HOA*. La familia Chávez—en cierta medida, extensión de los Márez—, inmersa ya en un sistema capitalista, se ve obligada a vender sus posesiones para cubrir unas deudas, mudarse a Albuquerque y trabajar en el ferrocarril.[25]

A partir de aquí, sin embargo, Anaya empieza a ofrecer una visión distinta del contexto. Si al referirse a épocas anteriores, las causas de la migración y expropiación quedan explícitamente relacionadas con la invasión y la sociedad industrial norteamericana, a la hora de señalar las causas inmediatas Anaya evade el problema:

> "You did not fail us, Clemente. It was Moises who squandered away the ranch after el abuelo Chavez died. He drank and gambled away everything the Chavez family had worked for." (*HOA* p. 5)

Es un primer síntoma de la trayectoria de eliminación del contexto que indicaba al principio de este trabajo. La cita pone de relieve una internalización de las razones que provocaron la pérdida de la tierra. Las causas no se encuentran ya objetivadas en un proceso histórico, sino asumidas por la propia familia. La culpa reside en el seno de los Chávez y no en las profundas presiones socio-económicas de la segunda mitad del siglo XX. Esta idea cobrará mayor relevancia en *Tortuga*.

En cualquier caso, lo que sí queda en evidencia es que el mundo que sustenta el concepto de "paraíso perdido", de un Aztlán idílico anterior a la diáspora, tiene estrechas relaciones con la "tierra perdida" y las subsiguientes migraciones a los centros industriales.[26]

## V

Visto este panorama, es lógico que la ciudad—foco del desarrollo industrial—adquiera una importante funcionalidad en la narrativa de Anaya. Es, por supuesto, el tema central de *HOA*. Pero los términos del conflicto son expuestos, una vez más, en *BMU*.

La primera escena de esta novela ocurre bajo el puente: Lupito, que ha regresado loco de la guerra, es muerto a tiros. *BMU* representa un primer paso, la exposición de la crisis creada por el confrontamiento entre un mundo rural pre-capitalista y otro capitalista. El puente asume, simbólicamente, esta relación. Es el lugar donde el mundo rural termina y donde la vida urbana comienza:

> The two lightposts of the bridge were a welcome sight. They signaled the dividing line between the turbulence of the town and its sins and

the quiet peace of the hills of the llano.... Beyond was home and safety, the warm arms of my mother, the curing power of Ultima, and the strength of my father. He would not allow Tenorio to intrude upon our quiet hills. But could he stop the intrusion? The townspeople had killed Lupito at the bridge and desecrated the river. (BMU p. 158)

Frente a la tranquilidad y la paz del llano yace la turbulencia y el pecado del pueblo; gentes del pueblo mataron a Lupito; y Tenorio, la encarnación misma del mal, es tabernero y como tal símbolo de la corrupción urbana:

> Though assuming less importance in the narrative than Rosie's, the local bars also appear to function as agents of alienation and corruption, seeming intrusions of urban decadence into the rural New Mexican landscape.[27]

Aparece así expuesta en la obra la tragedia de una sociedad que, habiendo vivido aislada por circunstancias históricas, de repente se ve acometida por un nuevo modo de producción. El "refugio" de Guadalupe ha entrado de lleno en la infraestructura de los Estados Unidos. Como indica Elaine Johnson:

> The highways to the various major New Mexican cities such as Tucumcari and Las Vegas are in a very real sense the rural people's link with the outside world. These roads, however, do not represent positive outlets, routes to opportunity; instead they symbolize death and the destruction of a unified way of life.[28]

En los sueños IV y IX los hermanos de Antonio cruzan el río y se internan en el "mundo", y corren así el peligro de alejarse de la tradición y de la familia.[29] Por supuesto, a medida que la base económica de las aldeas mexicanas va desapareciendo, a medida que su población entra en contacto con el mundo anglo o emigra a las ciudades, las formas tradicionales de vida se ven afectadas. Al señalar Thomas R. López, Jr. que "the cultural forces which held them together—religion, language, ethnicity, kinship, ties with the land—were transplanted into an urban scene," lo que hace es sentar las premisas y el marco de la crisis que esas "fuerzas culturales" encaran al insertarse en unas relaciones sociales de producción distintas.[30] La familia se convierte en uno de los núcleos que más dramáticamente encarna esta situación:

> ... la falta de respeto a los padres ... como el cambio más lamentable dentro de los patrones tradicionales de comportamiento social.... También hubo unanimidad entre nuestros informantes a la hora de señalar a los anglos como los culpables directos de la nueva situación.[31]

El marginamiento y las borracheras de Gregorio Márez, su desilusión con respecto al futuro que eligen los hermanos de Antonio, son ya indicios del problema. En *HOA* los cambios son más radicales: Adelia se hace cargo de las finanzas, el patriarquismo es puesto en jaque—sobre todo en relación a las posturas de rebeldía e independencia de las hijas—, los hijos siguen cada uno ruta e intereses diferentes ...

> We have forgotten the old ways, and we have changed until we have become like the gringo. ... It is a generation of the city, and it is a lost generation. I know, I have lived long enough to see it. In the city we have forgotten the old ways, and we have changed until we have become like the gringo. (*HOA* p. 103)

Lo que he venido en última instancia indicando es que los conflictos culturales que asoman en la obra de Anaya—y de hecho en cualquier obra—no deben ser tomados como la problemática de fondo, sino como la expresión de unas condiciones de base concretas. Elaine Johnson reconoce esta situación—aunque desgraciadamente no la explora a fondo—cuando nota la existencia de un enfrentamiento entre el pasado tradicional y la nueva era "tecnológica".[32] Campo y ciudad entran en oposición en la medida en que encarnan o resumen las características de una economía pre-capitalista y de otra industrializada. Es desde esta base conflictiva que se pueden entender los problemas sociales, políticos y culturales. Y su correspondiente expresión artística.

## VI

Sin lugar a dudas, Rudolfo Anaya se identifica con "su" modo de vida y critica las nuevas relaciones sociales que vienen con el desarrollo capitalista nuevomexicano. Como ya apunté, el alambre de púas, las carreteras, el sistema monetario, el ferrocarril, etc., son vistos como símbolos negativos. ¿Cuáles son, pues, los elementos que adoptan un valor simbólico positivo en la representación del mundo rural?

A lo largo de *BMU* se menciona varias veces que Antonio debe elegir entre los modos de vida Márez o Luna. La verdad es que el muchacho no tiene esas posibilidades como alternativas reales. En el fondo, su elección consiste entre ser campesino o asalariado, porque los Márez han sido expulsados por el tejano y, por tanto, como "estirpe" ya no existen. Como indica Roberto Cantú, "el sueño IX pone de relieve la ineficacia del destino Márez, o, en otras palabras, ilustra metafóricamente la muerte de un linaje, de un modo de vida que se torna anacrónico."[33] Diez años después, en *HOA*, las alternativas se reducen aun más al entrar en jaque "el modo de vida Luna". La familia Chávez—familia Luna en la medida en que son pequeños agricultores—abandona el campo e ingresa al mercado laboral.

Simbólicamente, el matrimonio entre los Márez y los Luna podría representar el mestizaje de Antonio. Los Márez aparecen como descendientes de aquellos conquistadores que cruzaron los océanos; los Luna, como representantes de unas culturas apegadas a la tierra y sus ciclos.[34] Unos guerreros, los otros curas; unos vaqueros, los otros agricultores.

Si nos atenemos a la obvia simbología de los apellidos, nuestra percepción de los personajes va a quedar un tanto condicionada, esperando encontrar dos bloques anatagónicos con características simbólicas "puras". Nada más ajeno al mundo narrativo de *BMU*.[35] Más allá de lo que los apellidos impliquen, el padre y la madre de Antonio pertenecen a la realidad de Nuevo México, encarnando sus contradicciones y matices.

> Del destino paterno, Antonio hereda un instinto nomádico, contrario a todo intento de civilización; del materno, Antonio recibe como legado un instinto pasivo, propicio al nacimiento de la cultura. De estos dos extremos... el joven protagonista tendrá que forjarse luego su destino. Antagonismo, pues, de sangres y estilos de vida.[36]

No se trata de un enfrentamiento barbarie-civilización, como parece sugerir Cantú, pero sí estaría de acuerdo con el hecho de que el matrimonio Márez/Luna viene a representar dos estilos de vida; o, matizando algo más, dos funciones distintas dentro de un mismo estilo de vida. Lo que la cita pone de manifiesto no es tanto un antagonismo entre el nomadismo y la pasividad como la diferencia existente entre un vaquero y un campesino. En el marco de una sociedad pre-capitalista, estas dos posibilidades no representan oposiciones, sino más bien delimitan las características clasistas que separan a la población. Guerreros y campesinos son las dos grandes clases sociales que estructuran el modo de producción feudal. Indudablemente, los "conquistadores" Márez no son, en el universo social de *BMU*, la clase dominante. Son simplemente los descendientes. Sin embargo, en el nivel interno, en el microcosmos familiar, el hombre sí asume ese papel. A él le corresponden las connotaciones guerrero-conquistador-clase alta mientras que la mujer es asociada con la idea de campesina-conquistada-clase baja.

Más allá de la romantización que se hace de la vida de vaquero, resalta en la producción de Anaya el valor semántico de ciertas palabras:

> Always the talk would return to life on the llano. The first pioneers there were sheepherders. Then they imported herds of cattle from Mexico and became vaqueros. They became horsemen, caballeros, men whose daily life was wrapped up in the ritual of horsemanship. (*BMU* p. 119)

> But from my father and Ultima I had learned that the greater immortality is in the freedom of man. And that freedom is best nourished by the noble expanse of land. (*BMU* p. 220)

La tierra—aparte de la importancia que tiene, como ya indiqué, en la narrativa de Anaya—es el elemento básico de la riqueza en el mundo feudal. Así, se nos presenta como "noble", y el vaquero no como peón sino como "caballero" y "libre"—la mujer/campesino aparece normalmente "atada" o "sujeta", "sierva" de la tierra (BMU p. 219-220). No es de extrañar, pues, que tanto Cantú[37] como Johnson aludan a esa sensación de Edad Media presente en la novela.[38]

Este es un elemento básico en la obra de Anaya que no debe perderse de vista: el mundo referencial que sustenta su narrativa es el medieval. Los valores simbólicos positivos hacen referencia al modo de producción feudal. Y ello es lógico, pues surgen de sociedades rurales pre-capitalistas.

El dato es significativo, pues pone de manifiesto la perspectiva que adopta la producción de Anaya. Indudablemente, existe una crítica a los valores enajenantes de nuestro tiempo, a los valores impuestos por la sociedad dominante del anglo. Y sin embargo ensalza un mundo en el que las condiciones del ser humano distaban mucho de ser liberadoras. El universo de Antonio es realista en tanto que refleja unas condiciones de vida, pero a la hora de presentar alternativas, a la hora de ofrecer otro esquema de valores, ese universo es idealizado. Establecida esta premisa, el resto de la obra de Anaya consistirá, por un lado, en confirmar estos términos de la oposición en distintos contextos y, por otro, en encontrar una solución, en ajustarse a lo que inexorablemente se reconoce como un *fait accompli*.

Anaya se mueve en el juego de contradicciones propio, en última instancia, de su condición particular en tanto que profesional nuevomexicano de la segunda mitad del siglo XX. Por un lado, es producto del mundo agrícola y tradicional que representan ciertos condados del Estado; por otro, comparte los esquemas de los "nuevos tiempos". Paradoja ésta que se resuelve buscando unas leyes de vida abstractas, una manera de ser "natural" que explique la evolución social y las injusticias: la mitificación. Como el mismo Anaya dice,

> I define myth as truth in the heart. It is the truth that you have carried, that we as human beings have carried all of our history, going back to the cave, pushing it back to the sea.[39]

De alguna manera, la diáspora de los Chávez se identifica con la del pueblo azteca, y en el proceso desaparecen el complejo industrial militar, el National Forest Service y las demás causas concretas que lo produjeron. El resultado consiste en una cierta idealización del mundo rural pre-capitalista reconociendo al mismo tiempo lo anacrónico de su existencia. El gran intento de Anaya será reconciliar ideológicamente dos sistemas distintos y antagónicos: denunciar la destrucción de su universo de la infancia—universo querido y respetado—por un nuevo modo de producción sin poner en cuestión al sistema en el proceso.

## VII

Es a partir de esta reivindicación del mundo de la infancia que se puede empezar a entender el otro "gran tema" de la literatura chicana, también presente en la obra de Anaya: la búsqueda de la identidad.

Como tópico literario, la búsqueda de identidad no es un fenómeno único a la experiencia chicana. En la tradición occidental, está presente desde la épica caballeresca hasta la literatura de nuestros días, y aparece como expresión de situaciones concretas. Como indica Juan Rodríguez.

> Eso aparte, la búsqueda de la identidad sí se plantea en la literatura chicana; así como se plantea en el fondo de todas las literaturas occidentales desde que la Primera Revolución Industrial y su aparato político, social y económico minaron la integridad del hombre, momento en que los productos de la actividad humana, al igual que las propiedades y capacidades del hombre, se convirtieron en algo independiente y ajeno a éste.[40]

Ya señalé que sectores de Nuevo México sufren los efectos de una "revolución industrial" a partir de los años 40, de manera que la obra de Anaya, en particular, se suma al fenómeno general arriba indicado.

Esta búsqueda suele darse, inicialmente, como un intento de recuperación de un pasado idealizado:

> Este nuevo afán nos lleva a otra manifestación de la búsqueda: el volver al pasado en busca del *ubi sunt*, del *là-bas*, del paraíso perdido en el que el chicano, se supone, gozaba de su ser completo, poseía una identidad.[41]

Ya establecí la relación existente entre la idea de "paraíso perdido" y "tierra perdida". A otro nivel, la mirada al pasado se tiñe de nostalgia: "Ay, but those were beautiful years, my father continued. The llano was still virgin." El pasado—y recuérdese que éste implica un modo de producción pre-capitalista—es asociado con la virginidad, con la pureza. Es decir, con la infancia—no hay que olvidar que *BMU* es narrada por Antonio-adulto—, esa etapa en que el hombre es "inocente".

A partir de aquí, se plantea un dilema interesante: ¿qué ocurre al crecer?

> "Tony," Cico said softly, "all men sin."
> I had no answer to that. My own mother had said that losing your innocence and becoming a man was learning to sin. I felt weak and powerless in the knowledge of the impending doom. (*BMU* p. 111)

Con el tiempo, al crecer, se pierde inevitablemente la inocencia. El desarrollo histórico se convierte así en un proceso de degeneración o corrupción.

Esta postura no difiere mucho de la adoptada por otras literaturas enfrentadas con una problemática similar. Ocurre, sin ir más lejos, en los Estados Unidos, aproximadamente durante la misma época, con escritores no chicanos.[42] Ernst Fisher reconoce en el escapismo y en la mirada nostálgica al pasado una expresión literaria de ciertos sectores de la burguesía que, respondiendo a la enajenación e incapaces de ver en la evolución histórica una solución, miran a la historia como si fuese la realidad misma de su momento, creando unos eslabones que inevitablemente conducen al presente, pero dándole la espalda a un futuro que asoma todavía más tormentoso. Es el refugio en un "tiempo perdido", en su recreación:

> The same angel inspired Proust and Joyce, Kafka and Elliot: shattered fragments of the past, the past as reality, grew vast before the eyes of their creative imagination.[43]

Frase que puede compararse a la que dice el narrador de *BMU*:

> That shot destroyed the quiet, moonlit peace of the hill, and it shattered my childhood into a thousand fragments that long ago stopped falling and are now dusty relics gathered in distant memories. (*BMU* p. 245)

Como vamos a ver, esa labor de recrear el pasado va a convertirse precisamente en una de las soluciones individuales propuestas por Anaya.

Al establecer una identificación entre infancia y pasado idealizado —entre niñez y sociedad rural—, el progreso sólo puede ser concebido en términos cíclicos de recuperación de valores y estructuras anteriores. Esquemáticamente, la asociación podría representarse de la siguiente manera:

| *Nivel social* | *Nivel individual* |
|---|---|
| pre-capitalismo | pre-corrupción |
| capitalismo | corrupción |

Puesto que el transcurso del tiempo lleva inevitablemente a la degradación, la historia es rechazada, como fenómeno lineal, por un concepto regenerativo.[44] Aunque, dado el hecho de que es imposible en la realidad regresar al punto de partida, esta regeneración cíclica sólo puede llevarse a cabo idealmente, en el nivel individual. La solución colectiva propuesta en *HOA*, por ejemplo, no es de hecho llevada a la práctica, y la novela nos deja con las ganas de saber qué pasaría después de esa marcha "revolucionaria" del final.

El gran dilema de Clemente Chávez es, precisamente, el de poder reconciliar los conceptos de individualismo y colectividad. En palabras de Anaya, congeniar "cada cabeza es un mundo" con "el alma de la raza". Algunos críticos, como Roberto Cantú, afirman que Anaya elige "el destino colectivo como proyecto hacia el futuro".[45] Pero esta elección, en realidad, sólo se adopta de una manera espiritual. En el fondo, la propuesta última es la introspección, la mirada a los rincones del corazón. "There is no other redeemer than mother earth", dice Anaya (HOA p. 104). O, "once there would have been the land to make him *whole* again" (HOA p. 78). Ante la ausencia de esa realidad social—y económica—se opta por llevar esa idea de tierra en uno mismo: corazón de Aztlán. De esa manera se pretende recuperar la unicidad—la armonía—original.

De no existir esta escapatoria, se nos dice, el ser humano se encontraría en un callejón sin salida, sumido en disyuntivas esquizofrénicas. Sin lugar a dudas, la realidad, la forma de vida del "americano"—es decir, la sociedad industrial—provoca la enajenación:

> If we are to survive as a people, and if we are not to become like the americano, then the soul of the people must rise above the hell of individual alienation. (HOA p. 147)

Pero tampoco el encaramiento con la verdad ofrece una solución:

> Is it truth that makes a man mad like an animal? Yes, it was a wounded and dying animal they found, delirious with fever, shouting wild stories ... (HOA p. 134)

No hay que olvidar que enajenación, en su sentido más literal, significa pérdida de la razón.

La realidad es enajenante. Regresar al pasado, imposible. Esta situación sin alternativas—paralela a la que sufría Antonio frente a los destinos Márez-Luna—tiene como consecuencia coherente la incapacidad de acción. La idea de "parálisis" asoma ya en HOA. Cuando Clemente Chávez trata de destruir la torre de acero, los demás trabajadores lo contemplan incapaces de ayudarle, de "moverse":

> And some of the workers of the graveyard shift came, and like us they could only stand and stare. I tell you my friends, we have created something we cannot destroy; we are slaves to the steel. (HOA p. 203)
>
> Now, the greatest tragedy is the *paralysis* which injustice and oppression inflict on our people. (HOA p. 206)

Los pasajes revelan tanto el sentido de opresión paralizadora como la inutilidad de enfrentar la realidad que la provoca.

Es, sin embargo, en *Tortuga* donde Anaya elabora sobre el tema, esta vez en términos simbólicos o alegóricos:

> "Your folks are way up north ... don't expect too many visits."
> "I know," I nodded. How well I knew the poverty and misery which

surrounded us and suffocated us and *held us enslaved as the paralysis held me now.* (*Tortuga* p. 8)

El universo narrativo de *Tortuga* asume las características jerarquizantes de nuestra sociedad, con cada categoría—¿clase?—encarnando un cierto nivel de incapacitación—o de libertad—según la posición en la escala de valores: desde el poder máximo del gobernador hasta el pabellón de "vegetantes" totalmente impotentes.[46] La trayectoria del personaje principal consistirá en vencer la parálisis, en liberarse y dejar el hospital.

Vista desde esta perspectiva, es decir desde el triunfo de Tortuga, la obra parecería optimista, por lo menos en la medida en que Tortuga puede ser tomado como personaje ejemplificador de una sociedad. Sin embargo, el hecho de que sea únicamente Tortuga quien consiga liberarse crea, cuando menos, una dualidad en el mensaje. Anaya ofrece una salida, pero ésta se halla reservada para ciertas personas particulares—como veremos más adelante—. A los demás se les ofrece la resignación a través de una realización espiritual o mítica. La estructura del hospital—la estructura social—queda intacta. La libertad de Tortuga implica el sacrificio de los "vegetantes" y quizás incluso del liberal Steel, pero todo termina en su sitio: Tortuga tiene su función, encuentra su razón de ser como lo hizo Antonio.

Las tres novelas de Anaya suponen tres experiencias de adquisición de conocimiento. Las tres implican una resignación frente a la realidad: en *BMU*, aceptar que el mundo se encuentra fragmentado y es pecaminoso; en *HOA*, admitir que el ferrocarril no puede ser vencido; en *Tortuga*, aprender a vivir con la parálisis. La enajenación aparece como consecuencia de la realidad social. La injusticia, la opresión, el acero como símbolo del capitalismo industrial, asoman como responsables directos de que el pueblo se encuentre paralizado; pero Anaya no lleva el argumento hasta sus últimas consecuencias. Tal como ocurrió a la hora de indicar las razones de la pérdida de la tierra, las causas objetivas sufren un proceso de internalización: "*we* have created something we cannot destroy," dicen los hombres de Barelas. Y en *Tortuga*: "holy water caressing the cripples of the desert *we* had created."

Desde su formulación misma, este proceso de internalización apunta hacia el fracaso. Al asumirse la culpa a título personal—postura, por cierto, de carácter religioso—es lógico que se busque la redención al nivel individual. Las soluciones no se podrán encontrar tanto en la modificación de las condiciones de vida como en la purificación del *ser*, de la esencia—punto de partida de la proyección mística—, de la existencia: "They could never be beaten. Not as long as a single man dared to look for his humanity in the corners of his heart" (*HOA* p. 208). Le queda al lector decidir si se puede conseguir la victoria a través de esos recursos. Es decir, ¿logran realmente algo los obreros de Barelas?

Si precisamente las causas concretas de esa pérdida de la humanidad se deben a factores socio-económicos—pérdida de la tierra, migración forzada, imposición de un modo de producción capitalista, etc.—, ¿se puede acaso remediar el problema sin eliminar aquello que lo produce? *HOA* concluye sin ofrecer soluciones. Concluye al estilo de los viejos cuentos de hadas con un "se casaron y fueron muy felices". Concluye con un grito en el vacío que el propio Anaya se ve obligado a recoger con posterioridad. En *Tortuga*—y recuérdese que esta novela funciona como "continuación" de *HOA*—se admite que nada ha cambiado en Barelas a pesar de la marcha final de Clemente Chávez: "And the battle has continued. It is like a war. Nothing is settled. The workers are without work. But we have faith and we keep fighting and praying" (*Tortuga* p. 168).

Este mecanismo de internalización de las causas provoca un proceso de ensimismamiento que se va dando gradualmente en la producción de Anaya. Poco a poco, el mundo va desapareciendo—es decir, el contexto—hasta que en *Tortuga* los personajes se encuentran totalmente aislados, protegidos y enmarcados por el desierto, encerrados entre las paredes de un hospital.[47] Es la culminación del proceso: Salomón encuentra su verdad y su salvación; Tortuga su razón de ser y su destino .... Mientras, en Barelas, los obreros siguen sin trabajo.

Así, pues, la búsqueda de la identidad en los valores míticos o en el pasado glorificado, la internalización de la culpa y el ensimismamiento individual pueden ser consecuencias de las condiciones de vida de un momento. Son respuestas, pero no deben ser tomadas por soluciones, pues se ignoran o se dejan de lado en el proceso las causas que las fomentan.

¿Por qué elige Anaya este camino? ¿Por qué plantea un rechazo del desarrollo histórico a costa de un refugio en los supuestos valores eternos e inamovibles? ¿Por qué no cree en el cambio de la sociedad a base de un encaramiento con la realidad y de la transformación de sus estructuras? Es decir, ¿por qué no lucha por un "reino de este mundo" donde se produzca una "armonía terrenal" que tenga como base la desaparición de las desigualdades y de las injusticias?

## VIII

No todos los personajes en la producción de Anaya comparten un proceso de estancamiento o degradación. Algunos se mantienen fuera de él, permaneciendo en un estado de pureza y privilegio. Algunos consiguen liberarse de sus circunstancias y transcender sus limitaciones, romper conceptualmente con la opresión de su contexto. Algunos son seres especiales:

"Does he know about the golden carp?" I asked.
"The *magic people* all know about the coming day of the golden carp."
(*BMU* p. 101)

Cico smiled. "They can't see him, Tony, they can't see him. I know every man from Guadalupe who fishes, and there ain't one who has ever mentioned seeing the golden carp. So I guess the grown-ups can't see him."
"The Indian, Narciso, Ultima—"
"*They're different*, Tony. Like Samuel, and me, and you—" (*BMU* p. 108)

Ultima, Antonio, Crispín, Salomón, Tortuga... personajes que van a tener una característica en común: pueden percibir la realidad de una manera diferente, pueden "ver" en ella una magia que escapa a los seres comunes.

Christian Lenhardt hace un interesante estudio sobre la función social y política de la magia y la religión. Aparte de indicar que magia y religión no son conceptos opuestos sino que, por el contrario, tienen un tronco común y responden más bien a dos organizaciones socio-políticas diferentes, señala que:

> Only gradually did certain individuals gain recognition as public magicians. This transformation may have been one of the first qualitative steps taken by man towards a social division of labour.[48]

Y

> Viewed from the standpoint of the magician, the motive for the performance of magic was the domination of man and the perpetuation of social privilege.[49]

¿Gozan esos personajes a los que me refería de poder o privilegio social? En última instancia, sí, aunque aparezcan apartados de las estructuras reales de poder. Es decir, gozan de un privilegio dentro de la comunidad a la que pertenecen, aunque, por supuesto, esta comunidad se halla, en su conjunto, discriminada y apartada. En *HOA*, Crispín, para la maquinaria social de los Estados Unidos, no goza de ningún estatuto especial, pero sí para la gente de Barelas; y una vez que Clemente Chávez, después de su "viaje" iluminador, comparte o aprende el estatuto de Crispín, se convierte en líder de esa comunidad. Ultima se encuentra en una situación parecida, pues si bien el cura asoma como la autoridad establecida—y ella es en alguna ocasión desafiada—, la gente la respeta y acude a ella.

Este doble carácter contradictorio de Ultima refleja una situación donde se sobreimponen dos estructuras de dominación: la de la sociedad norteamericana sobre la tradicional chicana de Nuevo México, esta última a su vez jerarquizada. De ahí que la crítica de Anaya a la iglesia sea limitada, pues no se trata de poner en jaque la esencia de las estructuras mágico-religiosas, sino de reivindicar unos privilegios que ahora no se gozan en su plenitud.[50]

Ultima—personaje esencial para entender la propuesta final de Anaya—vive, debido a su avanzada edad, bajo la protección de la familia Márez. En cierto sentido, disfruta de un mecenazgo, si bien esto no impide que también "venda" sus servicios:

> "I will pay you in silver if you save my son's life," he said . . .
> "Forty dollars to cheat la muerte," she mumbled.
> "Agreed," he responded. (BMU p. 185)

En este diálogo de contratación yace una clave importante para la comprensión de la situación del curandero. Su estatus económico depende de que pueda ganarse la vida con sus "artes", lo que implica que la sociedad debe compartir una creencia en sus poderes y que, además, tiene que tener éxito con su magia, pues de lo contrario su funcionalidad y su existencia dejarían de tener razón de ser.

¿Cuál es el propósito de que Anaya ofrezca un universo donde lo sobrenatural es aceptado y defendido? ¿Por qué quiere perpetuar, en nuestra sociedad tecnológica-industrial de segunda mitad del siglo XX, la noción de magia?

Quiero regresar un momento al trabajo de Christian Lenhardt: "We also see that the successor of the magician is not only the scientist but the artist whose poetry is an outgrowth of the incantatory mumbo-jumbo."[51] Ultima—la última de su casta—es defendida y ensalzada en la medida en que es vista como antecedente directo del escritor moderno. El sueño visionario de Antonio cobra así mayor sentido: "he had been witness [the golden carp] to everything that happened, and he decided that everyone should survive, but in new form." (BMU p. 168). El poeta—en eso se convierten Antonio y Tortuga, este último sucesor de Crispín y Salomón—reemplaza al curandero.

BMU es el proceso de iniciación de Antonio no sólo como persona sino como escritor. La novela relata la trayectoria de un muchacho en "busca de su destino", destino que consiste precisamente en relatar su proceso. Por encima—o complementario—a los descubrimientos de que en el mundo hay polarización, fragmentación, otredad, etc., sobresale el hecho de contar esos descubrimientos. Roberto Cantú señala que "en el caso de Antonio . . . su inocencia se encuentra en el lugar de su nacimiento, en el espacio donde Ultima sepultó, junto con el cordón umbilical, el misterio que cubre el destino de Antonio."[52] Destino que no es tan misterioso:

> You know the signs of his birth were good. You remember, Grande,

you offered him all the objects of life when he was a boy, and what did he choose, the pen and the paper. (*BMU* p. 51)

De ahí que Antonio-narrador vaya a decir más adelante: "Sometime in the future I would have to build my own dream out of those things that were so much a part of my childhood" (*BMU* p. 248). Cosa que se lleva a cabo al escribir *BMU*. Lanzado Antonio a un mundo sin inocencia, sin armonía, su aprendizaje con Ultima le lleva a descubrir el camino de recuperación de esa armonía a través de la escritura. Dice Juan Bruce-Novoa:

> As Sor Juana Inés de la Cruz, Proust, Octavio Paz, García Ponce, Georges Bataille and a whole list of others have shown, art is one of the possible responses to the discontinuity of chaotic reality.[53]

El arte, claro está, sólo puede aspirar, como mucho, a crear la ilusión de armonía. El acto de contar o de narrar se convierte, en la obra de Anaya, en factor fundamental para encontrar un cierto sentido funcional, una razón de vida y una justificación que permita aceptar la realidad. Bruce-Novoa, en el mismo trabajo, señala acertadamente que Antonio, emplazado en un mundo que se presenta como dividido en dualidades opuestas, se esfuerza por entender las fuerzas caóticas y destructivas del mundo; otro tanto indica Vernon Lattin cuando, a propósito del noveno sueño, nota que Antonio adopta una postura de aceptación de la fragmentación de la realidad. Sólo que esa aceptación se da una vez descubierto que ello permite que exista el escritor como ser encargado de ofrecer la armonía. Como dice el propio Anaya en su artículo sobre la epifanía: "It is our task as writers to convey our landscape to our readers and to work through the *harmony of* this essential metaphor."[54]

Es decir, por un lado se reconoce la existencia de unas condiciones sociales de injusticia y enajenación; y por otro se propone al artista — mediante su magia — como remedio. El artista, desde esta perspectiva, no va a tener interés en promover el cambio de las estructuras sociales, pues ello significaría auto-negarse. De poder llegar a un mundo no-enajenado a través de la transformación del sistema socio-económico, el artista correría el riesgo de perder su funcionalidad.[55]

Aceptadas estas premisas, se hace más fácil entender tanto la evolución ideológica de la producción de Anaya como la insistencia con la que los personajes-poetas aparecen como sujetos principales e indispensables a la solución de los conflictos. Así, el acto de escribir, la creación artística, la metaliteratura, se convierte en tema principal, en objetivo y medio de la obra:

> At the end he [Antonio] is unable to prevent her death and the continuity of his childhood lies in pieces.... An actual return to childhood is impossible, but the space of literature is open to Antonio and he becomes the narrator of the novel.... He creates the novel to keep his promise to Ultima within a space of total harmony analogous to the one she revealed to him, and ultimately the same.[56]

El regreso a la infancia—al pre-capitalismo—es imposible, con lo que se recurre al arte como manera de llenar la distancia que separa al deseo de la realidad. Mecanismo absolutamente tradicional en las letras dominantes de la historia occidental. Los distintos personajes-poetas se cargan de características convencionales. Seres privilegiados que, como Cristo o como Dante, pueden bajar a los infiernos y así redimir a la humanidad—"redemption in the epiphany", dice Anaya[57]—: Antonio durante la curación del tío Lucas; Crispín y Clemente en el viaje a las cavernas de Aztlán; Tortuga en sus incursiones a los pabellones de los "vegetantes". Seres privilegiados, portavoces de la verdad absoluta, visionarios del futuro, malabaristas del tiempo: ¿quién puede ofrecer la verdad de la existencia? Crispín (*HOA* p. 83). ¿Quién sabe y conoce todo? Salomón (*Tortuga* p. 36). ¿Quién elimina el paso del tiempo, la evolución histórica? Tortuga o los cuentistas:

> I saw my past flash before me for the first time, and it was a past of whispered stories, cuentos told by the gaunt men and women of the sea of land ... words tying together past and present in the magic of the moment. (*Tortuga* p. 131)

¿Quién puede predecir el porvenir, asumir el futuro? Crispín: "But his guitar contained the poems yet to be sung, the simple truths to be discovered and the melody that would make time stand still" (*HOA* p. 126).

Seres privilegiados que se arrogan poderes mágicos, sobrenaturales. Seres elegidos:

> I knew he understood part of the reason Salomon had chosen me. There was something in me that he could force to become a singer, the man who would not only feel the misery of the hell we lived in, but also return to sing about it. (*Tortuga* p. 134)

A ellos les corresponde, pues, solucionar los conflictos de la sociedad. La alternativa de Lalo, el "revolucionario" de *HOA* que pretende, a través de la lucha de clases, transformar las condiciones objetivas de la enajenación, de la injusticia y de la explotación, es desechada. El poeta, sin modificar las estructuras, sin poner en jaque las transnacionales, la concentración de la riqueza en un reducido sector de la sociedad, el racismo institucionalizado, etc., ofrece—¿vende?— resignación y felicidad:

> Tortuga, I know it's a long journey ... and we don't know why *we're chosen* to walk the path of the sun.... It's a road of suffering and pain, but *we can bear it* now ... you've seen the mountain's heart ... you walked through the halls of the orphans and the cripples of this life ... and you held us in your arms and offered us love .... Our pain and suffering had meaning in your heart! We're *not concerned with why we're here anymore*.... Don't you see my friend, you're the one hope that the darkness will never cover us completely! Even battered, crippled we will follow the path of the sun ... sing its songs ... (*Tortuga* p. 172)

¿Es acaso el poeta un elegido? ¿Puede ofrecer soluciones factibles?

El problema surge al atribuirle al artista las características mágicas señaladas, pues su funcionalidad se encuentra estrechamente ligada a las injustas condiciones sociales. Su razón de ser depende precisamente de la perpetuación del sistema, cayendo así en contradicciones reales insolubles. Por un lado, representa una respuesta individual a las condiciones enajenantes. Es decir, ofrece unas soluciones subjetivas de los problemas: "Subjectively, the artist believes himself to be realising an ideal freedom derived from the 'magic' qualities of art works, and the unique features of the artist's mind."[58] Por otro lado, al no cumplirse objetivamente la resolución deseada—regresar a una infancia precapitalista donde, por cierto, el artista no dependía de un mercado—el poeta sigue confrontándose con la cruda realidad y sigue necesitando reproducir su esquema. En palabras de Christopher Caudwell:

> The doom of bourgeois poets in this epoch is precisely that the misery of the world, including their own special misery, will not let them rest, and yet the temper of the time forces them to support the class which causes it.[59]

Se llega así a entender los términos de la contradicción básica de la producción de Anaya: propuesta crítica desde una perspectiva precapitalista pero preservación, en última instancia, de los esquemas contemporáneos.

## IX

> art for art's sake—i.e. art
> for my sake.
>
> C. Caudwell

A lo largo de este trabajo, he querido insertar la obra de Anaya en los contextos particulares de su producción. En el proceso he evitado, en lo posible, discutir la experiencia chicana en su generalidad o en abstracto. Al hablar de valores literarios "universales", la crítica—y los autores—pretende dejar de lado el hecho de que esos valores corresponden a unos condicionantes clasistas y temporales. Decir que el "paraíso perdido" es un tema presente en toda la historia de la literatura no conduce a ninguna parte. Equivale a afirmar que el arte explora los problemas del ser humano. Lo que interesa es analizar la expresión concreta del tópico, a qué se debe, cómo se manifiesta. Es decir—y por lo que a este trabajo interesa—lo chicano se define, precisamente, en la medida en que responde a unos condicionantes socio-económicos concretos. El paralelismo entre la temática chicano y otras, más que confirmar valores universales, lo que hace es señalar la semejanza de estructuras y problemáticas históricas. La mayor aspiración de universalidad que se puede indicar, consiste, por ahora, en la existencia de una clase dominante que comparte, más allá de las restricciones nacionales, unos intereses y unos problemas comunes.

La trayectoria novelística de Anaya refleja la evolución histórica de Nuevo México de la segunda mitad del siglo XX. A partir de la segunda gran guerra, el país ha sufrido profundas transformaciones estructurales. Cambios que han afectado, por supuesto, a la población chicana:

> The World War II period brought a rather impressive improvement in the occupational position of Mexican-Americans, and this change was undoubtedly accompanied by absolute and relative income gains.[60]

La cita no pretende desmentir, en ningún momento, la situación de opresión y discriminación. Pero da pie a que se pueda aceptar el nacimiento de una muy pequeña clase media y profesional chicana en las últimas décadas. Sector éste que va a tratar de acomodarse en la estructura social norteamericana y que, al enfrentarse con el racismo institucionalizado, va a responder críticamente, rescatando para ello en parte los elementos y los símbolos de una lucha que el pueblo chicano llevaba ejerciendo desde décadas. Postura crítica, sin embargo, que sólo pretende reclamar su derecho a participar y disfrutar del sistema, sin modificarlo substancialmente.[61] Esos son, sin más, los límites de la crítica propuesta por Anaya.

Decía al principio de este análisis que las tres novelas de Anaya conforman una trilogía. *BMU* es el punto de partida; en ella se reflejan las condiciones inmediatas de la post-guerra, el origen de los profundos cambios infraestructurales que afectaron a la población chicana de los últimos años; en ella asoman ya las vías de resolución del conflicto a través de la "salida" que Antonio encuentra en su destino de escritor. *HOA* corresponde al momento de auge de las luchas reivindicativas de los 60. Agudizadas las contradicciones del país por, entre otras cosas, la guerra de Vietnam, surge en los Estados Unidos un amplio frente de resistencia. *HOA* lo recoge en la medida en que refleja la respuesta de un pueblo bruscamente enajenado por el proceso de industrialización. Pero es una novela que trata de rechazar esa respuesta, negando la lucha de clases. Es una obra que termina en el vacío de un idealismo espiritual que rehuye confrontar la realidad objetiva. *Tortuga* cierra el círculo, regresando al punto de partida, al destino de Antonio: en la realización individual del escritor encuentra el pueblo entero la solución a sus problemas.

Exposición-clímax-conclusión: trípode literario absolutamente convencional que nos lleva de la injusticia a la resignación, de la denuncia a la aceptación, de la miseria a la felicidad. Todo ello, claro está, gracias a los poderes mágicos de una guitarra azul. Esta evolución, en realidad, es una expresión de las condiciones de enajenación sentidas y compartidas por muchos escritores: privados de toda decisión sobre el proceso de producción material y distribución, discriminados social y políticamente, estos escritores adoptan una actitud crítica, denunciando su realidad. Y, sin embargo, paradójicamente, las mismas premisas de partida llevan a algunos a abandonar su postura original y a refugiarse en el idealismo. Terminan creando la ilusión de su propia realidad.

DARTMOUTH COLLEGE

## Notas

[1] Rudolfo Anaya, *Bless Me, Ultima* (Berkeley: Quinto Sol Publications, Inc., 1973). De ahora en adelante todas las citas harán referencia a esta edición y la designaré *BMU*.

[2] Rudolfo Anaya, *Heart of Aztlán* (Berkeley: Editorial Justa Publications, Inc., 1976). De ahora en adelante todas las citas harán referencia a esta edición y la designaré *HOA*.

[3] Rudolfo Anaya, *Tortuga* (Berkeley: Editorial Justa Publications, Inc., 1979). De ahora en adelante todas las citas harán referencia a esta edición.

[4] No hay duda que *BMU* transcurre durante 1945, pues se menciona el final de la segunda guerra mundial; *HOA* aproximadamente transcurre en 1955, quizás un par de años después, aunque sólo se puede deducir a través de pequeños detalles: por ejemplo, en la fiesta se baila al ritmo de Bill Haley, Little Richard y Bo Diddley, cantantes estos que coincidieron en auge entre 1955-57.

[5] Elaine Dorough Johnson, "A Thematic Study of Three Chicano Narratives: Estampas del Valle y otras obras, Bless Me, Ultima and Peregrinos de Aztlán" (Madison: Ph.D. Dissertation, University of Wisconsin, 1978), p. 92.

[6] Johnson, pp. 289 y 127. El subrayado es mío.

[7] Utilizo el término "realista" no en el sentido de novela burguesa del siglo XIX, sino simplemente en oposición a la idea de alegoría.

[8] Rudolfo Anaya, "A Writer Discusses His Craft", *CEA Critic*, 40, 1 (1977), pp. 39-43.

[9] Roberto Cantú, "Bless Me, Ultima", *Mester*, 4, 1 (1973), p. 67.

[10] Anaya menciona estos pueblos aunque con pequeñas variantes: Las Pasturas, Puerto de los Luna.

[11] Así, por ejemplo, Puerto de Luna se encuentra unas millas al sur de Santa Rosa, sobre el río Pecos, al igual que el Puerto con respecto a Guadalupe en *BMU*; Santa Rosa cruza la carretera 66, que es la que toma la familia Chávez al partir hacia Albuquerque en *HOA*. En general, muchas de las descripciones de Guadalupe coinciden con Santa Rosa.

[12] Clark Knowlton, "The Spanish Americans in New Mexico", *Sociology and Social Research*, 45, 4-7 (1964), p. 3.

[13] Alfredo Jiménez Núñez, *Los Hispanos de Nuevo México* (Sevilla: Publicaciones de la Universidad de Sevilla, 1974).

[14] Para un interesante estudio de la época de post-segunda guerra mundial véase Lawrence S. Wittner, *Cold War America* (New York: Holt, Rinehart and Winston, 1978).

[15] Wittner, p. 118.

[16] Thomas R. López, Jr., "New Mexico and Cultural Pluralism", paper prepared for the Midwest Regional Meeting, East Lansing, Michigan, April 16-17, 1971, pp. 7-8.

[17] Jiménez, p. 210.

[18] Véase, por ejemplo, *Maize*, 4, 3-4 (1981), pp. 6-23.

[19] Vernon E. Lattin, "The Quest for Mythic Vision in Comtemporary Native American and Chicano Fiction", *American Literature*, 50, 4 (1979), pp. 625-646.

[20] Egla Morales, "Símbolos y motivos nahuas en la literatura chicana", *The Identification and Analysis of Chicano Literature*, Francisco Jiménez, ed. (New York: Bilingual Press/Editorial Bilingüe, 1979), p. 179.

[21] Anaya, "A writer ...", p. 39.

[22] Knowlton, p. 3. Guadalupe se encuentra al sur de Las Vegas.

[23] "For years, huge firms like Tenneco, Purex, Coca Cola, United Brands, ITT, Union Carbide, Boeing Aircraft, Kaiser Aluminum, Aetna Life, and Dow Chemical had been moving into agriculture, furthering the exodus of family farmers from the land. From 1960 to 1974, the numbers of farms in America decreased by 25%, and the number of farmers dipped below 3 million." Wittner, p. 311.

[24] Knowlton, p. 5.

[25] No deja de ser irónico que Clemente Chávez tenga que trabajar para el ferrocarril, pues éste ya había sido mostrado como origen de los primeros despojos y migraciones.

[26] No quiero decir que esta correspondencia esté explícitamente incluida en la obra. Simplemente señalo la relación. Por supuesto, hay que tener en cuenta las posibles diferencias entre el "mundo reflejado" y el "mundo representado".

[27] Johnson, p. 128.

[28] Johnson, p. 121.

²⁹ Véase, por ejemplo, Vernon E. Lattin, "The Horror of Darkness: Meaning and Structure in Anaya's *Bless Me, Ultima*", *Revista Chicano-riqueña*, VI, 2 (1978), pp. 50-57.
³⁰ López, pp. 7-8.
³¹ Jiménez, pp. 114-115.
³² Johnson, pp. 132-133.
³³ Cantú, p. 33.
³⁴ Aunque en este trabajo no voy a tocar el papel de la mujer en la obra de Anaya, a primera vista da la impresión de que nos encontramos en este matrimonio Márez-Luna con otra expresión del "malinchismo". La mujer es vista, en general, con ojos tradicionales: símbolo de la fertilidad, ama y señora de la cocina, ser generalmente pasivo que sólo alcanza a ser, como mucho, burda "adelita" en *HOA*. Para un análisis más detallado, aunque breve, puede consultarse Regina Unpingo-Garrett, "Images of Women in *Bless Me, Ultima*", *Vision* (1976), pp. 41-42.
³⁵ "Gregorio Márez is characterized as a descendant of conquistadores.... Nevertheless, he feels a deep reverence for the earth, a characteristically indigenous trait in Anaya's scheme." Johnson, p. 136.
³⁶ Roberto Cantú, "Estructura y sentido de lo onírico en *Bless Me, Ultima*", *Mester*, V, 1 (1974), p. 28.
³⁷ "[BMU es] la primera novela chicana que a diferencia de las anteriores, se ha propuesto alcanzar un nivel poético, repleto de mitos y cargado de una buena atmósfera medieval." Cantú, '*Bless Me, Ultima*", p. 66.
³⁸ "Within the allegorical framework of the narrative there are certain elements which are to be regarded as intrusions from the outside, fracturing the medieval unity of Antonio's closed rural world." Johnson, p. 44.
³⁹ *Maize*, 4, 3-4, p. 11.
⁴⁰ Juan Rodríguez, "La búsqueda de identidad y sus motivos en la literatura chicana", *The Identification and Analysis of Chicano Literature*, Francisco Jiménez, ed. (New York: Bilingual Press/Editorial Bilingüe, 1979), p. 170. Difiero con Juan Rodríguez en el hecho de que el fenómeno se haya dado a partir de la Revolución Industrial, aunque sí es posible que haya cobrado particular relevancia a partir de ese momento.
⁴¹ Rodríguez, p. 173.
⁴² "Even 'serious' fiction writers skirted America's social problems. Mary McCarthy, Bernard Malamud, and Saul Bellow devoted their talents to novels of manners and personal life, offering individual, often improbable solutions to the quest for personal identity and freedom. In his immensely popular *Catcher in the Rye* (1951), J. D. Salinger posed no alternative to the adult world of hypocrisy and corruption except withdrawal into the innocence of childhood or the consolation of Zen." Wittner, p. 130.
⁴³ Ernst Fischer, *The Necessity of Art* (Penguin Books, 1978), p. 203.
⁴⁴ Roberto Cantú, "Degradación y regeneración en *Bless Me, Ultima*: el chicano y la vida nueva", *The Identification and Analysis of Chicano Literature*, Francisco Jiménez, ed. (New York: Bilingual Press/Editorial Bilingüe, 1979), pp. 374-388. Cantú señala acertadamente la existencia de este mecanismo estructural, pero no ve en él una expresión escapista.
⁴⁵ Roberto Cantú, "Chicano Authors: Inquiry by Interview" (1981).

Desgraciadmente he perdido la ficha de la publicación donde aparece esta reseña de Cantú sobre el libro de Bruce-Novoa. La fotocopia que tengo no indica el lugar de origen.

[46] Se podría trazar a grandes rasgos un cierto paralelismo entre la jerarquización del hospital y la división clasista de la sociedad. La comparación arrojaría conclusiones interesantes. Por ejemplo: (1)La clase más baja es la más incapacitada, la menos activa, la más marginada, la que menos disfruta de la vida, etc. Sin embargo, el hecho de que exista permite y justifica la existencia del "hospital". Anaya ofrece a este grupo la resignación como forma de consuelo y de paz. Véase, por ejemplo, todo el pasaje, pp. 159-160, donde en una de las "transmisiones oníricas" Salomón arremete contra los héroes que rehusan reconocer su culpa interna y buscan las causas en las circunstancias: Prometeo, Cristo, Sísifo.... No hay que ver la incapacitación como castigo, sino aceptarla y justificar la existencia a partir de ella. (2)Dr. Steel es el doctor americano liberal. El valor semántico de su nombre—acero—podría ser considerado como representación simbólica de la sociedad industrial, al igual que ocurre en *HOA*. De ser así, sería interesante estudiar la evolución del signo y, por tanto, la posible, transformación o matización que experimenta la ideología de Anaya.

[47] Por supuesto, la eliminación del contexto provoca una actitud de rechazo de las condiciones sociales objetivas. Como dice Salomón, "we're not concerned why we're here anymore."

[48] Christian Lenhardt, "Magic and Domination", *Domination*, Alkis Kontor, ed. (Toronto: University of Toronto Press, 1975), p. 165. No toma en cuenta la separación sexista como división social del trabajo.

[49] Lenhardt, p. 174.

[50] Lo que vengo a insinuar es que se trata de un tipo de reivindicación que no intenta eliminar las divisiones sino reclamar unos privilegios.

[51] Lenhardt, p. 174.

[52] Cantú, "Estructura...", pp. 29-30.

[53] Juan Bruce-Novoa, "Portraits of the Chicano as a Young Man: the Making of the Author in Three Chicano Novels". Paper in the Mexican-American Collection, University of Texas, Austin, p. 2. Vernon Lattin, en su artículo "The Quest..." también señala la característica metaliteraria de la producción de Anaya.

[54] Anaya, "A Writer...", p. 43. Hay que añadir que lo máximo a lo que puede aspirar el escritor es a crear una "ilusión" de armonía. El problema consiste en hacer creer a los lectores que no se trata de una ilusión sino de la realidad misma. Tarea, por cierto, similar a la del mago. El propio Anaya, sin embargo, cae en contradicciones. En el mismo artículo, un poco antes, escribe: "as one learns how to receive that energy one also learns how to give of one's energy to dissolve the polarity of metaphor and create the unity of epiphany." ¿Es, pues, la metáfora armonía o dualidad?

[55] Entiéndase que el punto de partida de la definición del artista que estoy usando no es el mío sino el propuesto en la obra de Anaya.

[56] Bruce-Novoa, p. 13.

[57] Anaya, "A Writer...", p. 42. Es el sentimiento de enajenación el que pone en marcha el proceso.

[58] Christopher Caudwell, *Illusion and Reality* (New York: International Publishers, 1973), p. 127.

[59] Caudwell, p. 112.
[60] Leo Grebler, Joan W. Moore, and Ralph C. Guzman, *The Mexican-American People. The Nation's Second Largest Minority* (New York: The Free Press, 1970), p. 189.
[61] Expresión verdaderamente significativa de esta problemática es la reciente película de Jesús Treviño, "Seguín", donde se plantean propuestas similares.

# The Function of the La Llorona Motif in Anaya's *Bless Me, Ultima*

Jane Rogers

In *The Odyssey,* Circe warns the homeward-bound Odysseus of the menace of the Sirens, who, surrounded by the mouldering skeletons of men, lure and bewitch the unaware man with the music of their song. Yet just beyond their lovely voices—which Odysseus escapes by having himself lashed to the mast of his ship—lurks peril, a choice between annihilation on the sheer cliffs of the Wandering Rocks or a meeting with the double menace of Scylla and Charybdis, the former hideously fishing for a passerby with her twelve dangling feet, the latter but a bow's shot distance away threatening to suck men down into the deep waters near the foot of a luxurious fig tree. Certain death is the fate of the man who succumbs to the sweet lure of the sirens. The peril of life, and yet the promise of home, is the alternative.

A similar theme is developed by Rudolfo Anaya's use of the *la llorona* motif in *Bless Me, Ultima.* In the novel, Antonio, symbolically both Christ and Odysseus, moves from the security and from the sweet-smelling warmth of his mother's bosom and kitchen out into life and experience. As he weighs his options—priesthood and the confinement represented by the farms of the Lunas', or the Márezes' freedom on the pagan sea of the llano—and as he grows from innocence to knowledge and experience, the *la llorona* motif figures both on a literal mythological level and as an integral part of Antonio's life.

As "literal" myth, *la llorona* is the wailing woman of the river. Hers is the "tormented cry of a lonely goddess" that fills the valley in one of Antonio's dreams. *La llorona* is "the old witch who cries along the river banks and seeks the blood of boys and men to drink."[1] This myth is closely related to Cico's story of the mermaid.[2] The mermaid is the powerful presence in the bottomless Hidden Lakes. Her strange music is a "low, lonely murmuring . . . like something a sad girl would sing" (p. 109). Cico relates that all that had kept him from plunging into the bottomless lake when he heard the sound was the Golden Carp, whose appearance caused the music to stop. Not that the singing was evil, he relates, but "it called for me to join it. One more step and I'da stepped over the ledge and drowned in the waters of the lake—" (p. 109). Cico continues with the story of the shepherd taken by the mermaid. A "man from Méjico," working on a neighboring ranch, not having heard the story about the lakes, had taken his sheep to water there. Hearing the singing, he ran back to town and swore he had seen a mermaid.

> He said it was a woman, resting on the water and singing a lonely song. She was half woman and half fish— He said the song made him want to wade out to the middle of the lake to help her, but his fear had made him run. He told everyone the story, but no one believed him. He ended up getting drunk in town and swearing he would prove his story by going back to the lakes and bringing back the mer-woman. He never returned. A week later the flock was found near the lakes. He had vanished—. (p. 109)

As an integral part of Antonio's life, the *la llorona* motif emerges in his experiences with nature. *La llorona* is the ambivalent *presence* of the river, which Antonio fears and yet with which he senses a sharing of his own soul and a mystic peace. *La llorona* speaks in the owl's cry and in the dove's cou-rou. Even the dust devils of the llano bear *la llorona*'s signature, embracing Antonio in swirling dust as the gushing wind, which imprints evil on his soul, seems to call his name:

> Antonioooooooooooooooo . . . (p. 52)

But more significantly for Antonio, the *la llorona* motif emerges in his relationship with his mother and in the imagery of the women in the novel. It is the primary image associated with the mother, Maria. Her frequent extended calls of "Antonioooooo," like that of the whirlwind, reflect the wailing call of the *llorona* of Tony's dream:

> *La llorona* seeks the soul of Antonioooooooo . . . (p. 24)

In the same dream, Tony hears his "mother moan and cry because with each turning of the sun her son [is] growing old . . ." (p. 24). On his first day of school Antonio awakens with a sick feeling in his stomach, both excited and sad because for the first time he will be away from the protection of his mother. As he enters the kitchen his mother smiles, then sweeps him into her arms sobbing, "My baby will be gone today" (p. 50). At Ultima's stern but gentle persistence, Antonio is separated from his mother, yet as he leaves, following the sisters Deborah and

Theresa up the goat path, he hears his mother "cry" his name. Maria, as she prays around the Virgin's altar for Antonio and his three older brothers, is *la llorona*. On the return of Andrew, Eugene, and Leon from the war, Maria alternately sobs and prays until Gabriel complains, "Maria ... but we have prayed all night!" (p. 58). Mother and Virgin both assume the mournful aspect of *la llorona* in one of Antonio's dreams just prior to the three brothers' return:

> Virgen de Guadalupe, I heard my mother cry, return my sons to me.
> Your sons will return safely, a gentle voice answered.
> Mother of God, make my fourth son a priest.
> And I saw the virgin draped in the gown of night standing on the bright, horned moon of autumn, and she was in mourning for the fourth son. (p. 43)

Similarly, the *la llorona* motif is echoed in the tolling of the church bells and in the imagery of the mourning, lonely women as they are called to mass on the morning following Lupito's death. "Crying the knell of Lupito," the bell "tolled and drew to it the widows in black, the lonely, faithful women who came to pray for their men" (p. 32).

*La llorona* emerges in the patterns of imagery that surround the episode at Rosie's on the day of the Christmas pageant and of Narciso's death. The "single red light bulb" which shines at the porch door over the "snow-laden gate of the picket fence" is "like a beacon inviting weary travelers in from the storm." Light shines through the drawn shades, and from "somewhere in the house a faint melody" seeps out and is "lost in the wind." Antonio knows he must get home before the storm worsens, yet he is compelled to linger "at the gate of the evil women." The music and laughter intrigue him. His ears "explode with a ringing noise," and he is paralyzed to flight (p. 155). Instead, he must remain to learn that he himself has lost his innocence. The cry of the sirens prevails over Andrew, too, as the red-painted woman calls him from the back of the house:

> Androoooooo.... (p. 156)

When Andrew is summoned by Narciso, it is the giggling girl, her voice "sweet with allurement," that holds Andrew back. He fails to assume the responsibility that would have meant help for Narciso. Instead he succumbs to the allure of the siren.

Wherever it emerges in the novel, the *la llorona* motif harbors ambivalence. *La llorona* invites with music and warmth, and she offers security. Yet, like the mermaid in the hidden lakes, *la llorona* threatens death. For Antonio, his mother offers warmth, fragrance, security. But his own maturity demands that he deny it. To succumb would mean the death of his own manhood and—like the fate of William Blake's Thel, unwilling to accept the consequences of the generative life of experience—withdrawal to an original state of primal innocence. Yet this world holds an even darker fate because it becomes at once prison and paradise, a state of natural innocence and a state of ignorance.[3] This is the choice Antonio must make. He moves from the fragrance and the warmth and the security of his mother's kitchen, from the reassurance of her call, out into the world of experience, the world of school and his companions.

Antonio is introduced into the inferno of school life by Red, who leads him on the first day into the dark, cavernous building, its radiators snapping with steam and its "strange, unfamiliar smells and sounds that seemed to gurgle from its belly" (p. 53). Antonio races the Kid and Time across the bridge to and from school as the years pass and he matures chronologically. With the tutoring of Samuel he learns of the Golden Carp which is to provide apocalyptical knowledge and understanding, an illumination which burdens him with doubt and responsibility. Cico leads Antonio to Narciso's magic garden where he tastes of the fruit—the golden carrot—and to El Rito Creek where he at last experiences the Golden Carp, the "sudden illumination of beauty and understanding," an understanding he anticipated but later failed to find in the ritual of the Holy Communion. Coincident with his vision of the carp, Antonio doubts his own Christian God when he suddenly realizes that Ultima's power had succeeded in curing his Uncle Lucas where the Christian God had failed.

Antonio sees the powers of good and evil contend in Ultima, who serves as his guide through life, and in the dark, diabolic Tenorio. He experiences the deaths of Lupito, of Narciso, and of the angelic and heretical Florence. He sees his brother Andrew deny his responsibility at the summons of the girl at Rosie's, of *la llorona*. Andrew remains to indulge in pleasure, yet the knowledge that he has failed in his responsibility to Narciso drives him, finally, away into the death, the world of lost wanderings, of his other brothers, Eugene and Leon.

The experience at Rosie's is equally ambivalent for Antonio. He is at once lured and repulsed. It marks for him the beginning of a ritual death as he becomes abruptly aware of his own loss of innocence.

> I had seen evil, and so I carried the evil within me. . . . I had somehow lost my innocence and let sin enter into my soul, and the knowledge of God, the saving grace, was far away. (p. 158)

The illness which follows is a "long night" as Ultima sits by, "powerless in the face of death."

> A long, dark night came upon me in which I sought the face of God, but I could not find Him. Even the Virgin and my Saint Anthony would not look at my face.
> ... In front of the dark doors of Purgatory my bleached bones were laid to rest. (p. 167)

But, unlike Andrew's death, Antonio's experience at Rosie's becomes one that leads to death and ultimate rebirth. Antonio recovers from his illness, and though the events of the spring, of catechism and first communion, do not provide the enlightenment he finds with the carp, Antonio is a new man. His life has changed; he feels older. He faces directly the question of the existence of evil, and he is ready to accept his father's explanation that "most of the things we call evil are not evil at all; it is just that we don't understand those things and so we call them evil. And we fear evil only because we do not understand it" (p. 236). Antonio learns to accept the greater reality of life, that he is both Márez and Luna, that he does not have to choose one but can be both. He accepts his father's explanation that the understanding he failed to find in the Holy Communion will come with life. He comes to realize that one's dreams are "usually for a lost childhood" (p. 237). More importantly, he learns from Ultima that "the tragic consequences of life can be overcome by the magical strength that resides in the human heart" (p. 237).

Antonio spends the summer working on the farms with his uncles in El Puerto. Finally, as he struggles to get back to Guadalupe and his family to warn Ultima of Tenorio's threat when his second daughter dies, Antonio encounters *la llorona* once more:

> With darkness upon me I had to leave the brush and run up in the hills, just along the tree line.... Over my shoulder the moon rose from the east and lighted my way. Once I ran into a flat piece of bottom land, and what seemed solid earth by the light of the moon was a marshy quagmire. The wet quicksand sucked me down and I was almost to my waist before I squirmed loose. Exhausted and trembling I crawled onto solid ground. As I rested I felt the gloom of night settle on the river. The dark *presence* of the river was like a shroud, enveloping me, calling to me. The drone of the grillos and the sigh of the wind in the trees whispered the call of the soul of the river.
> Then I heard an owl cry its welcome to the night, and I was reminded again of my purpose. The owl's cry reawakened Tenorio's threat ... (p. 243-44).

Free of the call of *la llorona*, of the "dark *presence* of the river" which called to him, Antonio runs "with new resolution." He runs "to save Ultima" and "to preserve those moments when beauty mingled with sadness and flowed through [his] soul like the stream of time." Antonio leaves the river and runs across the llano feeling a new lightness, "like the wind" as his strides "carried [him] homeward" (p. 244). No longer does he feel the pain in his side, the thorns of the cactus or the needles of yucca that pierced his legs and feet. Yet Antonio knows his childhood is over as the report of Tenorio's rifle shatters it "into a thousand fragments" (p. 245).

Antonio has come home to himself. He has eluded the death call of *la llorona*, and as he buries the owl, Ultima's spirit, he takes on the responsibility of the future in which he knows he must "build [his] own dream out of those things which were so much a part of [his] childhood" (p. 248). Antonio has avoided annihilation on the sheer cliffs of the Wandering Rocks—the fate of his brothers—and he has moved through the narrow strait and evaded the menace of Scylla and Charybdis as he comes to face the reality of his manhood.

# Notes

[1] Rudolfo A. Anaya, *Bless Me, Ultima* (Berkeley, Calif.: Quinto Sol, 1972), p. 23. All quotations from *Bless Me, Ultima* are from this edition; page numbers will henceforth be cited in parentheses within the text.

[2] Joseph Campbell, *The Masks of God: Primitive Mythology*, notes the association between the water image in mythology and "goddesses, mermaids, witches, and sirens," who may represent either the "life-threatening" or "life-furthering" aspect of the water. The use of water imagery to represent the theme of rebirth, Campbell says, is a "mythological universal" imprinted at the moment of birth when "the congestion of blood and sense, of suffocation experienced by the infant before its lungs commence to operate give rise to a brief seizure of terror, the physical effects of which ... tend to occur, more or less strongly, whenever there is an abrupt moment of fright.... The birth trauma, as an archetype of transformation, floods with considerable emotional effect the brief moment of loss of security and threat of death that accompanies any crisis of radical change. In the imagery of mythology and religion this birth (or more often rebirth) theme is extremely prominent; in fact every threshold passage—not only this from the darkness of the womb to the light of the sun, but also those from childhood to adult life and from the light of the world to whatever mystery of darkness may lie beyond the portal of death—is comparable to a birth and has been ritually represented, practically everywhere, through an imagery of re-entry into the womb" (New York: Viking Press, 1959), pp. 61-62.

[3] See Harold Bloom's commentary on "The Book of Thel" in *The Poetry and Prose of William Blake*, ed. David V. Erdman (Garden City, N.Y.: Doubleday, 1965), pp. 807-08.

# C. Miguel Méndez

## Miguel Méndez: Voices of Silence

*Juan D. Bruce-Novoa*

> La historia en su versión escrita es una puta vulgar. Desdeña a los pueblos que no otorgan la lisonja del oro y del poder.
>
> Miguel Méndez, "Tata Casehua"

Chicano culture, in spite of a traceable tradition of written expression, is considered an oral culture. Its wealth of political, social and familial history has been passed down by word of mouth for countless years, and in some instances for centuries. The oral tradition takes many forms, for example, the *corrido*, the folktale, religious theatre on the formal level, or on a more basic, popular level there is the humorous story or jokes, the *chisme* or gossip, and the most common form, the stories told by the *viejitos*, especially the grandparents, to the children. Once we believed that the oral tradition was enough to maintain our culture, but more recently we have realized the severity of the threat which the Anglo-American dominant social system represents. I doubt that anyone would be surprised to hear that the younger generation no longer knows much of our history or traditions.

The voice as vehicle of our tradition no longer functions effectively because the dominant society's pressures have weakened the basic link in the oral chain; that is to say, the communication between the *viejitos* and the young children is each time less. In too many cases the grandchildren, even when interested in the past, no longer speak the language of their *abuelos*. The oral tradition is in danger of disappearing into the silent past, and the Chicano, cut off from this door to his heritage, could lose his cultural identity, his place in the present, and thus, disappear in the future as well. In other essays I have demonstrated how Chicano literature gives this danger central, thematic importance in its total range of genres.[1] Chicano literature rescues our threatened cultural images, fixes them in the word, thus free of the flow of time, and holds them up for us to contemplate, enjoy, study and, in a mutual process, invest with new life as they give our own life meaning. In this way Chicano literature itself constitutes a response to the threat of cultural annihilation—the most eloquent and perhaps in the long run the most effective. The rescue of our cultural images has taken varied directions in many writers, but of those who engage in the effort, two, Miguel Méndez and Tino Villanueva, make silence itself a central theme. Here I propose to study silence in the work of Miguel Méndez.

In his short story "Tata Casehua,"[2] Méndez states that the cruelest death of all is to be forgotten, as has happened to the Native American. The protagonist, an old Yaqui who wanders the Sonora desert like a walking corpse, cannot rest until he finds an heir—a son—to whom he can pass on the tribal history. However, the influence of the white man's blood has weakened his people, who now fear Casehua as a disruptive presence in their poor lives. The first *son* Casehua chooses dies during this initiation ritual. He betrays his race when he forgets the mission to follow some blonde women, who in reality are the golden disguise of death. Casehua's second son, faithful and brave, successfully passes the test and wins the right to hear his ancestors' voices that vibrate in the desert, "las que se perdieron en el tiempo, las que arrastra el viento y las voces que se levantan de las tumbas dialogando eternamente con el silencio" (39). These voices were silenced by the white man, who invented "aparatos para fabricar voces crecidas, voces que quiebran los tímpanos escondiendo su engaño bajo las conciencias . . . ¡Hipócritas! . . . los hombres de la palabra mecanizada escupen a las multitudes cuando glorifican la raza y la justicia" (39). The white man, be he the Anglo-American with his manifest-destiny-white-man's-burden-racial-superiority, or the Mexican with his Catholic-*mestizaje-hermandad-y-Revolución Mexicana*, imposes a distorted version of history, silencing the indigenous voices. Written history hides the fact that the present societies were (and still are) founded on the massacre and oppression of the indigenous peoples. Tata Casehua himself, feared and rejected by his own people, turns out to be the heroic warrior Tetabiate, who fought against the Mexican army at Mazacoba in 1900. When Casehua's newfound heir hears the voices in the desert, he rescues them from the silence of the forgotten past; he becomes the guardian of an oral tradition of cultural affirmation and resistance to encroachment, the guardian of identity.

However, when Méndez explicitly denounces written history as a vulgar whore who disdains the poor, implicitly he raises a question: how can we rescue the lost, cultural images if the oral tradition is almost dead? The answer is not only found in the story—the young must listen to the old—but in a very real sense it *is* the story. Méndez creates a space where the silenced voices speak, fixed outside of time in written literature. But the story needs to be read or silence will again engulf the voices. Like Tata Casehua himself, the story waits for someone capable of listening to and actualizing the voices of the past. The pages of the story are like the silent desert—one must give them what they demand before they will reveal themselves as the space where the voices of the past vibrate with life, in spite of death. Every reader who proves himself worthy of the message will be Casehua's heir, but he/she must pass a strenuous test. The reader's initiation rite is the reading of Méndez' poetic language and fragmented story. A weak reader will drown in the story's apparently muddy waters, as the traitorous first son drowned in the river during his unsuccessful initiation. He will question Méndez' purpose, even deny his value, angered by the difficult reading of this *nothing*, this *useless*, poetic tale. He will never hear the silent voices speak. On the other hand, the strong reader, the faithful, persistent reader will prove himself in the arduous reading by understanding Méndez' real message; and for him the story reveals its essence in which silence takes a form, the written work, through which it finally speaks. The story resists superficial readings, demanding a careful one—to be listened to with care. In this way, the written word incarnates the voice of silence, breaking silence itself, but without losing its mystery and essence.

In the novel *Peregrinos de Aztlán*[3] Méndez expands his scope to include many more characters, but the essential theme remains the same: the poor disappear silently, without anyone knowing the truth about their lives. The poor of whom Méndez speaks are pilgrims who he hopes will establish the nation of Aztlán, the country that "como madre que ama y guarda por igual a todos sus hijos [será la] República de Mexicanos Escarnecidos" (101). If Aztlán is to succeed, the images of its founders cannot be lost, and their rescue is what the novel proposes.

*Peregrinos* relates the suffering of some dozen victims of social oppression which Méndez sums up as war, prostitution, unemployment and hunger. The voices of these victims float freely through the novel's fragmented structure, like the characters who wander the streets of Tijuana, the Sonora desert, or the migrant labor camps. Aztlán will be home for all types of poor people; so Méndez no longer limits his victims to Native Americans, as in "Tata Casehua," but rather, includes the outcasts, Indian as well as *mestizo*, from both sides of the border. The variety of human types is reflected in the many different styles of speech used by Méndez' characters, like *pachuquismo*, lyric prose, hollow rhetoric, and others. What these types have in common is their shared suffering under capitalism which predominates in the United States as well as Mexico. Whatever their origin, they are really one people without place in either country. The poor Mexicans are "en tierra ajena olvidados y proscritos en la propia" (52). El Buen Chuco sums up the Chicano situation: "Allá [en los Estados Unidos], ése, pos es uno 'greaser,' 'un mexican,' viene uno acá [a México], ése, y quesque uno es 'pocho'; me empieza cuadrar que me llamen 'chicano,' bato; me cai a toda madre, carnal; siquiera ya es uno algo" (29). But Méndez' point is not that these poor suffer, but that their suffering is unknown, ignored by even their fellow victims around them. No one knows who or what they are. When they die they disappear into oblivion.

The novel contains a series of deaths which culminates with that of the protagonist himself. In each case we are confronted by two versions of the character's life. From their actions or their words we know the characters and appreciate their human value. However, society does not acknowledge their worth, and the written record denies it. When El Cometa, once a successful comic and friend of the poor, dies, the detectives who try to find out who he was can locate no one who knows anything about him other than he was a crazy old man who claimed he had once been someone. His official epitaph reads: "era un vago, de esos inútiles que ni siquiera tienen historia" (153). Pedro walks across the Sonora desert to find his sister who was raped and sold into prostitution. When he kills the owner of the house where she works, an immoral man who has achieved wealth through political opportunism and even prostituting his wife, the newspapers praise the rich, vile victim, without explaining who Pedro was or his motives for the killing. El Vate also crosses the desert in search of his love, Alma, another victim of prostitution. When he is found dead, a lawyer investigates the case, trying to establish the identity of the corpse, but in the end he can only dictate an official report from which any hint of El Vate's poetic sensibility and lyric talents are missing. And then, the lawyer does not even finish the empty report. Moreover, with El Vate dies all trace of another poet, Lorenzo, because the elegy El Vate wrote for Lorenzo's death, telling how he came north in search of work to save his family from poverty and hunger, will only be read and discarded by the indifferent lawyer. Frankie, a young Chicano, dies alone in Vietnam, with no one to help or listen to him. For society he is just one more number on the casualty list. Other deaths in the novel function in the same fashion.

The poor who manage to survive are, however, likewise ignored, and their true human drama is unknown even to those around them. La Malquerida is a prostitute whose real name no one knows. When the police arrest her, we learn that she is the sister of the murderer Pedro. The dialogue with the police clearly reveals society's attitude toward the poor. When quizzed about her activities, she asks the policemen if they really want to know her story; they respond: "No su historia. Sólo lo relacionado con el señor Cocuch [the murdered owner of the house of prostitution]" (144). Only the stories—the histories—of the rich matter. El Buen Chuco is known as a drunken, vagrant troublemaker; but by listening to a friend talk or from Chuco's own words we come to know him and sympathize with him. He was once a champion of the *pisca*; he supported his family with his earnings. His health now prematurely broken from a life of hard labor, he can no longer work and has no means of support; he becomes a drunk despised by society. When he steals three bottles of wine, he is sentenced to prison for three years by the same judge who had earlier pitied and pardoned a rich, young woman who had killed her illegitimate baby. A bartender sums up the dual view of the characters in the book when he explains the change in his attitude towards El Chuco: "A mí me caía sangrón, para serle franco, ahora que me cuenta estas cosas lo veo de otro modo" (38). We, the readers, could say the same thing about all the novel's poor characters, whose appearance often causes a reaction of repulsion, but whose human quality wins our sympathy. But society's official record will reject them, because written history, "coqueta liviana, los desdeña como toda puta que no otorga favores si no pulsa el oro de la paga" (177). A false, written history contradicts and annuls the true, oral history.

The oral histories, unacknowledged in society's official records, vibrate in the head of the protagonist Loreto, the old Yaqui who lives in the lowest level of poverty in Tijuana. Loreto is the center for the loose voices of the novel. Méndez gives us this structural key to the novel when he describes the feverish Loreto:

> Las fiebres lo dejaban chupado, pero le hacían el efecto de purgas de voces invasoras. Como murciélagos se iban colgando de su cerebro todo el palabrerío maldiciente, amargo; quejas y llantos de seres angustiados ... salían las palabras como almas que carga el diablo de las greñas ... Cosas de seres adoloridos; entre todas las voces ajenas, claro, las del mismo indio Loreto, porque también él navegaba como los demás desgraciados en el mar sanguinolento del dolor. (52)[4]

Believing that the history of the poor is found in the oral tradition, Méndez needs a human center to contain it, to be its focus; and although other possible centers for the voices might be identified, like the cantina Happy Days or Tijuana itself, Loreto is the only human center possible. He is the Tata Casehua of Tijuana, though it is not always exactly clear how he could have heard every story in the book. His role as the custodian of oral history is underscored by the fact that only Loreto knows and remembers the semi-mythical deeds of Coronel Cuamea, another Yaqui hero of the Mexican Revolution, who fell in love with Death and managed to rape her when she finally came to claim his life. In a process mirroring that of El Vate and Lorenzo explained above, Cuamea disappears into the forgotten past when Loreto, the only man who could tell the world of his life, dies; and Loreto himself was, also, a revolutionary hero.

In his old age, Loreto's image was that of a poor, ragged vagrant who many mistook for a beggar, though he refused to accept charity, washing cars to sustain his meager existence. No one know that he, like Cuamea, had been a colonel with Pancho Villa; Loreto is another of those authentic revolutionary heroes who, according to Méndez, "habían ganado la Revolución y se les pagaba con hambre y Jaramillazos" (50).[5] The garbage collectors who come to tear down Loreto's shack and take away his body discover a photograph of Loreto with Villa, but they throw it away because it has no monetary value. Loreto will not be included in the official accounts of the Revolution, a history written to justify those who took advantage of the war to get rich, or to convert the popular heroes, like Villa and Zapata, into antecedents of the P.R.I. (Partido Revolucionario Institucional), Mexico's ruling party, which has betrayed many of the revolutionary ideals it purports to embody. No; like all members of the poor class, Loreto disappears, and with him all those oral histories he would have passed on to a younger generation if the oral tradition still functioned as it should.

Méndez restates the fundamental threat to the culture: the oral tradition, once the receptable and process of our identity, has ceased to function, and the poor are in danger of being devoured by the chaos which for them the order of a strange and oppressive socio-cultural system represents. But Méndez' novel offers responses.

The first response is political. The young people have formulated a new, socio-political and cultural consciousness, the Chicano Movement, which resists acculturation, assimilation, and, in some cases, capitalism. Méndez argues for the foundation of Aztlán—another ideal of Chicano Movement—in northwestern Mexico and southwestern United States, which, as seen above, will include the poor from both countries. However, how can the Chicano Movement triumph if our history is being forgotten? Méndez posits another answer: the literary alternative, although in his own way. He demands a literature committed to social struggle, a literature *engagée*. The author has the responsibility to recover the oral tradition and, fixing it in a written media free of the uncontrollable contingencies which threaten the spoken word, make it available to the people, so they can know their identity, gather strength, and resist oppression. Méndez criticizes poetry of the strictly lyric type: "¡Mentiras!" says El Vate, "No hay poesía ni poetas, todo es una mascarada para no ver la tragedia humana; sólo los holgazanes que ignoran el dolor y el crimen, aduladores del poder, le cantan a las flores" (150). Méndez insists that literature should not be the white man's noisy shouting of the mechanized word we saw in "Tata Casehua," nor the beautiful word of art for art's sake, but rather, the committed word of struggle which expresses the silenced suffering of centuries of injustice. This literary ideology explains Méndez' themes and the form they have taken.

Finally, the most eloquent and effective answer is the book itself, which is a wealth of oral tradition. The reader retains the images rescued in the novel's literary space; the characters do not disappear when Loreto dies, because they now exist in the reader who has gathered them up as he reads, or should have. For this reason Méndez utilizes the different, distinctive styles of speech within the novel's fragmented structure. The images presented must not idealize the situation: there is much human suffering unknown to the people themselves, who find themselves disorganized by the pressures of an oppressive socioeconomic system, and therefore, helpless, unable to resist the oppressor. Méndez recovers their voices, but he does not falsify them by giving them an orderly, linear structure; the fragmentation of the narrative reflects the confusion and disorganization of the people, whereas a chronological, orderly structure would reflect more the supposed order of society into which the Chicano is being pushed. The structural tensions of the novel reflect the structural tensions of the socio-cultural (and economic) struggle. Moreover, Méndez never trusts the lazy reader who would take advantage of the novel to amuse himself without committing anything in return. As in "Tata Casehua," the style and structure are difficult; *Peregrinos* is not easy reading. The reader must prove himself worthy of being the guardian of the oral tradition. Méndez is not interested in entertaining him but moving him emotionally to compassion and intellectually and socially to action. To require an active participation in the reading is the first step. In another respect, as in all rituals, complexity and even confusion are codes hiding and protecting the secrets of a culture from the outsider. Those secrets reside in the voices vibrating in Loreto's head, which like the Sonora desert in "Tata Casehua" is the space where the silenced voices wait to be actualized by an heir to the tradition, in this case the reader. The novel's space and Loreto's mind-space are one and the same. Upon reading, the reader really hears the silent wealth of stories Loreto would have liked to tell him, and thus the book responds to the disappearance of the oral process.

In the last few pages the reader comes to a change in the narration. It is as if the narrative voice of the oral tradition now abandons the veil of secrecy and the masks of indirect address, and directly, clearly speaks to the reader who has proven capable of reaching the end; and to the survivors of the pilgrimage through the difficult passages of the novel, if they have listened carefully, the voice reveals the purpose of the voyage. The reading has been an initiation rite in which the reader becomes a "Peregrino de Aztlán," worthy of the revelations to be made to him.

This last segment begins with a *resumé* of the conflict: History "nos dejó varados en la isla del olvido, presos. No sólo eso, han quedado encadenados los genes que guardan la cultura, esencia de nuestra historia ... ni dignidad ni letras para los esclavos" (209). Méndez links writing to culture, offering the first as a path to the second. And when, in the historical process, the people realized they had lost their identity, they shouted out "para que el eco nos volviera los nombres y las voces que se iban ... dejándonos vacíos ... íbamos preguntando si el cielo sabe a dónde vamos, o de dónde venimos" (209). The forgotten, silent ancestors can give meaning to the present, because their *voices* know a tradition which can project itself as a path to the future. This is obvious when those voices respond from their silence with instructions to the faithful:

> Regresad más allá de la cruz de caminos; romped el silencio de las centurias con la agonía de nuestros gritos; veréis campos floridos donde plantastéis niños y árboles que se han bebido la savia de los siglos ... ahí donde moran las voces de los sucumbidos. El destino es la historia y la historia es el camino tendido ante los pasos que han sido. ¿Quién les ha hecho creer que sois corderos y bestias para el yugo?
>
> ¡Caballeros tigres, caballeros águilas, luchad por el destino de vuestros hijos! Sabed los inmolados, que en esta región, seréis alborada y también seréis río ... (209–210)

Méndez recapitulates his ideology explicitly: a true version of history will justify us; our lost traditions can grant significance and meaning to time and death, and they can project a viable path towards the goal of human dignity. But only the reader who has proven himself in the reading will be able to understand, will have enough energy to still listen to this final message, which, in truth, is an exhortation to action, to take the message beyond the reading into the world, to continue the "Peregrinaje de (a) Aztlán."

Both "Tata Casehua" and *Peregrinos de Aztlán* achieve the purpose of converting the oral tradition into fixed images. Faithful to his people, Méndez creates a synthesis of the *voices* of the poor and a *written text* which can compete in its complexity and beauty with contemporary literature. And ironically, in the final analysis, Méndez is most effective, most convincing, not when treating social themes or satirizing the rich, but when he writes the beautiful descriptions of the desert. And in every part what seduces us is not simply what is said, but how it is said. Méndez' art helps cover and compensate for some oversimplified, social moralizing. Méndez, while remaining faithful to his people and their situation as the silent ones, breaks the silence to rescue their images and preserve them. His literature—his writing—is the voice of silence crying for justice in the desert.

TRINITY UNIVERSITY, SAN ANTONIO

# Notes

[1] "The Space of Chicano Literature," *De Colores*, Vol. 1, No. 4; "Literatura Chicana: Una Respuesta al Caos," *Revista de la Universidad de México*, agosto, 1975.

[2] Miguel Méndez, "Tata Casehua," *El Espejo/The Mirror*, first ed. (Berkeley: Quinto Sol Publications, 1969), pp. 30–43. All quotations from this work come from this text and will be cited in parenthesis.

[3] Miguel Méndez, *Peregrinos de Aztlán* (Tuscon, Arizona: Editorial Peregrinos, 1974). All quotations from this edition will be cited in parenthesis.

[4] Other cases of Loreto as the center of the voices or memories can be found on pages 14, 33, 42–43, 54, 78, 87, 119, 130–131, 164–176.

[5] Jaramillo, a political activist who would not abandon the ideals of the Revolution, was murdered along with his family by government troops.

*Peregrinos de Aztlán:*
# Dialéctica estructural e ideológica

*Miriam Bornstein*

Desde su publicación en 1974, *Peregrinos de Aztlán* ha sido objeto de una gran variedad de visiones críticas.[1] Los enfoques de tales esfuerzos gravitan alrededor de acercamientos culturales, sociológicos, psicológicos, marxistas, lingüísticos y demás.[2] Tales aciertos críticos están configurados, sin embargo, dentro de un corpus tangencial a la obra misma; y si nos han mostrado la visión del mundo a partir de la obra, han fracasado en demostrar cómo surge tal visión.

Nuestro estudio parte de un concepto de la obra como entidad semiautónoma. Partimos del postulado de que la obra posee una estructura o un sistema de elementos interrelacionados jerárquicamente y que se caracteriza por los principios de totalidad, transformación y autorregulación.[3] Por lo tanto el estudio de la relación intra-estructural de los elementos variables e invariables nos revela el sistema operativo contribuyente a la carga informativa responsable de la significación.[4] De esta manera se puede aseverar que la obra crea su propio mundo, su propia realidad. Sin embargo esto no significa de ninguna manera que el texto exista únicamente en su materialidad. La obra como producto de un contexto social se proyecta a una realidad extra-literaria. Efectivamente, la posibilidad de aprehender toda la gama connotativa de significados depende precisa e indiscutiblemente de la relación entre el contexto textual y el contexto extra-textual.

Al proponer un acercamiento estructuralista-ideológico creemos estar insertados en un procedimiento más rigurosamente metódico, de mayor consistencia sistemática. Conjuntamente se intenta evitar que la obra se cierre sobre sí misma. Así es como la orientación general de este trabajo constituye la aplicación de un método que considera las leyes inmanentes que organizan la estructura de la novela, a la vez que su consecuente relación con las estructuras sociales generadoras.

A pesar de que hemos sentido la necesidad de exponer ciertas premisas, la naturaleza de este estudio no es teórica. El propósito principal es el de demostrar la existencia de un sistema contrastivo como principio estructurador en la organización interna del texto. Notamos que en *Peregrinos de Aztlán* el mecanismo dialéctico del texto es aparente en todos los niveles, pero especialmente a nivel de la composición. La reducción del conflicto a ciertas constantes proyecta el texto contra un fondo de estructuras semánticas que se activan por medio del contraste. Las asociaciones semánticas crean un mundo complejo revelado por la existencia de varias perspectivas. La reiteración de estructuras semánticas conflictivas establece un paralelismo en la perspectiva que se va intensificando hasta culminar en la significación ideológica del texto.

El estudio de la perspectiva del narrador representa uno de los aspectos más importantes ya que por medio de ésta se desentraña la específica visión del mundo, se actualiza el significado totalizador y se despliega la llamada "metáfora de la humanidad". En *Peregrinos de Aztlán* la perspectiva se responsabiliza de la organización dialéctica del relato. Sin embargo no se trata de una sola perspectiva sino de un conjunto de visiones enlazadas: la estética, la cultural, la religiosa y la moral, que culminan en la ideológica. La amplitud y complejidad de la perspectiva ideológica se debe a que no solamente unifica a las demás perspectivas sino que nos entrega simultáneamente una imagen de la realidad desde una postura socio-política, racial, histórica y económica. El narrador implícito, por medio de su relato y el de varios narradores ficticios, nos proporciona tal imagen a través de la ironía, el humor y hasta el melodrama. Las modalidades estilísticas como el retoricismo, la emotividad y la evaluación de los acontecimientos son producto de este enjambre de perspectivas construidas a partir de la dialéctica semántica del texto.

Primero analicemos la perspectiva estética. En un ensayo titulado "La alienación en la literatura chicana" Miguel Méndez declara que empezó a escribir *Peregrinos*... en un español "puro". Sin embargo se dio cuenta de "que está enajenado al lenguaje y a las formas impuestas y que el mundo chicano novelado en inglés o en español puro, resultaría a medias falso".[5] Este comentario apunta a la marginalidad que según el criterio de algunos es inherente a la literatura chicana ya que se inscribe lingüística y estéticamente en contra de las imposiciones de la cultura dominante; de aquí la sistemática "práctica de exclusión" de la literatura chicana. Es preciso notar que a través de la historia literaria la existencia de una literatura establecida ha sido producto de concretas situaciones socio-económicas favorables a la clase dominante.[6] Esta literatura se convierte en vigilante del *statu quo* y justifica la exclusión de la "otra literatura", según criterios y prejuicios tanto ideológicos como estéticos que influyen en la actividad del escritor, el editor, el librero, el maestro, el crítico, el historiador, el antólogo y en todas las personas responsables de la producción, diseminación, organización y análisis de la obra literaria. Por consiguiente el autor tiende a ajustar la escritura a los requisitos del editor receptivo a las leyes de demanda del mercado.

En el prólogo y a través del relato encontramos indicios del "ars poética" del autor que apunta al carácter rebelde de *Peregrinos...* como una novela ajena a un lenguaje único y a las "formas impuestas". Resalta una marcada actitud antagónica en la manera de entender y escribir la novela en relación a la novela tradicional. Aunque notamos treinta y seis casos en que el discurso pertenece a un narrador omnisciente no representado, característico de la novela tradicional, asimismo encontramos cuatro casos de un narrador-personaje, cuatro monólogos y doce unidades narrativas compuestas únicamente de diálogo. Por lo tanto, el uso de narradores ficticios representados del estilo directo narrativo, del cambio de tipografía, del correlato referente a otra obra o signo cultural y de la fragmentación espacial y temporal atestigua una oposición a la narrativa tradicional, donde se manifiesta un sólo narrador que generalmente es omnisciente y un hilo narrativo lógico guiado por una relación de causa y efecto.

Aun la rebeldía se proyecta a una autoconciencia autorial de compromiso. Rehusando la enajenación el autor declara en el prólogo que la escritura la "dicta el hablar común de los oprimidos" (p. 10). Y en boca del vate oímos "No hay poesía ni poetas, todo es una mascarada para no ver la tragedia humana; sólo los holgazanes... aduladores del poder... pagan brillo y oropel con arte prostituido" (p. 150). Esto ciertamente se contrasta con el relato caracterizado por el autor como "sublimador de lo muerto en bellas esculturas de mármol" (p. 9).

El autor, por medio de una delicada sensibilidad, intenta crear una novela asequible al público general y no sólo a un público afortunado. De aquí la importancia del uso de un lenguaje no alienado ni alienante, que se opone al lenguaje académico o "standard" como el único código narrativo posible. El mismo autor declara que su inicial inclinación hacia un lenguaje académico fue motivada por "alcanzar... [la] aprobación... de académicos de la lengua". Sin embargo resulta que "las palabras rebeldes... arguyeron ser la fiel expresión de las mayorías..." manifestando de esta manera todo un abanico de matices lingüísticos. En efecto las variadas capas lingüísticas son producto de un nivel de escritura estéticamente antagónico hacia lo convencionalmente establecido.

De esta manera afirmamos que la perspectiva estética se compone a partir de dos contextos diferentes. *Peregrinos...* representa un acto creativo comprometido, en oposición a una estética humanamente insensible y a un solo código socialmente "aceptable". Por lo tanto la perspectiva estética construye desde el comienzo un modelo dialéctico que establece el principio de estructuración para la obra.

En cuanto a la perspectiva cultural, notamos la continuación del principio de oposición en torno a la problemática del lenguaje. Primeramente el hecho de que Méndez escribe la novela en español representa un esfuerzo de mantener el idioma. En una conversación entre pizcadores leemos: "¿Por qué la raza que jala de foreman es más gacha que los mismos bosses?... Estos batos son funny, al recle te teoriquean pura totacha" (p. 49). Repetidamente se registra el conflicto lingüístico y el peligro de la asimilación. Pánfilo Pérez le dice a su hijo: "Perder el idioma materno, hijito, es como perder el alma" (p. 200). Finalmente el Chuco resume la problemática al quejarse de que "Nacimos sin palabras, nosotros los chicanos. A los jefecitos se les ha olvidado su luenga [sic]. En las escuelas gabachas nos apartan como a retardados por no hablar totacha" (p. 85). Efectivamente, a través de la novela notamos una profunda preocupación por mantener la identidad lingüística.

También dentro de esta perspectiva notamos que los valores culturales chicanos resultan superiores a los de los anglos. Analicemos el concepto de la familia. La mamá de Chalito, aunque cargada de hijos y de pobreza, cuida de su familia a toda costa y hasta el último sacrificio personal. Sin embargo la mamá del *hippy* rehusa su responsabilidad materna a favor de bienes materiales, y hasta llega a reemplazar a su hijo con un perro en quien deposita su amor y cuidado. El contraste entre las dos familias se aclara aún más cuando notamos que Chalito, integrado a su familia, lucha contra la pobreza, mientras que el *hippy* que se encuentra enajenado de la suya, escapa por medio de las drogas.

Este juego de oposiciones nos revela el deseo de implantar la importancia del lenguaje como conductor de valores culturales chicanos y de plasmar la tradición y realidad chicana a nivel literario.[7]

El contenido cultural se asocia cercanamente con una perspectiva religiosa contrastiva. Por medio de esta perspectiva el narrador nos indica la hipocresía religiosa de los explotadores. Doña Reginalda sale de la iglesia llorando de emoción mística mientras que vende a "La Malquerida" al prostíbulo. Mr. Smith se cree "Padre Eterno"; su casa es descrita como "espacio de santidad"; el narrador nos dice que su esposa "estaba convencida que a su consorte lo iluminaba la gracia divina" (p. 137). Sin embargo a pesar de creerse un hombre cristiano y moral, le perdona el crimen de su hijo ilegítimo a una muchachita adinerada. En comparación, Mr. Smith demuestra un profundo racismo detrás de su careta religiosa al condenar al Chuco a cuatro años de cárcel por quebrar un vidrio e insultar al juez. Mr. Mac Cane es otro caso de falsedad religiosa. Mientras leía la Biblia a la hora de comer y su familia se inclinaba respetuosamente en agradecimiento a Dios, sus hijas se bañaban desnudas en la alberca y la familia de Pánfilo Pérez apenas tenía alimento, aunque los animales de Mr. Mac Cane "resplandecían de salud". Finalmente se expone el fingimiento religioso dentro de un contexto histórico cuando Bobby, el *hippy*, le dice a su padre: "Me contaste... que tus abuelos habían llegado abrazándose con los indios como buenos cristianos; pero no me dijiste nunca que después los asesinaron para robarles sus posesiones" (p. 128). Es así que en la ética religiosa de los *Pilgrims* no entra en consideración la colonización y actividades imperialistas que persisten hasta nuestros días.

Dentro de esta perspectiva religiosa encontramos dos tipos de caridad contrastivos. Por un lado tenemos la falsa caridad que motiva a la Sra. Dávalos de Cocuch a darle limosna al orgulloso Loreto. Este acto está ocasionado por razones materialistas que al ser rechazado por Loreto, inspira en los Dávalos de Cocuch el desprecio social y la altanería. Ella y su esposo son representantes de la degradación moral y personal. No obstante asisten a la iglesia y continúan practicando la falsa caridad al comprarle el ataúd a Chalito quien muere a causa de la pobreza provocada, entre otras cosas, por la estratificación social que perpetúan los Dávalos de Cocuch. El narrador dice, "El con sus finanzas, atesorando, aseguraba la gloria terrenal; ella, administrando las cosas del espíritu, ganaba la del cielo" (p. 89).

Esta perspectiva abarca inclusive la religión institucionalizada. El uso del correlato bíblico nos da la clave para la interpretación de Jesús de Belén, una narración aparentemente tangencial al relato. Las coincidencias entre la vida de Belén y la de Cristo hacen que el yaqui sea propenso a la explotación. Cuando le preguntan: "¿Por qué has llegado a decir que eres Dios?" él contesta, "Porque a mí mismo me hicieron creer... Me asusté y quise huir; no me dejaron mis padres porque no les convenía... en cuanto me volví divino a ellos les empezó a relumbrar la barriga" (pp. 109-110). Dentro de este contexto vemos la fe expuesta en un doble plano. Los pecadores, enfermos del alma y del cuerpo, sufrían a causa de sus remordimientos. "Llegaban los sórdidos arrastrándose... Cuando los curaba de la sugestión... corrían a pregonar mis poderes divinos sin darse cuenta que tan sólo habían tropezado con su propia fe" (p. 114). El narrador repudia la fe institucionalizada y ritualizada, y apoya el concepto de la fe verdadera como parte de la integridad personal y la fuerza espiritual interior.

Jesús de Belén rechaza la identidad sagrada atribuida al afirmar que es "Ni más ni menos que cualquier humano" (p. 112). Efectivamente, él roba, bebe, dice malas palabras y hasta tiene mujer. El narrador dice "su maldita sensualidad y picardía le rebosaban la panza... le escurría la malicia burlesca... De pronto veo en su cara todo el dolor de la humanidad, todas las angustias y lágrimas sumadas a través de los siglos, la tragedia entera del indio torturado" (p. 112). Es aquí donde nos damos cuenta que Belén no es Cristo, sino un hombre revolucionario que vive dentro de su propio tiempo histórico. El grita que "al trabajador hay que pagarle con justicia" (p. 113); pide caridad y lo acusan de hablar contra "las instituciones del gobierno, contra la policía y el alcalde de este pueblo, contra las gentes honorables; alborotando a la plebe y sonsacando a la indiada pa que se alcen" (p. 117). En realidad Belén es un redentor, un redentor social cuya actividad compromete no sólo a los poderosos sino a la iglesia misma, que tradicionalmente se opone a la humanización de lo sagrado y a la verdadera reforma social.

El esquema contrastivo dentro de la perspectiva religiosa demuestra que las sinceras creencias cristianas ocupan una posición muy baja en la jerarquía de valores e intereses de los poderosos. Efectivamente, el materialismo egoísta se contrasta con la espiritualidad interior por medio de la oposición del código cristiano oficial y la verdadera caridad. El narrador, a través de su perspectiva, resuelve este conflicto al proponer un tipo de cristianismo humanitario que responda a las imperantes necesidades sociales.

Al considerar la perspectiva moral encontramos la continuación del contraste como recurso significativo. La Sra. Dávalos de Cocuch pertenece a la alta sociedad solamente "a base de una calistenia que la obligaba a abrir las piernas a cada vez que un hombre cualquiera le mostrara algún dinero" (p. 16). Ella se ha vendido como mujer con todo y la complicidad de su marido. El contraste entre los beneficios por pertenecer a una casta privilegiada y la degradación moral de esos individuos se acentúa más cuando el lector descubre que Mario es el dueño del burdel donde Doña Reginalda vendió a "La Malquerida". El paralelismo entre la Sra. Dávalos de Cocuch y "La Malquerida" se hace bastante obvio ya que, según la perspectiva moral, las dos son mujeres degradadas. La primera, debido a la ambición material y la segunda como víctima de tal ambición.

Finalmente, percibimos que la desintegración moral de algunos de los personajes se relaciona directamente con el espacio. El *hippy* nos apunta un espacio envilecido al hablar contra el aborto, el dinero, el poder, las drogas, la guerra y las orgías en Estados Unidos. Sin embargo este espacio corrupto afecta a otro, que en este caso es Tijuana. Un personaje lo resume todo: "¿Quién tiene más culpa? ¿O los cabrones estos que vienen con su dinero a corromperlo todo, o nosotros? Vienen con mucha, muchísima lana, suficiente para pagar quien haga malparir a sus hijas coscolinas, para pagar divorcios al plumazo, tirar en el juego, en la tomada, drogas, putas..." (p. 82).

La interpretación moral de la realidad es la de un burdel lujoso, espejo de la sociedad en cuyo ambiente se da la degradación a causa de la falta de escrúpulos morales de los poderosos quienes crean un estado de extrema necesidad y vulnerabilidad en los débiles.

Esta perspectiva moral, junto con la estética, la cultural y la religiosa, se incorporan a la perspectiva ideológica. El predominio de la perspectiva ideológica parte de que ésta cumple con una doble función: como eje unitivo e integrador de las demás perspectivas y como entorno generador del texto.

En este estudio definimos la ideología como parte de la superestructura: las imágenes social e históricamente determinadas con las que percibimos e interpretamos el mundo. Por lo tanto, la literatura como perteneciente a la superestructura, representa consciente o inconscientemente una crítica o propaganda que favorece una manera específica de concebir e interpretar la realidad. De esta manera la ideología no solamente está presente en el texto sino que funciona como factor normativo que impone reglas de selección durante el proceso de construcción de la obra. Debido a esto, resulta algo simplista afirmar que la ideología en el texto es la de la clase social del autor. Por otro lado, resultaría igualmente simplista afirmar que el autor está completamente desligado de su clase, ya que escribe a partir de su particular posición social y su posición ideológica hacia la doctrina imperante, la cual dispone tanto de los medios de producción material como intelectual y domina a través de éstos.

Sin embargo, es preciso apuntar que la obra no se reduce a ideología ya que dicho sistema es transformado internamente en el contexto del arte.[8] Así la perspectiva ideológica en *Peregrinos*... se construye a partir de un principio dialéctico organizador en relación a los personajes y el espacio.

Existe tal multiplicidad de figuras que la ausencia de un personaje central, con la posible excepción de Loreto, nos proporciona la clave para acertar el valor representativo de los personajes. Efectivamente, si consideramos a los personajes en relación al acontecer se pudiera decir que la mayoría son "personajes planos y estáticos" ya que solamente se conoce un aspecto de su personalidad o se desarrollan levemente o no evolucionan nada.[9] Notemos por ejemplo que Frankie Pérez, el Chuco, "La Malquerida", doña Candelita y otros personajes funcionan como representantes de un grupo racial y una clase social determinada. Esta categoría se puede aplicar a los anglos y mexicanos influyentes, con la única diferencia de que éstos son caricaturizados mientras que el narrador ve a los otros con simpatía. Quizá el personaje que se salva de estas clasificaciones sea Loreto, ya que funciona como centro unificador del acontecer.[10] En realidad todos los personajes son ideas o figuras alegóricas de conceptos y situaciones socio-económicas. Es por esto que notamos una clara polarización de los personajes, que dentro de una situación racial, social y económica se agrupan en buenos o malos. Los estereotipos de los anglos malos como Mr. Smith, Mr. Foxy y Mr. Mac Cane se oponen racialmente a personajes buenos como Loreto, El Chuco, Chayo Cuamea y otros más. Sin embargo, la oposición racial se rompe al considerar la clase social de los personajes. Los anglos se unen a los Dávalos de Cocuch para crear y perpetuar la pobreza en que viven los chicanos y mexicanos de la clase baja. Es por esto que la polarización racial y social no se puede desligar de la económica puesto que los personajes ricos, tanto anglos como mexicanos, se dedican a explotar a los pobres. Mr. Smith justifica la explotación de los trabajadores agrícolas y dice: "Qué sería de nuestros chicanos si no tuvieran el alivio de estas labores" (p. 136). Igualmente el narrador nos indica que la dueña de "Siesta's Chili Dogs", "Se daba aires de caritativa... pues gracias a ella comían aquellos pobres mexicanos, por primera vez, hasta que se les saltaba el ombligo y conocían lo que es ponerse zapatos..." (p. 39). Esta actitud paternalista y opresora perpetúa las diferencias raciales, sociales y económicas además de garantizar una fuerza laboral barata.

Por otra parte, tal polarización se proyecta al espacio ya que los dos grupos gravitan en entornos distintos. De esta manera el espacio funciona como principio de caracterización. Existe el espacio de los explotadores y el espacio de los explotados. Un sueño de Frankie expone la existencia de los trabajadores agrícolas en un espacio cerrado que describe como "los malditos viñedos que aprisionaban los testículos". El narrador, que en esta sección hace uso del lenguaje pachuco, dice: "El chante donde cantoneaban, era de pura pinchi wood; no tenían ni madre en que caise muertos" (p. 167). Sin embargo, Mr. Mac Cane vive en lo que el narrador llama, "palacios de fábula". Citemos otro ejemplo: mientras que los Dávalos de Cocuch se daban el lujo de adornar su baño con espejos y tomar baños de espuma con perfumes finos, la casa de Loreto en el barrio de Río Muerto está construida con los desperdicios de la sociedad de consumo los cuales incluyen irónicamente retratos de la comida que le hace tanta falta. Por último, a un nivel más abstracto, la casa al estilo mexicano de Mr. Smith se contrasta con la cárcel real y simbólica que su sentido de justicia y racismo logra crear para el Chuco.

Estos ejemplos representan la dialéctica entre el espacio de los ricos y el de los pobres, ayudando al lector a configurar una imagen más completa del sentido de la obra. De esta forma el espacio como "entorno cultural" manifiesta las deficiencias de la vida cotidiana, la lucha y el sufrimiento de una clase social. Su ignominia, pobreza y desesperación por razones de opresión, explotación, racismo y discriminación social, los cuales marcan el espacio en que viven los personajes.

Desde el punto de vista histórico-geográfico, el espacio de *Peregrinos*... incluye el noroeste de México y el suroeste de los Estados Unidos, o en otras palabras, se trata de Aztlán en la época contemporánea. En este sentido el espacio funciona como generador de conciencia social, racial y económica. Los personajes toman conciencia de su identidad según las condiciones de vida dentro de su espacio. Hablando del término méxico-americano el Chuco nos dice: "Chale, ése es puro pinchi madera, lo de Mexicano [sic] domás pa' meterlo al surco, a las minas, nel, pos otra chinga pior. Lo de americanos, pos ya te darás cola, camarada, pa' darnos en la madre en sus pinchis guerras puercas" (p. 29). El espacio del chicano en Estados Unidos es los campos agrícolas donde entrega su alma el Chuco, y es Viet Nam, donde sacrifica su vida Frankie Pérez. En este contexto notamos la continuación de la oposición espacial. En las conciencias ilusorias de los mojados, la pobreza de México y el sufrimiento en el desierto se oponen a "la selva cuajada de hojas verdes con signos de dólares"; o sea, a la imagen ideal de Estados Unidos, donde sólo allí la prosperidad es posible para el mexicano pobre. La sierra del Bacatete y la posibilidad de materializar el lema de "tierra y libertad" se oponen a la dura realidad; la revolución traicionada y los grandes latifundios de los exrevolucionarios. El ámbito mental y espiritual en el que gravitan los sueños de Loreto se caracteriza por la aventura, la posibilidad de un futuro que ciertamente se contrasta con un presente de lucha para sobrevivir un día más. Igualmente, el espacio metafórico de valores trascendentales en el que se revela la conciencia poética de Lorenzo y el vate, se opone a ambientes hóstiles que conducen a la autoaniquilación.

Se trata de un espacio físico y mental casi determinista en relación con el acontecer de las figuras. Los personajes cuál es su posición en la jerarquía racial, social y económica según su respectivo espacio, que funciona dialécticamente como contorno moldeador, generador de definidas existencias y personalidades dentro de un contexto socio-histórico estratificado. Así es como la edificación reiterativa y contrastiva de significados intensifican la continuidad semántica que desemboca en la perspectiva ideológica.

Para resumir, diremos que el paralelismo de las varias perspectivas se construye a partir de un eje horizontal bipartito que organiza los elementos semánticos en una relación dialéctica. El recurso de la dialéctica como principio organizador queda incrustado dentro de contextos intra y extra-textuales, revelándonos dos realidades cerradas aunque dependientes. Las apuntadas interacciones culturales, morales, religiosas, raciales, sociales y económicas sirven para destacar las diferencias entre los dos grupos, para registrar un espacio cerrado en el que la movilidad es nula. El mundo novelístico de *Peregrinos* ... queda escindido en dos hemisferios opuestos cuya interacción es posible solamente en términos de la explotación, el racismo, la degradación y la deshumanización. Los poderosos apoyan un mundo envilecido ya que de esto depende su supremacía; así todo y todos quedan en su debido lugar. Sin embargo, el narrador llama al lector a la lucha, a la protesta, a la creación de sus propias condiciones de vida. De aquí la nota final esperanzada a pesar del pesimismo imperante a través de toda la obra.

De esta manera el estudio de las constantes estructurales nos revela un texto multifuncional poseedor de diversas voces.[11] La obra responsable, ajena a la sublimación intelectual, cumple con una de sus funciones al cuestionar su entorno social. La expresión literaria no es solamente un acto creativo sino que es también una forma de conocimiento y transformación de la realidad. *Peregrinos de Aztlán* cumple con esta función. Miguel Méndez ha conseguido inscribir su obra en el cambio social; y aunque la novela no pueda suplantar la acción política, rehusa presentarse únicamente como entidad estética.

DENVER, COLORADO

# Notas

[1] Miguel M. Méndez, *Peregrinos de Aztlán* (Tucson: Editorial Peregrinos, 1974). Todas las citas textuales provienen de esta edición.

[2] Para una discusión teórica de la metodología crítica predominante y su aplicación en torno a la literatura chicana, véase Joseph Sommers y Tomás Ybarra-Frausto, *Modern Chicano Writers* (Englewood Cliffs, N.J.: Prentice-Hall, Inc., 1979).

[3] Jean Piaget, "Introduction and Location of Problems", *Structuralism* (New York: Harper & Row, 1970), pp. 3-16.

[4] Yury Lotman, "Purposes and Methods of the Structural Analysis of the Poetic Text", *Analysis of the Poetic Text* (Ann Arbor: Ardis, 1976), pp. 10-16.

[5] Miguel M. Méndez, "La alienación en la literatura chicana", *De Colores*, 4, Nos. 1-2 (1978), p. 151.

[6] La problemática del escritor y el medio político en relación a la producción literaria ha sido ampliamente estudiada por Eliana Rivero, "Hacia una historia integral de la literatura latinoamericana: reflexión e implementación", Taller de Ideología y Literatura, Universidad de Minnesota, abril de 1978, y

Víctor Godínez, "El escritor y la política", *Literatura, ideología y lenguaje* (México: Editorial Grijalbo, 1976), pp. 127-177.

[7] Para un análisis profundo sobre los valores culturales a nivel literario, véase Oscar U. Somoza, "Visión axiológica en la narrativa chicana", Tesis Doctoral, Universidad de Arizona, 1977.

[8] Julia Kristeva, *Semiotike* (Paris: Seuil, 1969), p.309.

[9] René Jara Cuadra y Fernando Moreno, *Anatomía de la novela* (Valparaíso: Ediciones Universitarias de Valparaíso, 1972), p. 67.

[10] Juan Bruce-Novoa, "La voz del silencio: Miguel Méndez", *Diálogos*, 13, No. 3 (mayo-junio, 1976), p. 29.

[11] Yury Lotman, "'The Alien Word' in the Poetic Text", *Analysis of the Poetic Text* (Ann Arbor: Ardis, 1976), pp. 107-113.

# D. Ron Arias

## Ron Arias'
## *The Road To Tamazunchale:*
## A Chicano Novel
## of the New Reality

*Eliud Martínez*

> Quiero decir que yo estoy convencido de que, si yo soy mexicano y vivo en México y escribo en México, mi obra será de México, lo mismo si me refiero a una anécdota de mis coterráneos del Bahío que si trato de enfocar, sinceramente, desde yo mismo, los efectos de la revolución francesa o mi admiración por el milagro griego.
> —José Rojas Garcidueñas, "El mexicanismo y nuestra literatura."

The critical reception of *The Road To Tamazunchale* has to date been uniformly enthusiastic.[1] In addition to its having been nominated for the National Book Award, the novel has been justly praised for its magic realism; its lean, crisp prose style; its blending of fantasy, magic and reality; its affinities with contemporary Spanish American fiction; its careful craftsmanship; its mock-heroic parody and humor; its faithful rendering of spoken conversational idioms; and for its humane and compassionate treatment of Death, the novel's central theme. The author has also been rightly praised for his simple, joyful, storytelling gifts—in the most praiseworthy sense—and for his commitment to art and truth which transcends but does not preclude social commentary on facets of the Chicano experience.

Equally deserving of praise is the novel's contemporaneity, which reviewers comment upon but do not emphasize. Ron Arias' *The Road To Tamazunchale* brings contemporary Chicano fiction into an association with international literature and the arts that it has never before enjoyed. The purpose of this paper is to examine some of the outstanding contemporary qualities of this novel.

*The Road To Tamazunchale*, first of all, obeys a conception of fictional reality which Robbe-Grillet, Carlos Fuentes, and others call "the new reality."[2] This term, which subsumes "magic realism,"[3] calls to mind the art of Pirandello and Genet; Buñuel, Fellini, Bergman and Antonioni; Borges, Robbe-Grillet, Rulfo, Cortázar, Fuentes, and countless others. The new reality, then, is a contemporary conception of artistic reality which has its origins in Modernism. It provides the esthetics for much of what is considered Post-Modern—that is, contemporary—art, including the novel, theatre, film and painting. The esthetic ideas, doctrines and techniques of the new reality cut across schools and movements such as surrealism, expressionism, the theatre of the absurd, the "new novel" (French and Spanish American), and so on.

In the novel the new reality represents a continuation and culmination of the modern novelist's preference for depicting interior reality and states of consciousness as opposed to exterior reality. Much of the action of *The Road To Tamazunchale* takes place in the imagination and dreams of Fausto, the novel's protagonist. "Are you awake?" is a constant refrain in the novel. Fausto is about eighty years old and he knows that he is dying. In fact, as the reader learns at the very beginning of the novel, Fausto, since his retirement six years earlier, has been leading what might be called a death in life.

> For six years he had shuffled to the window, to the bathroom, down to the kitchen, through gloomy rooms, resting, listening to the radio, reading, turning thin, impatient, waiting for the end. Six years ago she had convinced him to stop work. (p. 14)

Chapter One also describes Fausto's symbolic "change of skin," of which his niece Carmela remains unaware. "She must be blind, she didn't even notice.... Next time I'll give her my heart, and she'll say ... Tío, don't play games. Put it back" (p. 13). This change of skin and the symbolic sound of a flute, heard only by Fausto and associated throughout the novel with the theme of Death, propel the novel forward. Both symbolize the old man's determination to make his remaining days meaningful; his first impulse is to take a voyage to Cuzco, Peru (p. 15).

The new reality is also characterized by an emphasis on play and make-believe. The lovable Fausto therefore is able to journey back and forth in time; as he stumbles up the stairs to his bedroom in his Los Angeles home, he arrives in Peru, where buses, taxis, airplane terminals, concrete, train tracks and telephone poles co-exist with colonial viceroys, archbishops, and a procession of foot soldiers, arquebusiers and lancers. The ripoff of a pack of cigarettes at the local black market leads Fausto to compose "an elegant, detailed report to the viceroy" (p. 16). Another example of make-believe is described in a later part of the novel. Fausto says to one of the wetbacks in the group which (he dreams?) he is smuggling into the United States: "When we get to where we're going, all of you must pretend you're dead" (p. 70). And toward the end of the novel when a young priest comes to give the dying Fausto his last rites Fausto blesses him. "He's a strange man," says the perplexed priest to Carmela. "He likes to play games" (p. 95) is her reply. In this novel, death is the most serious game of all, and Fausto plays it with great frequency.

One of the most delightfully humorous episodes in the novel describes Fausto's encounter with two girls at a bus stop. Wearing his dead wife's pink nightgown as a cape and carrying a hoe which he believes to be a staff, Fausto boards the same bus that the girls take. Both girls are described as dark, one of them with dyed blonde hair. When the suspicious bus driver is rude to Fausto, Mario, an "apprentice wizard," a goateed teenager, intervenes and befriends Fausto. As Fausto takes a seat, Mario waved and

> ... gave him the thumbs-up sign. "Good try," he said as Fausto sat down. "But I'll tell you what's wrong."
> "What?"
> The boy slid over to Fausto's side and tugged at the cape.
> "This."
> "My cape?"
> "Yeah, it don't look too cool. I mean it's not the thing to wear when you're trying to score. They don't dig capes no more. That went out two years ago. (p. 25)

An extremely important convention in the arts of the twentieth century which emphasizes make-believe is the story within a story. This convention is followed in the theatre and film as well as in the novel.[4] A work of art becomes, as in Hermann Hesse's *Steppenwolf*, a "magic theatre," a spectacle in which the imagination is allowed complete liberation. In a work of the new reality, vision, fantasy, hallucination and dream are celebrated. Everything imaginable, even the impossible, is possible.

In this connection, *The Road To Tamazunchale* contains a play within the novel that is extremely important for an understanding of the novel's esthetics. It is a device which allows Arias to comment upon the esthetics of his novel and to make that commentary an integral part of the work itself. All of Chapter Eleven (pp. 84-90) is important for this reason, and it is intended in addition to prepare the reader for the impossible events depicted in Chapter Thirteen, the last chapter of the novel.

Several possible titles and settings for Arias' play within the novel are discussed by the characters. Tiburcio, one of them, proposes "Vida y muerte." After some discussion he also adds that "the title should have some mystery to it, maybe something about a man with a mask" (p. 83). The play is to be performed to entertain the heavy-hearted group of wetbacks smuggled by Fausto into Los Angeles. It takes place in an abandoned theatre, and as it turns out, the title of the play is "The Road To Tamazunchale." This is important for reasons that will be taken up later.

This chapter contains a great number of expressionistic details: to begin with, an abandoned theatre. There are improvised props, such as the simulated bus; makeshift costumes; theatrical make-up; ambiguous dialogue; and a carnival or circus atmosphere—popcorn, candied apples, footlights, whistling, laughter, applause and bewilderment. Tiburcio, like the barker at the circus, announces the play. Everyone is in a playful, make-believe frame of mind.

At the end of the play illusion and reality meet and overlap. Like at the end of Fellini's film 8½ or in a "happening," the child plays the role of Fausto, gestures to the audience, and invites them to join the actors. The play, therefore, discards in an expressionistic way the convention which separates performers from audience and projects beyond the physical limitations of the stage to incorporate the spectators. Chapter Eleven closes with Fausto in his own bed, asleep and dying, clapping and clapping his hands, much to the bewilderment of Carmela and Mario (pp. 90-91). Arias makes a cinematic transition at this point in the novel. He links the two chapters and establishes a subtle artistic continuity between them by shifting the scene or the situation and having Fausto clap his hands in both. The theatrical or make-believe nature of the play within the novel and the fictional nature of the novel itself are made apparent for the attentive reader by this overlapping of illusion (in this case, dream) and reality. There are other examples of the story within a story principle in *The Road To Tamazunchale*.

Illusion and reality overlap in other ways in Arias' handling of some of his characters. In passing from modern to contemporary, the arts of the novel, theatre and film are characterized by a noteworthy development, the emergence of what I call *the new breed of character*. Antecedents for the new breed of character may be found in a number of symbolist, dada, expressionistic and surrealistic works. They are exemplified in a great number of contemporary works—films, novels, plays.[5] Ron Arias' use of the new breed of character constitutes another praiseworthy aspect of his contemporaneity as a novelist.

Characters of the new breed are illusory, contradictory and ambiguous. When they are compared with traditional characters their complexity becomes even more pronounced.[6] Pure fictional creations, as Robbe-Grillet has pointed out in *For a New Novel*,[7] are true in proportion to their falseness. And they are subject to the most extravagant mutations in the mind of the creator and to the whims and fancies of the characters themselves. *The Road To Tamazunchale* offers generous evidence of the new breed of character.

Characters of the new breed, for example, are frequently fictions in the minds of other characters. Ana, for example, one of several Vergil-type guides for Fausto in the novel, appears to him in his imaginary voyage to Cuzco. She ambiguously fuses with Carmela in Fausto's mind, and whether she is a prostitute who brings warmth once again to the loins of the aging Fausto remains unclear (pp. 18-21). The Buñuelian shepherd from Peru, Marcelino Huanca, with his flock of alpacas offers another example of the new breed of character. The music from his magical flute is a recurrent leitmotif throughout the novel. It keeps Fausto's imminent death present in the reader's mind, for Marcelino is a Bergmanesque messenger from the other world. One of the most humorous and surrealistic episodes in *The Road To Tamazunchale* takes place on the Los Angeles Freeway; it is reminiscent of Buñuel:

> "What's that?" Mario said, jumping up.
> Fausto hurried to the sidewalk. "Vente, don't be afraid," he told Mario, then stepped off the curb into the mass of bobbing, furry heads. The shepherd, lagging behind, seemed confused by the traffic lights and horns. At the intersection leading to the freeway on-ramp the frightened alpacas blocked a row of funeral cars, headlights on. Fausto, shouting and waving his hoe, stumbled up the ramp and tried to turn the herd from disaster. Mario ran after him, catching a glimpse of the motorcycle escort racing to the head of the funeral procession. (pp. 28-29)

In this episode Marcelino exists for both Fausto and Mario, but not for the policeman. In other parts of the novel Marcelino seems to exist only for Fausto (p. 35), and the flute music is heard only by him, as at the very beginning and other parts of the novel. In another part Fausto introduces Marcelino to Carmela and her boyfriend Jess (p. 47).

Alive or dead, moreover, the new breed of character wends in and out of the narrative, appears and vanishes and reappears like Rulfo's characters in *Pedro Páramo*. Fausto's dead wife, Evangelina, for example, appears to Fausto in several parts of the novel, once inside the van in which he and Mario have hitched a ride (pp. 72-73), and another time in his bedroom in a hallucination brought on by fever (pp. 80-81). Another excellent new reality fictional device, the logical development of an absurd premise,[8] is used in combination with the new breed of character in Chapter Seven (pp. 57-62).

Chapter Seven develops around the discovery of an anonymous dead wetback by several of the novel's characters. The cause of his death is never established, and even though there is no water anyplace near, the wetback's death is attributed to drowning. David is the name which Mrs. Rentería, a spinster, finally decides on. This name, whether deliberate on Arias' part or not, is most suitable in view of the wetback's Michangelesque beauty:

> Everyone was silent. David was certainly the best looking young man they had ever seen, at least naked as he now lay. No one seemed to have the slightest shame before this perfect shape of a man; it was as if a statue had been placed among them ... Some of the men envied the wide chest, the angular jaw, and the hair, thick and wavy; the women for the most part gazed at the full, parted lips, the sun-baked arms, the long, strong legs and of course the dark, soft mound with its finger of life flopped over, head to the sky. (p. 58)

The spinster adopts the beautiful corpse. She bathes and shaves David, cuts his hair and powders his face, manicures his hands, and displays him. Everyone comes several times to shake the dead man's manicured hand and to admire his beauty, until he begins to decompose and smell. In the end David is not buried: "A body so perfect should not be buried," Fausto tells Marcelino (p. 62), and so the shepherd, using ancient Inca knowledge, restores David's decomposing beauty. And David, in perfect condition, is taken to a place near a river, "where others can find him" (p. 62).

In this chapter magic and fantasy overlap. One is reminded of Borges' "The Circular Ruins" and of a statement made by the narrator of "The Garden of Forking Paths." This statement offers a good commentary on the new breed of character: "This book—says the narrator—is an indeterminate heap of contradictory drafts. I examined it once: in the third chapter the hero dies, in the fourth he is alive."[9] In Arias' novel Fausto dies in Chapter Twelve; in Chapter Thirteen he is "alive" again.

The new breed of character, in addition, is aware of his existence as a character. As such he or she consciously plays one or several fictional roles. In the play within the novel, Smaldino, a character, dresses as Smaldino; Mrs. Rentería, another character, plays the role of Mrs. Rentería; and "someone, probably Robert, Smaldino's eldest son, hobbled out from the side, a hoe in one hand and wearing a shabby pith helmet, a moth-eaten cape and baggy trousers. Black, crayon wrinkles were drawn above and below the eyes and at both sides of the mouth" (p. 85). Robert plays the part of Fausto.

In the novel of the new reality the intrusion of "real life" into a fictional work ruins the artistic effect: "Get him off the stage," says one of the characters to another character in the play within the novel, referring to a third character. "He's ruining everything" (p. 86). Earlier in the novel, when Fausto and Marcelino walk into a Hollywood film in progress, as far as Fausto is concerned they are back in colonial times, in Colombia or Trinidad or Santa Marta (p. 52). But as they walk across the set a filmmaker cries out: "Get those guys out! ... What kind of costumes are those anyway?" (ibid). And when an actress mistakes them for actors playing the role of beggars, Fausto is offended:

> "Madame, do we look like beggars?"
> "Well, I'm a whore."
> "Madame, we are visitors."
> "I also play a flower girl. I did that yesterday."
> "I hoped we would get treated with respect."
> "Don't get touchy. One day a beggar, another day a soldier. And don't call me *madame*. I'm just a whore." (p. 53)

But in a novel of the new reality, as the above examples show, the intrusion of dream and fantasy into real life, the overlapping of illusion and reality, is both desirable and artistically sound. In many parts of *The Road To Tamazunchale*, as one can see, Arias skillfully blurs the boundaries between art and reality. His characters suddenly appear, disappear and reappear in the minds and perceptions of other characters.

It was noted above that whether or not the drowned wetback's name had been deliberately selected by Arias to suggest classical beauty, the name itself invites the kind of interpretation set forth. In *The Road To Tamazunchale* certain names are extremely important. This is certainly true of the novel's title and of the play within the novel. The latter tends to multiply the novel's levels of reality. First of all, the name itself is real, as the author points out in his *Postscript* (p. 108); Tamazunchale is a former Huastec capital and its precise location on the map is fixed. It is briefly described in *Frances Toor's New Guide to Mexico*. It is pronounced like "Thomas and Charlie" (p. 106). But Tamazunchale makes an extraordinary visual and psychological impact upon the reader, from whom this information is withheld until the very end of the novel; one had never heard of it until Arias' novel came along. And Arias artistically exploits that quality of the unknown which inheres in the unfamiliar name.

The title of Arias' novel has some mystery to it, as Tiburcio had wanted for the play within the novel. The title does not say *A Road*, but *The Road* to Tamazunchale. Tiburcio, in his introduction of the play, stresses that coming from or going to Tamazunchale, whether they know it or not, it's the same road. Thus, there is *only one* way to get there!

Consider, secondly, the characters' discussions of the name. Tiburcio explains the reason for the title of the play:

> You see, whenever things go bad, whenever we don't like someone, whoever it is ... we simply send them to Tamazunchale. We've never

really seen this place, but it sounds better than saying *the other*, if you know what I mean. (p. 84, my emphasis)

And the person who plays the part of Carmela says to the person who plays the part of Fausto:

> There's a boy who sits next to me in school, and he's always using *that word*. The other day the teacher heard him, and he had to stand in the corner for an hour. The teacher really got mad because he even wrote it on the wall. But that's nothing, I see it in the bathroom all the time. (p. 89, my emphasis)

But the character who plays Fausto expresses a different view:

> "Mijita ... everyone should go to Tamazunchale."
> "What's it like?"
> "Like any other place. Oh, a few things are different ... if you want them to be." (p. 89)

In Tamazunchale, he says, she can be anything she wants to be, a flower, the sun, the moon, the stars, a song of a million sounds or a little girl. She will be able to see all her friends there. When she asks whether they are going to die, he replies that no one dies in Tamazunchale. Some people pretend to die and others, he admits, do die and are buried. But then "they usually see how stupid it is to die, so they come out of the earth and do something else." In Tamazunchale there is complete freedom to be everything and everyone, even to be nothing (pp. 89–90).

In these commentaries, taken in connection with Fausto's "voyage" toward death, the name *Tamazunchale* acquires a serious vagueness and a deadly strangeness. Tamazunchale becomes a metaphor for the other world, to which there is only one road, only one way to go—by dying! Since no one has ever come back from there, no one knows what it is like. The novel as a whole, its central theme of death and dying, the strange events depicted in the last chapter, Fausto's final arrival in Tamazunchale where the impossible is possible, all this strongly supports the interpretation that Arias has used the name as a metaphor for the world beyond. According to the views of the characters Tamazunchale can be hell or limbo or purgatory or paradise. It is one and all of them because the novel itself admits them all as possibilities.

For Fausto, then, Life is a one-way journey toward Death. His journey is a quest for knowledge and beauty. The events through which Fausto passes and how he passes through them offer a commentary on Death. In a dying person, while he sleeps, while he drifts in and out of consciousness, life flickers off and on. In the process of dying the body remains while the soul wanders in and out, like consciousness, until the person dies. Then the soul remains outside.

*The Road To Tamazunchale* raises but does not answer the question concerning the state of souls after death. Where does the soul go? Is the grave the final "home" of the soul as well as of the body? At the end of this novel Fausto goes to Tamazunchale. For Fausto, Tamazunchale is Paradise. Hence, the last chapter communicates an exuberant joy and closes with a message of hope.

Tamazunchale names the afterlife without specifying its geography; it points to it symbolically. Another very important name is that of the main protagonist. *Fausto* is charged with significations. Even if the author never intended any reference to these significations, Fausto's discontent with his death in life, his aspiration to transcend earthly knowledge and physical limitations—these invoke Fausto's legendary namesake. In the same way, because Fausto Tejada is a dreamer and an adventurer, because he wears a "helmet" and a "cape" and carries a "staff," because he is a mock-hero who fights imaginary battles, not with windmills but with shadows, Fausto reminds one, in addition, of the knight-errant of the sorrowful countenance. Noticeable, too, in *The Road To Tamazunchale* is the number of guides—Ana, Carmela, Mario the apprentice-wizard, Marcelino Huanca (Fausto himself is a guide for the wetbacks)—who lead Fausto through his imaginary and real experiences. In the end, Fausto is himself the guide in Tamazunchale.

In a large sense, as one can see, the novel deals with universal themes that bring the Chicano experience into focus. The language of Arias' characters, particularly that of the disarming Mario, conveys an aspect of that experience, its linguistic reality. Arias has captured the special flavor, the rhythm and idioms of Chicano popular and conversational speech. The sprinkling of Spanish throughout the novel is always natural, never forced. There is a sense of shared cultural values among the characters. For example, Mexican superstition, folk medicine and the Catholic religion amalgamate in the characters' attitudes toward death. Arias even gently pokes fun at the drinking that takes place at a funeral and at the attitude toward Mexico that Evangelina expresses. The atmosphere of Los Angeles, the largest Mexican city outside of Mexico, is also felt in this novel.

Even the little episode describing Fausto's encounter with the two girls at the bus stop—they are both dark but one has dyed blonde hair—even this little episode makes a significant commentary on a facet of the Chicano experience in the United States. Very significant is "the wetback problem," a theme that runs through the novel. Illegal immigration is a vital and sometimes explosive issue today. The Indian heritage of Chicanos and the identification with Spanish American ethnic and cultural values are also mentioned. In the case of the former, mirrors are important in Chicano novels. Fausto

washed himself in the bathroom. Puro indio, he thought, looking at
the hairless face in the mirror. You're more indio than a Tarahumara,
his wife used to say. (p. 15)

These and other facets of the Chicano experience are given artistic expression in the novel.

*The Road To Tamazunchale*, as a Chicano novel, has liberated itself from dogmas, as Tomás Rivera says in the Foreword to the novel. Chicano writers, in Rivera's words, "need to represent and make concrete every angle and side of the Chicano. Our intent in literature, then, has to be totally human." Ron Arias responds successfully to that need.

In terms of craftsmanship and artistry, no Chicano novel before *The Road To Tamazunchale* has tapped the artistic resources of the modern and contemporary novel (and the arts) in a comparable way, deliberately and intuitively. Arias' understanding and command of new reality forms and techniques is daring and commendable. His handling of the new breed of character is most deserving of praise. Other traits of the novelist are equally commendable: the skillful way that he develops episodes logically from absurd premises, the imaginative use of the play within the novel, his employment of cinematic transitions, the blurring of illusion and reality in a number of unusual and ambiguous episodes, his structural handling of time, the effective depiction of numerous processions—processions of *alpacas*, of funeral cars, of torchlights, of foot soldiers, of actors, of wetbacks—, the expressionistic rendering of certain scenes, the defamiliarization of real places, and in general the admirable compression of a wealth of detail into 107 pages, among others.

*The Road To Tamazunchale*, moreover, contains surrealistic and "nonsense" images. It includes a Borges-type inventory of books, among which are books not yet written, "an early cosmography of the known and unknown worlds," "a neglected, indexed history of historiography," and "an anthology of uninvented myths" (p. 101). There are, admittedly, noticeable imperfections in the last chapter, in the handling of imagery related to the new breed of character. In Arias' handling of this extraordinary and complex literary device, however, such imperfections are to be expected in the case of a first novel, successful in so many respects, as this study tries to demonstrate. These imperfections are due to the attempt, I believe, to employ the humorous imagery of English nonsense verse in prose fiction without the forcefulness of rhyme, and they need not be adversely criticized.

*The Road To Tamazunchale*, then, is a carefully crafted work which exhibits and places in the service of Chicano literature a large number of artistic resources. For this reason it is a pace-setter and marks a new direction for Chicano literature. Given the generous evidence which the novel affords it seems safe to say that *The Road To Tamazunchale* points toward the conviction that all literatures, all cultures and all the arts cross-fertilize one another. This conviction, I believe, is what is fundamental to artistic contemporaneity. Properly appreciated, *The Road To Tamazunchale* will undoubtedly influence the future course of Chicano literature and literary criticism. This international novel is a significant contribution to American literature by a Chicano.

Finally, it does not seem out of place to call attention to the fact that Ron Arias' writing of *The Road To Tamazunchale* was a direct and highly personal response to the deaths of his mother, father and grandmother within the period of a single year. And even as this novel was going through its second printing Death visited again; Jonathan Arias, the novelist's six year old son, was struck and killed by an automobile.

This is no ordinary novel, then. *The Road To Tamazunchale* is a safety valve, a novel of necessity. And one is left with a number of unanswerable questions, to which Arias has responded creatively and personally, with an incomparable largeness of compassion and a quiet, soft-spoken strength. Surely the words of another compassionate man speak comfortingly to the author for those of us who know him. In the fourth letter to a young poet, Rainer Maria Rilke says:

> Here where an immense country lies about me, over which the winds pass coming from the seas, here I feel that no human being can answer for you those questions and feelings that deep within them have a life of their own; for even the best err in words when they are meant to mean most delicate and almost inexpressible things.[10]

University of California, Riverside

## Notes

[1] The reviews that have come to my attention to date are Alan Cheuse, "Death of Chicano Everyman," *Los Angeles Times* (December 7, 1975); C. K. Firman, "Realism, Fantasy Combined in Novel," *Progress Bulletin* (Pomona, Calif.: Nov. 2, 1975), p. 30; Arturo Islas, "Magic Realism in East Los Angeles," to be published, according to Islas, in the *New Mexico Sun*; Chris Preciado, "A Time to Die: A Look at Death in *The Road To Tamazunchale*," (unpublished ms.); and Bernice Zamora, "A New Departure: *The Road to Tamazunchale* by Ron Arias," to be published, according to Zamora, in *Mester* (UCLA).

[2] Carlos Fuentes, *La nueva novela hispanoamericana* (México: Joaquín Mortiz, 1969). Alain Robbe-Grillet, *For A New Novel* (New York: Grove Press, 1965).

Sections of Fuentes' work appear in slightly different form in Juan Loveluck, ed., *La novela hispanoamericana* (Santiago de Chile: Ed. Universitaria, 1969), pp. 162-192. See also Vivian Mercier, *A Readers Guide To The New Novel From Queneau To Pinget* (New York: Farrar, Straus and Giroux, 1971 ed.), espec. the Introduction, pp. 3-42, and the fine article by María Teresa Babín, "La antinovela en Hispanoamérica," *Revista Hispánica Moderna*, XXXIV (1968), pp. 523-532.

Cortázar's *Rayuela* (Buenos Aires: Ed. Sudamericana, 1963) [*Hopscotch* (New York: NAL Plume Books, 1966, excellently translated by Gregory Rabassa)] discusses throughout, but particularly in the third and final section beginning with Chapter 57, the esthetics of the anti-novel. The esthetics of the new reality consitutes a significant theme running through Fuentes' novel *Cambio de piel* (México: Joaquín Mortiz, 1967) [*Change of Skin* (New York: Capricorn Books, 1968)]. This very ably done translation misses some of the subtleties of Fuentes' style and technique, particularly the novelist's cinematic transitions where shifts in time and place occur in the narrative, and Fuentes' withholding of information or names to create ambiguity for the reader. Compare the first two or three pages of the novel, for example.

[3] See Alejo Carpentier, *Tientos y diferencias* (Montevideo: Arca Ed., 1967). Sections of this work appear in Juan Loveluck, ed., op. cit., pp. 137-161, under the title, "Problemática de la actual novela latinoamericana." The journal *Nueva Narrativa Hispanoamericana*, Vol. I (enero 1971), contains two articles which deal with the new reality: Eduardo Camacho Guizado, "Notas sobre la nueva novela hispanoamericana," pp. 133-135; and Jaime Giordano, "Hacia una definición del realismo en la novela hispanoamericana contemporánea," pp. 127-132.

[4] The convention-in several of the arts-of a story within a story or of a work of art that deals with the subject of the creative process has not, to my knowledge, been the subject of a book or monograph-type study as it deserves. There are, however, a few studies that recognize and deal with this convention. Roger Shattuck's admirable *The Banquet Years* (New York: Anchor Books, 1961) has a chapter called "The Art of Stillness," pp. 325-352, that relates self-reflexive art about art to a number of significant artistic forms and preoccupations in the arts from 1885 to 1918. Elizabeth Sewell has isolated and discussed commendably this convention in her study, *Paul Valéry: The Mind in The Mirror* (New Haven: Yale Univ. Press, 1952). She has mistakenly concluded, however, that the use of this convention has lapsed after Valéry. T. S. Eliot has attributed this convention to Edgar Allen Poe and traced its transmission in modern poetry in his essay "From Poe to Valéry," *To Criticize The Critic* (New York: Noonday, 1965), pp. 27-42. We know that Miguel de Cervantes and Laurence Sterne preceded Poe.

Pirandello's *Six Characters in Search of An Author*, Gide's *The Counterfeiters*, Fellini's 8½, Octavio Paz's *Sun Stone*, and other works attest to the continued use of this convention in the arts.

[5] It is not possible to mention the great many antecedents of the new breed of character in modern experimental novels, plays and films. Symbolism, dada, surrealism, expressionism and the modern psychological novel have all contributed immeasurably to this significant development in the arts of the twentieth century.

[6] For a comparison of traditional and modern characterization, see David

Daiches, *The Novel and The Modern World* (Chicago: Univ. of Chicago Press, 1967 ed.) Chap. 2, pp. 12-24.

[7] Robbe-Grillet, *For a New Novel*, pp. 27-29, 62.

[8] Perhaps the best known example of the logical development of an absurd premise is Kafka's *The Metamorphosis*. Literary methods related to absurdity and the irrational are discussed in Michael Benedikt's introduction to *Modern French Theatre*, edited by Benedikt and George E. Wellwarth (New York: E. P. Dutton, 1966); and by Martin Esslin, *The Theatre of The Absurd* (New York: Anchor Books, 1969, revised ed.). *Modern French Theatre* is an anthology of avant-garde, dada and surrealistic plays which exemplify several facets of these artistic methods.

[9] *Labyrinths* (New York, New Directions, 1964 ed.), p. 24.

[10] *Letters To a Young Poet* (New York: W. W. Norton, 1962 ed.), p. 34.

# The Dialectics of Textual Interpolation in Ron Arias' *The Road to Tamazunchale*

*Eva Margarita Nieto*

Ron Arias' short novel *The Road to Tamazunchale* (1975) experiments with a number of established narrative structures, all of which are familiar to readers of Hispanic literature. These experiments, which create a mental (internal) and representational (external) simultaneity in the work, have been likened to the novelistic techniques employed by Gabriel García Márquez and Carlos Fuentes. What has not yet been analyzed is the similarity of their readership and the presence of what has been traditionally called "influence" and "tradition" in this readership. Critics have, on the contrary, referred to the direct influence of the contemporary Latin American narrative on Arias' work and his acknowledged acquaintance with that body of narrative. Yet it is evident that Arias shares a much broader and deeper understanding of narrative structures with that group of writers. It is this shared understanding that creates a type of dialectic between the texts and structures that Arias has drawn on and the text he has produced.

The presence of interpolations and intertextualities has already been established with regard to the works of the Latin American authors. It is still an undetermined factor with regard to the established group of Chicano authors, despite their presence in academic circles and their obvious readership. What I propose to analyze in this brief study is the use of these structures in this novel, for I think that *The Road to Tamazunchale* can be read both as a sampler of narrative structures and as a key to Ron Arias' readership.[1] Most importantly, I think that the analysis of these techniques can cast new light on the novel and its relationship to its readers.

Arias' studies in literature at the University of California, Los Angeles, and his continuing friendships with academicians and critics are evidenced both in articles on his work and by interviews.[2] In this, I again assert, he is not unique among Chicano writers. The relationship of the Chicano movement to the university has long been understood. Yet the relationship between that experience, the readership, and the text produced has been a factor too long ignored by critics of Chicano literature. Although Latin American critics and readers understand the literary background of a Mario Vargas Llosa or a Carlos Fuentes, the emphasis on the sociopolitical context and circumstances of Chicano literature has created a false impression of social popularity that has limited its readership.

I do not pretend to suggest that these works are lacking in social commentary or meaning. As narrative, as novels, their relationship to the reader involves a commitment to social reality. In another place, I will analyze the functions of the structures that I propose to read in the text with regard to that very important issue. For now, I would like to refer to that very text in order to elucidate my contentions.

*The Road to Tamazunchale* is a short novel set in Los Angeles, with abrupt place changes to the Peruvian Andes (Cuzco), trips to Tijuana and the Coast, and a protagonist who is an old, lonely, retired door-to-door book salesman. Fausto Quiroga, the protagonist, lives with his niece, Carmen, in the Lincoln Heights barrio. Fearing the nearness of death, he decides to make his final days meaningful. With the acquaintance of Mario, a *vato* from the barrio, he sets off to activate his sedentary existence. A series of real and imagined episodes concludes with the characters jumping into a television screen that someone forgetfully turns off.

Within the context of this plot and structure, the title itself, "The Road to Tamazunchale," becomes an introductory metaphor. The road that Fausto follows is an apparent simulation of life, formulated through action and episode and creating a type of exemplification through mimetic devices. The concept of text=road=life is an established literary tradition, not only as a narrative in the modern sense, but in the didactic and prenovelistic traditions of England, Italy, and Spain. In avoiding the more common "historia," "vida," or even, in contemporary terms, "muerte," Arias seems to return to the structures set forth by Juan Ruiz in his *Libro de buen amor* (1350), in which the narrator explains that his book is a type of road-life and that the reader-traveler should embark upon it as one would on a journey. The remarkable thing is that Juan Ruiz' work is also a sampler of poetic form and meter, a concept that *Tamazunchale* seems to share on a narrative level.

There is still another aspect that the two works have in common. The medieval example ends with the narrator suggesting that the reader carry on with the text-road-life, thus passing the wand of creation on to him. In *Tamazunchale* the characters pass from the narrative/novelistic structure into the visual and dramatic structure of the television screen. I will not comment on the ominous meaning of this episode with regard to the written text's demise, but what does seem apparent is that this kaleidoscopic ending correlates to some extent with the open-endedness of Juan Ruiz' text.

Passing on to the pretextual quotation, which is taken from López de Gómara's history of the conquest of Mexico, the question of "historia" again comes up, for it is this version precisely that Bernal Díaz del Castillo refers to consistently. The author of *La verdadera historia de la conquista de La Nueva España* (1569) contends that he writes this "true" history to refute the lies and exaggerations that appear in the López de Gómara version. By using this quotation, the tone of *Tamazunchale* takes on new dimensions; not only are we involved with the word "historia" in terms of a personal history or account, but the question of fictional narrative versus history is also being raised. By alluding to the chronicle genre (moreover, a historical genre that is generally accepted as the first European literary documentation in America), the invention of history, the fictionalization of "truth," becomes a part of the problematic structure within the work. It is a question that consistently appears in the Latin American narrative of the sixties and seventies.

One has only to turn to Gabriel García Márquez' *Cien años de soledad* (1967) and Carlos Fuentes' *Terra Nostra* (1975) to find two immediate and viable examples. It is a problem, moreover, that extends throughout Arias' work, appearing again in the posttextual quotation, the description of Tamazunchale taken from Frances Toor's guidebook to Mexico. In inserting the mispronunciation of "Tamazunchale" in the theatrical representation toward the end of the novel ("Thomas and Charley"), the ironic dimensions of definitions per se are maintained. By questioning the function of valid historical data in the first quotation and geographical references in the second, Arias questions the relationships between stable and solid, temporal and spatial values.

If these phenomena already suggest a knowledgeable interplay of narrative experiments, the chapters themselves, separated as they are into episodes, also suggest prior structures. The novella, the collection of tales, the picaresque, the pastoral, and the novel of chivalry are all episodic; so for that matter is the *Quijote*. These genres also have in common a concept of hero (or antihero), a form of narrative, and some sense of spatial and temporal representation.

The first chapter of this novel, the reader's introduction to Fausto, sets into motion the series of choices he will put into action in order to determine his own novel or life. In the opening paragraph, the omniscient third-person narrator describes him carefully removing his entire skin, like a finely knit suit. The sense of shock the reader experiences is somewhat mitigated where that action is viewed within a broader context. A "change of skin" in Nahuatl terms corresponds to a change of life. The parallel between this representation and the presence of the same phenomenen in Carlos Fuentes' *Cambio de piel* (1972), in which the characters are caught in the sententious repetition of the lives and frustrations of their ancestral counterparts, the pre-Hispanic inhabitants of the Valley of Mexico, extends Arias' readership toward both ancient and contemporary Mexico. Fuentes' novel refers directly to Xipetotec, the Nahuatl diety who suffers flagellation in order to change skin and thus undergoes a transformation into a new life.

Fausto's symbolic change of skin begins with a mimicry of this ancient rite and also corresponds to the change of name in the classic European structural model, *Don Quijote*. For just as the taking on of a name and the rites of knightly ordination (with the subsequent humiliation and physical abuse) correspond to a baptismal rite for Cervantes' character, the stripping off of the old skin, which also embodies anguish and pain, renews Fausto for his initiation into a new life.

At the end of the first chapter, the opening ritual and the reader's realization that the act has been entirely imagined also open up new dimensions of Fausto's personality. The imagined act, for instance, has been made up to try to attract his niece's sympathy and attention. Her reaction, which is ordinary and mundane while still somewhat loving, serves to notify the reader that Fausto's grisly act has been imaginary and that Fausto is lonely and in need of love. The far-off sound of a flute at the end of the chapter is the device that opens up the old man's closed and lonely world to a reality of action and dialogue. Through it the narrator begins the next structural experiment, the invention of a strange combination of Fausto's contemporary world view and the active ideal world of the fifteenth century conquistador.

This combination of the pastoral, the novel of chivalry, and the *crónica* also serves to introduce one of the mainstays of the novelistic experiment within the novel. Marcelino, the Andean shepherd, is the shadowy and mysterious figure whose flute was heard at the end of Chapter 1. His name as well as his existence conjure images of Cervantes' interpolated novel. Rather than telling his story, Marcelino intertwines his existence into that of the characters living in Los Angeles. His presence then serves to transform their reality, their space; Elysian Park becomes the Elysian Fields.

Yet, as in the narrative models that precede Cervantes, the predominance of narrative over dialogue, the need for a dialectical opposite, creates a search for a counterpart. The archetypical duo of the knight-squire is realized when Fausto meets Mario, a lowrider *cholo* from the

Frogtown barrio of Lincoln Heights. Like Don Quijote and Sancho, Fausto and Mario represent harmonic opposites in terms of their socio-economic circumstances. By creating the harmonic duo on a conflictive level, Arias puts into motion the process of character dynamics and interaction through the use of dialogue. Communication and growth can now happen.

The blend of elements, models, modes, and narrations, drawn as they are from European and American sources, defines the rich and original dimensions of this novel. When it focuses on the dynamics of the knight-squire archetype, the process of dialectic (and dialogue) rather than narration also comes about. The knight-squire focus also begins to draw the novel closer to the *Quijote* in its strong parallels in characterization and dynamic process. Like Don Quijote, Fausto begins his novel-life-road-search just before his death. The process of becoming becomes *materia* through the process of writing and retelling, through mimesis and re-creation. The apparent absurdity and comical deeds of an imaginative old man draw on similar models in Cervantes' masterpiece. In this melange of the comic and the ideal, Fausto moves on, however, toward his own destiny, toward the formation of his own reality. Thus, despite the taking on of a "Faustean" name—thus implying the generic definition of Goethe's work as yet another feasible model—the selection of the young counterpart, the process of dynamic action through dialogue, and the idealism that pervades the novel also set its course.

This narrative experimentation probably reaches its climax in the middle of the novel with the interpolation and retelling of an episode that bears a strong resemblance to a short story by Gabriel García Márquez. In the seventh chapter of the novel, the barrio children, playing in the dry riverbed, come upon the body of a drowned *mojado*. The subsequent succession of events, the "baptism" (taking on of a name) of the drowned man, his integration into the society that functions in the novel, the night of passion between Mrs. Rentería, the old woman, and the beautiful corpse-lover, are all, except for the latter, variations on García Márquez' short story "El ahogado más hermoso del mundo."

As is the case with the other examples cited, this interpolation should be seen as yet another novelistic experiment that Arias undertakes. Yet, because it is so clearly tied to the model that precedes it, it deserves some reflection on the mythopoetic meanings it arouses.

The differences that exist between the two examples lie in the setting, the languages (Spanish, English), and Arias' insertion of the night of love that takes place between the spinster and the dead man (hinted at in the García Márquez model). The similarities consist of the following: the initial discovery of the corpse by the children (in both cases, a drowned man); the women's admiration of the physical beauty of the corpse and the envy and desire the corpse arouses; the bestowal of a name, and thus an identity, on the corpse; the transformation through death (transfiguration) that takes place in the barrio (village), that is, the new sense of purpose through the presence of death.

What the reader initially questions, however, is the function of this interpolation in Arias' novel. What is accepted with regard to the other examples of novelistic experimentation I have already mentioned here becomes a puzzle. Moreover, one remembers that the preceding model (and I purposely do not use the word "initial" or "original") is a short story, complete in itself. This example, however, appears within the structure of the novel, directly in the center. I must elaborate once again on the techniques I have referred to at the beginning of this study.

I have already spoken of the dynamic process behind the formation of Fausto's character. I observed that the road of the novel is akin to life itself, that the first chapter sets into motion the process of exploration and selection that creates meaning out of the old man's life. The complication occurs in the emphasis on old age as a factor in the novelistic process. Like his model and archetype Don Quijote, Fausto seeks the meaning of human purpose in this twilight stage of life. Significantly, in terms of this novel's structure, that process becomes more insistent from the seventh chapter on. The passage from one life to the next becomes more and more the *materia prima*, whereas the search for the narrative form, the election of one form of novelizing over another, had been the novel's preoccupation up to Chapter 7.

As the novel's mainstay, then, this interpolation merits some discussion. Certainly, the theme itself, which focuses on transfiguration through death, is familiar enough; what is far less familiar are the circumstances of the death, which make it difficult to accept if one has a traditional Western perception of this event. Both narratives, first of all, place the event within a familiar, ordinary framework of time and space. Moreover, the cause of death is not known; the identity of the corpse is also unknown. Consequently, neither violence nor tragedy, those two great poles of literary distance, are present to create a sense of pathos or anguish. The question of an initial detachment is important to both narratives, for the absence of knowledge about or familiarity with the person the corpse once was allows for the imaginative dimensions of growth, wonderment, and invention.

There is in Arias' example, moreover, a difference as to the circumstances surrounding the death; the corpse is found in a dry riverbed; still, he is David, the "drowned mojado," and reference is made to someone being swept downstream several winters ago. The invention of the cause of death by drowning is important in that the discrepancy between fact and invention lies in the reader's interpretation of the event, but not in the neighborhood's collective belief in it. Moreover, David is a "mojado," a wetback. Is David's death related to his "mojado-ness"? That is to say, is death in the dry riverbed a symbol of the anguished death of the exploited Mexican undocumented worker? Since the answer to that question lies only in our "reading" of the narrative, I would point out that one of Fausto's ensuing preoccupations after this episode involves protecting undocumented workers and that it becomes a raison d'être for him. It is also significant that this ambiguity does not exist in the García Márquez example. Since the corpse in that version is found on the beach and reference is made to waves and to seaweed, the sense of wonder has a different focus; the question of the corpse's origin becomes important.

Still, the distance between what I have called the Western perception of death and the familiarity with it in the context of Arias' novel rests on the use of the following devices: the children playing with the corpse; the perception by the older participants of the "normalcy" of that act; and the acceptance of the corpse by the society of the narrative to the point of baptizing it, dressing it, and elevating it to the role of a person, thus giving it an identity. The sense of familiarity and innocence projected in these two examples nonetheless has a parallel in the mythic structures of the Western tradition.

What has seemingly been lost by Anglo culture is the Hispanic belief in the marvelous. What I mean by this concerns the importance of the Christian belief in resurrection as demonstrated in the Gospel narration of the death of Christ and in the legend of St. James the Elder (Santiago de Compostela). In the Gospels, the function of belief lies in its power to convince that even physical death through the crucifixion does not deny the possibility of resurrection. It is thus basic to the belief in death and transfiguration. Still, as a myth, it relies on distance—a time and place far enough removed from our daily lives so as to create either a chasm of disbelief or a permission to believe. Furthermore, the distance between that event and our present lies in the language of narration. Even contemporary translations of the Bible cannot overcome that distance.

The legend of St. James of Compostela offers other possibilities. It begins with the arrival of a corpse borne on a small boat or raft that is deposited on the beach near Santiago in Spain, and from that point on the legend develops, for this body is the body of St. James, an apostle of Christ. The result of that event is the cult of St. James, one of the most powerful social and artistic manifestations of the European Middle Ages. More importantly for my intention here, the legend of

Santiago is one of the most powerful myths functioning in the Hispanic tradition; hence, its retelling here, its participation in the infinite textures and texts that make up literature.

What is compelling about the levels of meaning in Arias' novel, however, concerns the manner in which it constructs a dialectic between the reader and itself. I interpret this demand on the reader as an intention toward participation, not on an elitist level of meaning that rejects one group of readers for another, but as a challenge toward understanding, toward developing perceptions about the bridges and chasms, the fragments and traditions that make up Chicano culture. The novel focuses on an ordinary reality, but episode after episode of marvelous daily occurrences (for example, the snowstorm that falls only within the barrio) function as transformations of Fausto's ordinary existence, and through him and with him they transform that reality and that life into the extraordinary. The novel focuses on death, from the anticipation of death at the beginning to the novel's structural apex, the seventh chapter, and finally to its culmination, Fausto's passage from the narrative into the television screen (I repeat, a new "visual" dimension, perhaps?). Death and its transformation embody the meaning of Fausto's life and the mythopoetic levels of the novel. Both are an affirmation of the ordinary in the marvelous. What we share in that process is a unique experiment within the space of the Chicano narrative, a shared reading into broader areas of ourselves and of human understanding.

CALIFORNIA STATE UNIVERSITY, NORTHRIDGE

# Notes

[1] In formulating my approach to this study, I have used readings of Jacques Derrida's *Of Grammatology* (Baltimore: Johns Hopkins, 1977), as well as the trajectory concerning readership of the novel as discussed by Carlos Fuentes in *Cervantes o la crítica de la lectura* (México: Joaquín Mortiz, 1976).

[2] Much of the background concerning Ron Arias' readership has been taken from conversations during my long association with him. The documentation for many of my assertions is from the Symposia on Chicano Literature sponsored in February 1981 by the Department of Spanish and Portuguese at UCLA.

# E. Aristeo Brito

*El diablo en Texas:*
Structure and Meaning

*Marvin A. Lewis*

## Introduction

*El diablo en Texas* is divided into a prologue and three principal sections: Presidio 1883, 1942, and 1970 – the epilogue. Following techniques of the new novelists, Aristeo Brito sets forth themes in the prologue which he will develop in the text. Presidio brings to mind Juan Rulfo's Comala. The town is somewhere between heaven and hell. Occasionally "ánimas en pena" meet at an old 17th century fortress to discuss a massacre of Mexicans perpetrated by Ben Lynch, one of the early barbarians to enter the territory. Presidio is "far from everywhere" and records the highest daytime temperature in the United States several times each year. The inhabitants are in a constant struggle for survival against odds created by both the human and natural orders. They live a hand-to-mouth existence in agrarian country.

Characters are presented as mere caricatures of humanity, although the Lynch family, the exploiters, and Francisco Uranga, lawyer and defender of Mexican rights, are clearly drawn. Principal characters appear in both the 1883 and 1942 segments. The author seems to regard individuals as not that important, but instead values their collective contributions to the novel's overall meaning.

Since structure is broadly defined as the "sum of the relationships of the parts of a literary whole to one another,"[1] my purpose is to demonstrate how these relationships function to make *El diablo en Texas* a coherent whole. My approach to the novel entails an examination of (1) narrative technique, (2) imagery and symbolism, and (3) the relationship between form and meaning. It is generally agreed that technique and form are virtually inseparable from theme and world view.

## Narrative Technique

Chronological delineation is not one of the author's major concerns, as readers have to make their own chronology. Action oscillates between two poles: Ojinaga on the Mexican side of the Río Bravo and Presidio in the United States. This spatial juxtapositioning accounts for some of the fragmentation in the novel's structure. Through the thoughts and conversations of the protagonists and occasional straightforward narration the reader is able to piece together important historical events from the late 19th century to the present. The conquest and colonization of the Chicano emerge as the principal preoccupations. In the background one feels the presence of the omniscient author controlling and manipulating his world.

The principal plot thread winds around several generations of Urangas: Francisco and his son Reyes; José, son of Reyes; and the unnamed son of José who is the principal narrator in the 1970 segment. In the 1883 section, which spans the early twentieth century, Francisco Uranga is the focal point of activity. Through treachery, Ben Lynch is able to buy land that belongs to Paz, Francisco's wife. Rumor has it that their son Lázaro is involved in the crooked dealings. The effect of these early manipulations is seen in the 1942 section, where José and his family, rightful owners of the land, are forced to survive as field hands. Thus, the plot is constructed in a manner that shows the cause and effect relationships of exploitation on past, present, and future generations of Chicanos.

The device of having a fetus address a monologue to the host mother and relatives is quite thoughtful and effective. To achieve this end, Brito employs a stream of consciousness technique—interior monologue—that is

> used in fiction for representing the psychic content and process of character, partly or entirely unuttered, just as these processes exist at various levels of conscious control before they are formulated for deliberate speech.[2]

In *El diablo en Texas* the unborn baby of Marcela, José's wife, rationalizes the reasons for his mother's discomfort. "Es que trae cien años de historia indignada en la panza. Su enfermedad es de palabras que no pueden salir de aquí, de sus entrañas" (p. 79).[3] Marcela, representing the long-suffering Mexican mother, bears witness to 100 years of ignoble history. Yet she is unable to articulate her frustrations. The child will be left with the burden of writing the legacy of his people.

Broken chronology, interior monologue, and juxtapositioning of episodes in the narrative all reflect, to a degree, the characters' precarious existence. For the most part, they are unsure and unable to assert themselves in the living hell of Presidio.

Language is another important internal structural device in the novel. Brito's use of Chicano Spanish and portrayal of the actions of his characters is on a level with that of Méndez, Morales, Hinojosa, and Rivera. Mental attitudes and believable reactions are manifested convincingly through popular language. In a work situation, Chale, the crew chief, urges the cotton pickers on in the following manner:

> —Orale ésos, ya oyeron el jefe, ¿qué nel? Así que nada de perra. Aviéntensen o si no, los reporto.
> —Uuuu, que zurra el bato, vamos a empelotarlo pa que no se madereye el güey—brincó el Jusito, mientras que las mujeres se enrojecieron y pronto se escurrieron por los zurcos. ¡Chamaco descarado! ¡No tiene pelos en la lengua!
> El Chale, al notar el enojo en las caras de los otros, soltó la carcajada.
> —Puros mitotes, ésos. ¿A poco me creyeron? Este bato no está lurio ni come lumbre, ésos. ¿Pos quién les dijo que soy amigo del jale? La viuda es corta ésos. Llévensenla suave, al cabo no te dan premios. (p. 59)

The novel is a unique mixture of Chicano Spanish, "standard" Spanish, and English—all used to reflect different realities and levels of awareness. Tours of the fort are conducted in English and Francisco Uranga uses official Spanish. In the above scene there is a combination of comic and serious expression, for the intent is to relieve some of the frustration inherent in the working conditions. Throughout, scene and situations are accurately reflected by language, thereby contributing to the novel's verisimilitude.

## Imagery/Symbolism

Two central images dominate the novel: a fort built in 1863 and a 20th-century bridge spanning the river. Both represent divisiveness between the two cultures. The fort remains as a vestige of the early Spanish conquerors and explorers and the bridge symbolizes a general tendency of officialdom to control the movement of Chicanos. An examination of these two symbols reveals that they form an integral part of the novel's structure. The fort, for example grows to nearly mythic proportions within the closed environment of Presidio. It is described in the following manner:

> Allí cerca de Presidio donde llaman la Loma Pelona se levanta el fortín como castillo podrido. Es un castillo de adobe sin puertas que usa el viento como pito de barro. No falta quien pase por allí alguna noche con pelos de puercoespín y diga: el castillo está espantado. Hay espíritus

y hay diablos que pasan de cuarto en cuarto botando. Los incrédulos lo niegan diciendo que son mitotes pero lo cierto es que la historia se intuye. Las leyendas de la gente son las páginas de un libro que se arrancaron y se echaron a la hoguera.... (p. 36)

The existence of the fort gives rise to a set of popular beliefs that equate the fort with evil and the presence of the devil. The spoken word, or oral tradition, forms an important structural element in the novel, as maintained by the assertion that "Las leyendas de la gente son las páginas de un libro que se arrancaron y se echaron a la hoguera...." From a creative standpoint, the combination of fact, fiction, and rumor provides the conceptual basis of *El diablo en Texas*.

The bridge is another unifying image. Two key passages reveal its importance in the narrative.

El puente son cosas del diablo. (El puente es el arco iris del diablo: dos patas de chivo puestas en dos cementerios.) (p. 9)

Entonces todos éramos iguales. No es que no séamos, pero ha cambiado desde que pusieron el puente. Qué curioso, Vicke. La gente se siente separada ... ¿pa qué son esos papeles, Vicke? ¿Por qué los piden esos hombres todo el tiempo? ¿Quiénes son? ¿Y el diablo lo has visto, Vicke? ¿Es cierto que estamos en el infierno? Hace mucho calor aquí pero no es verdá, ¿verdá, Vicke? (p.19)

Interrelated as internal structural devices are the metaphorical prison and the devil himself: "Presidio, prisión, infierno. Diablo que se carcajea en silencio. Shhh!" (p. 26). These brief excerpts reveal the importance of the bridge, devil, and prison images to the structure and meaning of the novel. Life in Presidio is controlled by both human and natural limitations. That is to say, Presidio inhibits mobility because of a lack of social opportunities. The bridge restricts the free movement of people along the borders. Both the bridge and the fort are viewed as products of the devil himself, whose omnipresence pervades the novel. Hardly an episode takes place which does not concern the bridge, the prison/fort, or the devil.

The snake and the devil—equated with Ben Lynch—appear as evil omens several times, with no apparent effect on the narrative except for representing the evil side of human emotions and behavior. Symbolically, however, they represent the central metaphor in the novel's overall meaning. This revelation comes out in a conversation between two residents: "Pero lo importante es que la víbora era el enemigo de Diosito. Era el mero diablo" (p. 63). In Presidio, too, the proverbial battle between good and evil is being waged. From the opening paragraphs, the víbora/diablo keeps watch over the town and its inhabitants, appearing to derive satisfaction from human suffering.

## Conclusion

A noted critic has written that "Time affects every aspect of fiction: the theme, the form and the medium—language."[4] These remarks are certainly applicable to *El diablo en Texas*. The repetition of selected events gives the impression that not much has changed in Presidio for more than a century. That is why actors in the 1883 drama can play roles without difficulty in 1942. Eternal suffering seems to be the Chicano's plight. The novel's temporal fragmentation is due, for the most part, to the direct relationship between past and present in Presidio. The theme of the repression of Chicano culture and values pervades the work. Resistance takes place on an individual basis only.

The novel's message is that over the centuries there has not been much progress in Presidio. Time has been suspended. This point is brought out in the thoughts of José Uranga's son after a hard day's work in the field with his father.

> Así ha ocurrido siempre, padre. Siempre se ha quedado esta tierra maldita con tu sangre, con tu sudor. Y me duele que en cada gota de tu cuerpo vaya parte de tu alma, de una vida que muere para vivir mejor. Yo sé que tus pasos apuntan a un vacío día tras día y yo los sigo también.... Pero ya me cansé papá, y no te he dicho que me voy. Me voy porque estoy seguro de que hay otro mundo mejor que Presidio.... presidio, tejas. Hasta el nombre me suena enfermo para haber visto la luz primero, bajo tejas de presidio. (p. 96)

The presidio/prison image remains constant throughout the novel. Characters are portrayed as trapped and drained of life-sustaining forces. Escape is the easiest alternative. But in spite of the cyclical and deterministic nature of events, Brito does not deny his characters their humanity. Rather they are imbued with a tremendous capacity for survival and understanding.

José Uranga's son has returned to Presidio for his father's burial. He decides not to leave again but rather "encender la llama, la que murió con el tiempo" (p. 99). Thus the novel ends on a positive note, calling for Chicanos to assess their cultural and historical circumstances in an effort to bring about change. Based on what has happened in the novel, this is not likely to occur. But where there is life, there is hope, and the fragmented, schizophrenic existence reflected in *El diablo en Texas*'s structure will continue until Chicanos control their own destinies.

University of Illinois

## Notes

[1] *Princeton Encyclopedia of Poetry and Poetics* (Princeton, N.J.: Princeton University Press, 1974), p. 812.

[2] Robert Humphrey, *Stream of Consciousness in the Modern Novel* (Berkeley: University of California Press, 1968), p. 24.

[3] Aristeo Brito, *El diablo en Texas* (Tucson: Editorial Peregrinos, 1976).

[4] A. A. Mendilow, *Time and the Novel* (New York: Humanities Press, 1972), p. 31.

# Las metamorfosis del diablo en
# El diablo en Texas de Aristeo Brito

*Justo S. Alarcón*

La novela de la cual nos ocupamos aquí es una de las novelas más cortas de la narrativa chicana. No queremos sugerir con esto, sin embargo, que sea limitada en expresión, fuerza y mensaje. Todo lo contrario. *El diablo en Texas*, a pesar de sus cortas dimensiones, es una de las novelas chicanas más "apretadas," y esto debido a la concepción y esquema que el autor se trazó. Nos referimos, en particular, al personaje-símbolo central: el diablo.

Son varias las posibilidades analíticas que se presentan para el estudio de esta obra pero nos restringiremos a dos acercamientos: el arquetípico y el socio-marxista. Las razones por las cuales nos hemos decidido a enfocar la presente novela desde estos dos puntos de vista fueron debidas a la relación íntima que tienen con la temática y la disposición novelística. Dejando para otra ocasión algún estudio particularista sobre *El diablo en Texas*, ofreceremos a continuación una presentación descriptiva y general basada en estas dos aproximaciones.[1]

Sin necesidad de entrar en pormenores de trama, narradores, caracterizaciones y otros aspectos técnicos, creemos necesario, sin embargo, recrear el escenario. Un pueblo, llamado real y simbólicamente Presidio, que se sitúa en un valle al sur del estado de Texas y que linda con Ojinaga, México. Ambos pueblos fronterizos, divididos geográficamente por el Río Bravo y, artificialmente, por la política de dos países, son la fuente indispensable de la mano de obra necesaria para el cultivo de los campos del Valle. En Presidio, como realidad-símbolo, levanta la cabeza el semifeudal y burgués Fortín. A un lado, la sierra con su capilla religiosa y su cueva diabólica, y, a otro, los campos del hacendado Ben Lynch. Sobre este escenario geográfico, demográfico, histórico, económico e internacionalmente político, "se columpia el diablo."

El "diablo" es el personaje por excelencia simbólico y, al mismo tiempo, real que domina, se filtra, se goza, se ríe de una situación económico-religiosa opresiva y subhumana. El es el mago explotador que, con su varita, juega con las mentes y las pasiones humanas, con la flora y con la fauna, con los medios de producción y con la plus-valía, con la abundancia y con la escasez, con los elementos naturales y con los sobrenaturales. El diablo, bajo creencia, aparece en otras novelas chicanas, como ... *y no se lo tragó la tierra, Bless me, Ultima* y *Pocho*, pero no adquiere la dimensión abrumadora que se observa en la presente novela. Aquí tan pronto se encarna como se volatiliza. Es un ser a veces palpable y a veces escurridizo. Se metamorfosea con asombrosa facilidad.²

## La metamorfosis del diablo

La presencia del diablo en toda la novela es abrumadora. El lector no sólo la siente a través de los personajes, conscientes en mayor o menor grado de tal presencia, sino que la percibe también, y en grandes dosis, por medio de las descripciones del omnisciente narrador. La técnica narrativa, sea en el uso sintáctico, léxico, o bien semántico, como también en la concatenación de los leit-motivs literarios, hace que esa presencia, muchas veces intangible, llegue a ser escurridiza y sutil. Refirámonos, como ejemplo, a la primera página de la primera parte.

El sujeto de todas las oraciones de ese pasaje es la víbora, o sea el diablo. El número de verbos es de 22, de los cuales 17 son netamente reflexivos. De los cinco restantes, que no aparecen en la forma reflexiva, tres se acercan, por implicación y contexto, a la naturaleza reflexiva: "recuerda" (se acuerda), "continúa" (otra vez) y "empieza" (de nuevo). La acción de estos verbos no es transitiva. Se puede decir, pues, que de los 22 verbos del pasaje, 20 son reflexivos. Por medio del reflexivo el sujeto se auto-define, la acción se refleja en el sujeto y se hace autosuficiente, adquiere poderío. Cualidades todas de la víbora-"diablo."

De los 22 verbos, nueve, es decir más de la tercera parte, denotan personificación ("se sonríe," "se jacta," "se pone a pensar," etc.), con lo cual se establece una vez más la ecuación y metamorfosis víbora-diablo. Los restantes, 13, implican movimiento espacial. Unos cargados de significación sutil: sinuosa, escurridiza, pegajosa ("se retuerce," "se desliza," "se arrastra") y otros connotan intromisión, búsqueda y adquisición ("se cuela," "se trepa," "se ciñe"). La naturaleza y el valor semántico de estos verbos implican y nos describen las características, no sólo de la víbora al principio de la novela, sino también de las cualidades que posee y de la estrategia que empleará el diablo a través de toda la narración para enseñorearse de las relaciones humanas y prenderse de las mentes de la gente.

Si nos fijamos otra vez en la primera página de la novela podremos observar uno de los aspectos más importantes en el estudio de la metamorfosis: el de la multivalencia de los elementos y de los motivos literarios que afloran, se esfuman, para reaparecer más tarde por toda la narración. Esta polivalencia, que sobrepasa con frecuencia la simple metáfora para convertirse en alegoría, hace difícil catalogar categóricamente los niveles o planos del análisis. Por ejemplo, "la cueva," que se halla en la sierra, es, como en la mayoría de los casos, una entidad física y real, causada por fenómenos geológicos, de erosión. Pero en Presidio, y en la mente del pueblo, se convierte en morada del diablo. Por otra parte, la misma cueva puede muy bien servir, en el orden natural, de escondrijo a una culebra, cosa real y física, pero, al transformarse en "víbora-diablo," adquiere doble valor sobre/metanatural.

La dicotomía se trifurca al extenderse la metamorfosis de la cueva a la capilla, que también se encuentra en la sierra. Si la cueva es efecto de una actividad geológico-natural, la capilla es resultado de la tecnología-industria humana. Si aquélla es la morada del diablo, ésta, en cambio, es la morada de Dios. Dos fuerzas-poderes antitéticos que se conjugan-conjuran sobre las mentes del pueblo. Pero estas fuerzas, aparente y eternamente irreductibles entre sí, llegan a una síntesis cuando la víbora se adueña de la capilla y se enrosca en la cruz. En resumen: la sierra, realidad física y natural, base y albergue de la cueva y de la capilla, dicotomía de fuerzas opuestas, se convierte ahora en señorío exclusivo y absoluto del diablo. Las dos creencias del pueblo en dos valores sobrenaturales e irreductibles (Dios/Diablo, esperanza/miedo), nudos que aprietan la mente de los personajes pueblerinos, quedan ahora íntimamente entrelazados en un solo nudo: el poderío de la "víbora-diablo."

Pero la metamorfosis del diablo no se limita a la apariencia de víbora que se encuentra en la primera página. Continúa metamorfoseándose por las otras cien restantes. Enumerar y analizar todas las transformaciones por las que pasa el diablo necesitaría un largo estudio. Aquí se señalarán algunas de las principales. Las agruparemos en cuatro categorías generales. El diablo se metamorfosea 1) en los elementos naturales, 2) en los animales, 3) en la gente e instituciones sociales, y 4) en el campo y la tecnología.

## *Metamorfosis del diablo en los elementos*

Se entiende aquí por elementos naturales no sólo los cuatro tradicionales (agua, tierra, aire y fuego) sino también los derivados de estos, como nubes, tormentas, lluvia y río, para el agua. Voces, ruidos, susurros y viento, para el aire. Valle, campo, sierra y cueva, para la tierra. Y noche, luna y sol, para el fuego. Hay que hacer notar que la transformación del diablo en los elementos es una técnica literaria basada, sin duda, en la milenaria creencia de que el diablo tiene poderes sobrenaturales para controlar estos elementos naturales. De los siete enumerados creemos que los más logrados literariamente, desde el punto de vista de la metamorfosis del diablo, son la noche, el viento y la lluvia, aunque desde el punto de vista real, es decir del efecto opresivo, la transformación en sol, tormenta y río, es de lo más pernicioso. Es de gran interés observar que el efecto opresivo de las tres primeras metamorfosis se limita solamente al chicano y que el control o dominio diabólico es de orden síquico-religioso. Los otros tres elementos, sol, tormenta y río, ejercen dominio tanto sobre la carencia económica del chicano como sobre los sembradíos-posesiones del anglo. Este último efecto es, por consiguiente y en ambos casos, de orden físico-económico.

Presentaremos, a guisa de ejemplo, dos elementos combinados, que denominaremos síquico-religiosos: el viento (voces, ruidos) y la noche. Presidio está envuelto en un "sopor eterno," por donde se filtra el "ruido de almas en pena" que sale del Fortín (Intro.). El Fortín es un castillo "espantado," en donde "hay espíritus y hay diablos," cuyas voces las usa el "viento como pito de barro" (36). Son las "voces del diablo," "las nuestras," las de "Jesús del Río . . . hijo de la Llorona" (44). Marcela se imagina al río como un gato engrifado, pero que sólo deja salir de su hocico "un zumbido de abejón en lejanía" (92), mientras que Teléforo oye que "el rumor del río se convierte en una carcajada gigante" cuando el diablo regresa a su cueva (93). Todo esto se oye en las altas horas de la noche.

Poéticamente el autor nos describe la noche como "un chicle negro y pegajoso que envuelve al río, los árboles, las labores. Luego llega hasta los barrios y allí enreda a la gente y la pega fuertemente a las camas, a los pisos . . . en donde se quedaron dormidos. La noche se estira larga hasta el infinito" (19). Físicamente observamos que, cuando "entra la noche gigante y negra . . . con deseo de estrangular," la gente que estaba afuera se mete dentro de sus casas de adobe, que "se engarruñan, se encogen con la noche. Sólo así podrán resistir su peso" (64). Síquicamente la noche-diablo se convierte en "sombra" perseguidora (78). Durante la noche, al cruzar el río, Marcela "llevaba la mente como pescado muerto en una red" (93). Años más tarde, el protagonista que acompañaba a su padre de vuelta de la labor, nos dice que "la oscuridad nos apresaba los cerebros castigados" (96). En otros términos, la noche-diablo se estira, se enreda, se ciñe y se pega al cerebro y a la mente oprimiéndolos.

Además de las semejanzas sintáctico-metafóricas vemos la identidad, a través del metamorfoseo, entre la noche, la víbora, el diablo y la muerte. La noche "se enreda" en la gente del mismo modo que la víbora "se enrosca" en la cruz. La noche "se estira" por el espacio mientras que la víbora "se desliza" por la sierra y la capilla. La noche "se enreda" en la gente como el pescado muerto se queda en "una red." La noche "apresa los cerebros," parte superior de la persona, al mismo tiempo que la víbora "ciñe la parte superior de la cruz," en donde se encuentra la cabeza-cerebro. Para resumirlo, la noche "se estira," la víbora "se desliza," la muerte (alma separada) "se desliza" por la alfombra, y el viento "estira" al alma (28). Víbora, noche y viento son metamorfosis del diablo que busca la opresión sicológica y la muerte. O sea, el diablo se transforma en los elementos para controlar y oprimir al chicano.

## Metamorfosis del diablo en los animales

Aparecen, con mayor o menor frecuencia e importancia, una veintena de animales en *El diablo en Texas*. Los más sobresalientes son los que se han asociado tradicionalmente con el malagüero y con la muerte, sea por su ponzoña, como la víbora y la araña, sea por estar asociados con la noche, o porque son o aparecen con frecuencia negros, como el gato, el murciélago, la lechuza y el tecolote. También hay animales voraces, como el lobo, el perro y el gato. De la veintena se han contado y relacionado con el chicano solamente tres: el pescado, el ratón y el conejo. Se hallan asociados con los animales voraces por razones de dependencia, éstos, y de aparente instinto de superioridad, aquéllos. Aquí, a causa de la similitud y alegoría literarias, se traspone este nivel de dependencia antinatural, irracional y grotesca. Se degradan y animalizan las relaciones humanas. Del grupo de animales feroces se tratará en la siguiente sección, al hablar de la metamorfosis del diablo en las instituciones sociales. Ahora, como muestra, citemos algún ejemplo de animales malagoreros.

En el velorio del niño Chente, y entre rezadoras mujeres enlutadas y dicharacheros hombres bebedores, hay intervalos de silencio. En uno de estos momentos el "silencio (es) interrumpido por un mosco gigante. El mosco rodea el cajoncito del muerto dos veces y se para. Vuelve a reinar el silencio" (29).

> El mosco gigante ... se torna murciélago indeciso (que) desciende hasta el velorio como cometa ciego. Vicke lo ve diminuto al principio pero se hace más grande, más y más y más hasta que ... se estrella en su frente. Los aleteos en los ojos y en los brazos se estremecen. El murciélago se va. (33)

Ambos incidentes, de la misma realidad, ocurren en el mismo velorio. Del sonido del mosquito se pasa a la visión-sueño del murciélago. Como se desprende de la narración éstas son metamorfosis malagoreras del diablo que se lleva el alma-vida de un niño que muere a consecuencia de la explotación económica en las minas.

Algo semejante sucede con la metamorfosis del diablo en lechuza. Marcela, ya en la lancha para cruzar el río, se imagina a éste como "gato engrifado" y, a continuación, oyó el "zumbido de abejón en lejanía" (92). No ve nada. Pero es Teléforo el que, al subirse a su troca, "nota un par de luces que se vienen haciendo más grandes." Se acerca y no ve nada. Busca y nada. Y "es entonces que oye el fuerte golpe contra el parabrisas. La lechuza queda pataleando al lado del camino ... (y) el rumor del río ahora se convierte en una carcajada de gigante" (92, 93). El "zumbido" (sonido) de un abejón se transforma en visión ("nota") de "dos luces" del carro patrullero, que, a su vez, se supone eran los ojos de una lechuza, y que, por fin, se metamorfosea en una gigante "carcajada" (sonido) diabólica. Semejante al caso anterior, en donde ocurre la muerte de Chente, ahora la muerte de Marcela viene acompañada de una triple metamorfosis del diablo en "gato," "abejón," y "lechuza." La gigantesca "carcajada" final descubre al metamorfoseado y su victoria sobre la vida-muerte del oprimido. Esta vez la opresión es síquico-supersticiosa e institucional-policiaca.

## Metamorfosis del diablo en la gente-instituciones sociales

En la estructura social del Valle de Presidio, teniendo en cuenta la división del trabajo y las clases sociales, nos encontramos con un hacendado, Ben Lynch, para quien trabajan cientos de campesinos chicanos y mexicanos. Existe también una serie de diferentes cuerpos policiacos, como los rangers, el sheriff, la "migra," la patrulla fronteriza, el FBI, la policía local-estatal, los soldados y, al fondo, el ejército. En el mundo de la diversión nos hallamos con un payaso y un galán. También en la estructura y organización social, pero desde el punto de vista de las interrelaciones de dependencia, existe un cacique, Ben, a cuyas órdenes y servicio se ponen los diversos cuerpos policíacos. En este apartado se presentará el modo cómo el diablo se transforma para manipular no sólo cada peldaño de la jerarquía social sino también, y más importante, las interrelaciones de dependencia que consigo lleva esta jerarquía de clases sociales. Como ejemplos de metamorfosis se escogerán al sheriff, a un "rinche" (ranger) y al mismo Ben Lynch.

La metamorfosis del diablo en el sheriff de Marfa es una de las transformaciones más ridículas y, al mismo tiempo, brutales que haya salido de la pluma chicana, y esto debido a lo que la función de este personaje-oficio implica, sobre todo teniendo en cuenta al chicano y su historia en uno de los pueblos de los estados fronterizos. El contraste entre lo cómico y lo trágico es sin duda un acierto literario. Se podría decir que no sólo el diablo sino que también el autor nos está guiñando el ojo. La perplejidad y confusión del diablo son obvias. No sabe qué hacer. Parece que está aburrido. Y para matar el aburrimiento se mira en el espejo. Un lago pequeño que hay en su cueva le sirve de espejo. Lo que ve de inmediato es su cuerpo desnudo. Se sorprende al darse cuenta de que "no tiene sexo." Si esto no fuera bastante, el escarnio aumenta al imaginarse que su sexo se parece a "un bizcochito de niña recién parida." Esta "incapacidad" física se suma a otra de orden mental. Pronto se le ocurre vestirse de "payaso." Lo hace y le parece un "juego demasiado pueril." El mismo diablo se percata de que este juego es un juego de niños y que "no le vale afuera." Este "afuera" es la línea divisoria, la línea que separa al hombre-diablo como individuo y al sheriff-diablo como miembro de la sociedad que representa una clase social dada con una función social dada: la de salvaguardar la ley, pero que en este caso se convierte en salvaguardar los intereses económicos del capitalista agrícola. O sea, la supraestructura en función y, al mismo tiempo, esclava de la infraestructura económica. Entonces "debe ponerse más serio" el diablo para poder "seguir burlándose de la vida humana" (71).

Creemos necesario transcribir el pasaje para que pueda verse el contraste trágico-cómico y el impacto que lleva consigo. Después de que el diablo decide dejar el "traje de payaso" sigue otra metamorfosis:

> Ahora se arquea las cejas puntiagudas con un negro pincel y enseguida estira el brazo para rascar el azul de cielo. Este se lo talla en las pupilas. Como último toque a la parte superior del cuerpo, se casca una peluca rubia y un sombrero tejano. Luego busca un traje para cubrirse lo demás y encuentra el verde oscuro, su preferido. Cuando ya se lo puso, a pujidos se mete unas botas que le cubren las patas de gallo. ¡Ah! Allí está. De pronto se guiña el ojo en el lago que usa como espejo. Ya fuera, se monta en su columpio.... Se cimbrea alto, alto, hasta que alcanza una estrella. De inmediato la arranca y se la prende donde debe palpitar el corazón. ¡Listo! El diablo está listo para seguir su chiste eterno. (71, 72)

Tenemos aquí un retrato del salvaguardador de la ley. De pies a cabeza: cejas negras, ojos azules, pelo rubio, sombrero tejano, uniforme verde, botas tejanas y una estrella sobre "el corazón." Representación de uno, cien más. De una institución salvaguardadora de la ley. Semejante a este retrato, pero ya en acción, vemos a la fuerza policial-patrullera. El siguiente incidente ocurre dentro de la iglesia, durante la misa:

> Afuera, el agua menudita sigue picoteando mientras que la congregación se pone de pie. En este momento nota Marcela a un señor que entra sin quitarse el sombrero y se pasa hasta el frente como si ésta fuera su casa. Luego se regresa con unos ojos de águila que se columpian de lado a lado. Ella siente un fuerte estremecimiento pero lo

disfraza componiéndose el velo. Cuando el señor la nota, se detiene momentáneamente frente a ella y le sonríe. Luego le guiña el ojo y sale. (77)

En este segundo pasaje notamos que "los ojos de águila ... se columpian," como había hecho el diablo-sheriff momentos antes del pasaje anterior ("se monta en su columpio ... se cimbra alto"). También, como en el pasaje anterior ("se guiña el ojo en el lago"), ahora "le guiña el ojo a Marcela" después de sonreírle, como indicándole que su muerte se avecina. Este personaje, sheriff-patrulla-policía, aparece más tarde transformado en carro-lechuza cuando "un par de luces" se acerca hacia la troca de Teléforo, acto seguido se "oye un fuerte golpe contra el parabrisas (y) la lechuza queda pataleando" en la carretera (92).

La última transformación de que nos ocuparemos en este apartado de metamorfosis, gente-instituciones sociales, es la del gran hacendado, Ben Lynch. La transcribiremos en dos partes. En la primera personifica al diablo, "El Diablo Verde."

> Benito sonríe al pasar por el barrio oscuro .... Sonríe con el triunfo en la boca. Esa sonrisa hecha de mueca que no engaña a nadie .... Pasa el jinete por los cuadritos de adobe .... Casas que piden misericordia a Dios .... Sólo les falta a las casitas una cruz al frente para que sean cementerios .... Luego la calle polvorosa, sin brea. Burla, burlados todos, el diablo verde sonríe. El diablo manipula títeres. El diablo juega con la vida humana .... Se alejó el Diablo Verde como sombra. (25, 26)

En la segunda cita observamos la múltiple metamorfosis del gran hacendado. Por medio de voces muertas, nos enteramos del tremendo poder económico, social y legal, y también del señorío que tiene sobre la vida y la muerte de los siervos/proletariado campesino de sus ranchos.

> —A ver muchachos, vamos a darle una porra a Don Benito el de las barbas de chivo. Vamos todos ...
> —¿Y por qué se te ocurrió?
> —Porque ayer lo vi pasar con su traje de catrín, con una pata en el suelo y la otra tocando las barbas blancas del pecho.
> —Otra vez muchachos. Don Beniiito, don beniiito, don benito el de la *tienda* ...
> —don benito el del *graffitti* ...
> —en los escusados, en paredes de la calle, en los *cheques*, en los *lomos del ganado* ...
> —en el *cielo* y en el *infierno*, en las *tierras* de los padres de la Vicke que perdieron en la *corte* del condado ...
> —en los *papeles de cuero*, don benito el hacendado, don benito el soldado ...
> —... vamos a darle porra otra vez, por su astucia con el pobre, por sus *robos* y por los *asesinados*. (36, 37)[3]

El gran hacendado es la personificación del diablo (El "Diablo Verde"): "sonríe" en la oscuridad del barrio, con una "sonrisa hecha de mueca" y de "triunfo," y tiene las "barbas de chivo," que va "con una pata en el suelo" y con la otra tocándose "las barbas blancas," de chivo. Pero también es la transformación del diablo en la infraestructura económica del sistema capitalista agrario y en la subsistencia y la vida/muerte del siervo/proletario campesino.

## Metamorfosis del diablo en el campo y la tecnología

Bajo esta sección se podrían considerar las metamorfosis del diablo en los campos de cultivo, las minas, el puente, la lancha, el tren, las tiendas y las gasolineras, los aviones y autos, y también el cine y el salón de baile. Como ejemplo de estas transformaciones escogeremos los campos de cultivo, por hallarse relacionados aquí los campos y el trabajador.

> Varias figuras... se echan el costal al lomo como un chorizo gigante y lo ponen a la orilla del surco.... Los hombres se arrastran por la luz de la luna. Se cuelan, se retuercen por entre las plantas. Las plantas verdes, con sus motitas blancas, parecen arbolitos de Navidad. Los pizcadores quieren treparse hasta la cumbre como si fueran enanos. No pueden escarparla. La larga cola los ata a la tierra. Ahora serpiente, ceñida a la cintura quiere, con su hocico abierto, tragárselo pero no puede. El pizcador se la tapa con algodón, motitas que la pondrán repleta para que deje en paz a la gente. Las manos, rápidas, rápidas se rasguñan. Quieren despojar al árbol, llevarse esas esperanzas en las bolsas.... El diablo se las quita. Después viene otra serpiente tan hambrienta como la otra y otra y otra.... Por ahora los pizcadores platinados seguirán reptando entre mar verde y serpientes blancas. Capullos blancos, billetes verdes. Ojos verdes, dientes verdes. Podridos, podrida el alma, verde, verde. Verde mar, cuerpos verdes, verde muerte, descomposición. (27, 28)

Las dos transformaciones importantes de este largo pasaje son las "plantas verdes-mar verde" (Ben/"Diablo Verde") y el "chorizo gigante-serpientes blancas" (Ben/víbora/diablo). Más tarde (pág. 49), el sueño que tiene un conejo, que se sueña dormido en la luna, se transforma en realidad. En el sueño, el "conejo" representa a los campesinos y la "Luna" a los Estados Unidos y la Gran Depresión. Pero cuando la Luna "gruñe" el conejo despierta y los perros (patrulleros) lo persiguen y lo balacean, para volver a caer en otro sopor en donde se sueña "ratón" (campesinos) perseguido por la "víbora" (patrulla)-diablo, y, por fin, un "gato zalamero" lo devora.

En estas dos citas vemos, a través de las repetidas transformaciones del "Diablo Verde," el histórico robo de tierras, la desposesión del fruto que consechan los trabajadores por la hambrienta serpiente/diablo/patrón/sociedad capitalista, y la pérdida de la vida de los chicanos por el balaceo de los "perros" y la boca del "gato."

## Niveles de la actividad del hombre

Dentro y sobre el escenario natural del Valle se lleva a cabo la actividad del hombre. Esta actividad se perfila en la doble vertiente de tiempo-historia y espacio-geografía. Ambas quedan encuadradas en la narrativa. En cuanto a la vertiente tiempo-historia, sus límites son los explícitos de la novela: 1883-1970. Implícitamente, sin embargo, hay un *antes* y un *después* (2, 44, 80, 99), puntales de un posible orden edénico y de un posible retorno, si no al orden primigenio, al menos a otro semejante. Entre estos dos límites o puntales se desarrolla el *presente* novelado: la caída, el desajuste, el desequilibrio, causados por la explotación.

La segunda vertiente de la actividad humana la compone el espacio-geografía que, en la narrativa de que nos ocupamos, está circundada por el Valle de Presidio-Ojinaga. Varias son las realidades que saltan a la vista.

*Lo socio-económico.* En cuanto a los estratos, castas o clases socio-económicas se destacan dos: el señor/los peones, el hacendado/los siervos, y el capitalista agrícola/el proletariado agricultor. El de la clase baja (peón, siervo, proletariado), además de ser contundentemente mayoritario, se divide en dos grupos: el sedentario, que radica en Presidio y el inmigrante estacional, que procede de Ojinaga. Chicano y mexicano, respectivamente. Hay un anillo o peldaño en la escala de la clase social que, aunque procede de la clase baja, desempeña el papel de eje entre ésta y la clase alta. Es el tradicional "coyote," que en *El diablo en Texas* se haya encarnado en Lázaro.

Otro aspecto socio-económico que salta a la vista es la orientación o base económica de casi cien años (1883-1970). Aunque pueden suponerse ciertos cambios y adelantos tecnológicos, la base sigue siendo la misma: una economía agrícola servil, semi-feudalista. El contraste, e ironía, entre el avance tecnológico y el servilismo feudalista se hace más patente al observar que aquél no sólo no mejora a la clase baja sino que la hunde más en la escala socio-económica. Para corroborar este aserto baste citar, como ejemplo, la dicotomía contradictoria y real, aunque no necesariamente funcional, de la lancha-puente. La lancha, aún después de que Ben Lynch se hubiera apoderado de las tierras de Presidio, era el medio de transporte para cruzar el Río. Estaba en manos de la familia Uranga. Con la construcción del puente (avance tecnológico) los Uranga no sólo perdieron el negocio y la independencia económica, sino que se les prohibió el uso de la lancha. De semejante modo ocurrió no sólo con la desposesión de la tierra sino con el servilismo creado por la aparición del tractor, las gasolineras, las empacadoras, las tiendas, las bombas de regadío y hasta con el sistema monetario (cheques) y prestamista (deudas crónicas). O sea, cada adelanto tecnológico traía consigo un nuevo nudo que ataba, circundaba y acorralaba cada vez más la autodeterminación-servilismo económico de la clase baja.

*Lo político.* Una actividad humana necesaria en la sociedad es la política. Intimamente entrelazada a ésta se halla la legal y el salvaguardo de la misma, o sea la fuerza policial. En las sociedades occidentales, en general, se observa la interdependencia e incluso la supeditación de éstas a la actividad económica. Este fenómeno se hace patente en *El diablo en Texas.* Si Ben Lynch, Sr. y Ben Lynch, Jr. son los hacendados por excelencia, símbolos y realidad del sistema en cuestión, se sigue que el salvaguardo de la ley y el orden institucionales se pondrán al servicio del gran hacendado. Es el caso de los rangers y de los patrulleros que, de acuerdo a las necesidades económicas del terrateniente, no vacilan en importar o dejar pasar a no ciudadanos (no-documentados) o de expatriar a residentes descontentos (los Uranga). Hasta el mismo Gobernador Jones, al menos al principio, siguió el juego de los intereses económicos. Y, como si esto no bastara, el mismo erario federal y público se pone al servicio del terrateniente (Ben, Jr.) al concederle un cuarto de millón de dólares por dejar las tierras baldías mientras que los que las trabajan padecen consunción y hambre sin ningún subsidio gubernamental. Aparece claro a todas luces que la infraestructura económica rige y controla ciertos aspectos, por no decir todos, de la supraestructura social-legalista. Visto desde el orden mítico-literario, el gran hacendado, Ben Lynch, es la encarnación suprema del diablo: es "El Diablo Verde."

Se podría, pues, establecer el siguiente raciocinio: si el hacendado Ben es el epítome del sistema capitalista agrícola, y si, al mismo tiempo, es el "Diablo Verde," se sigue que el sistema capitalista agrícola "es el diablo." Lógicamente se establecería la ecuación: la infraestructura económica se equipara/es el diablo. Pero esta ecuación parece improbable dado que la infraestructura económica es de orden real-material y el "diablo" es de orden mítico-sobrenatural, ambos valores irreductibles. Además de que, en el orden temporal, no está claro cuál de los dos es el que precede y cuál el que sigue. No hay relación visible de causa-efecto. Pero dejando de lado esta disquisición abstracta y filosófica, el hecho es que en la presente obra narrativa nos encontramos con dos fuerzas opresoras de la gente: la física-económica, de una parte, y la síquica-espiritual, de otra.

*Lo sicológico-espiritual.* Esta doble situación opresiva surte efectos diversos en la miriada de personajes que afloran en las páginas de la novela. Hay que repetir que sería difícil, dentro de la narración, demostrar la relación de causa-efecto cuando se quiere analizar el trauma sicológico por el que atraviesan los personajes. Que si el "diablo," elemento de la supraestructura, es producto/condición de la infraestructura, o que si el "diablo," entidad teológica, precede al pensamiento humano, o que si el "diablo," realidad mítica, es producto de la inventiva humana, y, por tanto, posterior a ésta. El hecho es que el "diablo" *existe* en la mente de la gente de Presidio. Por tanto es, además de un valor religioso, una realidad síquica. Bajo este apartado citaremos tres fenómenos de sicología anormal. El primero es un fenómeno síquico-económico (crueldad), que se manifiesta en el niño Chente. El segundo, síquico-biológico (imbecilidad), es el caso del imbécil Chava. El tercer fenómeno, síquico-religioso (locura), se observa en la situación patética de Marcela, la madre del feto.

El primer caso, representativo de la correlación síquico-económica, es el de Chente, hermano de Vicke. A la edad de doce años le toca morir. La muerte fue debida a una enfermedad pulmonaria, causada por la polución de la mina, en donde trabajaba (32). Podemos suponer que llevaba varios años trabajando, es decir que debió comenzar a la edad de seis o siete años. Es un caso patente de la explotación económica que no respeta la tierna edad de los niños, debido al beneficio lucrativo materialista de una empresa capitalista en Presidio. Pero, además de la material, se puede ver la otra parte de la correlación, la síquica, si nos fijamos en el diálogo monologado entre Chente y su hermana Vicke. En una serie de preguntas, a las cuales Chente no recibe respuesta, aquél recorre una retahila de temas difíciles de hilvanar entre sí. Se puede suponer que la mente del niño está delirando, pero lo importante es observar el estado de anormalidad síquica debido a la explotación económica. En el espacio de una página nos habla de la vida y la muerte, por qué tiene que morir tan temprano, la crueldad hacia los animales, si el hombre debe o no llorar, del puente, de los juegos, de los "papeles," del diablo y de la cueva. La descripción literaria del miedo y la angustia que siente Chente ante lo desconocido de la muerte, causada por la explotación económica y diabólica, es una de las páginas más logradas de toda la novela (18, 19).

Dentro del segundo caso, que representa la correlación síquico-biológica, se puede citar a otro personaje que, a pesar de su edad indefinida, parece ser joven, de incipiente barba. Es la situación de Chava, sicótico, atrasado mental e imbécil. No sabemos nada de su historia, pero podemos suponer que es fruto de una de aquellas funciones que el "parir allí (Presidio) es parir medio muerto" (i, 3, 4, 10). Esta parece ser la historia de la mayor parte de sus habitantes-personajes. Por consiguiente podría deducirse que la imbecilidad de Chava es debida, entre otras cosas, a la consunción y al raquitismo biológico que, a su vez, es derivativo de la explotación económica y a las quince o diecisiete horas diarias de trabajo de la gente campesina.

El tercer caso de anormalidad síquica es el relacionado a lo religioso. Aunque hay otros factores influyentes, parece ser que la obsesión y creencia en el "diablo" es la causa, si no inmediata, remota de la locura de Marcela, esposa de José y madre del feto,[4] con quien se identifica el autor. José, para evitar ser reclutado al ejército, se escapa a México. Llegado el momento de dar a luz, quería unirse a su esposo, pero la lluvia no cesaba e, incluso, derretía la "casa de Dios." Fue a la iglesia antes de cruzar el Río. Ve que entra "un señor sin quitarse el sombrero . . . , sus ojos de águila columpian . . . , le sonríe," luego "le guiña el ojo y sale" (77). Perseguida por el "diablo," se fue corriendo a casa "agazapándose y echando manotadas al aire." Aterrorizada, pedía que le "quitaran el diablo, que se reía y reía como loco." Como una posesa, Marcela corre por la casa volcando la mesa y rompiendo todo lo que encuentra delante. Después se quedó con "las manos engarruñadas . . . y los ojos paralizados en la pared" (78).

## A modo de conclusión

Intentaremos resumir algunos de los aspectos más sobresalientes de *El diablo en Texas* que ya hemos señalado en nuestro estudio de las metamorfosis del "diablo." Pero antes queremos hacer una indicación sobre el aspecto formal de la novela, que se relaciona claramente con el tema presentado. Nos referimos a la estructura *fragmentada* de la narración.[5] Esta fragmentación corresponde, por una parte, al mundo fragmentado de que se ocupa la novela: la fuerte y distinta división de clases sociales y el juego engendrador de un caos en los valores religioso-económicos. Precisamente, y por otra parte, este mundo caótico fue creado por "el diablo," bajo sus muchas transformaciones y, al mismo tiempo, se presta para "el juego" diabólico, creando circular y sistemáticamente más confusión y desorganización socio-económica. Paradójicamente, y a pesar de una externa fragmentación de la forma, la unidad estructural interna puede recobrarse por medio del sutil y complicado hilo de las transformaciones y del proceso de los des-enmascaramientos respectivos. Parte de nuestro estudio, aunque indirectamente, ha sido precisamente éste: tratar de recobrar la yacente estructura interna.

Hemos presentado una serie de metamorfosis en este ensayo y lo que intentamos ahora es mostrar qué es lo que entraña la metamorfosis. En esta novela implica, además de un cambio de formas en sí, un poder que controla. El metamorfosearse lleva consigo un propósito: el de esconderse y disfrazarse para *confundir*. Al confundir se crea un caos y este caos es campo propicio para desarrollar el *control* y poder deseados. Este poder y control se ejerce en el nivel sicológico y en el nivel económico, como queda dicho.

En la trayectoria del tiempo nos encontramos en la novela con un *presente* y un *antes/después*. El primero es explícito y el segundo es implícito. Explícitamente nos hallamos ante dos realidades globales y, al mismo tiempo, contradictorias pero necesarias para que la contradicción subsista. De un lado tenemos la supraestructura que, en *El diablo en Texas*, la componen la Religión (fe, Dios/Diablo, Iglesia), la Política (Gobernadores tejanos y mexicanos, partido demócrata), los representantes de la Ley (el sheriff, la patrulla, el FBI, la cárcel, e, incluso, la Corte), los medios de Comunicación (los periódicos chicanos, el cine/Tarzán, y la música/Elvis Presley), y el arte (el periodismo/Francisco Uranga, el corrido de Joaquín Murrieta/Reyes Uranga y la novela/Autor). De otro lado nos enfrentamos con la infraestructura económica que, en la narración, está compuesta por el capital y la mano de obra. Entran, dentro del capital, además del capitalista, las tierras, las semillas/cosechas, la maquinaria, el dinero y el subsidio gubernamental por el rastrojo de las tierras valdías. Comprenden la mano de obra los chicanos y mexicanos. Los medios de producción y la riqueza acumulada del capital quedan bajo el control de Ben/clase alta, mientras que los bienes producidos, en lugar de ser distribuidos al productor chicano/clase baja, pasan a formar parte del capital. La supraestructura (Religión, Política, Ley), que en el sistema capitalista se alía a la infraestructura para llevar a cabo su meta de opresión/explotación, en la presente narración no sólo se *alía* a ésta sino que, por la intervención literaria/metamorfosis del "diablo," se *conjura* con ella. El diablo se convierte de este modo en el prestidigitador, el gran farsante en la tragicomedia de la condición humana, cuya escena se desarrolla en el Valle Presidio-Ojinaga. El "diablo" *es* Ben, es Texas, es el Capitalismo americano, que crean un "infierno" presente y real en el dicho Valle.

Además de un presente explícito hay también en la narración un *antes* y un *después* implícitos, como se observó antes. Se supone que había un *antes* paradisíaco, pero no parece claramente señalado. Se habla, sí, de una especie de paréntesis pretérito en la "perennidad" del tiempo, pero no surte efecto porque "nada ha cambiado" (2). La víbora, desde la cima de la cruz, "recuerda que desde un principio quisieron defraudarla, quitarle el dominio" del Valle. Se refiere el "diablo" a los misioneros que llegaron a Junta de los Ríos/Presidio en el siglo diecisiete. Pero "nada ha cambiado . . . (porque) sólo el tiempo es permanente" (2). El "nada ha cambiado," *después* de la llegada de los misioneros, implica que *antes* de su llegada el "diablo" tenía un dominio tan fuerte como el que reconquistó después de que se hubieran ido los misioneros, pues "nada ha cambiado." La aparición o advenimiento del hombre occidental parece haber interrumpido el orden natural al desempeñar su papel basado no en la presunta ley natural sino en unas leyes racionales y arbitrarias y, con frecuencia, contradictorias.

De la segunda y tercera parte de la novela se desprende un *después* futurista en donde se supone que habrá una especie de liberación del chicano. En la segunda parte se anuncia concretamente este *después* por boca del feto y de los muertos. "Algún día y ya pronto, encenderé la chispa, les quemaré los pies, y los muertos les invadirán la mente, los harán llorar, los harán reír, los volverán locos ..." a los poetas/demagogos/historiadores (80), le dice el feto a Chonito. Otro muerto, Jesús del Río, resucitará bajo el nombre de José "para aplacar las llamas de este infierno" (44), es decir para vengarse de la opresión/genocidio.

Pero es el narrador (feto/Jesús del Río/adulto) el que anuncia el comienzo de la liberación. Después de haberse "arrancado de las garras" de Presidio/Diablo, "vuelve" para asistir al entierro de su padre. Este quiso "vengarse" pero no pudo en vida. Será su hijo el que llevará a cabo el desquite. Para conseguirlo le dice a su difunto padre "he decidido quedarme porque hay que quitar la corona de espinas en Presidio ... ir hasta el río y lavarse las llagas y ... regresar fuerte.... El milagro obrará y necesitará contarles del diablo que se desató y que todavía anda suelto.... Habrá que encender la llama, la que murió con el tiempo" (99).

Nos parece ver en este pasaje la pre-figuración de un Alter Christus: el río Jordán, el bautismo, y el mensaje, más bien de lucha/desquite que de amor. Su misión será la de destronar las fuerzas del mal en Presidio: Diablo/Anticristo. El paralelismo religioso Cristo-Anticristo parece obvio si lo colocamos en el síquico-religioso, perteneciente a la supraestructura. Pero desaparece si lo bajamos al nivel de la infraestructura socio-económica, porque no hay ni mensaje ni programa de acción concretos. El mensaje es el de "contarles," "decirles" lo que ocurrió, que se supone será la "historia" verdadera de la opresión en Presidio. Pero esto no basta si es que no va acompañado de un programa de acción. Se puede suponer, sin embargo, que el programa de acción del Nuevo Cristo será paralelo al del Anticristo. Así como el de éste fue/es un programa de desrupción caótica y de explotación socio-económica el de aquél será, antitéticamente, un plan de liberación socio-económica.

ARIZONA STATE UNIVERSITY

## Notas

[1] Las citas de *El diablo en Texas* (Tucson: Editorial Peregrinos, 1976), aparecerán entre paréntesis en el cuerpo de este ensayo.

Del diablo, como personaje y tema literarios, se han ocupado, en mayor o menor grado, todas las literaturas. La obra de José María Souvirón, *El Príncipe de este siglo* (Madrid: Ediciones Cultura Hispánica, 1968), trata este asunto por extenso. La obra de Stith Thompson, *Motif-Index of Folk-Literature*, (Bloomington: Indiana University Press, 1955), es una obra clásica para el estudio del diablo en las diversas literaturas. Nos parece esencial, como libro de consulta, el *Dictionary of Symbols*, de Juan E. Cirlot, o cualquier otro diccionario detallado y extenso para cualquier estudio de esta novela.

[2] Charles Tatum, en su reseña de *El diablo en Texas*, aparecida en *World Literature Today*, 51, 4 (Autumn 1977), 592-93, comenta: "He (el autor) does *not fully develop* the demonic figure of the Anglo, nor does he shift comfortably between reality and the scene in which an *impish* devil appears" (Lo subrayado es nuestro). Es increíble que un lector, por muy distraído que esté, pueda hacer tal afirmación después de haber visto la serie de transformaciones por las que pasa el diablo y el dominio devastador que esta criatura-personaje, que no tiene nada de "diablillo" ("impish"), ejerce en el Valle Presidio-Ojinaga. Y, en cuanto a la carencia de un completo desarrollo de la figura del Anglo, como nos quiere hacer creer el reseñador, refiero al lector de este trabajo a las tremendas figuras metamorfoseadas, en particular, a la del "Diablo Verde" (Ben Lynch) y a la del Sheriff.

[3] Lo subrayado es nuestro. Con ello queremos llamar la atención al poderío y control económicos, bajo sus diversas formas, que el "Diablo Verde" ejerce sobre la gente y el Valle.

[4] En la reseña antes mencionada, Charles Tatum nos dice también: "The second section focuses on the anguish of a young Chicana who is *abandoned* by her *lover* shortly *after the birth* of their *illegitimate* child." (Nuestro el subrayado). Nos vemos forzados, para disipar errores, a aclarar varios puntos: 1) Parece desprenderse de este pasaje un estereotipo de que el chicano/latino debe/tiene que tener su "amante" ("lover"). 2) Marcela tiene su legítimo esposo. José no es su amante, es *su legítimo esposo*, y que, 3) por tanto, *su* hijo *no* es ilegítimo. 4) José no "abandonó" a su esposa sino que se escapó a México para evadir el reclutamiento (ver Tercera Parte de la novela). Y 5) la escapada de José no fue *después* ("after the birth") sino *antes* del nacimiento de su hijo.

[5] Queremos referirnos aquí otra vez a la reseña de Charles Tatum que dice: "In short, the novel lacks cohesiveness." Quizá el análisis hecho en el texto ayude a aclarar esa aparente falta de "cohesión" a que se refiere el crítico en su reseña.

# F. Estela Portillo Trambley

## Estela Portillo Trambley's Fictive Search for Paradise

*Tomás Vallejos*

Much Chicano fiction can be seen as a search for values in a world that is hostile to those values. In the case of the Chicana artist, the hostility is twofold. She is the target of both racism and sexism. It is no wonder, then, when a Chicana's literary expression is rooted in dissatisfaction. One outstanding case in point is Estela Portillo Trambley's collection of short fiction and drama, *Rain of Scorpions and Other Writings*.

One aspect of Portillo Trambley's writing which distinguishes her from many male Chicano writers is her criticism, not only of American society, but of some Chicano traditions and social structures as well. Dissatisfied with the inferior position of women advocated by many Chicano traditionalists, Portillo Trambley turns to ancient mythical structures as models of an ideal balance in the cosmos. This original balance, she seeks to inform her readers, precedes and excels the inequity she exposes in traditional Mexican customs and social structures that aggrandize men at the expense of women. She also uses this primordial model as a basis for criticizing American corruptions of it, such as the exploitation of the land and workers by American industry in the novella "Rain of Scorpions." Portillo Trambley envisions a paradise—an ideal state of mind and spirit—that turns to ancient mythical models as a basis for urging reform in both Chicano and American social attitudes and structures.

In applying the paradise motif to *Rain of Scorpions*, one can place most of the stories within it in either of two categories: those illustrating the failure to find paradise and those illustrating the successful quest. Paradise in Portillo Trambley's writings is a vision of cosmic wholeness within human consciousness. The author posits for her readers an ideal world where conflicting elements—male and female, reason and instinct, order and chaos—coexist in dynamic balance. In some stories she suggests this balance by creating characters who recognize and accept this world view. In others she creates characters in social environments that deny such a world view and demand the subjugation of one element by its opposite. When such an imbalance occurs, the result is destruction.

This world view is derived from ancient Nahua cosmology, for the opposing forces of Portillo Trambley's works are remarkably similar to the ancient Mexican belief that the world is governed by the struggles for supremacy among the four sons of Ometeotl, the gods of the four directions. The domination of one god and his attendant qualities over the others is responsible for the cosmic cataclysms in the Nahua myth of the Five Suns.[1] In *Rain of Scorpions* destruction occurs on a microcosmic level, for it is men and women, not gods, who inhabit her fictive world and give it motion.

Motion is fundamental to interpreting the work of Estela Portillo Trambley, for the paradise of her vision is dynamic, not static. While a balance between opposites is crucial to the attainment of wholeness, this balance is paradoxically achieved, not through harmony, but through struggle. In these works destruction inevitably leads to regeneration in essentially the same way the destruction of one sun in ancient Mexican myth resulted in the creation of a new one. Thus, despite the tragic fates of some of her characters, the tragedy often becomes a source of affirmation, for the author is by no means a nihilist. Like the ancient Mexicans, she expresses a belief in the unending cyclical regeneration of the universe.

An example of Portillo Trambley's treatment of the paradise motif is "The Trees." Containing elements of both ancient Mexican cosmology and Western myth, the story's symbolism alludes to the Garden of Eden.

"The Trees" is literally and figuratively the story of a fall from paradise. The main character, Nina Ayala, is a destructive woman who disrupts the harmonious Eden of the Ayala family, leading to its fall and, ultimately, her own suicidal fall from a cliff. The Ayalas' world before Nina's intrusion is described as a paradise where harmony prevailed:

> Don Teófilo Ayala was sole owner of six hundred fertile acres. He had four sons who worked in love and harmony with him from dawn to dusk to help with the creation of life's fruit. The simple laws amongst them were not vain, or seeking profit for self. It was a wholesome venture of unity where trust and giving came first. The profit in money was but an aftermath, never the due course of the ultimate incentive. The apple trees came first; they represented a task of God and for God, and in this belief the brothers worked.[2]

An important variation on the Eden motif is the revelation that even before Nina's arrival, the Ayalas' "Eden" was inherently flawed. Its very structure, a patriarchal order, is inequitable and thus doomed to final disintegration.

> The family, with its elementary tie to the earth, had established a working patriarchal order. The father and sons lived for a fraternal cause, the apple orchards. Their women followed in silent steps, fulfilled in their woman ways. If ambition or a sense of power touched the feminine heart, it was a silent touch. The lives were well patterned like the rows of apple trees and the trenches that fed them. Men and women had a separate given image until Nina came. (p. 13)

Furthermore, the patriarchal order of the Ayalas depends upon the power of the father. Thus, when Teófilo dies, the cohesive family order is suddenly thrown into chaos: "Unwittingly, he had willed the lives of his sons who had obediently followed his direction. A dependency was left behind with the death of the father. Someone needed to take strong reins. None of the brothers dared" (p. 14).

Into this false Eden, a male-dominated social order where there is harmony without balance, Nina enters and undoes the unity of the Ayala brothers, bringing total destruction to the valley: "... the Garden of Eden became a desolation" (p. 23).

Despite the final desolation of "The Trees," Portillo Trambley leaves no doubt in her readers' minds that there is more to the story than the destruction of a false Eden. This story, like several in *Rain of Scorpions*, begins with prefatory statements which provide an interpretation of the story that is akin to ancient Mexican cosmology, for it denies the prospect of final cosmic destruction and nothingness. Instead, it affirms a belief in a better world rising from the ashes of its predecessor:

> The dead valley. Tombstones sprouted on a hill ... a dead stream....
> Clusters of dry weeds ... jumbled skeletons of brush.... There was no desperate plea for life in this deadness, but it was far from nothingness. A nothingness ... can the mind and heart conceive of such a thing? Even dead valleys cling to traces of something. This something is new because it is now an instance of process. The process, in this case, was a part of eager lives until ... human error? Nature's error? No one ever thinks in terms of nothingness or *is* in terms with nothingness. All is part of the change in process, errant and eternal. (p. 11)

Death and destruction are essential parts of the unending cycles Portillo Trambley calls "change in process." Their crucial role in the restoration of balance and the creation of a new and better world is suggested in the comparison of Nina to the Quinteco apple: "There is a quality in experience that is very much like the Quinteco apple. It is the quality of creation, of innovation, of that something new. The newness itself, nevertheless, be it creation or destruction, finds its way of changing people, apples, ways" (p. 12). The result of change is the quality Portillo Trambley sees in a true paradise: balance. The ideal balance the author envisions is suggested in the Quinteco apple's physical properties. "Its softness had the quality of mangos in ripeness, and its green sweetness surprised at intervals with streaks of gentle, bitter strains that calmed the fullness of the sugar . . . a bittersweet goodness of surprise" (p. 12). Like Portillo Trambley's paradise, the apple's multiple symbolism encompasses the fertility of the Ayalas as well as the changes toward equality represented by Nina.

This vision of a world in which men and women are resilient and in union with the cosmos recurs in many variations throughout Portillo Trambley's writings. Her best work, *The Day of the Swallows*, explores this theme negatively in a lyrical dramatic style reminiscent of García Lorca's *Bodas de Sangre* and *La Casa de Bernarda Alba*. The play's central character is driven to lesbianism by a male-dominated society just as Nina is driven to an inordinate thirst for power by a social order that has denied that to her. Both characters become unbalanced as a result of a social order that is itself inequitable and unbalanced.

Another story from *Rain of Scorpions* following this pattern is "If It Weren't for the Honeysuckle." Beatriz, the protagonist, kills the brutally oppressive Robles as an assertion of her right to freedom. However, her act of defiance against a social order that negates women is excessive, for it negates and excludes men. In the final analysis, Beatriz replaces one unbalanced order based on violence with another, equally violent and unbalanced. Her obsessive order is described as "something without roots . . . something lost in the course of evolution" (p. 109).

In this story, as in "The Trees," characterization is developed archetypally as a set of antitheses. One may visualize their structure as a scale in which the overbalance of one characteristic (e.g., masculinity, darkness, reason versus femininity, light, instinct) leads to overcompensation of the other, a catastrophic tipping of the scale in the opposite direction. In these cases, the ideal balance, the wholeness, the paradise Portillo Trambley envisions, is lost.

In other works within *Rain of Scorpions* the search for balance and wholeness is achieved and kept intact. The best examples of this are "The Burning" and the title work. Both stories, especially "Rain of Scorpions," portray characters on a successful journey toward oneness, and in both this destination is represented in paradisiacal imagery.

Lela, in "The Burning," is a Tarahumara Indian from Batopilas with the magical healing powers of a *curandera* (p. 90). Her personal history is presented as a quest for a "larger self" that she cannot find in her native village (p. 92). Lela first comes upon this "larger self" entering into communion with her "little gods." The following passage describes this communion as a euphoric discovery of paradise:

> One day, she had walked too far towards the pines, too far towards a roar that spoke of rushing life. She followed a yellow butterfly that flitted towards a lake. As she followed, she looked for little gods in the glint of the sun, and in the open branches that pierced the absoluteness of the sky....
> When she had reached the lake, she stepped into the water without hesitation.... She began to swim more rapidly towards the turn that led to the cradle of the roar, the waterfall....
> She remembered the grotto behind the waterfall. It had been her hermitage of dreams, of wonder. Here her oneness had knitted all the little gods unto herself until she felt the whole of earth—things within her being. (pp. 91–92)

Lela's discovery of paradise, a balanced spiritual and mental magnanimity, is contrasted with the smallness of the people in the pueblo. As she lies on her deathbed, the women of the pueblo have decided that she must burn because she is a *bruja* (witch), "the enemy of God!" (p. 90). Lela's vision encompasses the totality of life and this is unacceptable to their orthodoxy. "One tired soul stood up to speak, 'Many times I see the light she makes of darkness, and that light is a greater blackness still.'" Another woman adds, "Yes, she drinks the bitterness of good and swallows, like the devil-wolf, the red honey milk of evil" (p. 89). Because the *curandera* never converts to Christianity, the people of the village are hostile and fearful of her, despite her many acts of kindness.

The main source of their hostility is her devotion to "little gods," imperfect, but approachable and lovable in their humanity. Unlike the omnipotent Judeo-Christian Yahweh, Lela's gods have much in common with those gods dear to the ancient Aztec commoners,[3] and the comical Pueblo divinities described by ethnologist Alfonso Ortiz.[4]

> They did not rule or demand allegiance. The little rural gods of river, sky, fire, seed, birds, all were chosen members of each family. Because they sanctified all human acts, they were the actions of the living, like an aura. They were a shrine to creation. (p. 91)

This humanness of Lela's gods is unacceptable to the townspeople, for it is a profanation of their sober, Christian God. One woman condemns Lela: "She took our holy saints, Mary, Joseph, and many others and made them obscene.... Drinking saints! Winking saints! Who can forgive the hideous suggestions of her clay devils?" (p. 95). Having reached a spiritual and mental paradise through her "little gods," Lela draws a conclusion: "Her larger self told her that the miracle of the living act was supreme, the giving, the receiving, *the stumbling, and the getting up*" (p. 95; emphasis added).

The story concludes on a note of supreme irony. While she is dying, a fact unknown to her executioners, preparations are made to burn her in her house as punishment for her alleged witchcraft. Ironically, Lela's last wish is to be cremated rather than buried. "If only . . . if only I could be buried in the tradition of my fathers . . . a clean burning for new life. . . . Oh, little gods, take me back to my fathers . . ." (p. 96). Meanwhile, the flames surrounding her house have begun to rise and through the petty maliciousness of the townspeople, Lela's dying wish is granted by her very executioners. Their enactment of a ritual reminiscent of the Spanish Inquisition ironically becomes a Tarahumara funeral rite. The story concludes with a strong suggestion that Lela is moving into a new form of life, a paradise like the one she has already found: "The little gods were racing to the waterfall" (p. 96).

A similar discovery of paradise also occurs in "Rain of Scorpions," which develops most extensively the paradise motif in terms of Indian cosmology. Like "The Trees," this novella presents a world view derived from Indian religions while drawing upon Biblical symbol and motif.

On the most superficial level, "Rain of Scorpions" is a variation of a story line common in children's literature: the treasure hunt. The hunt in this novella, however, is not for gold or jewels, but a map to paradise. The oppressive economic and ecological conditions of Smeltertown anger Fito, a veteran of the Vietnamese war who has lost his leg and acquired cynicism in its place. Consequently, he attempts to organize the people of this small mining town near El Paso, Texas, against their oppressors by unrealistically proposing an exodus from the town to shut down the smeltering plant and draw national attention to the problem. Prompted by this far-fetched scheme and the townspeople's objections that they have nowhere else to go, five boys decide to search for the "green valley," a paradise described to them by Papa At, an old man whose memory is rich in Indian legend. They hope to find the legendary map to the "green valley," so the people will have somewhere to go (p. 133). The boys mistake the "green valley where the nature gods live," Papa At's "answer to chaos," (p. 118) for an actual geographic location.

The boys seek a mythical solution to a social problem: ". . . they must find the map to the green valley. If the smelter fumes were poisonous, the green valley would be the ideal place; it would be the promised land for the people of Smeltertown" (p. 143). This notion, however, is revealed to be simplistic and illusory. In "Rain of Scorpions" Portillo Trambley makes no attempt to come up with magical solutions to such complex problems. She posits a paradise on a much smaller level, leaving the solutions of social problems to others. Portillo Trambley suggests that one cannot find the "promised land" for an entire population until one has found it within oneself. The quest for paradise must be made on a personal level.

Interwoven with the quest for paradise in "Rain of Scorpions" is the Great Flood motif borrowed from Genesis. In the interplay of these two Biblical themes, Portillo Trambley reconstructs in fiction a world view that is rooted in the same Indian cosmology developed to a lesser extent in "The Trees." "Rain of Scorpions" envisions a paradisiacal world of oneness in the balance of opposites and presents a cyclical and dialectical world view, one of endlessly alternating destruction and regeneration.

The key word, a concept which joins the paradise and the Great Flood themes, is chaos. The very title, "Rain of Scorpions," signals the importance of this concept. It is this curious freak of nature that helps the central characters, Fito and Lupe, find balance and wholeness. The "rain of scorpions" is actually a mudslide caused by a downpour which unearths a large nest of scorpions and carries the dead creatures along in its inundation of Smeltertown. This catastrophe joins Fito and Lupe in a symbolic restoration of balance between two people made unbalanced by misfortune. Lupe is a fat young woman who finds consolation for her unattractiveness in reading and eating; but her excessive reading is as unhealthy as her overeating. "The reading of too many books had grown into a madness, and that madness had grown wings" (p. 128). Fito's madness is his bitterness toward American society for sending him to a war that had taken his leg. This ultimately leads to his hatred of women after he is rejected by his beloved because of his war injury. Both Lupe and Fito are incapable of expressing their desires and feelings as a result of their misfortunes, but through the chaotic "rain of scorpions" they discover new feelings and the ability to express them. As the Biblical flood did for Noah, this flood provides the occasion for Lupe and Fito to begin anew. For Fito it is an end of bitterness: "She searched Fito's face and found the beginnings of peace" (p. 164). For Lupe it is a joyous shedding of her storybook illusions. "She stroked his head and knew that theirs would never be a great love story.... She felt very alive. She didn't want to be Cleopatra anymore. She wanted to be Lupe loving Fito the way she knew how" (p. 165). Chaos, in the form of a flood, has brought paradise to Lupe and Fito.

Moreover, chaos is revealed to the five young seekers of paradise as a sacred and essential aspect of nature. While Fito and Lupe are not spared the ravages of the flood, the boys unknowingly find deliverance from the "rain of scorpions" in the cave where the map of the "green valley" is supposed to be hidden. The boys' correspondence to Noah is suggested by the description of the rock next to the opening into the "crystal room," where the map had been left by the legendary Indio Tolo. The passage to this part of the cave is a small cleft near "an ark-like boulder" (pp. 151-52). When the boys enter the "crystal room," they discover chaos and in this chaos is beauty and sacredness. In the middle of this "room" is a stone resembling an altar: "They looked at the huge red stone shaped in tiers of small columns holding smaller skeletal arms of stone like a web . . . chaos finding order in stone" (p. 156). In the "crystal room," described as "a maze of stone" (p. 156), the boys discover the sacredness of chaos: "It demanded the silence of a cathedral . . . it demanded the awe for godly things" (p. 154). This "room" is testimony in rock to the chaotic order of divine creation:

> The rest of the boys were thinking about living in the cave . . . wild thoughts, free thoughts, thoughts of earthmen who know there is a wild god in the world, for the order of things lies in changing chaos, leaving only the most intricate patterns. Chaos of Man or chaos of Nature, it is a part of a deep wildness from a time when earth was taking form and creating changing life, all an orderly chaos. (p. 155)

After Miguel finds the map, he discovers, not the directions to a geographical site, but a simple Indian word, "KEAR," which he later learns is equivalent to the English word, "YOU" (p. 177). The "promised land" he and the other boys have found is a oneness within themselves and the world: "Miguel felt outside himself; his senses were crystallized. . . . Miguel felt a whisper inside himself, 'That's me . . . the stone, the light, the slab'" (p. 158). When his senses "crystallize," he is mystically becoming one with the chaotic crystal formations in the cave. Through the acceptance of his place in the totality of the universe, his sensibility has crystallized along with his senses.

Through the all-important element of chaos, Portillo Trambley's fiction discloses the passage to her visionary paradise. It is reached through an individual's inner acceptance of all aspects of life and awareness of being part of this "all." The search for paradise in *Rain of Scorpions*, sometimes successful and sometimes not, is a return to the primordial past, to the moment of creation. By holding the primordial wholeness of creation up as a model, Portillo Trambley makes her criticisms of social orders that are dead harmonies and not vital balances: "The balance existed before men tampered" (p. 135).

At the same time, she looks forward to future possibilities, to a world where both men and women can be complete and healthy—a world where no one is denied the freedom and ability to find a "larger self." For this reason, *Rain of Scorpions*, like *The Day of the Swallows*, is a timely literary work dealing with important contemporary social issues, most notably the Chicana's struggle for liberation.

However, as serious examination of her writing reveals, Estela Portillo Trambley is important not just because she grapples with the issue of the Chicana's struggles; the ideas she offers go beyond social criticism. Portillo Trambley leads her readers to unique explorations of extraordinary philosophical considerations relating to the social issues she explores. Thus, she should be considered a noteworthy figure in contemporary letters, as a woman, as a Chicana, as a thinker, and as an artist.

UNIVERSITY OF HOUSTON-DOWNTOWN

## Notes

[1] Miguel León-Portilla, *Aztec Thought and Culture: A Study of the Ancient Nahuatl Mind* (Norman, Okla.: Univ. of Oklahoma Press, 1963), pp. 35–43.

[2] Estela Portillo Trambley, *Rain of Scorpions and Other Writings* (Berkeley: Tonatiuh International, 1975), p. 12. All further references will hereafter be cited by page number in the text.

[3] Alfonso Caso, *The Aztecs: People of the Sun*, trans. Lowell Dunham (Norman, Okla.: Univ. of Oklahoma Press, 1958), p. 8.

[4] Alfonso Ortiz, *The Tewa World: Space, Time, Being, and Becoming in a Pueblo Society* (Chicago: Univ. of Chicago Press, 1969), p. 166.

# G. Nash Candelaria

## Time and History in Candelaria's *Memories of the Alhambra*

*Vernon E. Lattin*

A commonplace of literary criticism is the importance of time in the modern novel. With Bergson and Proust standing in the background, one thinks of Joyce, Woolf, Mann, and Faulkner to confirm this point. In the shadow of such giants, the recent development of the Chicano novel with its branch, the New Mexican Chicano narrative, goes unnoticed. However, a work like Nash Candelaria's *Memories of the Alhambra* must be read because it is one of a growing number of Chicano novels exploring time and history from a new perspective.

The New Mexican Chicano holds a unique position in American history and American letters. The Chicano looks at history and himself from multiple and often simultaneous angles of vision. From the first angle of vision he looks back to Spain and his emotional ties to Europe, to the Spanish language and customs, and to the early Spaniards in America such as Cortez, Coronado, Oñate, and Vargas. The date 1492 is etched into his soul. Perhaps he can trace his ancestors to the early settlers of New Spain. This emotional tie is reinforced by a prevalent Anglo racism which considers Spanish superior and Mexican inferior.

A second angle of vision turns toward Mexico, and his *mestizo* reality. Historically, the New Mexican territory was for a short period of time part of Mexico, and the New Mexican was a Mexican citizen. The New Mexican, from this angle, identifies with Mexico and sees Spain as the conquering country and the history of New Spain as the history of lies. As the Mexican writer Carlos Fuentes has said, "We are very conscious of the silence behind us. Our history is not written and there are a pack of lies concomitant with our abundant defeats. We have to rewrite it all over again."[1] The Chicano therefore joins the Mexican in seeing the Spanish language as the language of the conqueror and in taking pride in his Indianness.

Still another angle of vision results from the fact that in 1846 Mexico was defeated by the United States and that what is now New Mexico became part of the United States. As Candelaria has written: "Although Mexico lost this war, not all Mexicans lost their homeland as the New Mexican and Californian did. That is, the new migrants do not carry this defeat in their psyche as the New Mexican does."[2] From this angle, English is the language of the conqueror and Spanish is held in esteem.

When Carlos Fuentes says that Americans have never had to quarrel with their history because, except for the Southerner, they have never been defeated, he fails to account for the Chicanos and Native Americans who are defeated "American" people. Candelaria himself, who is married to a southerner who traces her history back to the defeated South, is very sensitive to this "quarrel." However, the New Mexican Chicano's quarrel is different. The double conquest (1492, 1846) creates ambiguities and uncertainties beyond that of the Southerner (one defeat, same race, same language), the American Indian (one defeat, one linguistic rape, one clear enemy), or even the Black (transferred to a land away from his native language and most cultural ties).

Finally, the modern Chicano must turn to see himself as an American living within a dominant Anglo culture. Today many New Mexican Chicanos, whose grandparents may have spoken no English, themselves speak little or no Spanish. Educated in English-speaking schools, they read history from the conqueror's perspective, and they remember the Alamo rather than the Alhambra.

Candelaria's novel deals with time and history from this multiple perspective. Having been influenced personally by the accumulated past of Spain, Mexico, and the United States, he speaks of Cervantes, Fuentes, and Faulkner as literary influences. His sense of the historical past, however, is balanced by an awareness of time as continuity and repetition.

*Memories of the Alhambra* has a circular structure, moving from the death and burial of José Rafa's father, "The patriarch was dead,"[3] to José's own death and burial at the end of the novel. This circular pattern includes a series of repeating episodes, images, verbal echoes, and thematic motifs reflecting a theory of the recurrent cycles of time as well as a sense of unity and wholeness that contrasts with the hero's fragmented self, his entrapment with clock time. The novel's thirty chapters are presented from three points of view (José, Theresa, Joe) which are echoed in other trilogies of the novel (Father, Son, Holy Ghost; United States, Mexico, Spain; past, present, future; Spanish,

Indian, Anglo), all reinforcing the separateness and division of José, but also reminding us that the three can mystically be one, that time and eternity can be reconciled.

The first three chapters of the novel, told from the successive points of view of José, Theresa, and Joe, establish the quest motif and refer the reader to the different concepts of time operating within the novel. Candelaria's basic understanding of time is that it is subjective and emotionally based: "All three characters flit back and forth in time guided by their feelings that revolved about the meaning to them of 'Mexicanness' and coming to terms with it and the Anglo world."[4] Yet within this general understanding of time, each character has his or her own concept of history and time; one can most clearly trace these attitudes toward time by following each individual's quest.

The novel begins with José in the present, being driven by his son from Los Angeles to his family home in Los Rafas (Albuquerque), New Mexico, for the funeral of his father. Suddenly transported in memory back to his childhood sixty years ago and then to the time forty years ago when he first moved from Los Rafas and broke with family and tradition, he realizes that now everything is different, changed: the city, his siblings, himself. Only the dust blowing on the way to the cemetery seems permanent and the same. After the funeral his old friend Herminio Padilla comes up to him, but he cannot "pierce the layer of years that covered the familiar voice with this alien flesh" (9). These reminders of lost time and mutability increase as he returns to the family home and views his greedy sisters and brothers, who do not even seem to be "members of the same race." The chapter ends with José standing by his mother in his childhood home, although not now at home at all, looking out the window, past the orchard, "toward the river," the symbol of both continuity and change, the ambivalent image of time as both duration (Bergson) and flux (Heraclitus). Stirred by all that has happened this day, he thinks: "And he had never traced back to the root of things, to the beginning—back to the conquistadors—back to the hidalgos, hijo de algo, son of someone" (12).

José's quest is doomed to failure because he is trapped by his view of lineal, chronological, clock time. His concept of self in time is actually spatial: he wants to find the exact place and date of this origin. To find himself he needs to know the when and where of his racial history. He is, in Sartre's term, "haunted" by a dead past and thus has as future only loneliness, fear, and death. Seeking an order that is spatial, he wants to arrange his life into neat successions of dates and categories. Specifically, as a Chicano, he wants to separate the Spanish from the Indian, to find his true origin in Spain at a specific date, linked to a specific father-figure. Bergson's concept of *durée* or Sartre's sense of an existential future are beyond his conscious powers.

José's attempt to place himself in space and time begins with "Alfonso de Sintierra," a *historical* consultant whose name means "without land," and who uses the "de" to signify "of someone, of somplace." For his $300 José gets a "top-heavy genealogical tree whose limbs, branches, twigs, and buds showed a complex tangle—a regular bird's nest of kinship" (22). This chart is not home (nest) for José since it is a spatial tangle (web, trap) whose few dates only keep José searching for himself. In chapter two, as Joe is questioning Sintierra in his search for his missing father, Sintierra points out that José Rafa, "a great-great-great something or other" has inscribed on a rock in Arizona: "Pasó por aquí." Later, when Joe asks Sintierra if José had indicated what he planned on doing with the genealogical information, Sintierra answers, "Pues no. No más pasó por aquí." This Joycean pun reveals the essential nature of José and raises the whole question of man's mutability: José is a man who is only passing by in this world, caught in time with no sense of future or timeless existence. He is all flux, "no más pasó por aquí."

José's journey takes him first to Mexico and then to Spain. Throughout his search he is continually made aware of important dates, dates which in Faulkner would suggest a timeless moment in history.[5] For example, in Mexico, Gómez, the supposed genealogist who turns out to be a limousine driver, reminds him of 1531 and the miracle of the Virgin of Guadalupe. The Basilica of Guadalupe is built on the site of the ancient Aztec temple of Tepeyac. Here Juan Diego met the Virgin Mary and began the conversion of Indians to Catholicism. To the fiercely Mexican Gómez, this event is a second betrayal: "We were betrayed by the Aztec woman, Malinche. Now the second. Betrayed to the Church by another woman. Hijos de la chingada. First they take the balls from your body, then they take the balls from your soul" (42). This event is real for Gómez because it lives in the present as a timeless moment, part of his racial history. But for José, who cannot integrate the event into his concept of self, it is merely a fixed date that proves that Mexico is not the home he seeks: "All wrong, we Spanish beat them. We were conquerers" (44).

José flees Mexico and his terrifying dreams of "an endless search—seeking, asking but never finding" (49). Trying to find in Spain his link to the conquistadores, he travels to Madrid, Granada, Sevilla, and finally Extremadura. The most significant event in Spain is José's meeting Señor Benetar. While they listen to the song "Recuerdos de la Alhambra," Benetar, who is of Moorish descent, tells his tale. When the

Moorish kingdom of Granada fell in 1492, his people were given the choice of leaving Spain or becoming Christians. They stayed, but always with the belief that the Moors would reconquer Spain. Finally, Benetar's father "accepted himself as a Christian Spaniard," abandoning the dream of reconquest. The son, who returned to Africa and the Muslim religion, rejected both the solution and the father. Now, however, Benetar comes back to Spain and accepts it as his home.

Pondering Benetar's story, José realizes for a moment the "magic" of 1492. "The Moors defeated and Christianized.... When Catholic-Islamic-Jewish Spain had become one nation—politically and spiritually. While in the New World they had initiated another trilogy of culture—Spanish, Indian, and later Anglo. As if the one God, the true god, sought balance" (159). This moment of awareness created by the unity of the song, which is of time and yet beyond time, by the magic of the timeless date which marks not a separation but a new unification, does not last, however; almost simultaneously he hears in his memory another tune of forty years ago, sung by an Anglo at Joe's first job in California:

> Mexico Joe.
> Mexico Joe.
> Crossed the river near the Alamo.
> Go back Joe.
> Not so slow.
> Across the river back to Mexico. (160)

With this song, panic and hatred assault José, destroying his moment of timelessness; ironically his thoughts flee back to his first success at his job of cleaning fish: "But he had shown them. They had let him help the *timekeeper*.... He had done the work so well, known his numbers so well, that soon he was helping the bookkeeper" (160, my italics). José is forced back into his prison of time, again unaware of time as more than sequential counting, life as more than timekeeping.

The above incident shows that José's cage of time and history is built with the pain and conflict of racial memories. Throughout his life he has been tormented by his race and the conflict of the New Mexican as Spanish, Mexican, Indian or White. This nationality "game" is repeated as a motif throughout the book, preventing José's accepting himself and finally killing him. As a second grader he feared the Anglo teacher's game of asking "about what it meant to be a citizen of a country. About nationality" (25). In high school, he worked in an Anglo drug store and wished he were light-skinned like Herminio. His Anglo boss knew he was "Mexican" yet was confused because José acted "Anglo" during a race riot. When he arrives in Mexico, the cab driver compliments him on his good Spanish and immediately identifies José as

"Cuban." In Spain, significantly sitting across from a statue of another endless quester, Don Quixote, José is approached by a dwarf with whom he is soon playing the nationality game. The dwarf proudly identifies José as from Mexico!

These repeating episodes of nationality are the cumulative experiences that keep José forever on a treadmill of time and pain. His thoughts of going "on like this forever—unfulfilled" are images of the self trapped within itself, the past as overwhelming.[6] Only in his dying thoughts does he come close for a moment to the possibility of home and peace: he goes back to his childhood when he and Herminio stole watermelons and then went swimming in the Río Grande. This is the same river he saw from his mother's window at the beginning of the novel, and he now recognizes it as a giver of life, "Feeder of cornfields, Sweetener of melons. Cooler of boys at the end of the hot summer days" (176). In a Proustian memory, he again feels the water, tastes the sweet melon, hears the laughter of childhood "along the banks of the quiet river. Flowed with barely a ripple, following the waters toward the south. Toward the river's home, its final resting place—the Gulf of Mexico" (126). Here the river images the movement of time to a point where time ends, where the river is at rest in the sea (ironically the Gulf of *Mexico*). Even in this final image of home and rest, however, José still expresses his limited concept of chronological time, time that can only stop, but which does not suggest a future or a repetition of time in a finer tone. José's life ends thus with a tragic question, "Where is home?" unanswered as he hears the bus driver announce "Sevilla in thirty minutes" (176).

The second point of view in the novel, the second concept of history and time, is that of Theresa. Theresa's quest is simpler and yet in many ways more profound. On one level her "quest" is often a running away from homes and a rejection of her past, both resulting from the scar she carries with her from childhood which prevents her from ever fully entering into the timeless reality she desires. This can be seen in the novel in the form of a series of earthly homes. Although her family has lived in New Mexico for over two hundred fifty years, she does not feel that "it was her home" (13), and her individual memories are often of moving. She remembers her childhood home, where her father was "mean and drank," as a place from which she wanted to escape (she climbed out the window to meet with José). She remembers the "home" of the Anglo for whom she cleaned and who fired her because she stole the can of tuna she was supposed to feed the cats. She remembers José's family home when he first took her there to meet his parents: "Theresa stared hard at the house, hoping to see what secrets it must hold that would foretell her future" (58). She remembers being told in this home that she was not good enough for José and that she should forget about marrying him. After their marriage, it was Theresa who convinced José to reject the adobe home the Rafas wanted to build for them on family land, and when they arrived in East Los Angeles, it was she who refused to live in the run-down home José wanted to rent. Theresa keeps the family moving to better homes and better neighborhoods until the present time of the novel, when she is temporarily home in an Anglo neighborhood in Whittier. From this home José runs away to find himself.

Basically, one part of Theresa is a woman trying to escape her past history, seeking security and a sense of "being" in different homes. Significantly, one of the songs attached to her memory is about traveling on Route 66: "Gallup, New Mexico, Flagstaff, Arizona. Winona. Kingman. Barsone. San Bernardino." She avoids the chronological past, always seeming in a state of "becoming." Running counter to this escapism, however, is a deeper awareness of timelessness, a sense of racial roots which cannot be measured in clock time, and a religious faith which assures her of an eternity outside of time. She achieves this understanding once during a visit to her grandparents in the Sangre de Cristo Mountains. Theresa has gone to her grandparents' house because she has miscarried and feels a deep sense of sin and guilt over her seduction of José and subsequent pregnancy. As she arrives in the mountains, she sees her grandparents' home, "Man-made, yet made from the earth so that it took its rightful place among the beans, chili, and corn in the small field." Repeating the image of the nest which was used ironically for José's genealogical chart, this house has a "nesting quality of comfort and refuge" (68). Life here is rooted in the past only in terms of the natural cycle of events and has a regularity that gives time itself a sense of eternity. Her grandmother, who measures time by generations of people and the changes of the seasons, seeks eternity in God.

Finally, a bird, a symbol that links the earth and sky, people and nature, time and eternity, serves as a catalyst to Theresa's understanding of her grandmother's sense of time. While talking to her grandmother, Theresa sees a one-legged bird, a friend of the grandmother, hop up to be fed. The bird intuitively accepts his place in space and time; he is at one with nature and all life. As Nana says, "He goes on living the best way he can." A few days later, while returning home from church with her grandparents, Theresa again encounters One Foot. Suddenly, in an epiphany, she moves beyond time into the eternal. "It was as if they were all one—the adobe church, the path, the two old people, the singing bird, the valley itself. As if they all throbbed with that same vibrant energy, that same vibrant life" (75). With this sense of oneness of eternity, Theresa finds a sense of peace and tries to live the rest of her life, like One Foot, as best she can, trying to help José break his barriers of time and Mexicanness, to make him see that all people are one and that time can be absorbed by eternity.

However, although Theresa does the best she can, her sense of eternity is never complete because she cannot escape her fears. Perhaps the image that best summarizes Theresa's struggle with time and eternity is her stealing holy water from the church to baptize her agnostic son's children. The drops of water symbolize eternity, but in this world they must be stolen. As a crying baby brings back these memories of baptism, she in turn recalls her grandmother and her own limited success in imitating her timeless existence: "What a beautiful old lady she had been. If I could only have been like that, she thought. Well, I tried. I tried. A sadness softly enveloped her, and tears ran down her cheeks" (109-110).

The novel's final point of view is that of José's son Joe, who throughout the novel is like Telemachus, seeking his missing father. He must come to grips with his individual personal history and with his father in that history. Joe's story is also about the generations of fathers and sons in an eternal pattern of love and hate. The book opens with Joe driving José to José's father's funeral and ends with Joe's son driving Joe to José's funeral. The pattern repeats itself.

Joe's story begins in chapter three as he sits in "his suburban ranch house" and hears by phone of his father's disappearance. By the end of the novel he has moved a long way toward understanding his place in time, as far as from his suburban home to the adobe home "that time had passed by," the home which belongs to his uncle Carlos:

> Even from inside he knew that it belonged to the earth. He felt from it a solid, heavy inertia that said: This is where I belong. No stone castles as in Spain on this new frontier, but the earth itself. Leaving no monuments after man has gone.[7] For then the elements will erode what was man-made, giving it back to the earth from which it came. It is proper that it should be so. (189-190)

This image obviously contrasts with his father's inability to find a place, a home, but also with Theresa's image of her grandparents' home. While Theresa's grandparents' home suggests a lasting security, an eternal rest, this image suggests an infinite series of cycles of time that subsume the individual into the whole. Each return renews and begins a new pattern of time, neither ending chronological time nor replacing it with eternity.

To understand Joe's journey toward this concept of time we need to understand his attempts to deal with his personal history that places him within the conflicts of Spanish, Mexican and Anglo identity. As a child he constantly overheard his father and brothers arguing whether they were Spanish, Mexican, Indian, or American. He experienced this conflict physically in Albuquerque when his cousins fought him because he could not speak Spanish. In Los Angeles he had to fight the Anglos who called him dirty Mexican. Later, his own father drove away his girlfriend Isabella because she was Mexican.[8]

Although while growing up Joe has learned to hate his father and has seen him as a traitor, he finally comes to realize he must accept and understand his father's pain if he is ever to understand himself as his father's son. He says, "I start out thinking about my father and his Mexicanness ... and end up thinking about myself" (86). He finally learns that his quarrel with his father is also a quarrel with history, a battle that cannot be won without a pragmatic acceptance of the past and a positive existential movement toward the future. He first comes to understand this in college, where he realizes that even with his liberal white friends he is a Mexican, their token. Although he cannot fully identify at this point with the Chicano Movement, when "El Chicano" asks him "¿eres Mejicano?" he can answer "Sí." (He wanted at first to say, "Hell no. I'm an American.") His freedom to answer yes moves him from the past into the future: "As if the bogeyman that had hung over his father for his entire life, and over Joe for so many years, had disappeared with that simple word: yes" (92).

This is Joe's pragmatic solution to his personal and racial history. In contrast to his father, who is on an endless search for the missing thread of his life, Joe escapes the labyrinth of time by simply stopping to look for himself. He finds it easier to say "Mexican" to the nationality game, and then forget it—to look toward a future where all Latinos are one: "Hispanos. The new race. The way of the future" (184). After his father's death he can formulate more clearly the intuitive understanding of his college days, realizing now that a new history can be written, the history of losers, Indians, Mestizos, Blacks, Southern Whites, who could form a new "pantheon, the rainbow of humanity as losers.... The brotherhood that would not be forged in peace had been forged in loss. If they could only recognize it" (181).

Complimenting this new view of history is Joe's growing awareness of time as cyclical. His accord with historical and personal time is pragmatic and oriented toward the future, yet he finally knows that no accord within time is permanent, no more permanent than an adobe home or man. Rejecting the Catholic Church, he cannot accept his mother's faith in an eternity beyond time, so he seeks a ballast to counter time's swift movement and the image of the river in constant flux.

Ultimately all time is caught in the pattern of death and birth. As his father before him had done so many times, Joe, at the end of the novel, looks out toward the Río Grande and thinks: "Like the river, life flowed on. Its headwaters replenished by the winter snows. Its winding course fed by the freshets of early spring. Surging with gathering strength toward the ocean where storm and sun sent it upward to the sky and moist clouds drifted back toward the source to begin the cycle again" (191). This last image of the novel looks back on all the images of rivers and water, revealing more fully Candelaria's final view of time.

Each of the three characters in Candelaria's novel must face an individual sense of time, his or her racial history, and the question of timelessness. Trapped and doomed by his chronological sense of time, José cannot escape his racial history and loses his quarrel with time. Theresa, who flees from home to home, still manages through her faith to grasp as much of eternity as her history allows. Finally, more fully representing Candelaria's view, Joe comes to practical terms with his individual and racial history, accepting his personal memories without being consumed by them. Moreover, rather than transcending time, he accepts time as a recurrent cycle. *Memories of the Alhambra* is both a uniquely New Mexican Chicano novel structured by the conflicts inherent in New Mexican history and a universal novel reflecting Everyman's struggle with mutability and death.

University of Wisconsin System

# Notes

[1] Carlos Fuentes, *Nuestro*, November 1978.

[2] Private correspondence.

[3] Nash Candelaria, *Memories of the Alhambra* (Palo Alto, Cal.: Cibola Press, 1977), p. 7. All future references are to this edition and will be included in the text.

[4] Private correspondence.

[5] See, for example, Margaret Church, *Time and Reality* (Chapel Hill: University of North Carolina Press, 1946), pp. 227–252.

[6] This is a common image in dreams and fantasies. See Thomas De Quincey's images of the terror of expanded space and time in *Confessions of an English Opium Eater* (1822; New York: New American Library, 1966).

[7] The futile quest of José to find himself in some point in time is mirrored by his encounters with statues and monuments that stop time in a static form, i.e., the statue of the Virgin Mary that his sister Juana tries to take from his mother's home; the stone shape of Tlaloc, the rain god; the statue of Don Quixote and Sancho Panza in Madrid; the statue of Hernán Cortés in Extremadura (while his body is buried in Mexico).

[8] Even in this incident Joe is more his father's son than he can admit. When he first meets Isabella at a dance where she is queen, he introduces himself as Ferdinand: "Isabella and Ferdinand . . . The King and Queen of Spain during Columbus' time." She counters with a foreshadowing of the end of their romance, "Ferdinand . . . that's the name of a bull isn't it?" (p. 100).

# H. Alejandro Morales

## *Caras viejas y vino nuevo:* Journey Through a Disintegrating Barrio

*Erlinda Gonzales-Berry*

Chicano fiction, whether written in Spanish or in English, demonstrates a broad sociological vision of the Chicano experience. The capture of the environment and social interactions are features that have emerged as constants in numerous works. While individuals may be portrayed as central figures, they function mainly as antennae designed to observe and to gather information which in turn is revealed to the reader. Even the young nameless boy in Rivera's novel . . . *y no se lo tragó la tierra*,[1] in whom we witness interior conflict, change and growth, does not acquire the dimensions of a fully developed character. Rather, Rivera's intent was to create a character whose story conveyed a broad universal significance, and for that reason he employs archetypal and mythical motifs which allude constantly to a deeper paradigmatic meaning lying beneath the surface of the story line.

*Caras viejas y vino nuevo* manifests a very new structural orientation while still focusing broadly on the Chicano experience. The vision the reader receives of that reality is screened through the psyche of one character, Mateo. It is not the vision of a participant narrator who tells the reader "here is what I have observed of Chicano reality," but rather it is the vision of a narrator who tells us "here is what Mateo thinks and feels about what he sees," and what he sees is often transformed according to what he thinks and feels. *Caras viejas y vino nuevo* gives us an intimate portrait of a *barrio* and can be classified as a novel of character which manifests internal evolvement of the protagonist,[2] the evolvement affecting or coloring his perception of exterior reality. My intent in this study is to explore the narrative technique employed by Morales to capture the light and dark and the many shaded aspects of a disintegrating *barrio*.

In a short story called "Las babas del Diablo," the Argentine writer Julio Cortázar begins the story by stating: "Nunca se sabrá como hay que contar eso, si en primera persona o en segunda, usando la tercera del plural o inventando continuamente formas que no servirán de nada."[3] In this utterance Cortázar expresses the major concern which faces any inventor of a fictional world—how to tell his story. The writer is generally interested in structuring his narrative in such a manner as to render an efficient, interesting and integrated work of art. These concerns are particularly apparent in modern fiction: "El *Cómo* ha de contarse la serie de hechos de que se compone una novela, la distribución y ordenación de las mismas, la—en definitivo—determinación de la estructura narrativa, es algo de que tiene hoy conciencia más aguda que nunca, cualquier novelista responsable."[4]

As we enter the fictitious world of Alejandro Morales we become more aware that we are facing a writer who has given a great deal of thought to the *cómo* of writing, and, as such, has created a work in the vein of modern fiction. The incorporation of mainstream literary techniques even in a first novel should come as no surprise given Morales' academic exposure to contemporary Hispanic literature. Before entering a discussion of the "how" of Morales' novel, let us briefly summarize its content.

Though many Chicano writers have dealt with the *barrio* as a literary topic, the majority so far has employed the pen to exhalt the positive aspects of *barrio* life and to elaborate it as a cultural womb which provides a center of security and protection against a hostile world. Morales, while not ignoring the positive elements of *barrio* existence, has painted a picture in which the sordid surfaces with unrelenting force. His portrayal of the *barrio* encompasses perfectly the following description offered by Luis Váldez: "A microcosm of a Chicano City, a place of dualities: a liberated zone and a prism: a place of hatred and violence, where most of *la raza* live out their lives. So it is a place of weddings, *bautismos, tardeadas, bailes, velorios*, and patriotic enchilada dinners. It is a place of poverty and self-reliance, of beloved *ancianos*, of *familias*, of *compadres*."[5]

The young protagonist experiences and embodies the positive elements of *barrio* life more fully than any other character in the novel. His family, one of the more fortunate in the neighborhood, represents the Chicano extended family, which has traditionally formed an integrative and supportive structure founded on love and mutual respect. Nurtured in this secure environment, Mateo has internalized a strong sense of humanistic love which impells him to feel concern for the *vagos* and *vatos locos* of the *barrio*, as well as for the unfortunate of the world at large. His deeply ingrained sense of *carnalismo* is most apparent in his attitude toward Julián, one of his childhood friends. Julián succumbs to *misticismo* (drug addiction) under the influence of an authoritarian father who believes that force and violence are the only means to bring up children. The death of Julián's mother is precipitated by her son's addiction and her husband's violence toward him. After her death, father and son engage in a cruel reciprocal vendetta through which each seeks to free himself of guilt. Mateo painfully observes the disintegration of this family which terminates in the nihilistic death of Julián and some other *vatos locos* in a car accident. The episodes depicting the activities of the barrio derelicts, men whom Mateo views with tender and sympathetic sentiments, some sordid erotic scenes, and Mateo's interior reflections, ranging from grotesque imagery to poetic lyricism, complete Morales' portrait of this *barrio*. In the end we learn that young Mateo, the "special" and different *barrio* boy, whose intelligence, dreams and ideals promise to be the ingredients of success, dies of leukemia, still a young man.

It is the inherent nature of summary to result in the reduction and over-simplification of complex phenomena. Morales' novel is by far more complex than a resumé of its contents may suggest; it is made into difficult *literatura para inciados* through the use of sophisticated structural and narrative techniques. The most readily apparent characteristic of its structure is the fragmentation of temporal continuity. A careful reading will reveal that there is, in fact, a chronological order to the novel. It is structured in reverse order, thus challenging our sense of rational sequence.

The fragmented episodes, once pieced together, reveal the basic story line—the gradual dissipation of Julián, the ensuing conflict between him and his father resulting in the death of the mother, and finally his own death. Interspersed between episodes of the main plot are fragments depicting scenes from the *barrio* and Mateo's personal life, lending the novel an apparently chaotic structure. The disorientation created in the reader by this complete process of fragmentation is increased in the beginning by a slippery narrator who keeps shifting the perspective without identifying typographically, or in any other way, the source of the interior perspective. Once the reader becomes familiar with the character who functions as the center of consciousness in the novel and learns to identify the syntactical clues which announce the shifts in perspective, the pattern of the novel emerges and the chaos gradually subsides. Yet the reader will continue to feel slightly disoriented because of the reverse chronological order of the work and some general stylistic ambiguities. At this point, a detailed analysis of the first four fragments should begin to reveal the structural plan of the novel.

The first fragment, narrated, as is the entire book, by a third person omniscient narrator, introduces the closing episode in the main story line. Briefly, what happens in this fragment is a violent confrontation between Julián and his father, each blaming the other for the mother's death. After the bitter confrontation, Julián rushes away in a car with two drugged brothers who are ironically named Buenasuerte. Laughing and shouting obscenities they speed away from the police to encounter their accidental death, which can only be viewed as the culmination of a suicidal tendency given impulse by a meaningless existence in an absurd world. The guilt feelings of the father and son and the subsequent emotional explosions or blaming each other for the mother's death is a theme introduced in this fragment, and one which will surface recurrently throughout the book providing one of the primary unifying elements.

The other recurrent leitmotifs are also introduced in this first episode, the first being the presence of the sinister Buenasuerte brothers, who might be seen as symbolic Horsemen of the Apocolypse, harbingers of evil and death. The haunting presence of *la llorona* constitutes the second unifying leitmotif. This theme, endemic to Chicano folklore and literature, appears transformed into a modern phenomenon.[6] The traditional wailing woman seeking her dead children becomes in the city the wailing of police car and ambulance sirens announcing the death of the sons of *la raza*. Thus, *la llorona* permeates the novel with a somber presence.

The most striking structural characteristic of the first fragment, one which leads in the beginning to a great deal of confusion, is the tendency of the narrator to move without warning from the exterior perspective of direct style to an interior position attained through indirect narrative, bringing to mind the narrative technique of Vargas Llosa and García Márquez.[7] The effect created by this style is that of a zoom photographic lense which shifts the point of view rapidly from exterior distance to a close-up of the action or center of consciousness. In Morales' use of this cinematographic technique, the traditional clues and devices employed to warn the reader of a shift in perspective are ignored. The change from mimetic to dramatic discourse is not indicated by the customary clues, as, for example, in the following quote: "El Turco estaba bien sonado; tan sonado que la cabeza no se mantenía sobre los hombros; se caía y luego volvía. Me quiero curar y abrió un paquetito (p. 13)."

The absence of any punctuation marks or typographical changes to indicate the shift from descriptive narrative to dialogue forces the reader to respond to different syntactic clues. If the flow of the reading process is not to be interrupted the reader must be quick to intuit the sudden shifts. In his study *Introducción al estilo indirecto libre en español*, Guillermo Verdín Díaz points out the various syntactical clues which announce such shifts.[8] The shift from third person to first person pronouns, as in the case cited above, is one warning. The use of words dealing with language also provides a warning, as exemplified in the following quote:

> Recibió la rociada en toda la cara; sintiendo el gargajo verde gelatinoso escurrirle por todo un lado de la nariz, desde el rincón del ojo derecho le golpearon *las palabras* de don Edmundo. Mira desgraciado si vienes otra vez a esta casa te voy a matar. (p. 12, emphasis mine)

Though this technique could constitute a potential danger, Verdín Díaz tells us that its positive narrative effects make it a worthwhile technique: "La carencia de verbos introductores explícitos hace que el estilo indirecto libre surja de manera espontánea en medio de la narración.... Bajo sus formas se desliga con toda naturalidad la intimidad pensante."[9] The potential for confusion inherent in the use of the unannounced indirect technique is compounded in the initial fragments of the novel by the device of the narrator's frequently shifting to an interior perspective without identifying immediately the center of consciousness; consequently, the reader must often stop and question the source of the perspective. The second, third and fourth fragments provide excellent examples of this process.

In the second fragment there is a long description of a city which appears initially to come from the perspective of the narrator observing at a distance. However, the subtle shift from the past descriptive tense in the first sentence to the present tense in the middle of the second sentence should provide a clue for the reader that the perspective is coming from the consciousness of an observing character. Zunilda Gertel, in describing the difference between descriptive narrative language and the language of interior lyricism, states that:

> El tiempo clásico de la narrativa como representación es el pretérito (lo dicho, lo hecho), el tiempo de la lírica es el presente (el hacerse). El punto crucial del cambio es, pues, el desplazamiento narrativo al modo lírico, expresivo y personal que manifiesta un existir que se desarrolla en el momento de la narración. Por lo tanto desaparece así el narrador cuya conciencia discurre desde una perspectiva teórica.[10]

Should the clue escape us, we must wait until the following page when the narrator, through direct representative language, describes the position of the observer. "Recostado ahora miraba a la de allá" (p. 15). Without any typographical warning he immediately zooms in, revealing the thought of his unnamed character: "Cómo quisiera, ay cómo quisiera...." He distances himself again through representative language: "La mano estaba entre las piernas, estaba mojado ahora" (p. 15), only to shift back immediately to the interior world of the character. This last shift is indicated syntactically by a change once again to the present tense. The intimate perspective reveals that the character's emotional state of mind is reflected in his appraisal of the environment he observes. The fact that he has been masturbating affects the imagery that flows through the mind and a grotesque pornographic panorama of the society contained within the city begins to unfold before his eyes.

> El crucifijo es usado como bastón o condón a través del delirio de la juventud por la ilusión de prostituirse por una causa. El maricón y su esposo se manotean en los cines. El asno de la humanidad sangriento y acojinado con toallas higiénicas de negociaciones de las reglas de la menstruación del período apareció anoche en la televisión. En los países inundados de bocas se recibe la verga para comer. (p. 16)

The effectiveness of this passage lies in that it does not represent the narrator's subjective or editorial intrusion but rather reveals the reflections of a character whose observation of the environment is in tune with his state of mind. It is the character's view and reflections of the environment that we experience, and so it will be throughout the novel that the disintegrating view of the *barrio* contained therein comes to the reader directly from the consciousness of this character. The grotesque imagery of the passage quoted above stands in sharp contrast to others that are highly lyrical and reflect the beauty inherent in the *barrio*. In fact, we are dealing with a complex character who is apt to pursue intellectual and reflective activities with the same gusto that he pursues the pleasures of street life, sex, drugs and violence.

In the third fragment there is a repetition of the process of interiorization without immediate identification of the center of consciousness. It is somewhat disconcerting to the reader not to know from the start whose sexual fantasies he is permitted to view. But by alluding to an action of a sexual nature present in the previous passage, the author provides a clue as to who the character may be. The character is finally identified through dramatic discourse as Mateo. It is through Mateo's activities that we meet the *barrio* derelicts and witness a very colorful description of a typical *barrio* wedding. Initially it is not a particular wedding that we witness, but rather Mateo's reflections concerning Chicano weddings per se, which he defines as "Una fiesta bacante, una orgía de comer y beber violenta" (p. 21). In order to support his generalizations about Chicano weddings he recalls a particular wedding and relives it in his memory. The highlight of this celebration is a free-for-all which ends in a shooting. Mateo recalls the details with relish, making no value judgments, but simply implying that those are the ways of *barrio* life.

At the end of this fragment the reader begins to suspect that Mateo is the axial character of the work, only to be disoriented once again at the beginning of the fourth fragment. The latter, a sweeping lyrical narration delivered once again from an unidentified center of consciousness, synthesizes through hermetic imagery the history of the Chicano. The use of ambiguous pronouns and temporal and spatial adjectives in an absolute sense permeate this passage with a rich biblical tone. There emerges in this passage the "scripturesque" metaphor *el filo de la estirpe*, which will appear repeatedly in the novel when Mateo is reflecting on Chicanos as a group. This metaphor suggests that the Chicano's past flows inexorably in his blood and that it is the strength of the blood flowing in his veins which has allowed him to survive the oppression inflicted by *aquéllos*.

As if emerging from the depths of a primordial level of consciousness, the language in the fragment gradually beomes concrete, allowing the appearance of the voice of the narrator who provides some descriptive clues regarding the spatial setting of this fragment. He never identifies the character responsible for the lyrical passage. However, by the end of the fifth fragment, what has previously been suspected by the reader becomes apparent—Mateo is in fact the character through whom we are experiencing the created world. Thence, we can identify Mateo in retrospect as the character responsible for the poetic reflections of the fourth fragment.

Beyond discovering Mateo's lyrical sentiments, this fragment reveals his anxieties concerning the future. The old man, a storehouse of insight and wisdom and also possessor of poetic talents, advises Mateo to make use of his talents, to go to the university and to stay clear of those *vatos locos*. Finally, Mateo reflects upon the nature of communion and love. Though he does not say it, he seems to realize that the kind of love he aspires to is anathema to the miserable existence of *barrio* life. It is only in the orbit of his inner world, or in the recluse of his *compadrito's* company, that he is able to experience momentarily that ideal.

The analysis of the preceding four fragments reveals that three basic themes constitute the novel: 1) the story of Julián, his family, and his acquaintances, other *vatos locos* of the *barrio*; 2) the activities of the *barrio* derelicts—all war veterans who upon returning to the *barrio*, unable to find their niche in society, seek solace in alcohol and each other's company; and 3) Mateo as the pivotal character who weaves in and out of the *barrio* reflecting on its condition and that of mankind. We have seen also Morales' technique of shifting subtly from a distant to a dramatic or interior perspective via an indirect narrative style. After completing the fourth fragment, the reader has been exposed to the major structural and thematic elements of the novel that provide the clues for its total reading. The reverse chronology becomes apparent only gradually and the initial chaos gives way to order at the end.

As we accompany Mateo on his wanderings through the *barrio*, language is the vehicle that allows us to penetrate the decadence of street life and the private spaces of his inner world. His retreats to the latter highlight his sense of loneliness from which is born a lyrical vision of life that stands in sharp contrast to the harsh reality of the exterior world. The threshold to his private world of sentiment and beauty is provided by the sanctuary of his home. It is always when Mateo finds himself in the seclusion of his home that he is able to move with ease into the realm of ideas and poetic visions. It is in this space, however, that he discovers man's condemnation to live in solitude: "Sabía que tenía cabeza, sabía que tenía que quebrar la cajita de vidrio, y no sentirse espiado. Se oía reír, ¿Cuántas cajitas de vidrio hay en este mundo, millones y millones, cómo ser para encontrar: el arma para que cada uno quiebre su cajita?" (p. 45). His attempts to transcend his human condition lead him to seek communion with his friends on the street or with *aquéllos* on the other side. While *aquéllos* view him as a pawn, his *barrio carnales* accept him, despite his "differentness." He accompanies them in their activities and participates fully in their way of life, especially their language, which corresponds perfectly to the surrounding misery and decadence. Though Mateo wants to be accepted by *los vatos*, he can only go so far before something moves him to reject that way of life as an answer to his search. We see this rejection after a sexual encounter with a prostitute friend of the derelicts. While he enjoys it thoroughly, afterwards he feels filthy and asks himself, "Ay Dios, ¿Por qué hice eso?" (p. 90).

Amidst the chaos and decadence of exterior reality, Mateo is able to catch a momentary glimpse of beauty and tranquility. A number of Mateo's humanistic reflections take place on *Nochebuena*, a time of magic which transforms the *barrio* into a place of beauty and peace for Mateo: "La vecindad lucía una belleza íntima; el barrio es un lugar bello si uno lo siente como lo sentía él" (p. 41). Mateo's sentiments toward the *barrio* are reiterated in the next-to-last fragment, and the reader is taken by surprise when he discovers that the source of the novel has been Mateo's memory as he lies dying in a hospital bed. This fact is made fully clear in the epilogue, which informs us of Mateo's premature death from leukemia and explains in part his special sensitivity and outsiderness. A re-reading of the fragment illuminates the following description which previously was a veiled one: "El cuarto está frío lleno del olor de loción masculina, y del otro lado emana el perfume de flores de la jaulasepultura vital de una anciana expósita" (p. 115). This revelation in turn sheds light upon the first part of the fragment:

> Pero encontré una tristeza bella que me llena el corazón con amor
> y felicidad, y tendré que expresarla para que todos los humanos la
> sientan y la griten. Aunque la vida sea sólo existencia, un rodeo
> solitario de la búsqueda de un hombre, de lo que ignora, una bús-
> queda que sigue por día y la noche, una búsqueda que termina febril-
> mente vacía a pesar de que quiere continuar. (p. 115)

Mateo realizes in these last days of his life that man's existential search leads ultimately to the nothingness of death. As he relives his life through memory, however, he recreates his *barrio* so that others might experience its horror and its beautiful sadness. That he has been able to recreate his life in this manner fills his heart with love and happiness and gives meaning to an otherwise meaningless existence.

In the last fragment of the book Mateo's memory takes us to the origin of the *barrio*, completing his reverse journey:

> Surgió un pueblo instantáneo como muchos otros durante las épocas.
> El ladrillo era la atracción, lo que realizaría todos los sueños con que
> vinieron. Pero en este lugar como en los otros latían problemas vie-
> jos y nuevos, quizás mayores de los que dejaron allá. (p. 126)

Morales' novel is the story of the development and disintegration of that *barrio*. Through the eyes of Mateo, a young boy embarked on a personal existential search for communion that would allow him to fill the void of solitude to which mankind is condemned, we witness this closed world surrounded by exterior oppression and destroyed by chaos from within. Through an excellent manipulation of perspective, Morales has eliminated the distance between reader and object, providing an interior vision of a vital social reality. While never strident in its protest, the novel stands as a strong comment on the dehumanizing conditions of the world we inhabit. It also stands as a monument to the survival and versatility of the mother tongue, although, ironically, the use of Spanish as well as the linguistic and structural difficulties of this artistically self-conscious novel may unfortunately make it accessible only to a very small minority of readers.

UNIVERSITY OF NEW MEXICO

## Notes

[1] Tomás Rivera, "... y no se lo tragó la tierra" (Berkeley: Quinto Sol, 1972).

[2] For an in-depth study of this type of novel, see Zunilda Gertel, *La novela hispanoamericana contemporánea* (Buenos Aires: Editorial Columbia, 1970), pp. 71–78. On page 72 Gertel points out that in the *novela de personaje*, "la proyección a la interioridad del personaje se encausa ya, predominantemente en el modo lírico, en lugar del representativo-narrativo, e inicia el cambio de la novela de espacio a la de personaje, que estructura la visión de un mundo cerrado, personal."

[3] "Las babas del Diablo," in *Las armas secretas* (Buenos Aires: Editorial Sudamericana, 1968), p. 77.

[4] Mariano Baquero Goyanes, *Estructura de la novela actual* (Barcelona: Editorial Planeta, 1970), p. 158.

[5] Luis Valdez and Stan Steiner, *Aztlán: An Anthology of Mexican American Literature* (New York: Alfred A. Knopf, 1972), p. 145.

[6] A similar treatment of *La llorona* appears in Anaya's *Heart of Aztlán*. Dick Gerdes comments on this phenomenon, pointing out that "from the Hispanic tradition there are new interpretations of the *La llorona* legend; traditionally—as in *Nambé–Year One*–the wailing image seeks her lost children, but in *Heart of Aztlán* the screeching cries are the piercing whistles in the shops at the railroad yard. Even more frightening, however, is another possibility: the legendary cries become the sirens of a police car." "The Evolution of Chicano Fiction: Three New Mexican Novels," paper read at the Thirtieth Annual Kentucky Foreign Language Conference, April 28–30, 1977.

[7] Commenting on this technique in *El otoño del patriarca*, John M. Lipski affirms, "The most striking stylistic feature of the novel in question is the rapid switching, abruptly or in the middle of a phrase, between narrator and a speech style evidently indicating the direct speech of another character." "Embedded Dialogue in *El otoño del patriarca*," *The American Hispanist*, 2:14 (Jan. 1977), 9.

[8] Guillermo Verdín Díaz, *Introducción al estilo indirecto libre en español* (Madrid: Revista de Filología Española, 1970).

[9] P. 80.

[10] Gertel, pp. 74–75.

# Choque e interacción en
## *La verdad sin voz*
## de Alejandro Morales

*Oscar U. Somoza*

La obra literaria de Alejandro Morales todavía no se ha dado a conocer en grande escala a pesar de ser uno de los escritores chicanos más prometedores. Hasta este momento (1982) han salido dos novelas suyas, ambas escritas en español y publicadas por la editorial mexicana Joaquín Mortiz. En *Caras viejas y vino nuevo* (1975), su primera novela, se percibe una constante y progresiva disolución de los lazos personales a pesar de un evidente afán por establecer nexos que hagan significativa la existencia y progresión humana. El anhelo y el fracaso evidentes en la novela se deben a la desorientación y desilusión que se percibe en la falta de respeto aun entre miembros de la misma familia y en el desmoronamiento continuo de los personajes hasta finalmente desgastarse. Como consecuencia de este fracaso surge el choque, la falta de auto-afirmación y enajenación de la realidad.

*La verdad sin voz* (1979), su segunda novela, continúa en parte la visión del mundo presentada por *Caras viejas y vino nuevo*. La preocupación básica en las dos novelas radica en la falta de voluntad revelada por los personajes, la negación de dar a otros o a sí mismos la oportunidad de conocer, reconstruir y convivir en el mundo.

En ambas hay una necesidad de analizar al ser humano que se despliega en un ambiente visto como laberinto que confunde y deprime al individuo al verse rodeado de una muchedumbre anónima.

Debido al gran interés que ha suscitado la segunda novela de Morales, por ahora trataremos de ahondar en algunos aspectos de la perspectiva que se manifiestan principalmente en relación a los personajes. En *La verdad sin voz*, los personajes se encuentran conscientes de esta confusión laberíntica, pero algunos hacen un esfuerzo por encontrar una mejor manera de subsistir. Hay una presentación más positiva, se busca la interacción, la aniquilación de tensiones y se trata de contribuir para formar un mundo menos degradado. Es un esfuerzo por examinar la sociedad y tratar de descifrar los problemas que asechan al individuo y lo vuelven brutal.

La novela funciona significativamente en torno a un eje estructurante que consiste en un choque constante entre y dentro de los personajes, pertenecientes a dos manifestaciones socioeconómica y culturalmente distintas; y de allí el proceso inevitable de interacción como consecuencia de tal choque. Morales sitúa a sus personajes dentro de un medio ambiente social y psicológico de una realidad urbana más que agraria y de consecuencias que se manifiestan en el presente. El pueblo de Mathis, localizado en el sur de Texas, es donde se inicia la novela. Este lugar es tomado como enfoque principal alrededor del cual las acciones se desarrollan. Hay una recurrencia o vuelta constante al mismo pueblo en las narraciones interpoladas que manifiestan la transformación interior de los personajes.

La visión que esta obra nos da de Mathis está enmarcada dentro de un ambiente que, a primera vista, establece una polaridad racial entre los anglos que controlan el pueblo y los chicanos, o la estirpe como los llama el narrador. Al tomar como fondo novelesco un grupo minoritario muy despreciado en los Estados Unidos, *La verdad sin voz* demuestra ser una manifestación social y colectiva. Pero la obra no permanece allí sino que refleja la intensidad del esfuerzo de los personajes por definir su propio ambiente como chicanos y angloamericanos condicionados por ese medio que los define como individuos dentro de una situación social conflictiva.

Morales propone una revaluación de lo que se ha escrito antes y plantea su propia visión estética, que consiste de un conjunto de aspectos creadores dominado por una visión más madura y compleja de la realidad en cuanto al desarrollo de los personajes en la dimensión personal y colectiva del ser humano en su trayectoria cotidiana. Desde un principio, los personajes que moldean esta visión son descritos como entes multifacéticos que expresan la incertidumbre de un ambiente tanto como sus propias inseguridades.

Los anglos que controlan el pueblo no quieren que nadie de afuera venga a ayudar a los chicanos con servicios médicos. Alegan que es gente que, por su ignorancia, no necesita de estos servicios y que bastante tienen con las curanderas. Ya desde el momento en que se introduce Leroy Hales, el primer personaje anglo, el ambiente es enfocado desde una perspectiva que va generalmente en desacuerdo con la anterior, donde los personajes anglos, a la vez que los chicanos, representaban, por la mayor parte, naturalezas opuestas. Es decir, en algunos casos los anglos eran los prototipos de entidades poseedoras de las peores características orientadas al abuso de los débiles y al afán exagerado de la acumulación de lo económico. En cambio el chicano por su parte era pintado como entidad prisionera dentro de ese mundo controlado por el gringo y sin posibilidades de escape.[1]

A través de toda la obra y en un ambiente de médicos, medicinas y enfermedades se establece dentro del discurso narrativo una serie de complejidades y conflictos circunstanciales entre las figuras que plasman la visión del mundo creado.

Leroy Hales desde un principio ha roto estos moldes tradicionales al manifestar el contraste entre él y otro anglo en cuanto al papel que debe desarrollar un médico en la profesión: "Cuántos años de estudiar, y qué ideas locas tengo, ¿pero quién le va a ayudar a esta pobre gente desgraciada?"[2] Así surge el conflicto entre sus ideales de hacer el bien como médico y la necesidad social de hacerse rico tan pronto como pueda, como lo expone su amigo y colega Harold Beesley: "–Leroy, mira, ya deja de jugar al humanitario; a esa gente no se le puede ayudar; ... si no te vas del pueblo, te morirás de hambre o los otros te matarán ... es muy sencillo, o vente acá conmigo y hazte millonario o quédate allí para que te entierren" (pp. 14-15). "Estas ideas locas idealistas pronto se le borrarán del cerebro. En esta profesión no hay sitio ni tiempo para idealistas" (p. 21). El conflicto entre el humanitarismo y los bienes materiales es resuelto cuando Hales opta por hacerse rico.

Michael Logan, personaje cuyo nombre inicialmente figuraba como título de la novela, es médico y dueño de una personalidad compleja. En oposición a Hales, Logan no está contento con la única posibilidad que tiene para lograrse como ser humano:

> ... no me gusta lo que veo en el futuro, un consultorio, mis pacientes, una casa bonita, vivir con mi familia, hacerme viejo y morir de un ataque cardíaco. "¡Qué vida tan aburrida! ¡Qué vida tan mala! ... Tengo miedo que me vaya a aburrir y a abandonarlo todo. Debo ser un bicho raro, ¿quién ha oído de un médico que ama a su profesión pero que también esté harto de ella? (pp. 75-76)

Se siente atrapado sin posibilidades de ejercer su voluntad en un mundo ya trazado por la tradición. A la vez cuestiona las motivaciones de sus colegas cuando le dice a Hales, "Y te mostraré que seré el tipo de doctor que tú querías ser antes de que tu interés se alejara de la medicina y te dedicaras a la acumulación de dinero" (p. 106). Esta alienación de sus colegas se transfiere al plano familiar. Se siente culpable por no cumplir con su papel de esposo ideal: "Pero lo feo es lo del día siguiente. No la cruda física pero la decaída mental, sicológica que me hace sentir como una cosa asquerosa, un paria. No puedo ver a mi mujer, a mis hijos" (p. 39).

Además de hacerles ver a otros sus errores, Michael está tratando de comprobarse a sí mismo que sus propios razonamientos son legítimos. Siente la necesidad de alejarse del materialismo y descubrir valores diferentes a los que lo rodean constantemente y con los que no está de acuerdo. Por esta razón decide ir a Mathis. Pero además de su noble rebeldía ante su presente situación y dedicación humana, se manifiesta una falla en su carácter al procurar la gloria:

> ... soy un falso, hago lo que hago para darme fama, para sentirme importante, pero... ¿pero por qué lo hago? ¿Qué estoy haciendo allá con esos, con esa gente cuando mi mujer, mis hijos me necesitan aquí?
> ... Me gusta... eso es todo, me gustan las cosas que hago; ... tengo suerte de poder escoger lo que quiero hacer; yo puedo escoger, otros no, soy libre; otros no. (p. 186)

Este anticonformismo y autoafirmación de su voluntad se proyecta también en su rechazo a las tentaciones materiales y manera de vestir; usa barba larga y tiene un Volkswagen y luego una motocicleta.

La novela logra exponer un auténtico intercambio de relaciones que se ven marcadas por la agresividad individual y la esperanza para que, por medio del auto-sacrificio, se alcance una mejor vida.[3] La búsqueda y encuentro de la solidaridad humana capacita al individuo para sobrevivir a pesar de los obstáculos impuestos por el elemento dominante, y comprueba en Michael su gran habilidad de amar y de sentirse humano. Su problemática se reduce al conflicto entre intereses humanitarios como el respeto, tanto a la persona común como a sí mismo, y el materialismo facilitado por su profesión, su afán de gloria, el posible alcoholismo y las dificultades familiares.

El proceso que se efectúa en Logan le otorga una configuración más lograda y más madura ya que se comprueba como figura humana con características multidimensionales que muchas veces se contradicen.

Fernando Rodríguez es el único policía chicano en Mathis. Su participación en el discurrir de la narración se reduce a una problemática que se divide en dos manifestaciones principales. Una es ayudar el cherif del pueblo y actuar contra su gente mientras que por otro lado siente culpabilidad por lo que hace: "Estoy espiando para el gobierno. Estoy espiando a mi propia raza" (p. 37). Luego se desarrolla hasta lograr un cambio de actitud: "No estés tan seguro que me importa... ese trabajo que me hace obrar contra mi gente. Ahora me doy cuenta de muchas cosas... Yo por tanto me he dejado manipular, manipular por ti y por todos los vendidos de este pueblo" (p. 169).

Pistola Gorda, el cherif, obedece a sus superiores al actuar como matón en contra de los chicanos, aunque luego se establece una relación personal entre él y una chicana del pueblo de la que él había abusado sexualmente: "Los dientes casi soldados de rabia que mandaron las manos contra la mesa suplicaron con lágrimas de cariño a la muchacha bella, sensual que ya se había dado cuenta de su poder sobre Pistola Gorda" (p. 198). Pistola Gorda es un personaje que al principio parece querer tomar un desarrollo por medio de una *caracterización onomástica*[4] porque al meditar un momento sobre el nombre del personaje, el lector tiende a ver una figura estereotipada ya que es el matón del pueblo y el que se encarga de desterrar a los médicos indeseables. Pero aun éste resulta ser un personaje que se desarrolla en el transcurso del relato. Cuando conoce a Teresa, la muchacha del pueblo, por medio del abuso, irónicamente su personalidad pasa a otro nivel más humano y al enamorarse de ella comprueba que es capaz de vivir la gama conflictiva de los sentimientos humanos.

Otro personaje en el que se manifiesta el proceso de choque e interacción es el Profe Morenito, Eutemio, que se debate entre producir artículos eruditos para obtener su promoción en el departamento de español y el esfuerzo que hace para sentir libertad de creación y hacer lo suyo como artista. Eutemio propone su propia visión de los departamentos de español y de literatura en las universidades norteamericanas. Cada departamento con programa graduado tiene un grupo de profesores que proponen y se adhieren a su formación crítica. Estos individuos están proyectados aquí no como entidades humanas e independientes sino caricaturizados con nombres como el Aristócrata, el Colmo Marxista, la Tortuga Chaparra, el Pelón Anteojado, el Romano Teórico, el Osito Coala, el Biciclista Onírico y el mismo Profe Morenito. Estos son los únicos personajes estereotipados que parecen ser reflejo de una realidad exterior y actual y que como consecuencia de su caracterización en la novela sufren de desprecio y odio por parte del Profe Morenito.[5] El énfasis que estos personajes creados por el Profe ponen en la publicación de libros y artículos eruditos y el desarrollo que cada uno hace de su especialidad en términos "goichanos, en vocablos goldmananos y lukachanos" (p. 152) es expuesto satíricamente al explicitar una fuerte crítica de parte del narrador.

Las mujeres como personajes principales toman un papel mucho más activo y participan más que los personajes femeninos en previas novelas chicanas al hacer más decisiones importantes.[6] A la doctora Kastura, que arriesga su vida al trasladarse a Mathis para ayudar a los pobres, y a Margarita y Teresa, que retan a Pistola Gorda para ayudar a los suyos como enfermeras de Michael, se les otorga el lugar que desde hace tiempo merecen en la literatura como verdaderas dirigentes de su propio destino. Como consecuencia se rebelan contra el papel que se les quiere imponer tal como lo manifiesta Pistola Gorda: "Teresa . . . se ha vuelto rebelde; piensa en lo imposible, en cosas que no puede hacer. Eso de querer ser enfermera, ahora habla de hacerse doctora, esas ideas son imposibles, no lo puede hacer, es incapaz" (p. 270).

La mayoría de los personajes apuntados hasta ahora, en relación a la acción interna de la novela, han modificado su manera de ser convirtiéndose en entidades que cambian de nivel de caracterización en el sentido que se hacen progresivamente más complejos. Su dialéctica interna se despliega hasta lograr las características de figuras vivas y reveladoras de las varias facetas del ser humano. La expresión de las necesidades y tensiones entre personajes pertenecientes a varios segmentos de la población se hace por medio de una delicada y sutil representación y desarrollo de cada situación. Es así como en cada uno de los personajes se establece una serie de elementos dialécticos que llegan a formar a una persona completa, redondeada. De allí el choque e interacción dentro de la personalidad conflictiva de diferentes facetas de cada uno de los personajes.

A nivel colectivo, la referencia directa al contexto étnico y socioeconómico del suroeste de los Estados Unidos propone una preocupación por el destino del individuo que habita este entorno. Por lo tanto, la mayoría de los personajes representan el afán por buscar la resolución de este conflicto como necesidad vital de llegar a una toma de conciencia social. La exposición de una problemática chicana y angloamericana a un nivel colectivo e individual permite interiorizar y concretizar en la conciencia de cada uno de los personajes para extraer de ellos, o para que cada uno exponga por sí solo, sus preocupaciones y necesidades. Esta técnica permite una profundización en los dos estratos culturales vigentes e íntimamente relacionados, y la integración de ambos contextos aproxima esta novela a una representación más real y más prendida de las cosas.

Es inevitable reconocer el esfuerzo que Morales hace en esta obra para llegar a una revaluación de las relaciones entre las dos manifestaciones culturales principales en el suroeste de los Estados Unidos. *La verdad sin voz* le da mejor forma a la imagen de un nuevo ser como manifestación de una nueva forma de escritura. Consecuentemente, la función del texto es llegar a una mejor comprensión humana de la crisis sociocultural que en el tiempo interior de la novela se lleva a cabo en el entorno chicano.

*La verdad sin voz* es el cuestionamiento y crisis del sistema de valores impuestos a la fuerza por los que dominan en Mathis. Michael Logan, al pronosticar por medio de sus acciones el surgimiento de un nivel de vida más equitativo, apresura la crisis de esta particular ordenación del mundo. Desde el momento en que Michael decide ir a Mathis, la novela toma una dirección más apresurada y las relaciones internas de los personajes dentro del texto se vuelven más agudas. De aquí la novela lleva a una formación nueva, no sólo de una persona, sino de toda la visión que se tiene de este ambiente social que evoluciona a una altura totalizante y positiva.

Así es como por medio de este autorreconocimiento se llega a una comprensión integrada y coherente del mundo circundante, a una nueva dimensión de la realidad para tratar de darle orden y formular una nueva estructuración de valores. En fin, se busca el restablecimiento de la unidad y armonía entre los varios elementos que la pueblan. Es la necesidad de ir más allá de la circunstancia actual para llegar a un entendimiento humano superior y reafirmar la fe en el mundo que los rodea.

UNIVERSITY OF DENVER

## Notas

[1] En particular nos referimos a la novela de Miguel Méndez M., *Peregrinos de Aztlán* (Tucson, Arizona: Editorial Peregrinos, 1974).

[2] Alejandro Morales, *La verdad sin voz* (México: Joaquín Mortiz, 1979), p. 13. Subsecuentes alusiones a esta novela pertenecen a la misma edición y estarán indicadas entre paréntesis.

[3] Cuando decimos auto-sacrificio nos referimos al hecho de que al final Michael Logan es asesinado por Pistola Gorda.

[4] René Jara y Fernando Moreno, *Anatomía de la novela* (Valparaíso, Chile: Ediciones Universitarias de Valparaíso, 1972), p. 111.

[5] El narrador ofrece un caso particular en esta obra. Su grado de conocimiento aquí demuestra al narrador como un observador que a la vez está totalmente inmiscuido dentro del acontecer. Es decir que la distancia entre la psique del narrador y lo referido parece entrecruzarse y en ocasiones hasta desaparecer. El Profe Morenito, Eutemio, al final comprueba ser el narrador y autor de la novela a la vez: ". . . y el Profe Morenito empezó a escribir: *La verdad sin voz*" (p. 300).

[6] Como ejemplo de una falta de participación de los personajes femeninos en la literatura chicana, véase: Francisca Chacón, "La caracterización de los personajes femeninos en . . . *y no se lo tragó la tierra*", *La Palabra*, 1, No. 2 (Otoño 1979), pp. 43-50.

# I. Orlando Romero

## The Concept of Time in *Nambé—Year One*

*Nasario García*

Time is a complex phenomenon, and scientific, philosophical and metaphysical theories are testimony to its complexity. Scholars from Plato, Plotinus, and St. Augustine to Bergson have yet to agree on a precise definition. Time continues to be a mystery to man, but it need not be treated only on a theoretical plane. Many fiction writers in modern literature have developed systems within which events unfold, and one of the built-in components has been time. To it the writer ascribes values or measurements according to his concept of time as it relates to the events depicted and the characters involved. My intent in this study is to show how Orlando Romero deals with time on three dimensions in the novel *Nambé—Year One* (the title itself is a clue to the complexity of time). I shall call the three categories Cyclical Time, Abstract Time, and Retrospective Time.

### Cyclical Time

Cyclical Time is probably the least complicated. It can also be classified, measured, or horizontal time. Other critics and writers have labeled it clock time, true time, chronological time, conceptual time, and so forth.[1] Notwithstanding the mulitiplicity of labels, Cyclical Time denotes objectivity, for it is absolute, conventional and fixed. It moves in a linear form uninterrupted and unaffected by external objects or events. Transience, sequence and irreversibility[2] characterize it further as moving on a continuum.

*Nambé—Year One*, an autobiographical novel about Mateo Romero, in reality Orlando Romero, begins in early spring and ends in early spring (a letter dated July 1975 at the end of the novel serves as an epilogue) within a three year cycle. From the outset Mateo Romero alludes to Nature's "cyclic pattern."[3] He traverses many obstacles in real life and whatever transpires in between in no way impedes the natural flow of time. Years, seasons, months, weeks, days, hours, minutes and seconds come and go routinely as life in the village of Nambé progresses, but, as he says, "Here in Nambé everything evolves in and around cycles" (p. 13). If Mateo did set back the clock, time would continue to elapse.

However, mechanical gadgets to measure the regularity of natural or invented events are not typical in Mateo's household, and for that reason time appears to go unchecked. He says: ". . . in this house there are no clocks or other man-made devices that try to measure time" (p. 13). Yet, there must be calendars because generally Mateo is very conscious of the chronology of time. He utilizes events such as Easter, Ash Wednesday, and local fiestas as signposts for the synchronization of time in Nambé.

If we parallel the continuity of time with man's existence on Earth, then the scope of time that Orlando Romero uses falls within a traditional mold of beginning and end, or ". . . the cyclic patterns of life and death" (p. 100). Time does not stand still in the world of reality. It is inevitable and the ultimate result for Man is death. Mateo recognizes this, so he is not afraid to die, for death does not symbolize the discontinuation of life. It represents the start of a new life, reincarnation. As he says: "Death is not dying, but coming back again to nourish living things" (p. 15). Death also represents the idea that past, present and future converge simultaneously to assure the perpetuity of his being. He reflects: "When I have completed my turn, I shall be buried under the apricot tree. My rot shall enrich its roots.[4] But, tomorrow, I must water all the trees, the garden, and also the thirst of ancestral memories that go down one thousand feet below Nambé" (pp. 13–14). Death becomes indistinguishable from the beginning of life and cyclical in nature because "the end will be like the beginning" (p. 25).

In assessing the contributions of the old people of Nambé who are dying—the completion of their life-cycle on Earth—Mateo does not shrug them off lightly. Their death is recognized as a tremendous loss, and he bemoans the far-reaching implications for *hispano* culture. The present, past and future[5] converge again: "If the old people are dying too, and with them the wisdom of the ancients, who will show the children the real sun that gives life to Nambé?" (p. 17). Mateo furthermore laments the fugacity of time, and he views his life as inane, in addition to feeling guilty because of not having left a legacy: "How quickly my life has passed, and I've not composed a great symphony, or painted a mural masterpiece reflecting the life of my people . . ." (p. 172).

Life is circumscribed by a beginning and an ending, and years, seasons, and the like are but entities that constitute the whole. That is

Cyclical Time, a kind of whirlpool of life whose movement and energy ultimately create a depression in the center as motion ceases. Thus, in *Nambé—Year One* one has Giant Cycles (Life-Death) made up of many Medium Cycles (Year-Year), with Miniature Cycles falling within a year's time span.

## Abstract Time

Unlike Cyclical Time, Abstract Time is not measurable and is much more complicated; its abstractness emanates from personal and subjective value judgments. Critics and writers have categorized it as psychological time, private time, inner time, or perceptive time.[6] No matter what classification one adopts or invents, Abstract Time is man's personal clock that measures time according to his perceptions rather than by conventional means. Values attributed to circumstances surrounding events of the past become important. In order to bring to the present a fictional past, a writer must rely on past memories.

Since memories tend to be somewhat vague in the writer's mind, regardless of the time that has elapsed between the writing and the actual occurrence of the event, he avails himself of his greatest literary weapon—imagination. Imagination affects memories and the values linked to them. Imaginary embellishment of memories in the abstract world of time is unavoidable. Three values germane to the complete understanding of Abstract Time in *Nambé—Year One* are the emotional, mental and physiological, and physical conditions as they relate to some of Orlando Romero's characters.

Time does not discriminate; it is ruthless in its physical encounter with Nature and Man. Time is all-powerful; it vanquishes and overcomes and destroys. Mateo, in talking about New Mexico, the ancestral land of serpents and ghosts, expresses that, despite Nature's fortitude, time is as destructive to It as it is to Man: "The rugged Bandelier Canyon vibrates.... The giant walls of the canyon, sharp and ravaged by time and the elements, destroy the twentieth century" (p. 30).

In the mystical land of New Mexico, Man and his legendary past are inextricably bound to the soil (*la tierra*); and the inhabitants of the village of Nambé are testimony to this unique relationship and dependency. Man can endure punishment inflicted by time but, unlike Nature, he eventually succumbs to it. The people of Nambé are no exception and the physical consequences of their suffering are evident. This is particularly true of those persons who become legends in their own right. Time does not spare them either.

La Bartola (*La Llorona*) is one such individual who, because of the mystique associated with the *llorona* in New Mexico, is shunned by her neighbors in Nambé and normally lives in isolation. *La Llorona* is very much a part of New Mexico's culture, and physically La Bartola in her old age becomes indistinguishable from the soil. As Orlando Romero says: "She looked like her adobe house. It was so weathered by time that most of the mud plaster was cracking and the wood of the windows had turned a soft, wild nappy gray" (p. 59).

But *La Llorona* is not the only person who forms part of the *hispano* culture in New Mexico. No village is ever without a *viuda*. A widow is very much an integral part of *hispano* culture and in most cases she is venerated, not scorned. Orlando Romero talks about *La Viuda* as an anonymous, nameless creature; the reason, no doubt, is to underscore her importance collectively instead of fragmenting the concept of *viudez*. By and large the widow leads a very introspective and personal life, in which time is relative. The punishment—or martyrdom— is partially self-inflicted, although culture is also responsible because mourning is inherent in it; hence the consequences for the *viuda* which are "total remorse, total isolation, total penitence . . ." (p. 163). All of these things contribute to physical deterioration, but time is the most devastating. *La Viuda* has been "bent by time" in ". . . the vast loneliness of her house" (p. 163).

One of the by-products of solitude is mental and physiological agony incurred by circumstances surrounding isolation, in which case time seems even more abstract. As Mateo states: "In my restlessness [physiological] I imagine [mental] the hour, for in this house there are no clocks or other man-made devices that try to measure time" (p. 13). Five minutes under duress may seem like an eternity and therefore not indicative of true time because the conscious activity is altogether different.

Proper conditions can also engender an inordinate expansion of time in the mind of an individual. Mateo, in recalling an unpleasant episode with his father, draws upon the expansion of time: "Centuries later, at age twelve or so, I hit him with a piece of firewood as he was about to beat my mother" (p. 26). The expansion of time is seen moreover in the context of Man's wisdom. In Nambé the person who stands out in that category is Don Agustín. His knowledge has transcended so many decades that his name strikes a legend remembered only in time and space. According to Mateo's grandfather, Don Agustín is ageless: "My Grandfather says he [Don Agustín] is about one-hundred-fifty years old. Everyone in the village knows he is a man of wisdom" (p. 93). Don Agustín himself talks to Mateo not in literal but abstract time: " 'Mateo, today for the first time in over a hundred years, I feel a little old but yet full of joy to see you a grown man and as exciting a child as when I used to hold you in my arms!' " (p. 97).

Feelings and emotions are values inherent in Abstract Time too. They are symptoms that emanate from within, or as the *hispano* would say, from the "heart and soul." Mateo's "adobe soul and spirit" rest in his adobe house "... where time means nothing and everything ..." (p. 9). However, it is the place where memories and nostalgia abound with emotion: "Its walls are alive with the tears of years forgotten to the meaningless word we know as time.[7] It was fact.... It caught time itself, made it stop, and its haunting memories were left as reminders" (loc. cit.). Mateo's soul at times reflects antiquity, but his spirit is rejuvenated. He states the following: "My years have been measured at twenty-seven though my soul is older than the world ..." (p. 17). He talks about his "weary yet joyous soul" (p. 21) and how time is meaningless in a world of illusion in spite of the many spirits he evokes from his adobe milieu. Time is priceless, an abstraction, to say the least, but "that's the way it is in this land of paradoxes, enigmas and solitude. In this land, time means nothing and everything. Every second is burdened with joy and sorrow" (p. 94).

Love causes joy and sorrow and makes time insignificant; love is witnessed in relatives, friends, or children. There is no question but that time that is lived and enjoyed intensely tends to elapse much more quickly, while in memory it lasts a lot longer because "only the memory lingers, always memory. It stays behind and sometimes jumps ahead of time, which we consider more valuable than wealth" (p. 57). Mateo constantly reminds us of this fact "... as if the time we shared with our loved ones will far outlast the time created by men ..." (p. 80). Mateo recalls his first love affair with an Indian-Irish girl as a means of measuring time: "She was my first. This is the way time is measured here. In seasons, love, joy, and pain" (p. 15).

Mateo asserts over and over the validity of time in its abstract form, saying that time is "precious and enigmatic" (p. 138). Conversely, if time is imbued with boredom, time passes slowly. In the final analysis, Abstract Time is very personal because, "Each one of us lives in his own time. Each one of us lives in his own world. It is the health of our own past and the health of our own world that will determine our future" (pp. 141–142).

## Retrospective Time

Retrospective Time may be defined as the block of time that the author selects to describe past and present events in a novel. Time, in this case, does not command a true beginning or a definite ending because something precedes and something follows. Because of the author's choice, time is irreducible and constant, yet he may wish to restrict or to expand time itself within that time frame either to underscore or de-emphasize certain episodes and thereby achieve the proper fullness and continuity in the work. In that context, time can vary in degree, with the basic difference being that here, unlike in Abstract Time, it is the reader who is affected (provided there are no external distractions) and not the hero or characters.

Retrospective Time, then, once the author establishes its boundaries, is not altered. In *Nambé—Year One* it covers twenty years. This period can be placed between 1955 and 1975, a time span that begins when Mateo Romero is seven years old and ends about the time he is twenty-seven. To be sure, the reader experiences two decades in a few hours of reading.[8] It is worth noting, moreover, that Mateo's age span is both arbitrary and coincidental, which is in keeping with the concept of Retrospective Time, because his physical presence on earth does not start or end at age seven and twenty-seven, or in 1955 and 1975, respectively. His intellectual and spiritual *raison d'être* does; it begins on the day he finds his identity and roots: "I am the incarnation of his wild-blood [his grandfather's] . . . There is Indian in us . . . I felt it the night I was seven years old" (p. 12).[9]

Where short periods of expanded or reduced time within Retrospective Time affect the reader, the author strives to bring into focus particular events that add texture and tempo to the novel. To do this he resorts to devices concerning time. These may include time-shift, flash-back[10] or historical reference. These devices are all important in *Nambé—Year One*.

Orlando Romero employs what I have chosen to call historical reference. This does not mean historical citations *per se*; instead, they are references made to history in a broad and purposely vague way. (This vagueness is in concert with the concept of time in general.) For example, in *Nambé—Year One* Romero does not refer directly to episodes in history, but the general and implicit hints that he does use manifest an impact on and an importance in the artistic development of the novel.

He begins his novel by purposely introducing the reader into a world of historical significance that sets, to a degree, the tone and prepares the reader for the kind of atmosphere that is prevalent throughout *Nambé—Year One*. He narrates: "In the time of the Gypsies and Payasos that wandered through the mountains of Northern New Mexico, there was one particular enchantress who came from Spain" (p. 7).[11] An amplification of the importance of the history of New Mexico in the novel is further witnessed in the longstanding archeological and anthropological vestiges of the Native American. As Mateo says:

> This is the land of Serpents and Ghosts. Ghost of Indians in their caves, children playing and crying. Old, ancient people dying, being

reborn in the blackness and stillness of cave society, as the great, primal essence is absorbed. The paintings in the caves remain as proof of man's mystery, love, and involvement in the sometimes bewildering events in nature. Here, man has taken a bit of himself and painted his fancy, fantasy, and his reality." (p. 30)

However, as Mateo proclaims, Man has a way of neglecting or distorting history: "There is an invader in this stream. He devours the young of the Rainbow and Cutthroat trout. He was brought here in the 1880's, but is considered by many as a native" (p. 31).

Time-shift is the other technique that Orlando Romero uses, and he does so successfully in giving balance to the structure of the novel. This device is a deliberate fragmentation of the sequence of events or the natural flow of time in a novel. It is time in the past laden with feelings that remain in the past. Two good examples are Romero's references to a couple of letters by Juan López Romero (Mateo's great-grandfather) that Mateo examines surreptitiously in the attic of his house. The first letter, dated October 18, 1863, is to a woman in Santa Fe who is ill and for whom help will come from a *curandero* enroute from Mexico (pp. 45–47). The second is a love letter written on August 21, 1862, addressed affectionately to Flor (pp. 47–48). The date indicates a time-shift within a time-shift. That is, the more recent letter comes first in the novel's narrative. This is a conscious interruption of the continuity of time and events that Romero uses by accentuating that interruption with two letters from yesteryear, out of sequence, and not within the 1955–75 time period chosen as Retrospective Time for the novel.[12]

The last device that Romero employs in dealing with Retrospective Time is flash-back; it is the depiction of past events inserted into a present situation. Unlike time-shift, where the emotional impact of the situation remains in the past, flash-back deals with events of the past, but the feelings are brought to the present.[13] For example, Bartola, the *Llorona* in the novel, encounters Mateo one early spring or summer day and tells him about the calamity that befell Tres Ritos in years past. "'In the middle of January,'" says Bartola, "'up in Tres Ritos, that's where we lived, a terrible plague terrified all the villages. Little children died every day.... We weathered that cruel winter of death, sorrow, and haunting, restless spirits'" (pp. 63–64). It is also a winter that brings back memories for Mateo in reflecting on his love for his Gypsy, his idealized love and Muse:

> It was at her doorstep, in the middle of Winter, that a small snow-filled man melted. He disappeared into the flagstones by her door. His little pebble eyes remained along with the same warm smile that caused him to melt. There in the middle of a cruel physical Winter, the bronze, golden sun of Nambé penetrated the solitude of enigmas

that constitute living in the land of ancient ghosts and paradoxes. . . .
Only the memory lingers, always a memory. It stays behind and sometimes jumps ahead of time, which we consider more valuable than wealth. (p. 57)[14]

After studying the dimensions of time in *Nambé–Year One* several observations and conclusions come to mind: first, Nambé, a Tewa word (*nambay-ongwee*) meaning "people of the roundish earth,"[15] prompts us to reflect briefly on the title of the novel as it relates to our study on time. Nambé implies antiquity, things of the past. Similarly, "year one" conjures up a kind of mystery and uncertainty about the significance of time. It suggests moreover an epoch in the past, but is it 1 A.D. or 1 B.C.? Or is it perhaps a year in the future? A concrete determination of the date may be irrelevant. On the other hand, it could be the fateful year 2001. By that time Nambé, after having been ravaged and destroyed by time and melted into the earth from which it once rose, may be nothing more than a symbol of history, as has become customary with other villages in rural New Mexico. To be sure, Orlando Romero used year one deliberately to dramatize the spirit of time and how it defies a concrete definition and is therefore open to a multitude of analyses and interpretations by anyone who is interested. Year one quite simply heightens what Mendilow calls the vagaries and varieties of time.[16]

Finally, we have learned that one should not take time lightly in a piece of literature, particularly the novel. Time demands more than casual attention. Cyclical, Abstract, and Retrospective Time and their respective nuances and preferences according to the values ascribed to them attest further to the complexity of time in the structure of a given work of art. Yet, in the total scheme of things, it cannot be controlled. Any manipulation of time is superficial at best, and this, coupled with all the other facets discussed in the course of this study on *Nambé–Year One*, accounts for the mystery that time generates and the bafflement it creates in human behavior, whether it concerns the writer, the critic, or the reader.

UNIVERSITY OF SOUTHERN COLORADO

## Notes

[1] A. A. Mendilow, *Time and the Novel* (New York: Humanities Press, 1965), pp. 63–65.

[2] *Ibid.*, p. 32.

[3] Orlando Romero, *Nambé – Year One* (Berkeley: Tonatiuh International Inc., 1976), p. 12. Henceforth, all references to *Nambé – Year One* in this study will be from this edition.

[4] Reincarnation surfaces as a leitmotif in the novel to underline the Christian beliefs of Mateo's people. Once again Mateo's thoughts on this matter are convincing: "Another Spring full of the smells of beginning life, another Summer, another Fall golden and dying, announcing that life will be born on the rot of the decaying remains, so natural to lose only to be found again" (p. 160); or, "When the Gypsy and I were together, I wondered who would devour who. Was it natural to us that one soul should live and feed on another? Or were we to transcend our natural bonds to a place where love meant the mutual joy and suffering of our souls?" (pp. 30–31).

[5] Other examples of the past, present and future coming together are reflected in Mateo's words as he contemplates his companionship with the Gypsy: "Ah! Yes, here we are. You and I sitting in this little car on top of this hill on the highest plateau. We can see my village, Nambé. We can see my past from here and to our right we can see my future, the camposanto. Or is it our future?" (p. 150); or, "It's good to have relatives! Especially to have those who remember the past. Today will be the past, and, since the future seems uncertain, we derive our strength to face each new day from the lingering warmth of what has gone by" (p. 141).

[6] Mendilow, pp. 31–32 and p. 118.

[7] Mateo mentions ". . . the many spirits that make time meaningless" (p. 81) in Nambé.

[8] One must remember that Cyclical Time denotes, among other things, chronology and absoluteness; it has a definite beginning and an ending as it moves uninterrupted. Conversely, Retrospective Time does not have an absolute start or a definite ending; they are both chosen arbitrarily for the sake of, let us say, giving the novel form and structure.

[9] In talking about his age Mateo does so in concrete terms with statements like "I was thirteen or so in measured years . . ." (p. 15), or "My years have been measured at twenty-seven . . ." (p. 17).

[10] Mendilow, p. 72.

[11] On page five, prior to the start of the novel, Orlando Romero includes a quotation (in English translation) on what Cervantes had to say about the Gypsies in 1614. I have traced this excerpt to *La Gitanilla* in *Novelas ejemplares* (Madrid: Espasa-Calpe, S. A., 1960), pp. 39–40. Orlando Romero surely had the gypsy Preciosa of *La Gitanilla* in mind when he invented his own character Gypsy. Moreover, they both possess some identical traits.

[12] Another example of time-shift appears on p. 118. The year is 1879. Mateo reflects: "My Great Grandmother on my Mother's side busied herself packing his provisions for the trip to Santa Fe. My Great Grandfather was saddling his horse in the corral . . . she stopped in her work and asked him for a reason."

[13] Mendilow, p. 90, categorizes this approach as that of a pseudo-author because the feelings expressed are not truly reflective of the past.

[14] Remedios, who had collaborated with her husband Gilberto in protecting the bandit Diego Trujillo, for whom they had sought refuge in the mountains, assures him of his freedom in a flash-back way: " 'There was a shootout in October, down in Las Cruces. Some bandits were surrounded in an old house at the southern end of that town. According to the news we got last month from a stranger passing our village on his way up to Taos, the officials are certain that you were among those they shot it out with. . . . Four days ago my Father returned from buying coffee at Santa Fe, and he said that the law has stopped searching for you!' " (p. 137).

[15] *New Mexico Place Names: A Geographical Dictionary*, ed. T. M. Pearce (Albuquerque: University of New Mexico Press, 1965), p. 106.

[16] Mendilow, p. 31.

# Bibliography

## A Selected Bibliography of Criticism of the Chicano Novel

*Ernestina N. Eger*

The recent flowering of Chicano fiction and its criticism has necessitated extreme selectivity in the compilation of this bibliography. Sources have been limited generally to books, journal and *festschrift* articles, and theses and dissertations. In addition, "individual author" listings are given only for the thirteen novelists considered in this collection. For news articles, short reviews, alternative media, unpublished conference papers, and in-progress materials, as well as for criticism of many other Chicano fiction writers, the reader may consult item 3.

Bibliographic control of Chicano narrative is progressing but remains somewhat spotty. Lomelí and Urioste (item 4), Tatum (item 7), Zimmerman (item 10), and others provide annotations of many book-length and some shorter works. Trujillo and Quiróz de González (item 9) have compiled the most extensive list to date of primary sources, which includes about half of the hundred prose fiction monographs published since the 1960s. Rojas (item 5) indexes short fiction, but unfortunately only in Chicano journals and newspapers, 1965-1972. Our book-length bibliography (item 3) covers literary criticism of Chicano prose fiction from the 1960s through mid-1979.

### Bibliography

1. Cárdenas de Dwyer, Carlota. "Chicano Literature: An Introduction and an Annotated Bibliography." Austin: University of Texas, 1974. ED 088 080.
2. Castro, Donald F. "Chicano Literature: A Bibliographical Essay." *English in Texas* (Texas Joint Council of Teachers of English, Houston), 7, 4 (Summer 1976), 14-19. ED 134 986.
3. Eger, Ernestina N. *A Bibliography of Criticism of Contemporary Chicano Literature*. Berkeley: Chicano Studies Library, Univ. of California, 1982. xxi+295 pp.

4. Lomelí, Francisco A., and Donaldo W. Urioste. *Chicano Perspectives in Literature: A Critical and Annotated Bibliography.* Albuquerque, NM: Pajarito Publications, 1976. 120 pp.

5. [Rojas, Guillermo.] "Toward a Chicano/Raza Bibliography: Drama, Prose, Poetry." *El Grito,* 7, 2 (Dec. 1973), 1–56.

6. Scott, Frank, et al., comp. *Chicano Literature: A Selective Bibliography.* El Paso: Univ. of Texas, 1977. 17 pp. ED 147 051.

7. Tatum, Charles M. *A Selected and Annotated Bibliography of Chicano Studies.* [Manhattan, KS: Kansas State Univ.,] Society of Spanish and Spanish-American Studies, 1976.

Second edition. Lincoln, NE: University of Nebraska, SSSAS, Modern Languages and Literatures, 1979.

8. Treviño, Albert D. "Mexican-American Short Fiction for the High School Program." *English Journal,* 65, 5 (May 1976), 81–84.

9. Trujillo, Roberto G., and Raquel Quiróz de González, comps. "A Comprehensive Bibliography (1970–1979)." In *A Decade of Chicano Literature (1970–1979): Critical Essays and Bibliography.* Eds. Luis Leal et al. Santa Barbara, CA: Editorial La Causa, 1982. Pp. 107–28.

10. Zimmerman, Enid. "An Annotated Bibliography of Chicano Literature: Novels, Short Fiction, Poetry, and Drama, 1970–1980." *Bilingual Review/Revista Bilingüe,* 9, 3 (Sept.–Dec. 1982), 227–51.

See also items 122, 135, 200, 228.

## Prose Fiction

11. Alurista. "Cultural Nationalism and Xicano Literature During the Decade of 1965–1975." *MELUS,* 8, 2 (Summer 1981), 22–34.

12. Armas, José. "Chicano Writing: The New Mexico Narrative." *De Colores,* 5, 1–2 (1980), 69–81.

Rpt. in this volume, section 1.

13. Avendaño, Fausto. "Observaciones sobre los problemas de traducción de la literatura chicana." *Bilingual Review/Revista Bilingüe,* 2, 3 (Sept.–Dec. 1975), 276–80.

14. Brito, Aristeo, Jr. "Paraíso, caída y regeneración en tres novelas chicanas." *DAI,* 39, 4 (Oct. 1978), 2268A.

15. Bruce-Novoa, [Juan]. *Chicano Authors: Inquiry by Interview.* Austin & London: Univ. of Texas Press, 1980. xii+292 pp.

16. _____. "El deslinde del espacio literario chicano." *Aztlán,* 11, 2 (Fall, 1980), 323–38.

17. _____. "Literatura chicana: Una respuesta al caos." *Revista de la Universidad de México,* 29, 12 (ago. 1975), 20–24.

18. _____. "México en la literatura chicana." *Revista de la Universidad de México,* 29, 5 (enero 1975), 13–18.

Rpt. in *Tejidos,* 3, 3 (otoño 1976), 31–42.

Rpt. in *Chicanos: Antología histórica y literaria.* Comp. Tino Villanueva. México: Fondo de Cultura Económica, 1980. Pp. 188–99.

19. _____. "Portraits of the Chicano Artist as a Young Man. The Making of the 'Author' in Three Chicano Novels." In *Festival Flor y Canto II.* Ed.

Arnold C. Vento, Alurista, José Flores Peregrino et al. Albuquerque: Pajarito Pubs., [1979]. Pp. 150–61.

20. _____. "The Space of Chicano Literature." In *The Chicano Literary World 1974*. Ed. Felipe Ortego and David Conde. Las Vegas, NM: New Mexico Highlands Univ., 1975. Pp. 29–58. ED 101 924.
Rpt. in *De Colores*, 1, 4 (1975), 22–42.

21. Cárdenas de Dwyer, Carlota. "Chicano Literature 1965–75: The Flowering of the Southwest." *DAI*, 37, 3 (Sept. 1976), 1582–83A.

22. _____. "Cultural Regionalism and Chicano Literature." *Western American Literature*, 15, 3 (Fall 1980), 187–94.
Revised as "Cultural Nationalism and Chicano Literature in the Eighties." *MELUS*, 8, 2 (Summer 1981), 40–47.

23. Carrillo, Loretta. "The Search for Selfhood and Order in Contemporary Chicano Fiction." *DAI*, 40, 7 (Jan. 1980), 4034A.

24. Castro, Donald F. "The Chicano Novel: An Ethno-Generic Study." *La Luz*, 2, 1 (April 1973), 50–52.

25. Dávila, Luis. "Chicano Fantasy Through a Glass Darkly." In *Otros mundos, otros fuegos; Fantasía y Realismo Mágico en Iberoamérica (Memoria del XVI Congreso del Instituto Internacional de Literatura Iberoamericana)*. Aug. 1973. Ed. Donald A. Yates. East Lansing, Michigan State Univ., 1975. Pp. 245–48.

26. _____. "Otherness in Chicano Literature." In *Contemporary Mexico: Papers of the IV International Congress of Mexican History*. 17–21 Oct. 1973. Ed. James W. Wilkie, Michael C. Meyer, and Edna Monzón de Wilkie. Berkeley: Univ. of California, 1976. Pp. 556–63.

27. Elizondo, Sergio D. "Myth and Reality in Chicano Literature." *Latin American Literary Review*, 5, 10 (Spring–Summer 1977), 23–31.

28. de la Garza, Rudolph O., and Rowena Rivera. "The Socio-Political World of the Chicano: A Comparative Analysis of Social Scientific and Literary Perspectives." In *Minority Language and Literature: Retrospective and Perspective*. Ed. Dexter Fisher. New York: Modern Language Assn., 1977. Pp. 42–64.

29. Gerdes, Dick. "Cultural Values in Three Novels of New Mexico." *Bilingual Review/Revista Bilingüe*, 7, 3 (Sept.–Dec. 1980), 239–48.

30. Gonzales, Lucy. "Conflict and Struggle: A Study of Themes in the Chicano Novel." Unpublished MA thesis. Univ. of Houston, 1974. 100 pp.

31. Gonzales-Berry, Erlinda. "Chicano Literature in Spanish: Roots and Content." Unpublished PhD diss. Univ. of New Mexico, 1978.

32. Grajeda, Rafael Francisco. "The Figure of the Pocho in Contemporary Chicano Fiction." *DAI*, 35, 8 (Feb. 1975), 5402–03A.

33. Johnson, Elaine Dorough. "A Thematic Study of Three Chicano Narratives: *Estampas del Valle y otras obras*, *Bless Me, Ultima*, and *Peregrinos de Aztlán*." *DAI*, 39, 6 (Dec. 1978), 3614A.

34. Lattin, Vernon E. "The City in Contemporary Chicano Fiction." *Studies in American Fiction*, 6, 1 (Spring 1978), 93–100.

35. _____. "Ethnicity and Identity in the Contemporary Chicano Novel." *Minority Voices*, 2, 2 (Fall, 1978), 37–44.

36. _____. "The Quest for Mythic Vision in Contemporary Native American and Chicano Fiction." *American Literature*, 50, 4 (Jan. 1979), 625–40.

37. Leal, Luis. "Mexican-American Literature: A Historical Perspective." *Revista Chicano-Riqueña*, 1, 1 (verano 1973), 32–44.

Updated version in *Modern Chicano Writers*. Ed. Joseph Sommers and Tomás Ybarra-Frausto. Englewood Cliffs, NJ: Prentice-Hall, 1979. Pp. 18-30.

38. Leal, Luis, and Pepe Barrón. "Chicano Literature: An Overview." In *Three American Literatures*. Ed. Houston A. Baker Jr. New York: Modern Language Association of America, 1982. Pp. 9-32.

39. Lewis, Marvin A. *Introduction to the Chicano Novel*. Institute Paper Series. Milwaukee: University of Wisconsin-Milwaukee, College of Letters and Science, Spanish Speaking Outreach Institute, 1982. [v]+74 pp.

40. _____. "The Urban Experience in Selected Chicano Fiction." *Selected Proceedings of the 4th Annual Conference on Minority Studies*, Vol. 6, "Minority Literature and the Urban Experience." April 1976. Ed. George E. Carter and James R. Parker. La Crosse, WI: Institute for Minority Studies, Univ. of Wisconsin, 1978. Pp. 85-94.

Rpt. in this volume, section 1.

41. _____. "Violence in the Chicano Novel." *Crítica Hispánica*, 2, 2 (1980), 53-63.

42. Lomelí, Francisco. "The Family Crisis in Three Chicano Novels: Disintegration vs. Continuity." In *Work, Family, Sex Roles, Language: The National Association for Chicano Studies, Selected Papers 1979*. Ed. Mario Barrera, Alberto Camarillo, and Francisco Hernández. Berkeley, CA: Tonatiuh-Quinto Sol International, 1980. Pp. 141-55.

43. López, Joe Raymond. "Religion in Selected Works of Chicano Literature." Unpublished MA thesis. Texas Tech Univ., Lubbock, TX, 1975. iii+134 pp.

44. Lyon, Ted. "Loss of Innocence in Chicano Prose." In *The Identification and Analysis of Chicano Literature*. Ed. Francisco Jiménez. New York: Bilingual Press/Editorial Bilingüe, 1979. Pp. 254-62.

45. Melville, Margarita B. "Family Values as Reflected in Mexican American Literature." In *Understanding the Chicano Experience through Literature*. Ed. Nicolás Kanellos. Houston, TX: Mexican American Studies, Univ. of Houston, 1981. Pp. 43-53.

46. Mickelson, Joel C. "The Chicano Novel Since World War II." *La Luz*, 6, 4 (April 1977), 22-29.

47. Mindiola, Tatcho, Jr. "Politics and Chicano Literature: The Views of Chicano Writers." In *Understanding the Chicano Experience through Literature*. Ed. Nicolás Kanellos. Houston, TX: Mexican American Studies, Univ. of Houston, 1981. Pp. 15-27.

48. Moesser, Alba Irene. "La literatura mejicoamericana del suroeste de los Estados Unidos." *DAI*, 32, 5 (Nov. 1971), 2648A.

49. Monahan, Sister Helena, C.C.V.I. "The Chicano Novel: Toward a Definition and Literary Criticism." *DAI*, 33, 3 (Sept. 1972), 1175A.

50. Monleón, José, ed. "Mesa redonda con Alurista, Rudolfo Anaya, María Herrera Sobek, Alejandro Morales y Helen Viramontes." *Maize*, 4, 3-4 (Spring-Summer 1981), 6-23.

51. Morales, Alejandro Dennis. "Visión panorámica de la literatura mexicoamericana hasta el boom de 1966." *DAI*, 36, 10 (April 1976), 6731A.

52. Ortego, Philip Darraugh. "Backgrounds of Mexican American Literature." *DAI*, 32, 9 (March 1972), 5195A.

53. Paredes, Raymund A. "The Evolution of Chicano Literature." *MELUS*, 5, 2 (Summer 1978), 71-110.

Revised and expanded version in *Three American Literatures*. Ed. Houston A. Baker Jr. New York: Modern Language Association of America, 1982. Pp. 33-79.

54. _____. "Mexican American Authors and the American Dream." *MELUS*, 8, 4 (Winter 1981), 71-80.

55. Rainey, Marianne Pettersen. "Un estudio del anglo y del chicano en cinco novelas chicanas." Unpublished MA thesis. Southern Illinois Univ., 1976. 55 pp.

56. Rascón Garza, María Luisa. "El tema de la religión en dos novelas méxicoamericanas." Unpublished MA thesis. Texas A & I, Kingsville, TX, 1975. 69 pp.

57. Reinhardt, Karl. "The Image of Gays in Chicano Prose Fiction." *Explorations in Ethnic Studies*, 4, 2 (July 1981), 41-50. Critiques by W. Thomas Jamison, Sara Bentley and LaVerne González, pp. 51-55.

58. Rocard, Marcienne. *Les Fils du Soleil: La minorité mexicaine à travers la littérature des États-Unis*. Paris: Maison-neuve et Larose, 1980.

59. Rodríguez, Joe D. "The Chicano Novel and the North American Narrative of Survival." *Denver Quarterly*, 16, 3 (Fall 1981), 64-70.

60. _____. "God's Silence and the Shrill of Ethnicity in the Chicano Novel." *Explorations in Ethnic Studies*, 4, 2 (July 1981), 14-21. Critiques by Neil Nakadate and Gladys David Howell, pp. 22-25.

61. Rodríguez, Juan. "El desarrollo del cuento chicano: Del folklore al tenebroso mundo del yo." *Mester*, 4, 1 (Nov. 1973), 7-12.

Rpt. in *Fomento Literario* (Congreso Nacional de Asuntos Colegiales), 1, 3 (invierno 1973), 19-30.

Rpt. in *The Identification and Analysis of Chicano Literature*. Ed. Francisco Jiménez. New York: Bilingual Press/Editorial Bilingüe, 1979. Pp. 58-67.

62. _____. "Notes on the Evolution of Chicano Prose Fiction." In *Modern Chicano Writers*. Ed. Joseph Sommers and Tomás Ybarra-Frausto. Englewood Cliffs, NJ: Prentice-Hall, 1979. Pp. 67-73.

63. _____. "Temas y Motivos de la Literatura Chicana." *Festival Flor y Canto II*. Ed. Arnold C. Vento, Alurista, José Flores Peregrino et al. Albuquerque: Pajarito Pubs., [1979]. Pp. 162-68.

Revised version, "La búsqueda de identidad y sus motivos en la literatura chicana." In *The Identification and Analysis of Chicano Literature*. Ed. Francisco Jiménez. New York: Bilingual Press/Editorial Bilingüe, 1979. Pp. 170-78.

64. Rodríguez del Pino, Salvador. "La novela chicana de los setenta comentada por sus escritores y críticos." *Bilingual Review/Revista Bilingüe*, 4, 3 (Sept.-Dec. 1977), 240-44.

Rpt. in *The Identification and Analysis of Chicano Literature*. Ed. Francisco Jiménez. New York: Bilingual Press/Editorial Bilingüe, 1979. Pp. 153-60.

65. _____. *La novela chicana escrita en español: Cinco autores comprometidos*. Ypsilanti, MI: Bilingual Press/Editorial Bilingüe, 1982. 159 pp.

66. Rojas, Guillermo. "La prosa chicana: Tres epígonos de la novela mexicana de la Revolución." In *The Chicano Literary World 1974*. Ed. Felipe Ortego and David Conde. Las Vegas, NM: New Mexico Highlands Univ., 1975. Pp. 59-70. ED 101 924.

Rpt. in *Cuadernos Americanos*, 34, 3 (mayo-junio 1975), 198-209.

Rpt. in *De Colores*, 1, 4 (1975), 43-57.

Rpt. in *The Identification and Analysis of Chicano Literature*. Ed. Francisco Jiménez. New York: Bilingual Press/Editorial Bilingüe, 1979. Pp. 317-28.

67. Saldívar, Ramón. "Chicano Literature and Ideology: Prospectus for the '80's." *MELUS*, 8, 2 (Summer 1981), 35-39.

68. _____. "A Dialectic of Difference: Towards a Theory of the Chicano Novel." *MELUS*, 6, 3 (Fall, 1979), 73-92. Rpt. in this volume, section 1.

69. Salinas, Judy. "The Image of Woman in Chicano Literature." *Revista Chicano-Riqueña*, 4, 4 (otoño 1976), 139-48. Revised and amplified as "The Role of Women in Chicano Literature." In *The Identification and Analysis of Chicano Literature*. Ed. Francisco Jiménez. New York: Bilingual Press/Editorial Bilingüe, 1979. Pp. 191-240.

70. Sánchez, Federico A. "Raíces mexicanas." *Grito del Sol*, 1, 4 (Oct.-Dec. 1976), 75-87.

71. Sánchez, Saúl. "La incipiente narrativa chicana: Un espejo de telarañas." *Cuadernos Hispanoamericanos*, No. 390 (dic. 1982), pp. 641-45.

72. _____. "Tres Dimensiones en la Narrativa Chicana Contemporánea." In *Canto al Pueblo: An Anthology of Experiences*. Ed. Leonardo Carrillo, Antonio Martínez, Carol Molina and Marie Wood. San Antonio, TX: Penca Books, 1978. Pp. 93-98.

73. Segade, Gustavo V. "Un Panorama Conceptual de la Novela Chicana." *Fomento Literario* (Congreso Nacional de Asuntos Colegiales), 1, 3 (invierno 1973), 5-18.

74. Sommers, Joseph. "Critical Approaches to Chicano Literature." *De Colores*, 3, 4 [1977], 15-21. Also in *Bilingual Review/Revista Bilingüe*, 4, 1-2 (Jan.-Aug. 1977), 92-98. Rpt. in *The Identification and Analysis of Chicano Literature*. Ed. Francisco Jiménez. New York: Bilingual Press/Editorial Bilingüe, 1979. Pp. 143-52. Slightly revised version in *Modern Chicano Writers*. Ed. Joseph Sommers and Tomás Ybarra-Frausto. Englewood Cliffs, NJ: Prentice-Hall, 1979. Pp. 31-40. Early version of first part of item 75.

75. _____. "From the Critical Premise to the Product: Critical Modes and Their Applications to a Chicano Literary Text." *New Scholar*, 6 (1977), 51-80.

76. Somoza, Oscar Urquídez. "Visión axiológica en la narrativa chicana." *DAI*, 38, 7 (Jan. 1978), 4203A.

77. Tatum, Charles M. *Chicano Literature*. TUSAS 433. Boston: Twayne Publishers, 1982. [xiii+] 214 pp.

78. _____. "Contemporary Chicano Prose Fiction: A Chronicle of Misery." *Latin American Literary Review*, 1, 2 (Spring 1973), 7-17. Rpt. in *The Identification and Analysis of Chicano Literature*. Ed. Francisco Jiménez. New York: Bilingual Press/Editorial Bilingüe, 1979. Pp. 241-53.

79. _____. "Contemporary Chicano Prose Fiction: Its Ties to Mexican Literature." *Books Abroad*, 49, 3 (Summer 1975), 431-38. Rpt. in *The Identification and Analysis of Chicano Literature*. Ed. Francisco Jiménez. New York: Bilingual Press/Editorial Bilingüe, 1979. Pp. 47-57.

80. Thomas, George Aaron. "Tres etapas en el desarrollo de la novela chicana contemporánea." *DAI*, 43, 6 (Dec. 1982), 1987A.

81. Valdés Fallis, Guadalupe. "Metaphysical Anxiety and the Existence of God in Contemporary Chicano Fiction." *Revista Chicano-Riqueña*, 3, 2 (invierno 1975), 26–33.

82. Vallejos, Thomas. "Mestizaje: The Transformations of Ancient Indian Religious Thought in Contemporary Chicano Fiction." *DAI*, 41, 4 (Oct. 1980), 1602A.

83. Vowell, Faye Nell. "The Chicano Novel [in English]: A Study in Self-Definition." *DAI*, 40, 3 (Sept. 1979), 1473A.

84. Willey, Michael Lee. "The Debt to Minority Literature: Images of Change and Action in Recent White Literature." *DAI*, 34, 12 (June 1974), 7792–93A.

85. Woods, Richard D. "The Chicano Novel: Silence after Publication." *Revista Chicano-Riqueña*, 4, 3 (verano 1976), 42–47.

# Individual Authors

## Oscar Zeta Acosta

86. Alurista. "Alienación e ironía en los personajes de Arlt y Acosta: *Los siete locos* y *The Revolt of the Cockroach People*." *Grito del Sol*, 2, 4 (Oct.–Dec. 1977), 69–80.

87. _____. "El Caso, la Novela, y la Historia en la Obra de Acosta: *The Revolt of the Cockroach People*." *Maize*, 2, 3 (primavera 1979), 6–13.
Rpt. in this volume in, English translation, section 2.

88. _____. "From Tragedy to Caricature . . . and Beyond." *Aztlán*, 11, 1 (Spring 1980), 89–97.

89. Bruce-Novoa. "Fear and Loathing on the Buffalo Trail." *MELUS*, 6, 4 (Winter 1979), 39–50.

90. Padilla, Genaro Miguel. "The Progression from Individual to Social Consciousness in Two Chicano Novelists: José Antonio Villarreal and Oscar Zeta Acosta." *DAI*, 42, 12 (June 1982), 5123A.

91. Ramírez, Arthur. Review of *The Autobiography of a Brown Buffalo* and *The Revolt of the Cockroach People*. *Revista Chicano-Riqueña*, 3, 3 (verano 1975), 46–53.

92. Smith, Norman D. "Buffalos and Cockroaches: Acosta's Siege at Aztlán." *Latin American Literary Review*, 5, 10 (Spring–Summer 1977), 85–97.
Rpt. in this volume, section 2.

93. Thompson, Hunter S. "Fear and Loathing in the Graveyard of the Weird: The Banshee Screams for Buffalo Meat." *Rolling Stone Magazine*, No. 254 (15 Dec. 1977), pp. 48–54, 57, 59.

94. Urista, Alberto Heredia. "Oscar Z. Acosta: In Context." *DAI*, 44, 2 (Aug. 1983), 497A.
See also items 18, 21, 59, 60, 63, 68, 77, 83, 172.

## Rudolfo Anaya

95. Anaya, Rudolfo A. "A Writer Discusses his Craft." *CEA Critic*, 40, 1 (Nov. 1977), 39–43.
Rpt. as "The Writer's Landscape: Epiphany in Landscape." *Latin American Literary Review*, 5, 10 (Spring–Summer 1977), 98–102.

Also in *Southwest: A Contemporary Anthology*. Ed. Karl and Jane Kopp. Albuquerque, NM: Red Earth Press, 1977. Pp. 175–79.

96. Cantú, Roberto. "Degradación y regeneración en *Bless Me, Ultima*: el chicano y la vida nueva." *Caribe* (Univ. of Hawaii), 1, 1 (primavera 1976), 113–26. Rpt. in *The Identification and Analysis of Chicano Literature*. Ed. Francisco Jiménez. New York: Bilingual Press/Editorial Bilingüe, 1979. Pp. 374–88.

97. _____. "Estructura y sentido de lo onírico en *Bless Me, Ultima*." *Mester*, 5, 1 (Nov. 1974), 27–41.

98. Carpenter, Lorene Hyde. "Maps for the Journey: Shamanic Patterns in Anaya, Asturias, and Castaneda." *DAI*, 42, 8 (Feb. 1982), 3588A.

99. Carrasco, David. "A Perspective for a Study of Religious Dimensions in Chicano Experience: *Bless Me, Ultima* as a Religious Text." *Aztlán*, 13, 1–2 (Spring–Fall 1982), 195–221.

100. Clements, William M. "The Way to Individuation in Anaya's *Bless Me, Ultima*." *Midwest Quarterly*, 23, 2 (Winter 1982), 131–43.

101. "A Dialogue: Rudolfo Anaya/John Nichols." *Puerto del Sol*, Vol. 17 (Spring 1982), 61–85.

102. Donnelly, Dyan. "Finding a Home in the World." *Bilingual Review/Revista Bilingüe*, 1, 1 (Jan.–April 1974), 112–18.

103. Eckley, Grace. "Folklore and Faith in Anaya's *Bless Me, Ultima*." *English in Texas* (Houston, TX), 9, 1 (Fall 1977), 10–12.

104. _____. "The Process of Maturation in Anaya's *Bless Me, Ultima*." *English in Texas* (Houston, TX), 9, 1 (Fall 1977), 7–9.

105. Elías, Edward. "*Tortuga*: A Novel of Archetypal Structure." *Bilingual Review/Revista Bilingüe*, 9, 1 (Jan.–April 1982), 82–87.

106. Gish, Robert F. "Curanderismo and Witchery in the Fiction of Rudolfo A. Anaya: The Novel as Magic." *New Mexico Humanities Review*, 2, 2 (Summer 1979), 5–13.

107. Gutiérrez, Armando. "Politics in the Chicano Novel: A Critique." In *Understanding the Chicano Experience through Literature*. Ed. Nicolás Kanellos. Houston, TX: Mexican American Studies, Univ. of Houston, 1981. Pp. 7–14.

108. Harris, Jim. "Writers in New Mexico Series: An Interview with Rudolfo Anaya." *Southwest Heritage*, 11, 3 (Fall 1981), 16–19.

109. Hoffman, María López. "Myth and Reality in *Heart of Aztlán*." *De Colores*, 5, 1–2 (1980), 111–14.

110. Lattin, Vernon E. " 'The Horror of Darkness': Meaning and Structure in Anaya's *Bless Me, Ultima*." *Revista Chicano-Riqueña*, 6, 2 (primavera 1978), 50–57.

111. Johnson, David, and David Apodaca. "Myths and the Writer: A Conversation with Rudolfo Anaya." *New America*, 3, 3 (Spring 1979), 76–85.

112. King, Scottie. "Rudolfo A. Anaya: Journey from La Pastura." *New Mexico Magazine*, 57, 7 (July 1979), pp. 42–43, 60–63.

113. Malpezzi, Frances. "A Study of the Female Protagonist in Frank Waters' *People of the Valley* and Rudolfo Anaya's *Bless Me, Ultima*." *South Dakota Review*, 14, 2 (Summer 1976), 102–10.

114. Mitchell, Carol. "Rudolfo Anaya's *Bless Me, Ultima*: Folk Culture in Literature." *Critique: Studies in Modern Fiction*, 22, 1 (1980), 55–64.

115. Monleón, José. "Ilusión y realidad en la obra de Rudolfo Anaya." In this volume, section 4B.

116. Pacheco, Consuelo. "A Conversation with Rudolfo Anaya." *La Confluencia*, 3, 3-4 (Feb. 1980), 8-15.

117. Reed, Ishmael. "An Interview with Rudolfo Anaya." *San Francisco Review of Books*, 4, 2 (June 1978), pp. 9-12, 34.

118. Rogers, Jane. "The Function of the *La Llorona* Myth in Rudolfo Anaya's *Bless Me, Ultima*." *Latin American Literary Review*, 5, 10 (Spring-Summer 1977), 64-69.

Rpt. in this volume, section 4B.

119. Testa, Daniel. "Extensive/Intensive Dimensionality in Anaya's *Bless Me, Ultima*." *Latin American Literary Review*, 5, 10 (Spring-Summer 1977), 70-78.

120. Treviño, Albert D. "*Bless Me, Ultima*: A Critical Interpretation." *De Colores*, 3, 4 [1977], 30-33.

121. Unpingco-Garrett, Regina. "Images of Women in *Bless Me, Ultima*." *Visión* (San Diego State Univ.), Spring 1976, pp. 41-42.

122. Vassallo, Paul, ed. *The Magic of Words: Rudolfo A. Anaya and His Writings*. Albuquerque: Univ. of New Mexico Press, 1982. xii+83 pp.

123. Waggoner, Amy. "Tony's Dreams—An Important Dimension in *Bless Me, Ultima*." *Southwestern American Literature*, 4 (1974), 74-79.

124. Wilson, Carter. "'Magical Strength in the Human Heart'—the framing of mortal confusion in Rudolph A. Anaya's *Bless Me, Ultima—*." *Ploughshares* (Watertown, MA), 4, 3[1978], 190-97.

See also items 12, 14, 15, 17, 19, 20, 21, 23, 25, 28, 29, 30, 33, 36, 39, 42, 43, 44, 45, 46, 50, 53, 56, 69, 70, 73, 76, 77, 81, 82, 83.

## Ron Arias

125. Arias, Ron. "El señor del chivo." *Journal of Ethnic Studies*, 3, 4 (Winter 1976), 58-60.

126. Bruce-Novoa, [Juan]. "Interview with Ron Arias." *Journal of Ethnic Studies*, 3, 4 (Winter 1976), 70-73.

Revised and amplified version in item 15.

127. Cárdenas de Dwyer, Carlota. "International Literary Metaphor and Ron Arias: An Analysis of *The Road to Tamazunchale*." *Bilingual Review/Revista Bilingüe*, 4, 3 (Sept.-Dec. 1977), 229-33.

Rpt. in *The Identification and Analysis of Chicano Literature*. Ed. Francisco Jiménez. New York: Bilingual Press/Editorial Bilingüe, 1979. Pp. 358-64.

128. Gingerich, Willard. "Chicanismo: The Rebirth of a Spirit." *Southwest Review*, 62, 3 (Summer 1977), pp. vi-vii, 302-04.

129. Lewis, Marvin A. "On *The Road to Tamazunchale*." *Revista Chicano-Riqueña*, 5, 4 (otoño 1977), 49-52.

130. Marín, Mariana. "*The Road to Tamazunchale*: Fantasy or Reality?" *De Colores*, 3, 4 [1977], 34-38.

131. Martínez, Eliud. "Ron Arias' *The Road to Tamazunchale*: A Chicano Novel of the New Reality." *Latin American Literary Review*, 5, 10 (Spring-Summer 1977), 51-63.

Rpt. in this volume, section 4D.

132. Nieto, Eva Margarita. "The Dialectics of Textual Interpolation in Ron Arias' *The Road to Tamazunchale*." In this volume, section 4D.

133. Saldívar, José David. "Claiming the Americas: Contemporary Third World Literature." *DAI*, 43, 11 (May 1983), 3589A.
See also items 15, 36, 39, 40, 68, 77, 82.

## Raymond Barrio

134. Barrio, Raymond. "Plum, A Novel About California Farm Workers." In *The Publish-It-Yourself Handbook*. Ed. Bill Henderson. Yonkers, NY: Pushcart Press, 1973. Pp. 108–16.
135. Eger, Ernestina N. "Bibliography of Works By and About Raymond Barrio." In *The Plum Plum Pickers*, by Raymond Barrio. Second edition. Binghamton, NY: Bilingual Press/Editorial Bilingüe, 1984. Pp. 227–32.
136. Geuder, Patricia A. "Address Systems in *The Plum Plum Pickers*." *Aztlán*, 6, 3 (Fall 1975), 341–46.
137. Lattin, Vernon E. "Paradise and Plums: Appearance and Reality in Barrio's *The Plum Plum Pickers*." *Selected Proceedings of the 3rd Annual Conference on Minority Studies*, Vol. 2. April 1975. Ed. George E. Carter and James R. Parker. La Crosse, WI: Institute for Minority Studies, Univ. of Wisconsin, 1976. Pp. 165–71. ED 125 799 or ED 138 668.
Rpt. in *Critique: Studies in Modern Fiction*, 19, 1 [1977], 49–57.
Rpt. in this volume, section 2.
138. Lomelí, Francisco A. "Depraved New World Revisited: Dreams and Dystopia in *The Plum Plum Pickers*." In *The Plum Plum Pickers*, by Raymond Barrio. Second edition. Binghamton, NY: Bilingual Press/Editorial Bilingüe, 1984. Pp. 9–26.
139. McKenna, Teresa. "Three Novels: An Analysis." *Aztlán*, 1, 2 (Fall 1970), 47–56.
140. Miller, Yvette E. "The Social Message in Chicano Fiction: Tomás Rivera's *. . . and the earth did not part* and Raymond Barrio's *The Plum Plum Pickers*." *Selected Proceedings of the 3rd Annual Conference on Minority Studies*, Vol. 2. April 1975. Ed. George E. Carter and James R. Parker. La Crosse, WI: Univ. of Wisconsin, Institute for Minority Studies, 1976. Pp. 159–64. ED 125 799 or ED 138 668.
See also items 21, 24, 30, 39, 46, 49, 52, 55, 69, 77, 83, 172.

## Aristeo Brito

141. Alarcón, Justo S. "Las metamorfosis del diablo en *El Diablo en Texas* de Aristeo Brito." *De Colores*, 5, 1–2 (1980), 30–44.
Rpt. in this volume, section 4E.
142. Febles, Jorge M. Review of *Cuentos i poemas de Aristeo Brito* and *El Diablo en Texas*. *Revista Chicano-Riqueña*, 5, 4 (otoño 1977), 55–58.
143. Lewis, Marvin A. "*El Diablo en Texas*: Structure and Meaning." In this volume, section 4E.
144. Rodríguez del Pino, Salvador. "Lo mexicano y lo chicano en *El diablo en Texas*." In *The Identification and Analysis of Chicano Literature*. Ed. Francisco Jiménez. New York: Bilingual Press/Editorial Bilingüe, 1979. Pp. 365–73.
See also items 31, 39, 41, 65, 77.

## Nash Candelaria

145. Bruce-Novoa. "Nash Candelaria: An Interview." *De Colores*, 5, 1-2 (1980), 115-29.

146. Lattin, Vernon E. "Time and History in Candelaria's *Memories of the Alhambra.*" *De Colores*, 5, 1-2 (1980), 102-10.
Rpt. in this volume, section 4G.

147. Shirley, Paula. Review of *Memories of the Alhambra*. *MELUS*, 6, 2 (Summer 1979), 100-03.

148. Trujillo, David F. Review of *Memories of the Alhambra*. *De Colores*, 5, 1-2 (1980), 130-32.
See also items 39, 77.

## Rolando Hinojosa

149. Alvarez García, Imeldo. "*Klail City y sus alrededores.*" *Casa de las Américas*, No. 99 (nov.-dic. 1976), pp. 126-30.

150. Brox, Luis María. "Los límites del costumbrismo en *Estampas del Valle y otras obras.*" *Mester*, 5, 2 (abril 1975), 101-04.

151. Bruce-Novoa, Juan. "Interview with Rolando Hinojosa-S." *Latin American Literary Review*, 5, 10 (Spring-Summer 1977), 103-14.
Slightly revised version in item 15.

152. _____. "Righting the Oral Tradition." *Denver Quarterly*, 16, 3 (Fall 1981), 78-86.

153. Gonzales-Berry, Erlinda. "*Estampas del Valle:* From *Costumbrismo* to Self-Reflecting Literature." *Bilingual Review/Revista Bilingüe*, 7, 1 (Jan.-April 1980), 29-38.
Rpt. in this volume, section 4A.

154. Guerrero, Yolanda. "Literatura y Sociedad: Análisis de *Generaciones y semblanzas.*" *La Palabra*, 1, 2 (otoño 1979), 21-30.
Rpt. in this volume, section 4A.

155. Hinojosa, Rolando. *Crossing the Line: The Construction of a Poem*. Institute Paper Series. Milwaukee, WI: Spanish Speaking Outreach Institute, Univ. of Wisconsin/Milwaukee, 1981. 16 pp.

156. Martínez, Max. "Por esas novelas que pegan: *Generaciones y semblanzas.*" In *Flor y Canto IV and V: An Anthology of Chicano Literature from the Festivals held in Albuquerque, New Mexico, 1977, and Tempe, Arizona, 1978*. Ed. José Armas, Justo Alarcón et al. [Albuquerque, NM]: Pajarito Publications/Flor y Canto V Committee, 1980. Pp. 157-65.

157. Medina, Rubén. "Entrevista con Rolando Hinojosa." *Maize*, 5, 1-2 (Fall-Winter 1981-1982), 16-31.

158. Randolph, Donald A. "La imprecisión estética en *Klail City y sus alrededores.*" *Revista Chicano-Riqueña*, 9, 4 (otoño 1981), 52-65.

159. Tatum, Charles. Review of *Klail City y sus alrededores*. *Latin American Literary Review*, 5, 10 (Spring-Summer 1977), 165-69.
See also items 11, 13, 15, 22, 27, 28, 31, 33, 39, 41, 53, 65, 66, 67, 69, 73, 77.

## Miguel Méndez

160. Alarcón, Justo S. "Miguel Méndez M.: Entrevista." *La Palabra*, 3, 1-2 (primavera-otoño 1981), 3-17.

161. Bornstein, Miriam. "*Peregrinos de Aztlán*: Dialéctica estructural e ideológica." *Cuadernos Americanos*, 39, 4 (julio–ago. 1980), 23-33.
Rpt. in *Revista Chicano-Riqueña*, 8, 4 (otoño 1980), 69-78.
Rpt. in this volume, section 4C.

162. Brito, Aristeo. "El lenguaje tropológico en *Peregrinos de Aztlán*." *La Luz*, 4, 2 (May 1975), 42-43.

163. _____. "El paraíso en *Peregrinos de Aztlán*." In *Flor y Canto IV and V: An Anthology of Chicano Literature from the Festivals held in Albuquerque, New Mexico, 1977, and Tempe, Arizona, 1978*. Ed. José Armas, Justo Alarcón et al. [Albuquerque, NM]: Pajarito Publications/Flor y Canto V Committee, 1980. Pp. 174-81.

164. Bruce-Novoa, Juan. "En torno a Miguel Méndez." *La Palabra*, 3, 1-2 (primavera–otoño 1981), 77-83.

165. _____. "La voz del silencio: Miguel Méndez." *Diálogos*, 12, 3 (mayo–junio 1976), 27-30.
Shortened and tr. as "Miguel Méndez: Voices of Silence." *De Colores*, 3, 4 [1977], 63-69.
Rpt. in this volume, section 4C.

166. Cárdenas, Lupe. "La ciudad como arquetipo de la madre terrible en *Peregrinos de Aztlán*." *La Palabra*, 3, 1-2 (primavera–otoño 1981), 33-49.

167. Gaardner, A. Bruce. "Análisis crítico de *Peregrinos de Aztlán*." In *Bilingual Schooling and the Survival of Spanish in the United States*. Rowley, MA: Newbury House Publishers, 1977. Pp. 191-224.

168. García, Esteban Herman. "Un análisis de una novela chicana: *Peregrinos de Aztlán* by Miguel Méndez M." Unpublished MA thesis. Pullman: Washington State Univ., 1977. vi, 37 pp.

169. Johnson, Elaine Dorough. "El papel de la naturaleza en *Peregrinos de Aztlán*." *La Palabra*, 3, 1-2 (primavera–otoño 1981), 50-57.

170. Johnson Stephenson, María Mercedes. "El tema del destierro en *Peregrinos de Aztlán*." *DAI*, 43, 5 (Nov. 1982), 1539A.

171. Leal, Luis. "Méndez y el *Calila y Dimna*." *La Palabra*, 3, 1-2 (primavera–otoño 1981), 67-76.

172. Lewis, Marvin A. "*Peregrinos de Aztlán* and the Emergence of the Chicano Novel." In *Selected Proceedings of the 3rd Annual Conference on Minority Studies*, Vol. 2. April 1975. Ed. George E. Carter and James R. Parker. La Crosse, WI: Institute for Minority Studies, Univ. of Wisconsin, 1976. Pp. 143-57. ED 125 799 or ED 138 668.

173. Marín, Mariana. "*Pocho* y *Peregrinos de Aztlán*: Contradicciones textuales e ideología." *Revista Chicano-Riqueña*, 6, 4 (otoño 1978), 59-62.

174. Méndez M., Miguel. "La alienación en la literatura chicana." *De Colores*, 4, 1-2 (1978), 151-54.

175. Quiroz, Roberto R. "The Images of Miguel Méndez M." *Raza Art & Media Collective Journal* (Univ. of Michigan, Ann Arbor), 1, 2 (1 March 1976), 1-2.

176. Rodríguez, Juan. Review of *Peregrinos de Aztlán*. *Revista Chicano-Riqueña*, 2, 3 (verano 1974), 51-55.

177. Segade, Gustavo. "Chicano Indigenismo: Alurista and Miguel Méndez." *Xalmán*, 1, 4 (Spring 1977), 4-11.

178. _____. "*Peregrinos de Aztlán*: Viaje y Laberinto." *De Colores*, 3, 4 [1977], 58-62.

Rpt. in *Festival Flor y Canto II.* Ed. Arnold C. Vento, Alurista, José Flores Peregrino et al. Albuquerque: Pajarito Pubs., [1979]. Pp. 143-49.

179. Somoza, Oscar Urquídez. "El marxismo subyacente en *Peregrinos de Aztlán.*" *Xalmán,* 2, 1 (Spring 1978), 17-22.

180. _____. "The Mexican Element in the Fiction of Miguel Méndez." *Denver Quarterly,* 17, 1 (Spring 1982), 68-77.

181. Ubilla-Arenas, Cecilia. "*Peregrinos de Aztlán:* de la crítica social al sueño humanista." *La Palabra,* 1, 2 (otoño 1979), 64-76.

See also items 11, 14, 15, 27, 31, 33, 39, 41, 55, 63, 65, 66, 76, 77.

## Alejandro Morales

182. Benavides, Ricardo F. "Estirpe y estigma en una novela chicana." *Chasqui,* 6, 1 (Nov. 1976), 84-93.

183. Gonzales-Berry, Erlinda. "*Caras viejas y vino nuevo:* Journey Through a Disintegrating *Barrio.*" *Latin American Literary Review,* 7, 14 (Spring-Summer 1979), 62-72.

Rpt. in this volume, section 4H.

184. _____. "Doctor, Writer, Warrior Chief." *Bilingual Review/Revista Bilingüe,* 9, 3 (Sept.-Dec. 1982), 276-79.

185. Herrera-Sobek, María. "Barrio Life in the Fifties and Sixties." *Latin American Literary Review,* 5, 10 (Spring-Summer 1977), 148-50.

186. Lewis, Marvin A. "*Caras viejas y vino nuevo:* Essence of the barrio." *Bilingual Review/Revista Bilingüe,* 4, 1-2 (Jan.-Aug. 1977), 141-44.

187. Monleón, José. "Dos novelas de Alejandro Morales." *Maize,* 4, 1-2 (Fall-Winter 1980-81), 6-8.

188. _____. "Entrevista con Alejandro Morales." *Maize,* 4, 1-2 (Fall-Winter 1980-81), 9-20.

189. Somoza, Oscar U. "Choque e interacción en *Caras viejas y vino nuevo* de Alejandro Morales." *Cuadernos Americanos,* 39, 4 (julio-ago. 1980), 34-40.

Rpt. in this volume, section 4H.

See also items 11, 31, 39, 41, 50, 65, 77.

## Estela Portillo Trambley

190. Castellano, Olivia. "Of Clarity and the Moon – A Study of Two Women in Rebellion." *De Colores,* 3, 3 (1977), 25-30.

191. Fisher, Jerilyn Beth. "The Minority Woman's Voice: A Cultural Study of Black and Chicana Fiction." *DAI,* 39, 3 (Sept. 1978), 1565 A.

Revised as "From Under the Yoke of Race and Sex: Black and Chicano Women's Fiction of the Seventies." *Minority Voices,* 2, 2 (Fall 1978), 1-12.

192. Lattin, Patricia and Vernon E. "Power and Freedom in the Stories of Estela Portillo Trambley." *Critique,* 21, 1 (Fall 1979), 93-101.

193. Ordóñez, Elizabeth J. "Narrative Texts by Ethnic Women: Rereading the Past, Reshaping the Future." *MELUS,* 9, 3 (Winter 1982), 19-28.

194. Parr, Carmen Salazar. "Surrealism in the Work of Estela Portillo." *MELUS,* 7, 4 (Winter 1980), 85-92.

195. Ramírez, Arthur. "Estela Portillo: The Dialectic of Oppression and Liberation." *Revista Chicano-Riqueña,* 8, 3 (verano 1980), 106-14.

196. Rodríguez, Alfonso. "Tragic Vision in Estela Portillo's *The Day of the Swallows*." *De Colores*, 5, 1-2 (1980), 152-58.

197. Rodríguez Lester, Trinidad. "A Study of Women as Reflected in Estela Portillo Trambley's Writings." Unpublished MA thesis. Southern Illinois Univ., 1976.

198. Vallejos, Tomás. "Estela Portillo Trambley's Fictive Search for Paradise." *Frontiers*, 5, 2 (1980), 54-58.
Rpt. in this volume, section 4F.

199. Vowell, Faye Nell. "A MELUS Interview: Estela Portillo Trambley." *MELUS*, 9, 4 (Winter II 1982), 59-66.

See also items 15, 21, 23, 69, 77, 82.

## Tomás Rivera

200. Eger, Ernestina N. "Bibliography of Works by and about Tomás Rivera." *Carta Abierta*, No. 16 (abril 1980), pp. 2-7.

201. Grajeda, Ralph F. "Tomás Rivera's... *y no se lo tragó la tierra*: Discovery and Appropriation of the Chicano Past." *Hispania*, 62, 1 (March 1979), 71-81.
Condensed as "Tomás Rivera's Appropriation of the Chicano Past." In *Modern Chicano Writers*. Ed. Joseph Sommers and Tomás Ybarra-Frausto. Englewood Cliffs, NJ: Prentice-Hall, 1979. Pp. 74-85.
Rpt. in this volume, section 3.

202. Lattin, Vernon E. "Novelistic Structure and Myth in '... *y no se lo tragó la tierra*.'" *Bilingual Review/Revista Bilingüe*, 9, 3 (Sept.-Dec. 1982), 220-26.

203. Lizárraga, Sylvia S. "Cambio: Intento principal de ... *y no se lo tragó la tierra*." *Aztlán*, 7, 3 (Fall 1976), 419-26.

204. Menton, Seymour. Review of ... *y no se lo tragó la tierra*. *Latin American Literary Review*, 1, 1 (Fall 1972), 111-15.

205. Pino, Frank. "The Outsider and 'El Otro' in Tomás Rivera's '... *y no se lo tragó la tierra*.'" *Books Abroad*, 49, 3 (Summer 1975), 453-58.

206. ———. "Realidad y fantasía en '... *y no se lo tragó la tierra*' de Tomás Rivera." In *Otros mundos, otros fuegos; Fantasía y Realismo Mágico en Iberoamérica* (Memoria del XVI Congreso del Instituto Internacional de Literatura Iberoamericana). Aug. 1973. Ed. Donald A. Yates. East Lansing: Michigan State Univ., 1975. Pp. 249-54.

207. Ramos, Luis Arturo. "... *y no se lo tragó la tierra*." *Caracol*, 5, 5 (enero 1979), pp. 10-11, 14.

208. Rascón, Francisca. "La caracterización de los personajes femeninos en ... *y no se lo tragó la tierra*." *La Palabra*, 1, 2 (otoño 1979), 43-50.
Rpt. in this volume, section 3.

209. Rivera, Tomás. "Recuerdo, Descubrimiento y Voluntad en el Proceso Imaginativo Literario." Trans. Gustavo Valadez. *Atisbos*, No. 1 (Summer 1975), pp. 66-77.
Rpt. in *La Raza Habla* (New Mexico State Univ.), 1, 1 (Jan. 1976), 13-16.

210. Rocard, Marcienne. "The Cycle of Chicano Experience in '... *and the earth did not part*' by Tomás Rivera." *Caliban*, XI, in *Annales de l'Université de Toulouse/Le Mirail*, Tome X, Fascicule 1 (1974), 141-51.

211. Rodríguez, Alfonso. "Time as a Structural Device in Rivera's ... *y no se lo tragó la tierra*." In this volume, section 3.

212. Rodríguez, Juan. "Acercamiento a cuatro relatos de . . . y no se lo tragó la tierra." Mester, 5, 1 (Nov. 1974), 16-24.
213. _____. "La embestida contra la religiosidad en . . . Y no se lo tragó la tierra." PCCLAS [Pacific Coast Council on Latin American Studies] Proceedings: Changing Perspectives in Latin America, 3 (1974), 83-86.
214. _____. "The Problematic in Tomás Rivera's . . . y no se lo tragó la tierra." Revista Chicano-Riqueña, 6, 3 (verano 1978), 42-50.
Rpt. in this volume, section 3.
215. Sommers, Joseph. "Interpreting Tomás Rivera." In Modern Chicano Writers. Ed. Joseph Sommers and Tomás Ybarra-Frausto. Englewood Cliffs, NJ: Prentice-Hall, 1979. Pp. 94-107.
Condensed from second part of item 75.
216. Somoza, Oscar U. "Grados de dependencia colectiva en . . . y no se lo tragó la tierra." La Palabra, 1, 1 (primavera 1979), 40-53.
217. Testa, Daniel P. "Narrative Technique and Human Experience in Tomás Rivera." In Modern Chicano Writers. Ed. Joseph Sommers and Tomás Ybarra-Frausto. Englewood Cliffs, NJ: Prentice-Hall, 1979. Pp. 86-93.
218. Vásquez-Castro, Javier. Acerca de literatura (Diálogo con 3 autores chicanos). San Antonio, TX: M & A Editions, 1979. Pp. 39-53.
219. Vélez, Diana. "The Reality of the Chicanos." Bilingual Review/Revista Bilingüe, 2, 1-2 (Jan.-Aug. 1975), 203-07.
See also items 11, 15, 17, 19, 20, 22, 23, 25, 26, 27, 28, 30, 31, 32, 43, 44, 45, 53, 55, 56, 59, 60, 63, 65, 66, 68, 70, 73, 76, 77, 80, 81, 82, 84, 140, 172.

## Orlando Romero

220. García, Nasario. "The Concept of Time in Nambé–Year One." Latin American Literary Review, 7, 13 (Fall-Winter 1978), 20-28.
Rpt. as "Dimensiones del tiempo en Nambé–Year One." Explicación de Textos Literarios, 11, 2 (1982-83), 111-19.
Rpt. in this volume, section 4I.
221. Guerrero, Yolanda E. "La función del mito: Nambé–Year One." Maize, 4, 3-4 (Spring-Summer, 1981), 51-59.
222. Roeder, Beatrice A. "Roots in New Mexico: Nambé–Year One." La Luz, 6, 10 (Oct. 1977), pp. 18-19, 30-31.
See also items 12, 23, 29, 39, 76, 77, 80, 82.

## José Antonio Villarreal

223. Alarcón, Justo S. "Hacia la nada . . . O la religión en Pocho." Minority Voices, 1, 2 (Fall 1977), 17-26.
224. Alurista. "Entrevista con José Antonio Villarreal." Maize, 5, 3-4 (Spring-Summer 1982), 7-16.
225. Bruce-Novoa, Juan. "Interview with José Antonio Villarreal." Revista Chicano-Riqueña, 4, 2 (primavera 1976), 40-48.
Revised version in item 15.
226. _____. "Pocho as Literature." Aztlán, 7, 1 (Spring 1976), 65-77.
227. Dimicelli, Judith M. "A Chicano Twentieth-Century Book of Genesis." Bilingual Review/Revista Bilingüe, 3, 1 (Jan.-April 1976), 73-77.

228. Eger, Ernestina N. "Bibliography of Works by and about José Antonio Villarreal." In *The Fifth Horseman*, by José Antonio Villarreal. Second edition. Clásicos Chicanos/Chicano Classics 1. Binghamton, NY: Bilingual Press/Editorial Bilingüe, 1984. Pp. 399–410.

229. Farkas, David. "Novelist José Antonio Villarreal." *Phantasm* (Chico, CA), 4, 6 (1979), [cover, pp. 3–7].

230. Grajeda, Rafael F. "José Antonio Villarreal and Richard Vásquez: The Novelist Against Himself." In *The Identification and Analysis of Chicano Literature*. Ed. Francisco Jiménez. New York: Bilingual Press/Editorial Bilingüe, 1979. Pp. 329–57.

231. Jiménez, Francisco. "An Interview with José Antonio Villarreal." *Bilingual Review/Revista Bilingüe*, 3, 1 (Jan.–April 1976), 66–72.

232. Leal, Luis. "The Fifth Horseman and Its Literary Antecedents." In *The Fifth Horseman*, by José Antonio Villarreal. Second edition. Clásicos Chicanos/Chicano Classics 1. Binghamton, NY: Bilingual Press/Editorial Bilingüe, 1984. Pp. ix-xxvi.

233. Luedtke, Luther S. "*Pocho* and The American Dream." *Minority Voices*, 1, 2 (Fall 1977), 1–16.
Rpt. in this volume, section 2.

234. Ruiz, Ramón E[duardo]. "On the Meaning of *Pocho*." In *Pocho*, by José Antonio Villarreal. Second edition. Garden City, NY: Doubleday/Anchor, 1970. Pp. vii-xii.

235. Shirley, Carl R. "*Pocho*: Bildungsroman of a Chicano." *Revista Chicano-Riqueña*, 7, 2 (primavera 1979), 63–68.

See also items 14, 15, 18, 19, 21, 23, 24, 30, 32, 39, 42, 44, 45, 46, 48, 49, 52, 53, 55, 59, 60, 68, 73, 76, 77, 80, 81, 83, 84, 173.

CARTHAGE COLLEGE